STATE CRIMES
AROUND THE WORLD

A Treatise in the Sociology of State Deviance

Obi N. I. Ebbe

University of Tennessee at Chattanooga

Kendall Hunt
publishing company

Cover image © Shutterstock, Inc.

Kendall Hunt
publishing company

www.kendallhunt.com
Send all inquiries to:
4050 Westmark Drive
Dubuque, IA 52004-1840

DEDICATION

In memory of Distinguished Criminologist
William J. Chambliss

Contents

List of Figures

Figures

List of Tables

Tables

Acknowledgements

The author is very much obliged to David "Ebiz" Ebizie, who provided him with photos on starvation as a weapon of genocide in the Nigeria-Biafra War.

Also, the author thanks Dr. Dennis Miller, who spent over 15 years in the Soviet Union and Dr. Yakov Gilinskiy of St. Petersburg, Russian Academy of Science; both provided him with additional data on Soviet Russia and post-Soviet Russia, respectively.

As the adage goes, a person who encourages a fight for a good course is a greater fighter than the soldiers on the frontline. In this case, my kindest regards to Dr. Charles B. A. Ubah, who called me on several occasions to make sure that I was still on this project.

Undeniably, this book couldn't have been completed at this time without Ms. April Matthews's diligence and devotion to typing the manuscript.

Finally, "That which touches us most will be last served," Shakespeare wrote; my profound indebtedness goes to Kendall Hunt Publishing Company's Senior Acquisitions Editor, Terry Brennan, and his editorial team, Abby M. Davis, Amy Wagner, Ryan P. Brown, and others, whose guidance expedited the production of this informative text.

Introduction

Sociologists and criminologists have wasted too much time studying street crimes because of two factors: street crimes, in the main, are confrontational and scare the hell out of us. Lastly, street crime is a crime of poor, powerless individuals. Undeniably, of all the various categories of crime that we study in criminology, the most costly and dangerous to society is state crime. One egoistic policy of a head of state can take millions of lives. A lone, crack-head, street criminal or terrorist can kill 1 to 100 people using a bomb. That is less than what a state could destroy in genocide.

It is evident from history that individuals do not commit genocide. Genocide is a state crime. From the 1915 Armenian genocide, which took 1.5 million Armenians in the hands of Ottoman Empire soldiers, to the 1995 Srebrenica, Bosnia genocide in which 8,000–8,500 lives were lost in the hands of President Slobodan Milosevic of the Serbia/former Yugoslavia, there have been at least 30 genocides around the world. Stalin of the Soviet Union, Chairman Mao of China, Pol Pot of Cambodia, Yakubu Gowon of Nigeria, Adolf Hitler of the Nazi Germany, and so forth, led governments (states) that committed various types of genocides which took an estimated 3,000,000 to 20,000,000 lives, as you are going to find out in this text. Is genocide not a crime? Who says states don't commit crimes? By the United Nations Convention on Prevention and Punishment of the Crime of Genocide (CPPCG), genocide is a crime committed by some state parties of the United Nations.

Unmistakably, war crimes, crime against humanity, crime against peace, or crime of aggression, and genocide, are among the crimes charged at the International Military Tribunal (IMT) at the Nuremberg trial in 1945 after World War II, because they are crimes committed by a state or state agents.

A state is an organism. It can sue some of its subjects for certain violations of state law, and the state can be sued by individuals or groups for some of its excesses. Individuals administer the state (government) on behalf of the masses. Those individuals sworn in to handle the affairs of the state represent the state. They enforce the laws of the state. As individuals in society are subject to structural strain, those handling the affairs of the state also have their own strain. These state administrators are also vulnerable to strain and deviance. Executing state policies can run into a roadblock, and the state leaders may violate state laws to achieve state goals.

This book is full of instances where the head of state and his agents violated state laws with impunity. This book looks at the whole of the 195 member states of the United Nations. The text brought both developed and underdeveloped countries under one x-ray as to the type of deviances and crimes perpetrated by some of the heads of state, their cabinet members, legislators, civil servants, and law enforcement agencies. Those five categories of a state government represent what we call a state. Their crimes, collectively, or dividually, against its own people or other nations constitute state crime.

There are many dimensions of state crime. That is why the United Nations has so many Conventions and Protocols to control state deviance and crime. If states were not vulnerable to committing crime, we wouldn't need the United Nations Organization. If a state does not commit crime, then what killed the League of Nations? It was because some states violated treaty agreements, which have a force of law, that some League members withdrew their membership. For instance, Italy invaded Ethiopia, and the League of Nations did not do anything about it.

The state is made up of human beings who are vulnerable to greed, avariciousness, cult of personality, and inordinate ambition, and so forth. Therefore, humanity has seen some heads of state who took their country as their own personal property (President Trujillo of the Dominican Republic, 1930–1961; President Mobutu Sese Seko of Zaire, 1965–1997; and so forth), and the treasury of their country as their own personal bank account. If the masses harass him too much, he loots the national treasury and goes into self-exile (Duvalier "Baby Doc" of Haiti, 1971–1982; Idi Amin of Uganda, 1971–1979; Ferdinand Marcos of the Philippines, 1965–1986; and so forth). Furthermore, in this book, the modus operandi of state-organized crime is laid bare. Both developed countries and developing countries are involved in state-organized crime.

State crime did not emanate in the modern era. It is a crime that began in the ancient times, highlighted by the Roman Emperors. Then it passed to the medieval monarchs and dynasties. And the fall of Constantinople in 1453 passed it to the modern times. Unfortunately for the modern era, the ideas of Charles Darwin (1809–1882), Robert Malthus (1766–1834), and Niccolo Machiavelli contributed to throwing both developed and developing countries asunder.

The data for this book came from my years of travels all over the world. The data are collected in a space of over 20 years. Also, a review of relevant literature on various subjects concerning state deviance contributed to the data presented and analyzed in this text. In addition, ethnographic observations, as one who grew up and got into higher education in a developing, former colonial dependency (state), made an immense contribution to the data presented in this book.

State crimes around the world are presented and analyzed in 10 chapters. Chapter 1 provides an operational definition of state crime. It lays the foundation for the rest of the chapters. In this chapter, the nature of the phenomenon "state" is explained. The relevance of studying state crime, contemporary scholars' view of state crime, why traditional sociology and criminology ignored the study of state crime, and the theories of state crime are delineated.

Chapter 2 traces crimes of heads of state from the ancient times of the Roman Emperors to the medieval and modern era. Highlighted are the criminal atrocities of emperors Elagabalus (218–227 A.D.), Commodus (180–192 A.D.), Domitian (81–96 A.D.), Nero (54–68 A.D.), and Caligula (37–41 A.D.). This chapter notes that the unquenchable appetite for wealth, greed, and power that engulfed Emperors of the later years of the Roman Empire grew from them to medieval and modern times. Undeniably, the Kings, Queens, Presidents, and Prime Ministers of the modern times built empires in a way similar to that of the late Roman Emperors. This chapter notes that criminally minded politicians make criminal heads of state.

Chapter 3 deals with crimes of colonization. This chapter presents historic data on acts of terrorism and genocide in the process of trying to annex and colonize various nations of the world.

Chapter 4 analyzes state terrorism in various parts of the world motivated by greed, hate, ethnocentrism, and culminating in ethnic cleansing. In Chapter 5 is presented state genocides committed by many heads of state and their armed forces and law enforcement agencies. In this chapter, you see that holocaust was perpetrated in different parts of the world even before Nazi Germany of 1933–1945. In this chapter one also learns what constitutes war crime, genocide, crime against humanity, war against peace, or war of aggression.

Chapter 6 demonstrates that dictatorships create state crimes. This chapter shows how some heads of state, under the camouflage of democracy, kidnap a whole country and put the natural resources in their pocket.

Chapter 7 presents, with photographs, how states commit crimes in the process of law enforcement. In this chapter one learns how the state violated the "social contract" theory with impunity. State crimes of omission and negligence are demonstrated.

Chapter 8 presents deviances and crimes of the state in neglect, and differential enforcement, of environmental pollution laws. This chapter demonstrates state violation of Fundamental Human Rights of its citizens, and violation by some states of the Basel Convention in dumping of nuclear and industrial wastes in poor neighborhoods and poor countries of the world.

Chapter 9 presents irrefutable data on state-organized crime involving both rich and poor nations. The definition of state-organized crime comes with specific examples of heads of state who carried out such schemes with impunity across the globe. In this chapter one learns details of Russian Mafiya and Mexican drug cartels living in symbiosis with their states/ governments. In this chapter you will find the causes of state-organized crime and four of types of such crime.

Chapter 10, the last chapter, presents the mechanisms developed by the United Nations to control state crimes, the meaning of International Humanitarian Law, the various United Nations Conventions and Protocols to hold state parties in check, and the emergence of the various courts of the United Nations including the International Criminal Tribunals and the International Criminal Court (ICC). This chapter concludes with an explanation of victimology and the future of state crime.

This book demonstrates that political-criminal nexus is an endemic part of politics and state organization all over the world. The data presented show that no state is immune from criminal collaborations. As analyzed in this book, the development of "off-shore banks," coupled with its concealment and lack of meaningful control by the state for decades and centuries, demonstrate the magnitude of state-organized crime.

CHAPTER 1

Operational Definition of State Crime and the Criminology of State Crime

The Nature of the State

One cannot stage "Hamlet" without the Duke of Denmark. In a similar vein, we cannot talk about "state crimes" without an explanation of the meaning of a state. This is because some countries (states) are divided into states (substates) such as the United States (50), Nigeria (36), Brazil (26), Germany (16), India (29), Mexico (31), and so forth; others into provinces such as China (22), South Africa (9), Canada (10), or regions such as France (22), Ethiopia (9), Italy (20), and so forth. A country under which these states, provinces, regions, divisions, or prefectures (Japan) exist is called a "state."

Unmistakably, a state is a relatively autonomous, heterogeneous collectivity occupying a particular territory bound together by immemorial customs, heritage, or a common code of laws, rules, and regulations, whose members may or may not have ties to consanguinity. A state is a country with a legislative structure and a government that pilots the machinery of the country's domestic and international affairs. In principle, the government is the state.

The government of each country is the leader of the people inhabiting the country or state. The government is the eyes, the legs, the hands, and the voice of a country. It is expected to forge and execute domestic and foreign policies in the interest of its people. The activities of a government are the activities of the state in which it exists. The government and the state are inseparable. The government is the leader of the state. Sociologically, a state is made up of human beings. Therefore, the state is an organism and susceptible to the frailties of human nature.

1

Remarkably, individual human beings have their aspirations, ambitions, and goals. Unfortunately, some people have unfathomable ambitions and aspirations. And their ascendency to the epicenter of state or national leadership does not eclipse those aspirations and ambitions. Consequently, a state is vulnerable to being crushed in the hands of some egoistic pilots of state affairs, as we are going to see in this study.

There are different types of states. In modern times, we have communist, democratic, and socialist states. Unfortunately, none of them is immune from a state leader's abuse of power. Undeniably, it can be argued that democracies experience less state abuse of power than communist and socialist states. Communist and socialist states are dictatorships. In such regimes, the media and individuals have less freedom of speech and action than in democracies. Each of the three types of states has a legislature which makes laws that govern the people of the state without an exception. However, in principle, nobody is beyond incrimination, but not in practice, as we shall see in the following chapters.

Unmistakably, in communist and socialist states, there is an exception to the rule of law. The dictator piloting the affairs of the state is beyond incrimination, because he controls the police, the courts, the prisons, the military, and all of the other agencies of the state. Beyond doubt, there are camouflaged democracies, as we shall see in Chapter 6, where the state professes "democratic republic," whereas it is a dictatorship.

Undeniably, the state is an entity that needs to be studied just like any other organization. Why do we study organizations such as corporations, nongovernment organizations (NGOs), Ku Klux Klan, Organized Crime, United Nations, and so forth, and not study the state? The next section of this chapter presents the answer.

Why We Study State Crime

State crime is a part of the overall field of Criminology. The fact that traditional sociology and criminology ignored the subject does not inherently eliminate it from social science scholarly investigation. State crime is an affiliate of white collar crime. Edwin Sutherland (1949) ignored it, because medieval and modern state leaders did not tolerate being criticized. In effect, social scientists ignored investigating the crimes of heads of state and the civil servants.

When Sutherland came up with the concept of "white collar crime" in 1949 and engineered an avalanche of studies on the subject, why didn't he think about the crimes of heads of state? Notably, in addition to the above explanation, the focus of sociology in the study of crime was the crime of the underprivileged elements of society. During the Academy of Criminal Justice Sciences (ACJS) conference in Chicago in 1984, I presented "Crimes of Heads of State." When the Chair of the panel stood up to introduce me, and said, Obi Ebbe from Ohio Northern University presents "Crimes of Heads of State," a respectable professor (now late) from the University of Illinois, Chicago Circle (now University of Illinois at Chicago), spontaneously questioned: "Heads of state commit crime?" I stood up, and smiled, heading

AKA: govern... is corrupt

Some let Power go to their heads

do

toward the podium. In the presentation, by the time I pointed out a few instances of crimes of murder committed by some late medieval monarchs and the crimes of some contemporary heads of state like those of Ferdinand Marcus of Philippines, Idi Amin of Uganda, and Richard Nixon's Watergate to prolong the life of a government, the professor from the University of Illinois-Chicago Circle was nodding his head in agreement.

A state or government is a legal entity just like a corporation. It can sue individuals, groups, or corporations for violation of state law. In the same vein, in modern times, a state can be sued for violation of individual or group rights. The problem lies in the fact that the state is very powerful. In effect, sometimes individuals have no wherewithal to sue the state, or are afraid to sue the state for its vindictive repercussions. Who is the state or government in the context of state crime? The state is the head of state, his cabinet members, civil servants including social control agencies. When we say "Bush Administration," "Obama Administration," "Ferdinand Marcos Administration," or "Abacha Administration," we are referring to the state, which is the government led by the individuals mentioned.

The state makes laws and executes the laws made by its legislature. The state focuses on the enforcement of the laws violated by some members of the country. In some instances, crimes committed by state employees for personal benefits are enforced, while some are ignored. But crimes to forge the interests of the head of state or his political party are seen as normal by the state itself, as its modus operandi. In addition, we study state crimes to keep the state aware of its deviances or crimes and design a way to bring them under control. Furthermore, when crimes of state leaders and civil servants are not controlled, the underprivileged elements of society can use those crimes to neutralize their guilt (Sykes & Matza, 1964).

Contemporary Scholars' View of State Crime

We have sociologists and criminologists who do not follow the crowd. They are able to figure out that following the crowd is not always the right route. Such scholars have been referred to as conflict/Marxist/radical sociologists and criminologists. Leading this small group of criminologists are William Chambliss (1974, 1975, 1976, 1978, 1988, 2010) and Richard Quinney (1977, 2000, 2001).

In his radical text, Class, State, and Crime, Quinney (1977) argued that the ruling class made laws, but turned around and violated the laws they created. This he calls "contradictions of capitalism." Undeniably, the "ruling class" constitutes the "state." But that was not a frontal attack on the subject.

In his books titled *The State, the Law, and the Definition of Behavior as Criminal or Delinquent* (1974); *Toward a Political Economy of Crimes* (1975); *Whose Law? What Order? A Conflict Approach to Criminology* (1976); and *Making Law: The State, the Law, and Structural Contradictions* (1993); Chambliss was attacking the ruling class hypocrisies in making of laws, enforcing the laws, and violating the laws themselves with impunity. His major criticism was yet to come.

In 1988, Chambliss was the President of the American Society of Criminology (ASC). Before that year, he had traveled to many Third World and First World countries including Nigeria (1966) studying how the people were governed. In 1974, before the end of the Vietnam-American War, he went to Thailand to study how opium, from the Golden Triangle, was being flown out of Asia into the United States, and who were involved. He found out that there was a secret government in the U.S. operations in Vietnam, and that the secret government was run by the CIA agents (Chambliss, 1978, 1988, pp. 185–187). All of his various travels studying the modus operandi of government operations in developed and developing countries gave rise to mind-boggling and numbing revelations in his book captioned, *On the Take: from Petty Crooks to Presidents* (1978, 1988).

Challenging the world of criminologists and sociologists, at the American Society of Criminology annual conference 1988 captioned "State and Crime," Chambliss titled his Presidential Address "State-Organized Crime." In that presidential address, he defined "State-Organized Crime" as "acts defined by law as criminal and committed by state officials in pursuit of their jobs as representatives of the State." In a publication of "State-Organized Crime in a *Criminology* journal a year later, Chambliss urged criminologists as follows:

> "State organized crimes, environmental crimes, crimes against humanity, human rights crime, and the violations of international treaties increasingly must take center stage in criminology. . . . Criminologists must define crime as behavior that violates international agreements and principles established in the courts and treaties of international bodies" (Chambliss, 1989).

Since this Chambliss' groundbreaking address and its subsequent publications, some criminologists have responded with publications in line with Chambliss' explanations of state crime (Barak, 1991; Ross, 2000; Kauzlarich et al., 2003; Faust & Kauzlarich, 2008; Rothe, 2009; Bassiouni, 2011; and Rothe & Mullins, 2011). These scholars argued that states commit crimes with impunity, and in some cases commit crimes of omission to act, when they have a duty to act but failed.

Those who do not think that states commit crime (Cohen, 1990), or that social harm committed by a state is not a crime (Sharkansky, 1995) should think again. Undeniably, it is an established truth that no head of state or a political party in a position of power will criminalize a behavior that services their interests. We saw this fact in the United States during the President Clinton administration and W. Bush administration. Under the Clinton administration, possession of assault weapons by nonmilitary employees was banned and such an offense was a felony. The conservatives opposed the ban on lay persons possessing assault weapons. However, at the end of the President Clinton administration came the conservative W. Bush administration, which controlled the legislative branch of the state. Consequently, the W. Bush administration, in power, revoked the law that banned lay persons possessing assault weapons. Similarly, in Nigeria's civilian administration, possession and smoking of marijuana was punishable with seven years of imprisonment with hard labor. But when the military overthrew the civilian government, the military head of state reduced the penalty to a six-month jail term, because the long prison term did not serve the interest of the military officers and men, who were engulfed in drug abuse before they took over the government of Nigeria.

Unmistakably, a social harm is an injury to some persons. Therefore, if the social harm or injury is not defined as a crime by the state, it is simply because the act does not serve the interest of the ruling class (Quinney, 1977; Chambliss, 2011). The *Trail of Tears* of 1830, in which 2,000 to 6,000 out of 16,542 Native Americans from the southeastern part of the United States were forced out of their homes and died on their long arduous journey to Oklahoma, was a social harm and not a crime, because the ruling class at the time had decided that the order be carried out (Anderson, 1991; Foreman, 1989).

Also, the *Last Grave at Dimbaza* in which the "white" minority government of South Africa (apartheid regime) created a marooned location they called Dimbaza to house Black South Africans who were removed from their homes in a "white" residential area. There was no sanitation, no clean water supply, no jobs in the area, no health care, and, in fact, not meant for human habitation. That was a "social harm" and not a state crime? For those who think that it is a social harm and not a crime, it is so because the ruling class of the South Africa government did not define it as such. In both *Trail of Tears* and *Last Grave at Dimbaza*, the violations were of fundamental human rights of citizens (an international humanitarian law), and therefore a crime by international law (Miller, 2007). Therefore, those social harms are crimes against humanity. The President W. Bush administration's omission to act or act on time in "Hurricane Katrina," led to the death of over 1,833 people and an estimated $81 billion U.S. dollars lost in property damages was a crime against humanity (Spielman, 2007; Hartman & Squires, 2006). If such an omission is not a crime, it is because saving those lives and property was not in the interest of the ruling elite of the George W. Bush administration.

The Composition of the State and Definition of State Crime

What is the conceptual definition of the "state" or "government" for the purpose of this book? A state or a government is composed of the executive branch, the legislative branch, and the judicial branch. It is the responsibility of the executive branch, led by the head of state, to execute policy developed by the three organs of the state. The three branches are one. That is why we talk about a divided government when the executive branch and the legislative branch fail to cooperate in making policies. However, in some dictatorships, there is only one branch or two branches of the government. In a unicameral dictatorship, it is only one governing body with the head of state presiding. In a two-branch of governing dictatorship, it is the head of state and members elected or selected from a unit, and a handpicked judiciary is a second chamber. Therefore, a state crime is any crime committed by the executive branch alone or in cooperation with one or both other branches of the government in terms of overt illegal actions or omission to enforce the law. In a dictatorship, state crime becomes crimes committed by the governing body for the interest of the dictatorship.

State crimes, therefore, include any crime committed by the head of state personally or in collaboration with his aides or agents; or an order given by him to carry out illegal acts against the interests of the country; or illegal acts designed to enrich himself; acts by the head of state or his aides or agents that lead to loss of life, illegal detention or incarceration, or illegal search and seizure; pursuit of policies that violate domestic and international agreements; illegal acts committed by government officials for the benefit of the administration; illegal acts committed by state agents with the ulterior motive that such illegal or harmful acts would please the head of state; all illegal acts committed by state law enforcement officials or national security agents in the process of enforcing state law; the state's failure to enforce a law against individuals, groups, or businesses, when it has a duty to do so; and the state's failure to regulate small and big businesses.

There should be no controversy over the definition of state crime, because some states violate the law in contravention of the criminal code, and that is a crime (Barak, 1991; Sharkansky, 1995; Michalowski, 1985; Schwendinger, 1970; Michalowski & Kramer, 2006; Kauzlarich, Mullins, & Matthews, 2003; Green & Ward, 2000 and Rothe & Mullins, 2011). The lack of a consensus over a single, acceptable definition of what constitutes a state crime lies in the diverse political leanings of criminologists, plus "all like is not the same," as William Shakespeare put it. It is undeniable that what constitutes a crime is an act that majority members of a society agree to be a crime and put it as such in their criminal code. That's why we noted earlier that where an act is harmful to some members of a society, and it is not criminalized, it means proscribing the act does not serve the interest of the ruling elite of society.

Society makes the law. Therefore, an act of a state that is not criminalized in the criminal code, but the masses strongly agitate against the state's harmful act, criminologists should go with the masses to regard the harmful act as a serious injury that should be criminalized. This is because politicians are aware of certain behaviors that they should not get into against some segments of society. In effect, they make sure that such behaviors are not prohibited by law. Unmistakably, what constitutes a crime or state crime lies within the eyes and minds of members of society (Green & Ward, 2000). Democracy has been battling with this for years, because the masses may not have the opportunity to bring the issue to the table of the ruling class. And if it gets to the table of the ruling class, will it become a law of the land? That is the question. Criminologists should represent the masses in such a case by providing frequent research reports to the state leaders and the media about such a harmful act that the masses or groups agitated against. When a crime is committed and nobody reports it, or there is no complainant, then there is no court case. Criminologists, especially criminology organizations, therefore, should begin to play a part in determining what constitutes a crime and a state crime. It does not mean that the legislators will always agree with the criminology organization, but it makes a difference when the legislators and the government are aware that some organizations are there to question state omission and wrongful legislations.

Why Traditional Sociology and Criminology Ignored State Crime

Sociology gave birth to criminology. Among the sciences, sociology was a late comer. It was conceived only in the 18th century emanating from the Industrial Revolution and the French Revolution. And it was at a time when the absolutism of the monarchy had not totally given up the ancient and medieval political order. The vibrations of the murderous spirits of the monarchy were still being felt by potential challengers of the ruling elite.

Consequently, criminological inquiries focused on the crimes of the underprivileged elements of society. But heads of state are regarded as being beyond incrimination. Their crimes are ignored by criminologists and sociologists partly because traditional society regards Kings and Queens as having divine rights and partly because, in many regimes, the head of state is the custodian of the criminal code and has control of the law enforcement agencies. Besides, higher education, in other words "intellectualism," emerged from the bases and corridors of power, and a kingdom cannot fight against itself. For instance, entrance to medieval universities in Europe was a prerogative of the sons of kings and nobles. Thus, modern intellectuals are afraid to study the criminality of the ruling class. Consequently, the illegal and criminal political acts perpetrated by heads of state or by those in power in the government are seldom treated as a category of crime. In effect, social scientists ignored the criminogenic effect of the crimes of the ruling class, while crimes against persons and property, and all types of murder perpetrated by the underprivileged elements of society, were the subject of serious study. Political murder, however, like other political criminality, passes almost unstudied (Ebbe, 1990).

Undeniably, some social scientists are afraid to study state crimes or the crimes of the powerful, especially topics that will bring them in confrontation with the government or the head of state. For instance, in a colloquium of 22 scholars, including an FBI Special Agent, and a USAID Deputy Director, organized by Professor Roy Godson of Georgetown University and sponsored by the National Strategy Information Center, Inc., Washington D.C., held in the Ranch of a British Billionaire, Sir Goldsmith[2]; at Hacienda San Antonio, Colima, Mexico, from March 2–9, 1997, the topic, as charged by the British Billionaire was , "*Causes and Strategies for Control of World-Wide Corruption*" (see Roy Godson, 2003; *Menace to Society: Political-Criminal Collaborations in Global Perspective*). After my presentation on the third day, we had a short break. An Italian University Professor approached me and walked pari passu with me toward a direction, and he asked me, "Had anybody threatened your life for what you wrote?" I shrugged, and said, "no." He gave a chuckle of surprise.

A year later, 1998, I was at The Hague, the Netherlands, presenting at the fifth International Police Executive Symposium on "Crime Prevention," which I was coordinating. Once again, during a brief break, a German University Professor came to where I was standing by myself and asked me, "Had anybody threatened your life for what you wrote?" I laughed loudly, but he didn't know why I laughed so loudly, and I replied, "no." And he was astonished at my nonchalant composure about the dreadfulness of the question. But what he didn't know was that a different scholar from another country had asked me the same question a year earlier; and I didn't tell him, because I felt that it was not necessary.

The questions from the two different scholars made me aware of how dreadful it is to some scholars to call a spade a spade in criminology. I don't very much blame those early and contemporary scholars who were afraid to point out the crimes of heads of state and their governments, because many journalists have lost their lives in many countries especially in Third World countries, Russia, and Newly Independent States of the former Soviet Union (NIS), or lose their jobs in Western societies (DiLorenzo, 2012, p. 16).

Contemporary sociologists and criminologists should muster courage and make constructive criticisms against heads of states and their officials' brazen violations of law. And then provide them with recommendations to ameliorate the pains of the underprivileged elements of society.

Criminology of State Crime

State crime is a violation of law. The state, unfortunately, is a judge in its own case. Therefore, it cannot arrest itself or prosecute itself. Even when some individuals sue the state, it is always in a civil and not in a criminal court. When a state official or a legislator commits a crime, his peers call it unethical behavior and not a crime. Sometimes the crime of the legislator or an official of the government is sent to an administrative tribunal instead of a criminal court to avoid a criminal label on the politician or official. This is what happens in many countries.

In Third World countries, the head of state, his legislators, and top civil servants commit hard crimes with impunity, because the head of state controls all law enforcement agencies including the judiciary. A politician who is ever charged with a crime in some Third World countries is a greedy politician who does not share his booty with the head of state. Why is it that some countries like Nigeria, Zimbabwe, and so forth have been called "failed states" (Ebbe, 1999, 2003)? It is because they are predatory states. A predatory state is a state where the head of state governs like a "Mafia Boss."

Unmistakably, a failed state denies the majority of its inhabitants the basic needs of man: shelter, food, and water. A failed state does not bother itself about the supply and quality of water available to its inhabitants, the quality of food, and the adequacy of housing for its people. Also, a failed state ignores sanitation as city streets are fraught with heaps of rotten garbage, hospitals are denied regular supply of medicine, and corruption is the modus operandi of its governance. These are state crimes against humanity. Furthermore, in such regimes, assassination of investigative journalists is rampant. Also, such regimes do not see good roads and electric supply as necessary for everybody in the country for as long as they could provide electricity for themselves, and put the rest of the money in their pockets. The above characteristics of failed states are endemic in most of the Third World countries.

And all of those show a state failing its people. Therefore, they constitute a crime of omission and a crime against humanity.

The criminology of state crime should focus, among other areas, on how states' neglect of social services to some segments of society could lead to criminal acts by some members of society, and how state failures to prevent riots, bloody demonstrations, and strikes are state crimes of omission.

Furthermore, the criminology of state crime should engage in processes of making laws in different countries, and try to determine the various ways the governments, contradictorily, violate the laws they enacted. Also, investigate the degree of the state's omission to enforce the law in various corporations, other businesses, and individual violations. This type of criminological monitoring is very essential, because legislation without stringent enforcement of the law is tantamount to criminalization of the masses. That means, when the masses are aware that the government will not enforce a law, or that the state's law enforcement agents are willing to take bribes for the illegal acts, they will go along and violate the law whichever is more profitable than the other, which may lead to anomie (Durkheim, 1964).

In addition, criminology of state crime should investigate state crimes in the area of foreign aid to poor countries that continue to be poor despite millions of dollars claimed to have been pumped into those countries. This part of criminology should study state crimes involved in IMF loans to poor or developing counties, and the ramifications of poor nations accepting IMF loans.

The study of state crime should also involve the role of advanced economies in encouraging state crime in developing countries. For instance, some cabinet ministers in Third World states embezzled millions of state money and flew away from their countries and deposited the money in Western and Asian banks. And efforts to extradite the fugitive offenders are blocked by the host industrialized economy (Ebbe, 1999, 2003; Abbott, 1988a, 1988b). This is a very good area for the criminology of state crime instead of learning about the international crime from investigative journalism. Any study of state crime must include the analysis of the criminology of power and political crimes around the world.

Finally, this study of state crimes does not include crimes committed by individuals, groups, corporations, or other businesses against the government. Instead, this study focuses on crimes committed by a state or a national government against its citizens or other countries such as embezzlement, wholesale corruption, omission to enforce the laws of the land, torture, illegal search and seizure, illegal detention or incarceration of persons without due process of law, political exploitation and repression of political party opponents and ethnic groups opposed to the government, crimes against humanity, crimes against peace (war of aggression), war crimes in furtherance of a state policy, denial of fundamental human rights to some citizens or foreigners in state custody, acts of genocide, deliberate breach of treaties and other international agreements, forcible rape and trafficking of women and children by state soldiers of wars of aggression, flagrant violation of international law, and state-organized crime.

Theories of State Crime

The theories of state crime are part of the study of criminology of state crime. The theories of state crime emanate from the strain theory (Merton, 1968). The strain theory asserts that when a society lays emphasis on the values of success (cultural goals measured in terms of acquisition of wealth and living in affluent neighborhoods), and defined legitimate avenues (means) to success, but fails to provide the legitimate means equally to everybody, then, those who have internalized the values of success but have no legitimate means to the goals, will, inevitably, use alternative means which are illegitimate. This is the point at which strain occurs. The desire to succeed in life economically while the means to achieve that goal are not always there is a structural strain.

Mizruchi (1964) had argued that the strain is no more on the lower class because of the welfare system, but on the middle class whose anomie is boundlessness as against lower class anomie of bondlessness. Undeniably, the strain is more on the middle class who are the targets of all expensive industrial manufactured goods such as cars, private jets, super refrigerators, stoves, furniture, clothes, and so forth.

Unmistakably, the strain facing individuals also faces the state. The head of state, his cabinet members, his law enforcement agents, and other civil servants are individuals with needs and aspirations engulfed in structural strain. By a state's national policy, it has goals to be achieved. There are means to achieve those state goals, and those means are not always there for the state. Sometimes the state violates its own laws in order to achieve its goals. The state violates its laws when it re-zones an area, extortionarily acquires individuals' acres of lands, or demolishes their homes with little or no compensation.

The strain for a state to achieve a goal can be domestic and international. In state goals of international nature, the means to achieve the goal are never always available. Very often a state violates international law to achieve its goal. This occurs when a state illegally flies over the air space of another country/state to get some secret information, illegally enters the territorial waters of another state with a submarine, or dumps nuclear waste in a Third World country. Furthermore, heads of state were sworn in to uphold the constitution of their countries, to obey and enforce the law of the land by an oath, but on ascending the office, some lied to the masses by pursuing a policy they promised that they would never take. For instance, a head of state who said to his people, "watch my lips, no new taxes"; but after being elected, he raised taxes. What is that?

Other explanations of state crime are greed, inordinate ambition, and power.

Greediness pursues wealth for its accumulation and the power opulence will bring. This greediness leads to bribery and corruption from the head of state down to the lowest civil servant. Also, greediness is asserted in conspicuous consumption which is prevalent among Third World elite.

Inordinate ambition is demonstrated in high waves of assassinations of political opponents, very often engineered by the head of state and his cronies or party faithful (President

Abacha of Nigeria (1993–1998), Idi Amin Dade "the Butcher of Uganda" (1971–1979), Ferdinand Marcos of Philippines (1965–1986), Augusto Pinochet of Chile (1973–1990), Muammar Gaddafi of Libya (1969–2011), and so forth. The above national leaders' smiles before a rabble-roused mass of subjects were shrouded in deceit and fraud, as they have no cult of good manners.

Power blindfolds the greedy and the ambitious man. Greediness is a prerequisite of inordinate ambition, and both are the ingredients of a seat of power. When the epicenter of the powerful position is reached, arrogance and invincibility of his ability to rule grips him, then he scorns the lower bases that helped him ascend the highest office in the land. At this juncture, absolutism is born. He sees the country as all his own. He can, at this point, commit any crime to preserve his position and power. In reality, he doesn't see beyond his nose anymore, and his end may be near. That is reminiscent of dictatorships.

Review Questions

1. What is a state?
2. Is a state an organism?
3. (a) What are the various types of state/government? (b) What are the various characteristics of a state/government?
4. What is a social harm?
5. What is state crime? Can a state commit a crime?
6. What are the author's explanations for why traditional sociology and criminology ignored the study of state crime?
7. What are the theories of state crime?

Notes

1. Within some countries, in addition to the states, provinces, regions, divisions, they have subadministrative units such as territories, capital territory, districts, municipalities, and administrative units
2. On the valley of Colima Mountain is a hidden fabulous palace, surrounded by medieval styled buildings and vibrant ranch in Hacienda San Antonio, Colima, Mexico. This indescribable palace was a vacation home of the British real estate mogul, Sir Goldsmith.

The Building Blocks of 18th–21st Centuries' State Crimes

Introduction: The End of the Dark Ages and its Aftermath

The year 1453 marked the end of the Dark Ages and the beginning of modern times. That year saw the fall of Constantinople into the hands of the Ottoman Empire and the demise of the Byzantine Empire. The Ottoman Turks became a dominant power in southeastern Europe and eastern Mediterranean (Braudel, 1995; Mancel, 1997; Woolf, 2008).

In time, the old feudal order in Europe operated in such a way that decentralized power broke down, and power became centralized at the royal courts (Woolf, 2008). The kings grew in power by offering honorable positions to powerful nobles to secure their loyalties. The idea of nation state was virgin. A kingdom ruled by a monarch was the social, economic, and political order. Many places in Europe, known as countries today, were inhabited by many autonomous kingdoms often fighting against each other. Spain, for instance, had three kingdoms: Aragon, Castile, and Navarre. In all of Europe, a kingdom fought against other kingdoms to acquire more territories, and tried to dominate them for economic and military power. While the monarchs were heads of state, they endeavored more immensely to preserve their dynasties than the affairs of the state. While Renaissance was the aftermath of the fall of Constantinople, by 1494 wars of territorial control took its toll throughout Western Europe. The Holy Roman Empire, England, Spain, France, Scotland, Switzerland, the Papal

States, Venice, and many Italian city-states were engulfed in what is called "Italian Wars" (1494–1559). At the end of the wars, many Italian city-states collapsed, France declined, but Habsburg Spain became a dominant power in Europe (Woolf, 2008; Mallett & Shaw, 2012; Guerard, 1959).

Although the wars were for power and territorial domination, it was also about who pays tax to whom?

The European interest and advances in global exploration sharpened the European dog-eat-dog wars in different fronts especially when in 1519, Ferdinand Magellan led the first voyage to circumnavigate the globe, and Christopher Columbus inadvertently discovered West Indies and the Americas. Portugal discovered West Africa (1472) and left with gold, spices, and slaves from Benin Kingdom in Nigeria. In 1488, Bartholomew Diaz rounded the Cape of Good Hope in South Africa, and Vasco da Gama found a sea route to India (1497–1498) which eluded Christopher Columbus. While Spain and Portugal were in South and Central America, France and England fought it out in North America.

The age of discovery gave a final blow to feudalism in Europe, and that was the emergence of European Capitalism. As many Western European States had developed the banking system as far back as the 14th century in the rich cities of Renaissance Italy,[1] the motivation for accumulation of wealth by individuals and states was a major additional drive toward empire building. International trade proliferated by leaps and bounds. In effect, absolute monarchy reigned supreme. Dissidents or individuals or groups who opposed the dynastic monarchies were executed by the order of the King, for instance, the murder of William of Orange by the will of Philip of Spain; Mary Queen of Scots perished in the hands of Queen Elizabeth I of England; Henry VIII (1509–1547) executed tens of thousands of his English subjects during his 36-year reign, and his daughter who succeeded him as queen ("Bloody Mary") killed about 300 people during her six-year reign (Weir, 2003 Hall, 1954; Williams, 1964).

In Russia, Peter the Great came to power in 1689. From 1700–1721, Russia defeated Sweden, its strongest rival in the Baltic, and captured Estonia, Livonia, Ingria, Karelia, and the coastal ports of Vyborg, Reval, and Riga (Woolf, 2008). He established his capital at St. Petersburg on the Baltic. With control of the Baltic region, Russia embraced French culture and got deeply involved in English and Dutch commercial enterprises (Hughes, 1998, 2001; Bushkovitch, 2001; Woolf, 2008). In 1725, he succeeded in making Russia a great power in Europe. Consequently, Russia advanced to play a significant role in European wars. The seven years' war (1756–1763) nearly destroyed Prussia, but it drove the Ottoman Turks away from the territories around the Black Sea, and played a part in the partition of Poland in 1772 (Woolf, 2008).

The discovery of new lands around the globe, the Industrial Revolution, and the development of a medium of commodity exchange created unfathomable trading rivalries among European nations, which led to inexplicable wars of aggression, crimes against humanity, assassinations, political corruption, war crimes, genocide, and false charges to eliminate those who were threats to the monarchy such as Elizabeth I versus Mary Stuart[2] (Queen of Scots), Nero and his mother Agrippina[3] (Wilkinson, 2004). As Proal (1898) put it,

> Political passions have bathed the earth in blood, kings, emperors, aristocracies, democrats, republics; all governments have resorted to murder out of political considerations, those from love of power, those from hatred of royalty aristocracy, in one case from fear, in another from fanaticism.

Crimes of Medieval Roman Emperors as Stare Decisis of State Crimes of Modern Times

The criminal atrocities of Emperors Elagabalus (218–227 A.D.), Commodus (180–192 A.D.), Domitian (81–96 A.D.), Nero (54–68 A.D.), and Caligula (37–41 A.D.) have not eclipsed the atrocities committed by many contemporary heads of state.

Emperor Elagabalus raped vestal virgins. In his kingdom, he was the only man allowed to enter the house of vestal virgins. He had a brothel in his palace. Worst of all, he imprisoned and executed those who criticized him. In his sexual insanity, he married a vestal virgin, Aquilia Severa, and claimed that the marriage was going to yield "god-like children." But such a marriage was a flagrant violation of Roman law and custom. By Roman law and customary standards, a vestal virgin was buried alive if she engaged in coitus (Icks, 2011; De Arrizabalaga Y. Padro, 2010).

Emperor Commodus was a dictator to his senatorial order to a point that the senators feared and hated him. All those who conspired to assassinate him in 182 A.D. were executed. Perennis, an administrator of the state under Emperor Commodus, was very ambitious, and he had plotted to overthrow King Commodus. The plot leaked and Commodus gave an order that Perennis be executed along with his wife and sons. Commodus made himself the "fountainhead of the Empire, Roman life, and religion," and sold imperial honors and favors to the highest bidder (Spiedel, 1993; Freisenbruch, 2010).

Emperor Domitian developed unimaginable types of torture to deal with deviants, critics, and persons he hated. Philosophers and Jews were his arch enemies. He got vestal virgins executed or buried alive on charges of immorality. He impregnated his niece and forced her to have an abortion, and when she died, he deified her. Emperor Domitian depraved-heartedly executed officials who opposed his policies and confiscated their property. He was murdered in a palace conspiracy which was designed by his own court officials on September 18 in 96 A.D. (Jones, 1984).

Emperor Nero (54–68 A.D.), like Emperors Elagabalus, Commodus, and Domitian, was also bloody. He came to the throne through his mother's criminal design. Nero's mother, Agrippina the young, married her uncle, Emperor Claudius (41–54 A.D.), when she already had Nero in a previous marriage. In other words, Emperor Claudius married his niece and Nero became his grand-nephew and adopted son. In a horrendous move, Agrippina poisoned her husband, Emperor Claudius, so that her son, Nero, would become Emperor of Rome at the age of 17. When Nero became the Emperor of the Roman Empire, he persecuted Christians. He had Christians torn to death by dogs, while some Christians were burnt and used as torches to light his gardens on ceremonial occasions.

Nero executed many people he felt were threats to his throne. He poisoned Burrus, his Praetorian Prefect, because he believed Burrus was plotting to overthrow him (Gibbon, 2003). He even did not spare his own mother who brought him to the throne. In 59 A.D., he accused his mother of treason and ordered her executed, because he believed that his mother, Agrippina, was plotting to dethrone him and enthrone Rubellius Plautus. At a point, as a result of Nero's depraved-hearted executions, a group of senators banded together and formed the "Pisonian conspiracy" to murder Nero and replace him with C-Calpurnius. The conspiracy was discovered and he executed most of the conspirators (Griffin, 1984; Holland, 2000; Gibbon, 2003).

The last of the most atrocious and bloodthirsty emperors of the Roman Empire presented here is Emperor Caligula (37–41 A.D.). He killed for greed, and moved that he be treated as a god. He opened brothels in his palace, and raped whoever he wanted. He raped married women and reported the woman's sexual performance to her husband. Caligula committed incest with impunity. His cruelty, sadism, intense sexual perversity, and extravagance were unfathomable. He was regarded throughout the Roman Empire as an insane tyrant. He executed and exiled those he found were threats to his throne.

Among other atrocities of Emperor Caligula were the poisoning of his grandmother, Antonia Minor, because she opposed the Emperor's execution of his relatives; he executed his father-in-law, Marcus Julius Salinus, his brother-in-law, Marcus Lepidus, and exiled his two sisters. In 41 A.D., his Praetorian Guard, Roman Senate, and the Imperial Court conspired and assassinated him (Dunstan, 2010; Barrett, 1989; Hurley, 1993; Sandison, 1958).

The Roots of Modern State Crimes

The unquenchable appetite for wealth, greed, and power that engulfed emperors of the Roman Empire grew from them (ancient) to medieval and modern times. The state crimes of the Roman emperors formed a precedent for the state crimes of medieval and modern times.

The Medieval era began about the 5th century and lasted up to the 15th century. But the Roman Empire reached its peak in 117 A.D. So the Roman Empire was there in the Middle Ages, and so were the Armenian Empire of Tigranes the Great (83–69 A.D.), Mongol Empire (1206–1368), Sassanid Empire (224–651 A.D.), and so forth. The Roman empires had the characteristics of the early and late Roman empires.

The kings and queens of the early modern times built their empires in a way similar to that of the early and late Roman emperors. The Italian wars and other European wars, coupled with the Age of Exploration, gave impetus to the emergence of the modern empires of Spain, Portugal, Britain, France, Nazi Germany, Japan, Russia, Qing, Dutch, Ottoman, and so forth (Allsen, 1987; Backman, 2014). The empire building mania that spread around the globe rationalized exploitation of weak nations by the mightier ones, and brought about state crimes of immeasurable magnitude. The ancient and medieval state crimes spread and multiplied like cancer and permeated into the modern times. Some of the crimes of the Roman emperors are found in contemporary democracies and communist and socialist states of the world. Some of the state crimes of ancient and medieval times are simply modified by contemporary national leaders.

In this modern era, in Inca Empire, Atahualpa became the Emperor (1497–1533) and defeated and executed his half-brother, Huascar, in a civil war after their father's death. Then, Spain attacked the Inca Empire and defeated Emperor Atahualpa and executed him (Brundage, 1963; Hemming, 2003, Rostworowski, 1998).

In the late 19th century, France invaded Mexico in 1861. Soon after, at the invitation of Napoleon III, Archduke Ferdinand Maximilian left his Austrian naval position and traveled to Mexico and proclaimed himself the Emperor of Mexico on April 10, 1864 (Hall, 1868). In 1866, France withdrew its Army. The United States, in its own civil war, did not recognize the Maximilian regime. Instead, at the end of the American Civil War in 1865, it was able to give some aid to President Benito Juarez's democratic forces of Mexico. Consequently, Maxilimian's empire collapsed, and he was captured and executed. His wife, Carlota, who had gone to Europe to seek support for her husband's empire emotionally lost it and became insane (Haslip, 1972; Hyde, 1946; O'Connor, 1971; Ridley, 2001).

The same bloodthirsty ghosts that haunted the ancient and medieval emperors also engulfed early modern monarchs and contemporary presidents, prime ministers, and other politicians. In the contemporary regimes of the world, waging unprovoked wars for territorial control, and economic domination, has not eclipsed the globe. We still have some states waging wars not for trivial dynastic reasons of the ancient, medieval, and early modern times but for fictitious national security, power, ambition, greed, glory, reverence, economic exploitation, and monopolization of industries.

The above data are provided to demonstrate the origin and development of state crimes or government crimes. It must be a fit of intellectual bankruptcy for anyone, after reading this chapter, to still claim that governments do not violate their own laws and laws of other nations at the criminal level. It is unequivocal that there are state crimes when Proal (1898) noted, "Humanity has had for its governors slaughterers, fanatics, robbers, false coiners, bankrupts, madmen, men who have been corrupt, and men who have sown seeds of corruption."

Undeniably, some criminally minded politicians make criminal heads of state. That's what William Chambliss (1978, 1988) called "From petty crooks to presidents." It was the same greedy, power-hungry, empire-building ancient and medieval Roman emperors' mindset that affected the minds of 18th to 21st century heads of state which culminated, among others, in the World War I (1914–1918), (which America called the war of Europe) and World War II (1939–1945), which was still the war of Europe. The League of Nations emerged to control the excesses of some of the European States, but the League still failed because of the social, political, and economic pathologies that caused it. While Chapter 1 provided us with the working tool of this book, crimes of colonization in Chapter 3 nails down the validity of the concept of state crime.

Review Questions

1. How did the fall of Constantinople in 1453 A.D. give rise to the modern times?
2. How did the "Age of Discovery" give a final blow to feudalism?
3. How did the Roman emperors corrupt some heads of state of the modern times?
4. Why did the United States fail to recognize the Archduke Ferdinand Maximilian regime in Mexico (1864–1866)?
5. The same bloodthirsty ghosts that haunted the ancient and medieval emperors also engulfed early modern monarchs, and some contemporary presidents, prime ministers, and politicians. Discuss.
6. Which American intellectual spurred scholars around the globe to study "state crime"?

Notes

1. The oldest existing bank Monte dei Paschi di Siena, was founded in 1472 in Siena, Italy.
2. Queen Elizabeth I of England believed that Mary Stuart was a threat to her throne, and in effect, got her confined in a number of castles and manor houses in remote locations of England. Despite being incarcerated for eighteen-and-a-half years, Elizabeth I accused Mary Stuart of treason and got her executed.
3. King Nero (Emperor) ordered the murder of his own mother, Agrippina, and framed it as suicide, because he believed that Agrippina was plotting to dethrone him and enthrone Rubellius Polla.

CHAPTER
3

Crimes of Colonization

Colonization is a cancer that kills a nation. I was born less than 90 years after Britain colonized Nigeria. So, as traditional African history is based on oral history, I learned about precolonial Nigeria and Africa from my father who was 68 years old when I was born, and lived until 1962, when he was 94 years old. In addition, my maternal grandfather, who died in 1961, was 116 years. And I lived under British colonial administration, for at least 21 years. In effect, I am in a position to detect the crimes of British colonial administration in Nigeria, and the crimes of colonization elsewhere in the world.

On the basis of my experience with living through a colonial regime, colonization is the unprovoked criminal invasion of a peaceful autonomous nation or society by use of military or paramilitary force, crushing every resistance, forcing the traditional ruler, chief or king, to surrender his domain, or he would be sent to exile. Consequently, came the usurpation of the power and authority of the traditional leader, taxing and enslaving some of the natives, coupled with exploitation, expropriation, and appropriation of the natural resources of the people for as long as the colonial hegemony lasted.

Colonization involves denial of the native people the right to self-determination. In effect, some of the cultural values of the people were condemned and criminalized, while such behaviors are, by no means, a violation of fundamental human rights of anybody. Also, the colonists engaged in elimination of the religious beliefs and matrimonial standards of the people and qualified them as paganism (Sellin, 1938; Ebbe, 1988).

Remote Causes of Colonization

The ancient and medieval monarchies laid the foundation of early modern imperial ambitions. As noted above, Machiavelli's maxim, "the end justifies the means," prepared the minds of the national leaders of the 16th century through the 21st century to pursue their political ambitions and aspirations to infinity without considerations.

Undeniably, the ancient and medieval politics was shrouded in tyranny, deceit, and fraud. Both the ancient and medieval emperors achieved power and prestige through successful wars, oppression, assassination, and exile of those who were threats to their throne, corruption, and injustice (Proal, 1898). During the Middle Ages, Roman emperors were engulfed in using poison, cold-blooded murder, exile, corruption, torture, and oppression as the modus operandi of governance (Ebbe, 1990; Proal 1898). Both Caesar and Pompey caused the death of more than 2 million people in their foreign wars. And Charles IX (1550–1574) ordered the Saint Bartholomew Day Massacre to thwart a Huguenot plot against the Royal Family (Holt, 2002; Knecht, 2001; Benedict, 2004, Proal, 1898).

Machiavelli had advised heads of state and other politicians in his writings that whatever course of action that is for the good of the state should be regarded as a supreme goal, and should be pursued at all costs. He further asserted that such a course of action must not be stopped by "any regard to justice or injustice, cruelty, glory or ignominy" (Proal, 1898, p. 21). In effect, whatever domestic and foreign policy that medieval and modern heads of state considered to be in the primary interest of the nation were pursued with impunity at all costs.

The fall of Constantinople and the resulting Renaissance, and the emergence of the Age of Discovery brought a new phase of competition and conflict among European nations. The discovery of new lands across the globe by Portuguese and Spaniards, spearheaded by the voyages and discoveries of Bartholomew Diaz (1488), Christopher Columbus (1492), Vasco da Gama (1498), and circumnavigation of the globe by Ferdinand Magellan (1519–1521), brought unquenchable appetite for exploration and discovery of new nations to trade with or conquer and exploit, as the emperors promised the explorers that they would be appointed governors of the new nations to be discovered (Ames, 2004; Subrahmanyam, 1997; Russell-Wood, 1993; Phillips & Phillips, 1992; Cohen, 1969: Fuson, 1992).

In addition, the emergence of the Industrial Revolution in England in 1750 sharpened the desire to discover new lands, conquer them, and exploit them for the new industries in Europe. In effect, Britain entered the exploration of Africa, Asia, and the Middle East. Mungo Park (1771–1806) of Scotland led the way in entering the interior of the tailor-made country called "Nigeria," when he was searching for the source and mouth of the River Niger.

The Process of Colonization

In this section, the writer is going to use his Nigerian experience to demonstrate how many of the nations in Africa; Asia; the Middle East; and North, Central, and South America became colonized by various European colonists.

During the Age of Discovery, the initial encounter with new autonomous societies, in the main, was friendly. It was just like tourists meeting new people. For instance, in 1454, Prince Henry of Portugal obtained from Pope Nicholas V a Papal Bull granting to Portugal all lands and islands which had been, or might be, discovered south of Cape Bojador (i.e., Africa). In 1472, the land of Southern Nigeria was discovered by the Portuguese under the leadership of Ruy de Squira. In 1485, the ancient city of Benin was visited by another Portuguese, Joao Affonso d'Aveiro, who took back with him a Bini ambassador (Ebbe, 1982). "A great sensation was caused in Europe owing to the discovery of 'tailed' pepper at Benin and the rumor of a great king nearby, who was taken to be Prester John, but was in fact the Awni of Ife" (Talbot, 1929:33, 1967). At this time, the empire of Benin stretched from Kotonu in the west to the Bonny River in the east, and by the next century included Idah to the north.

Within a space of 200 years (1500–1700), the British, Portuguese, and the Dutch built trading posts along the Atlantic coast of West Africa. The Africans were bringing their articles of trade to the seaports and exchanging goods with the Europeans. By the mid-16th century, the Portuguese and the British had begun kidnapping West and East Africans for slavery. When Africans discovered that not all those who went to the seaport to sell their goods returned, the trading process slowed down in some areas, and was totally abandoned in others.

Between 1600 and 1700, the British and the French bought off the trading ports of other European countries who decided to leave the West African Atlantic trade, because the Africans were afraid of being kidnapped; and mosquitoes and tsetse flies were the greatest enemies of the Europeans. The death rate among the Europeans in West Africa due to malaria and yellow fever was too high for the Dutch and others to continue in the across-the-Atlantic trade. For Britain and France, the West Africans were a precious "cargo" to be abandoned, as they regarded men and women from Africa as "cargos."

The West Africans, at the Atlantic Coast, did not want the Europeans to penetrate inland. However, in the course of time, by coaxing and cajolery, they succeeded in getting the attention of the coastal kings and chiefs for an interview. They took to giving precious gifts to the chiefs to establish an intimate relationship. The British and French initial agreements were to come into the region to trade and nothing beyond that, but that was a fraud. This is because both the British and French governments flooded the territories with their military and paramilitary forces and began to dominate the trading at the seaports and posts in the hinterland.

On entering the hinterland close to the Atlantic Coast, the British and French traders were able to entice some Africans and employed them as middlemen to kidnap men, women, and children to be carried into slavery. At this point, the African chiefs' resistance to the European trade and relationship began. According to my nonagenarian father and maternal centenarian grandfather:

The Whiteman started attacking one village after another from the towns along the coast to towns inland. Natives ran away from their homes. The sound of the

Whiteman's gun was ear-piercing that everybody ran away. Some people were able to go back to their homes at night, when the Whiteman had withdrawn, but early in the morning, people left their homes to hide in the jungle. Nobody was going to the farm to work anymore, because in many instances, they had used their gun and surrounded everybody in a farm and took the young men and women. They left old men and old women.

Worse of all, they built fortresses in some towns like Brass, Opobo, Onitsha, etc; and from there they launched their offensives. Consequently, some towns came together and mustered courage, formed a large committee, and walked to the Whiteman's fortress to surrender and pledge an agreement of peace and non-violence. In some places, a chief signed an agreement of non-violence with the Whiteman, but the chief did not know that the Whiteman was going to settle in the region and be his governor, and interfere with his power and authority.

My father was born in 1868, and my maternal grandfather around 1845. So they saw a lot about how the British gained control of a region we today call "Nigeria." In addition, my mother was born in 1900 and died on November 5, 1999. She told us (her children), how she and other children were being hidden every day to protect them from being kidnapped and sold into slavery.

When an area of Nigeria has many kings and chiefs, after invading the area and conquering them, the British got the chiefs and kings to their fortress to sign an agreement of peace and cooperation. In all cases, before signing the agreement or treaty, the king or chief did not know that he would totally relinquish his political power and authority to the British.

After the Reformation, the Papal Bull was ignored; so in 1553, the first known English expedition to Benin (Nigeria) took place under Windham and Pintaedo, and English and French ships began to come in large numbers. The first chartered African company was granted a patent by Queen Elizabeth I in 1588, but its ship never reached Nigeria. In 1618, another British company was given a charter by King James I.

In 1631, what appeared to be the third British company was chartered by King Charles I. The English merchants began to share in the trade of palm oil, cotton, gold, ivory, bronze, and brass. When the traditional rulers of Southern Nigeria saw that their products were becoming very lucrative, the result was interborder conflicts to secure more palm trees and cotton. The traditional rulers exchanged their goods for iron spears, guns, gun powder, and other European goods. The increasing demand for more Nigerian goods escalated intertribal jealousy and envy.

When competition among European merchants proliferated, there came the need for an agreement to determine each company's territory. The treaty of Utrecht in 1712 secured a 30-year monopoly for Great Britain. British influence increased on the coast as a result of this treaty, and England began to take a leading part in gold, bronze, brass, cotton, and palm oil trade (Niven, 1937; Ebbe, 1982). In 1796, Mungo Park, a Scottish doctor of medicine, made his journey of exploration and saw a great river at Segu. He called it the river "Niger." Many expeditions were made to find the source, course, and mouth of this mysterious river. These attempts took many lives at Bussa Rapids, including that of Mungo Park. It was in 1830 that John and Richard Lander (The Lander brothers) succeeded in finding that the River Niger entered the Atlantic Ocean, not through an estuary as was theorized, but through a delta. Thus, from the River Niger, the British named the geographical area around it "Nigeria." By this time, trading stations, mainly British, were found all over the coast and up the rivers and creeks, especially in the oil rivers, Calabar and Cameroon Rivers (Talbot, 1967).

John Beecroft, Governor of the Island of Fernando Po,[2] was appointed consul and agent for the Bight of Benin and Biafra "to regulate trade between the ports of Benin, Brass, New and Old Calabar, Bony, Bimbia, and the Cameroons" (Ayandele, 1979).

In 1851, when the King of Lagos, Kosoko, refused to stop his annual raids against his neighbors and sale of POWs into slavery, the British attacked and captured Lagos. Benjamin Campbell was appointed Consul at Lagos for the Bight of Benin, while Beecroft retained the Bight of Biafra. Akintoye was enthroned as the Oba of Lagos (king). When he died, his son, Dosummu, became the king of Lagos. The British placed Dosummu as king of Lagos. In 1861, a British naval force seized Lagos in the name of Queen Victoria, and King Dosummu was exiled, because he refused to accede Lagos to the British, and consul William McCosky was installed as the acting governor. At this period, Lagos, as a British colony, was governed directly from Britain (Ayandele, 1970; Carland, 1985). At this stage, the British had invested a lot of men and money in Nigeria, but local resistance was still very high in many towns and tribes of Nigeria in both the north and south regions.

When peaceful takeover of the towns and tribes was not possible, the British Government decided to make peace by use of force (Ebbe, 1982). British troops attacked and defeated the Egba and Ijebu Ode near Lagos. By 1866, the British had reached all the three regions of Nigeria with trading stations but were not involved with governing the people. The traditional rulers in the hinterland still retained their power, except where there was resistance against British merchants; then war became the alternative. When a traditional ruler was defeated, another person from the tribe was crowned chief or king by the British merchants. The British Government had a consul at Lagos to coordinate trade and relations with the natives. When the native rulers opposed direct trade with the interior, the consulate dispatched troops to attack the particular kingdom.

In 1881, King Jaja of Opobo of the eastern coast attacked the Kwa-Ibo villages to bring them under his domain. He also obstructed trade with the British. The British made a treaty with King Jaja, which he violated, and so he was exiled to the island of Saint Helena. By 1875, the British consulate could not handle the problems of the British merchants in Nigeria because of the size of the country and the intertribal wars and native rulers' conflicts with the

European merchants. The consul himself was not always in his position, because the climate made it necessary for him to be frequently in England on leave.

In 1884, the British merchants on the Benin River complained that no consul had visited the river for five years, and in 1885 merchants on the other rivers pointed out to the British Home Government that no consul had been on the coast "for a long time" (Burns, 1967). After a series of negotiations and fake promises, the British signed a treaty with the chiefs of the Oil Rivers, placing their territories under British "protection." Similar treaties were obtained from the chiefs of the tribes on either bank of the Niger and from the Fulani Sultans of Sokoto and Gwandu.

The treaties were purely extortionary agreements. The kings and chiefs were not literate and did not understand what they were putting an "x" to as their signature in consent. Presented below is a treaty signed by eleven Kings, a Queen, and six Chiefs at the British fortress in Asaba located at the bank of the River Niger in 1884. The treaty has IX articles. The kings, queen, and chiefs were lured into putting an "x" by their names to indicate that they agreed to the clauses and Articles of the treaty. Here is the full treaty:

TREATY WITH ASABA, 1884

Treaty with Kings, Queen, and Chiefs of Asaba, signed at Asaba.

Her Majesty the Queen of the United Kingdom of Great Britain and Ireland, Empress of India, etc., and the Kings, Queen, and Chiefs of Asaba, being desirous of maintaining and strengthening the relation of peace and friendship which have for so long existed between them:

Her Britannic Majesty has named and appointed E.H. Hewett, Esq., her Consul for the Bights of Benin and Biafra, to conclude a Treaty for this purpose.

The said E.H. Hewett, Esq., and the said Kings, Queen, and Chiefs of Asaba have agreed upon and concluded the following Articles:—

ARTICLE I

Her Majesty the Queen of Great Britain and Ireland, etc., in compliance with the request of the Kings, Queen, Chiefs, and people of Asaba, hereby undertakes to extend to them, and to the territory under their authority and jurisdiction, her gracious favor and protection.

ARTICLE II

The Kings, Queen, and Chiefs of Asaba agree and promise to refrain from entering into any correspondence, Agreement, or Treaty with any foreign nation or Power, except with the knowledge and sanction of Her Britannic Majesty's Government.

ARTICLE III

It is agreed that full and exclusive jurisdiction, civil and criminal, over British subjects and their property in the territory of Asaba is reserved to Her Britannic Majesty, to be exercised by such Consular or other offices as Her Majesty shall appoint for that purpose.

The same jurisdiction is likewise reserved to Her Majesty in the said territory of Asaba over foreign subjects enjoying British protection, who shall be deemed to be included in the expression 'British subject' throughout this Treaty.

ARTICLE IV

All disputes between the Kings, Queen, and Chiefs of Asaba, or between them and British or foreign traders or between the aforesaid Kings, Queen, and Chiefs and neighboring tribes, which cannot be settled amicably between the two parties, shall be submitted to the British Consular or other officers appointed by her Britannic Majesty decision, or for arrangement.

ARTICLE V

The Kings, Queen, and Chiefs of Asaba hereby agree to assist the British Consular or other officers in the execution of such duties as may be assigned to them; and, further, to act upon their advice in matters relating to the administration of justice, the development of the resources of the country, the interests of commerce, or in any other matter in relation to peace, order and good government, and the general progress of civilization.

ARTICLE VI

The subjects and citizens of all countries may freely carry on trade in every part of the territories of the Kings, Queen, and Chiefs parties hereto, and may have houses and factories therein, subject to the agreement made on the 28th August, 1884, between the Kings, Queen, and Chiefs and the National African Company (Limited), of London.

ARTICLE VII

All ministers of the Christian religion shall be permitted to reside and exercise their calling within the territories of the aforesaid Kings, Queen, Chiefs, who hereby guarantee to them full protection.

All forms of religious worship and religious ordinances may be exercised within the territories of the aforesaid Kings, Queen, and Chiefs, and no hindrance shall be offered thereto.

ARTICLE VIII

If any vessels should be wrecked within the Asaba territories, the Kings, Queen, and Chiefs will give them all the assistance in their power, will secure them from plunder, and also recover and deliver to the owners or agents all the property which can be saved.

If there are no such owners or agents on the spot, then the said property shall be delivered to the British Consular or other officer.

The Kings, Queen, and Chiefs further engage to do all in their power to protect the persons and property of the officers, crew, and others on board such wrecked vessels.

All claims for salvage dues in such cases shall, if disputed, be referred to the British Consular or other officer for arbitration and decision.

ARTICLE IX

This treaty shall come into operation, so far as may be practicable, from the date of its signature.

Done in duplicate at Asaba, this 1st day of November, 1884.

(Signed)   EDWARD HYDE HEWETT

KING OBI AKATA, his X mark.
KING OBI NEZA OMUKRORU, his X mark.
KING OBI WABUNI, his X mark.
KING OBI OSUDEBE, his X mark.
KING OBI RAPU OKOSA, his X mark.
KING OBI NTEE, his X mark.
KING OBI MEMEKA, his X mark.
KING OBI OGASIE, his X mark.
KING OBI CHEGEA, his X mark.
KING OBI NEYA, his X mark.
KING OBI AUBA, his X mark.
QUEEN OMU WANUKA, her X mark.
KING OBI ONACHIA, his X mark.
        CHIEF OSADEBE, his X mark.
CHIEF ITOR OMORDIE, his X mark

CHIEF AFEHNAZA OMORDIE, his X mark.
CHIEF BALLIE OMORDIE, his X mark.
      CHIEF MBA ODIE, his X mark.
CHIEF AWUNOR ODIE, his X mark.

    Witness to the mark-signatures of the above thirteen Kings, of the Queen, and of the six Chiefs:

(signed)   REGINALD GOUGH PAYNTER

(Signature in Arabic of 'Mohamed Shitta,' a merchant of Lagos

where he is also known as William Shitta.)

Source: Nigerian National Archives, Vol. 3, pp. XI–XII.

Reading the Articles of the Treaty one can see the concepts and phrases such as "protection," "British subjects," "refrain from entering into any correspondence Agreement or Treaty with any foreign nation or power." The fact is nobody asked the British for protection. Why were they fighting against the British and asking them to leave? The Emir of Kano lost the lives of many of his subjects when a company of British invaders attacked the Emirate in 1804 and took his kingdom, and he had to flee for his life. He had to come back to negotiate to take back his throne under the British terms. That was the fraudulent and extortionary treaty the Kings, Emirs, Queens, and Chiefs signed. In other words, they signed the treaties under duress. In effect, by international humanitarian and criminal law, those treaties signed with an "x" in various parts of Nigeria in the 1800s were null and void and ultra vires *ab initio*.

At the Berlin Conference of 1884/1885, all of the Western European countries partitioning Africa in their scramble for the Dark Continent claimed that the African tribes needed protection from each other. The Africans were not there to refute their claims. And who were the judges at the Berlin Conference? They were the same European colonizers.

Unmistakably, at the Berlin Conference of 1885, the British representatives were able, successfully, to claim that British interests were supreme on the lower Niger and on the Oil Rivers. And their claim to Nigeria was recognized by the conference. A notification was accordingly published in the *London Gazette* of June 5, 1885, declaring the establishment of a protectorate over the "Niger District" (Burns, 1967). These districts were defined as including the territories on the coastline between the British protectorate of Lagos and the right of the western bank of the Rio de Rey, and the territories on both banks of the Niger from its confluence with the River Benue at Lokoja to the sea, as well as the territories on both banks of the River Benue, from the confluence.

Colonization was a business venture. As a result, Britain must find a way to spend less money in administering its colonies by selling the colonies to a business corporation by a Charter. That was the first approach in the colonial exploitation.

For six years, the Oil Rivers Protectorate existed only on paper, and nothing was being done to make it really effective. The consul continued to exercise a more or less nominal authority. The British Government was not yet prepared to provide the costly administration that would be necessary if the immense area were to be brought under control. The British Parliament felt that it was better to hand over the territory to those who were willing and anxious to administer the region. In effect, on July 10, 1886, a Royal Charter was granted to the National African Company Limited.[3] The name was later changed to the Royal Niger Company, Chartered and Limited, and later United African Company (UAC).

The delta tribes, who had objected to the European merchants trading with the interior, became more hostile than ever when the different firms were amalgamated into one powerful company. They did not cease in their efforts to hamper its trade. Eventually this company proved too strong for them. But from time to time, stations were sacked by the hinterland tribes, and the company suffered. Towns like Onitsha and Asaba, with strong traditional rulers, persistently refused to allow the company to operate in their territories. Both Onitsha and Asaba were attacked by the company's constabulary and conquered with the aid of the British Naval squadron. Other delta towns were subjugated and brought under control. Courts of justice were established and an armed constabulary, with British officers, protected the business locations. Custom duties and trade licenses were imposed to provide the funds necessary for administration. The company made regulations guiding the movement of people. Some tribes hated this, especially where some normative behaviors in the people's culture were proscribed (Ebbe, 1985; Sellin, 1938). The people of Brass on the eastern coast of Nigeria were the first to violate the company's regulations. The company sent some armed men, including some Brassmen serving the company, to warn the chief of Brass. This angered the King of Brass, but attacking the company's messengers would be killing some of his kinsmen. Mutual resentment increased, and there were frequent threats that Akassa, the company's trade headquarters, would be attacked. On January 27, 1895, Mr. Harrison, the Vice-Consul at Brass, received an anonymous letter in the following terms:

> Brass people leaving tomorrow to destroy Royal Niger Company's factories and lives at Akassa on Tuesday morning. Be sure you send troops at once to stop them.
>
> An Observer

Mr. Harrison had to alert the Agent-General of the company at Akassa. The Agent-General did not think it probable that an attack would be made. Before daylight on January 29, 1895, a fleet of canoes, containing over 1,500 men, left the various towns of Brass and, passing quietly by the consulate and the merchants' factories at Brass, entered the waters within the sphere of the company. The company's patrolling streamer was easily evaded in the darkness, and the heavy mist on the river provided additional cover, and Akassa was suddenly attacked. The Agent-General escaped in a steamer, and the other Europeans successfully defended themselves in a house, but the African servants of the company, mostly "crewmen," were not so fortunate. About twenty-four were killed and sixty carried off as prisoners (Burns, 1967). Most of the company's property at Akassa was destroyed and plundered. Several of the delta tribes joined in the looting after the fight was over, and only the timely appearance of a steamer, which was mistaken for a warship, put an end to the raid. The situation annoyed the British Government, because the Royal Niger Company, Chartered and Limited, went beyond the territory assigned to it. The Brass tribe and their territorial waters were not included in the company's administration.

Shortly after the Akassa raid, the company was involved in a struggle with the Fulani Emirs of Nupe and Ilorin in Northern Nigeria. The Emirs vehemently refused the Royal Niger Company infringing on their affairs. On January 6, 1897, a force of 500 men of the Royal Niger Constabulary, with two guns, and over 800 carriers, marched westwards from Lokoja in pursuit of a portion of the Nupe army (see Appendix A—map of colonial Nigeria). The force was accompanied by the Governor of the Company, Sir George Taubman Goldie. The war camp of the Nupe army was discovered and destroyed, but the Nupe soldiers scattered and fled before the company's heavy gunfire. The company engaged itself in a series of wars all over the country far beyond its territory. The company violated the articles of the charter, one of which was "never to interfere with the laws, customs, and traditions of the people as long as there were no human sacrifices involved" (Ebbe, 1982, p. 42). The time had, however, arrived when the existence of the Chartered Company could no longer be justified. All investigations made by Major MacDonald in 1889 about various allegations against the company confirmed the company's deviation from the articles of the Charter.

Consequently, in 1899 the British Government decided that the Charter should be revoked. The British Government felt that the company was no longer able to handle the administration of the area, and with the British-French agreement of June 1898, by which the present western frontier of Nigeria was established, the old Kingdom of Borgu was divided between the two powers. The British-French agreement and the manner in which the company's commercial monopoly pressed on the native traders, as exemplified by the raiding in Brass and Akassa, was among the things which led to the Charter being taken away from the company (Niven, 1937, p. 214; Burns, 1967). The British Government thought that it was necessary for a government to be set up in Nigeria to carry out the agreement with France and to control directly the West African Frontier Force. The Royal Niger Company had been forbidden by the Charter to set up a monopoly of trade, but it did; so the British Government revoked its Charter. On April 1, 1899, the Colonial Office took over from the Foreign Office, the Niger Coast Protectorate, which had been controlled by the Royal Niger Company. The laws of the Royal Niger Company were formally repealed by the High Commissioner under an Order in Council, and a number of new Niger Coast Protectorate laws were declared to be in force (Talbot, 1967, p. 72). Steps were taken to establish a Supreme Court, Commissioners Courts, and Native Courts now called Customary Courts.

On January 1, 1900, the Royal Niger Company's territories were transferred to the Crown. Colonel Lugard was appointed the first High Commissioner for Northern Nigeria by an Order in Council, and the Niger Coast Protectorate was constituted the Protectorate of Southern Nigeria. The Protectorate of Southern Nigeria was placed under Divisional Commissioners, and the Consul and Vice-Consul positions were abolished. By 1901, most areas in the hinterland of the eastern coast were still hostile to trade, and British penetration was almost impossible because of the military might of the local towns. In 1902, the colonial government took out what is known as the "Aro Expedition" and brought the cities of Aro-Chuku, Bende, Iko-Ekpene, Uyo, Aba, and parts of Owerri and Ahoada clans under control (see Appendix A).

The Building of a Totalitarian Unitary Government

In 1906, by letters patent of February 28, Lagos Colony and Protectorate were amalgamated with Southern Nigeria under a Governor and Commander-in-Chief, Sir Walter Egerton, with its capital at Lagos. Up to that time, Northern and Southern Nigeria were separate countries. The Yoruba intertribal fighting was stopped by the governor at Lagos, and a treaty drawn up by him was signed by all the tribal rulers (Talbot, 1967, p. 67). The Criminal Code of Nigeria was drawn up in 1904, patterned according to English law and custom. This Criminal Code had opposition from the natives, because some of the laws conflicted with the customary values of the people. For example, Section 370 of the Criminal Code prescribed seven years' imprisonment for anyone who marries another while the first marriage is still legal. This statute conflicted with polygamy, which was, and still is, a common cultural practice of all the tribes in Nigeria (Ebbe, 1985).

"On the first of January 1914, Nigeria came into existence" (Niven, 1937, p. 238). That day, Northern and Southern Nigeria were amalgamated under a Governor General and two Lieutenant Governors (one for the Northern and one for the Southern provinces), each with a secretariat. For the first time in its violent colonial history, Nigeria came under one government. Its diverse peoples and tribes (Niven, 1937, p. 238) had no choice and accepted the central dictatorship government, but not unanimously. Some accepted a united Nigeria, because no particular tribe was ruling, and some were hostile to anyone from outside their tribe. In June 1918, an Egba uprising occurred. The Egba people did not want to associate with their enemies, such as the Oyo, Ijebu-Ode, and Ibadan in the United Nigeria. The colonial government crushed the Egba in August of that year. In the year of the amalgamation (1914), there was fighting at Ogoja Province, Obubra Clan, and serious disturbances occurred in Aba, Okigwi, Owerri, and Bende (Talbot, 1967, p. 275). In short, the Nigerians did not want the alien government. They wanted to be left alone and live by their customs and traditions.

Furthermore, the introduction of taxation, called "Capitation Rate," brought about a series of opposition in different towns and clans. This is an infringement upon the kings' and chiefs' rights to determine the economic well-being of their subjects. This led to riots at Warri in 1928 and what is known as the "Women's War" or (because it all started in Aba) the "Aba Uprising." The rising by women took place when the government proposed that women should pay taxes, and women took to the streets destroying government and company installations. Some government police officers and some of the rioting women were killed. The women's riot against payment of taxes was countrywide, and it lasted from 1929 through 1930. The riot was more devastating at Abeokuta and Egbaland than any other place in the country. In effect, the women's taxation proposal was dropped.

Another serious problem came when the government started installing chiefs and kings in place of hereditary rulers who opposed colonial administration. The consequences of bestowing chieftancy and kingship title on individuals who were not in the line of chiefs or kings and sometimes bestowed on untouchables (*Osu*), were social structurally damaging to tradition. The rightful kings, who were set aside, "bit their fingers" and poisoned the British-imposed incumbents, an act reminiscent of some Roman dynastic emperors.

When Britain was involved in war in East Africa, Burma, and World War II, many Nigerians were recruited. When the survivors came back in 1947, they brought with them patterns of behavior such as rape, pocket picking, smoking marijuana, daylight robbery, burglary, and willful homicide.[4] In the writer's hometown, some people took to the nearby bush, when they saw an ex-soldier coming toward them. Women who saw an ex-soldier coming toward them trembled to a freezing point at his appearance, because he dressed as if he were going to war and carried a Mark-4 bolt action rifle which he had smuggled home. Some wives were taken away from their rightful husbands, and grudges still persist; the sons of such soldiers are visited with revenge by the sons of those whose fathers' wives were forcefully grabbed.

Both World Wars I and II resulted in many enlightened Nigerians' agitating for representation in the House of Representatives in Lagos. Representation in the House of Representatives became a new source of interethnic conflict. For instance, when the House of Representatives in Lagos under the Governor, Sir Hugh Clifford, wanted Nigerians represented in the House in 1930, the problem was which tribes should have representation. Only 21 Nigerians were members of the House, although there were more than 200 tribes. At this time, the Hausa and Fulani Muslims of Northern Nigeria started to hate any unity of Southern and Northern Nigeria. They had their problem of unwillingness and inability to learn the English language. The Hausas openly declared that they wanted a separate government, but the Governor General did not want that to happen. The worst political division was yet to be made. In 1946, a new Governor General, Sir Author Richard, divided Nigeria into three regions, East, West, and North, without a plebiscite and without granting them autonomy. The Governor knew that the system of representation in Lagos had, *ipso facto*, shown the tribes that they were to compete with one another. In fact, they were not ready to stick together for a united country. Interethnic conflicts became a regular occurrence.

In spite of the agitations against dividing the country into three regions under one central government, regional headquarters were opened at Enugu (East), Ibadan (West), and Kaduna (North). The Hausas insisted on pulling out of the latent Federation, but they were not allowed to. The leader of the Yoruba tribe, Chief Obafemi Awolowo, who graduated from the University of London, set up a slogan of "divide and rule." What he meant was, let each region remain a separate entity from the other because the major ethnic groups (Yoruba, Ibo, and Hausa) constituted the bulk of the population of each region. But that was not convenient for the British Imperial Government. From 1946, the three regions (three major tribes) continued to exist in intertribal antagonisms which got worse after independence.

Some people from one region went to live in another for government services and trade, especially the Ibos and Yorubas. Ibos like to trade, and some went to the new trading cities in the northern and western regions. Educated people had to be employed to work in any region where the colonial unitary government had vacancy. Ibos embraced Western education faster and to a greater extent than the other tribes (Kwitny, 1980), so the colonial government employed many Ibos all over the country.

The Ibo civil service domination sharpened the old tribal hatred. Yorubas fought Ibos at Ajegunle near Lagos, the Tivs fought Nupe in 1951, and Hausas killed many Ibos living in Kano City in 1953. Perennial skirmishes across the borders have not died away up to this date. Most Africans are not known for forgiving and forgetting their enemies, no matter how long ago the injury was perpetrated.

Monetary System and Migration

As soon as European merchants established trading posts in the delta areas and the hinterland of the coastal regions, money as a medium of exchange was introduced. Most people refused to accept the monetary system introduced and continued to trade by barter. Under this state of affairs, the British government levied taxes which would be paid in money rather than barter. As soon as the taxation system was initiated, coupled with imprisonment for failing to pay, people started to accept British money for their products. Some people who had no cash crops to sell to get money for the capitation rate had to go to the trading posts to work for the European merchants. Some people had to travel for many miles from their homes to the trading posts. As soon as they saved up the required amount to pay their capitation rate, they left for their towns and villages. Movement from the villages to the trading centers became an annual event for many adults. Thus, a new pattern of migration was established in Nigeria.

Both the colonial government and the missionaries built schools and stressed the importance of English language and Western education. A small amount was introduced as school fees in both church (private) and public schools, and money had to be used to pay the fees. Some parents felt bad about the problem of migrating to cities to get jobs and money to pay the school fees. In effect, they refused to send their children to school. Payment of school fees in the primary schools contributed to a low rate of literacy in Nigeria. Some parents, especially in Northern Nigeria, hated Western education so much that they swore that their children would never go to school, and this continues till date.

Colonial Exploitation of Their Dependencies

The British Colonial Government of Nigeria knew that bringing the three major ethnic groups (Ibo, Yourba, and Hausa), naturally separated by two large rivers, into one central unitary government was a bad idea; yet they went for it. The River Niger and the River Benue naturally divided the three ethnic groups into North (Hausa), West (Yoruba), and East (Ibo). By African religion and philosophy, "bush fire does not cross a river and burn a forest on the other side." That means, in African customary law, an individual or a tribe does not claim ownership of land across a river 300 kilometers wide. But the colonial government deliberately decided to sow the seed of perpetual conflict in Nigeria. To do so, they redesigned the boundaries of what constituted Northern, Western, and Eastern Nigeria. They knew that the Hausas of Northern Nigeria were backward in Western education and economic endeavors. In effect, they avoided the rivers in drafting regional boundaries for the north. They knew that Ibos and Yorubas are customarily capitalist societies with very high enthusiasm for Western education. In effect, the colonial administration avoided the River Niger on the northwest and the River Benue on the northeast and came down below the confluence of the tributary of the two rivers with such towns as Oturkpo, Lokoja, Idah in the Northern Region of Nigeria (see Appendix A). The colonial administration did that on purpose, so that when democracy was introduced in a tribal society, the backward north would lead the nation. And that is what happened to Nigeria when independence was granted October 1, 1960.

The main goal of British colonial administration was exploitation, expropriation, and appropriation of natural resources of Nigeria and any country in Africa, Asia, and the Middle East that they ever colonized. Take, for instance, the whole of Nigeria, which had a population of 55 million people in 1956, had only one University College which had less than eight hundred students. It was the same story in all of their colonies in Africa, Asia, and the Middle East. In addition, they built inexpensive hospitals, and some colonial districts like Orlu with six counties today did not have even a single government (general) hospital. In addition, they did not construct even a single paved highway or street throughout the colonial regime. No two vehicles could pass each other on colonial bridges built for Nigeria, and those narrow bridges took many lives before post-independence governments could reconstruct them. Where was the money from the palm produce; peanut-pyramid in Kano; cocoa, gold, other minerals; and agricultural export products? Such money was transferred to Her Majesty as tax revenue and to pay the colonial administrators.

In addition, in the colonial dictatorship, like all dictatorships, there was no accountability to the people about how their money was being spent. There is no deviance more serious than colonial exploitation and appropriation of its dependencies.

Worst of all, there were two types of taxes on the people: individual taxes (capitation rate) and income tax for business owners and employed persons. The colonial governments were accountable only to their home governments.

The Nigerian colonial cities were almost like the *Last Grave at Dimbaza,* in that while the British colonial administrators live in a segregated area of the city called "European Quarters" with a good water supply system and excellent sanitary conditions, the rest of the city had no good water supply system, no sewer, and no sanitation. The pit-latrines in the cities produced more diseases to the city dwellers than they could prevent. If such a policy was not criminal, it was a serious deviance.

The colonial regimes were out to make money for their home governments by all means. They used the police for intimidation and extortion. For instance, in 1948, my father was fined £5 (five pounds) in Orlu Magistrate's Court, because he "coughed" in the court while the court was in session. Think about that. Thank God my dad had the money at the time. Some Nigerians would have slept in jail that day, if they didn't pay the money on that day, or may remain in jail for weeks until somebody pays it to bail them out.[5] In fact, a colonial regime was a robbery and extortionary money-making machine for its home government.

The colonial police brutalized so many people in Nigeria. And most of the policemen were Nigerians being used against Nigerians. There were no women police in colonial Nigeria, because the colonial police force was not designed to help the people. Instead, they were instituted to force men and women to do what the colonial master wanted them to do, no matter how contrary the colonial law and regulation was to the cherished values of the people. The colonial police were used to raid villages and towns that refused to yield to the colonial administration. Consequently, the Nigerian police have been seen as enemies of the people even up to the year 2014. This negative police attitude to the masses is found in all former colonial dependencies of India, Ghana, Burma, Malaysia, Sierra Leone, and so forth.

The Granting of Independence to Former Colonial Dependencies

Again using Nigeria as an example of what happened in other former colonial dependencies at the time they wanted independence, the colonial master, especially the British style, laterally promised their colonies that they were going to collapse at the eclipse of the colonial regime. In the case of Nigeria, the British had divided the country in such a way that there would be trouble when they are gone.

When Dr. Nnamdi Azikiwe spearheaded the march to Nigerian independence with his *West African Pilot* newspaper immediately after he returned from his overseas university studies in the United States, the British colonial government sent him into exile in Ghana, West Africa. That was because Dr. Azikiwe was using his newspaper to tell the masses about the benefits of national independence from alien rule. Unfortunately, for the colonial administration, Dr. Azikiwe was able to publish his newspaper in Ghana and dump copies all over the three regions of Nigeria. He was able to publish facts about the negative consequences of colonial rule, which he would have not published if he were based in Nigeria. Consequently, in 1946, the colonial administration unilaterally revoked the exile and lured Zik (as he was called) back to Nigeria.

Undeniably, the colonial administration saw that it was better to have Dr. Zik reside in Nigeria than outside of Nigeria. Zik agreed to return to Nigeria on the condition that he be allowed to continue to publish his *West African Pilot* newspaper. The British colonial administrators granted him unconditional reentry into Nigeria (Ebbe, 2011).

Zik formed a political party called National Council of Nigeria and Cameroons (NCNC)[6] and agitated for Nigerian independence with a slogan: "One Nigeria One Destiny."[7] The British colonial administrators were profoundly very angry with Dr. Nnamdi Azikiwe. Consequently, on one occasion, the last colonial Governor General of Nigeria, Sir James Robertson (1955–1960), said to Zik in 1955 (five years before Nigerian independence), that "Nigeria will never get independence on a gold platter" (Ebbe, 2011, p. 13).

Sir Robertson's assertion and challenge to Zik did not take too long to materialize. In 1964, nearly four years after independence, Nigeria exploded. In 1966, Nigeria fell apart in a military coup d'etat, and was on the verge of the regions going their separate ways. Unfortunately for Nigeria, when the military head of state of Nigeria, Major General Yakubu Gowon, saw the handwriting on the wall, after Eastern Region seceded from Nigeria as a result of a pogrom against the Ibos in 1966, and announced on the Government Radio that "There is no basis for Nigerian Unity;" the British Foreign Minister told General Gowon, "Without the Ibos, there is no Nigeria," as if he and Britain loved Nigeria so much. Consequently, General Gowon changed his mind and announced on the same government radio that, "to keep Nigeria 'one' is an attack that must be done." And on July 6, 1967, Nigerian forces attacked Eastern Region which had declared itself "the Republic of Biafra." In the two-and-a-half years' war, Britain sold military war equipment to Nigeria and used their bomber jet planes to bomb open market places in Eastern Nigeria before my eyes, which killed innocent local women and children (more on this on "State Terrorism" and "State Genocide").

Since independence from Britain, Nigeria has had six coups d'etat. The six military regimes created a predatory state, or what David Satter (2003) described as a "criminal state." In effect, the successive civilian governments were also predatory states. The Nigerian military that has ruled Nigeria for 34 years want to make sure that no civilian government will ever probe them. As a result, they made sure that a puppet civilian politician was installed as the Nigeria head of state, and the predatory government system continues.

Undeniably, Nigeria is now a failed state, because, how can a colonial government be a dictatorship unitary system of government, and grant independence to a federal structure? That was a political abomination, a deviant act of the most serious magnitude. The British designed Nigeria to fail. They did not hide it. There was no training on federalism given to Nigerians before independence. The wholesale bribery and corruption in Nigeria was planted by the British colonial administrators. If that is false, why is it that official corruption is endemic in all former British colonies? Look at India, Kenya, Uganda, Malaysia, Burma, Sierra Leone, and so forth. Also, why is it that every country that was a British colony has had one or more coups d'etat? France, Spain, and Portugal are also guilty of creating criminal constitutions in their former colonies (Argentina, Brazil, Mexico, Chile, etc.), that would lead to coups d'etat and counter coups d'etat after they give up their colonial hegemony.

Colonial administration was fraught with a high degree of immeasurable deviances against the people of their dependencies. And many of the deviances were outright criminal acts and intrepid violations of international humanitarian laws and standards.

Finally, as can be seen from the data provided in this chapter, crimes of colonization include murder, aggravated assault, rape, violation of international humanitarian laws, aggravated robbery, embezzlement, extortion, violation of fundamental human rights, burglary and stealing of arts or cultural heritage materials of the people, slavery, denial of due process, war crimes, wars of aggression, and crimes against humanity.

Emergence of Peonage and Slave Trade

Historically, peonage emerged with colonialism in Latin America and other countries of Spanish and Portuguese hegemony. A peon was forced to expend his labor power on his master without pay. While peonage preceded slave trade, the two sprang up at the same time, with Spain and Portugal as the leading protagonists.

This system of labor exploitation continued for a long time, and remained in force throughout the slavery era and after. Peonage was a way to get cheap labor for the Spanish and Portuguese plantations in Latin American colonies.

At the same time, 17th and 18th centuries, Britain and France initiated indentured servitude. Young men would like to go to the British and French North American colonies but had no money for the ship captain to take them there. So they entered into a contract with an employer to work for him for a certain number of years. At the end of the contract term, he was free to sell his labor power to someone else. The employer bought the indenture from the sea captain who brought the youths to the new colony. According to Rusche and Kirchheimer (1939), some Western European countries sold some of their prisoners to the plantation owners in North American colonies for a large amount of money as indentured servants for a certain number of years based on their original prison terms.

All of these state-approved peonage and indentured services in the 17th and 18th centuries were deviance but not criminal. They were not criminal at the time, because the practice served the interests of the ruling class of the period.

One of the negative results of the Europeans discovering new lands in North and South America, Africa, Asia, and the Middle East was the forceful carrying away of some men and women as slaves from their native countries to Europe, North America, and South America. The newly discovered nations were colonized by use of force and fraud.

The first Europeans to engage in slave trade were the Portuguese and Spanish merchants. While slaves were acquired from both Africa and Asia, Africa, especially Western and Central Africa, was the center of the slave trade. In the 16th century, Portugal and Spain began trans-Atlantic slave trade. Their plantations in their new colonies in South and Central America and elsewhere were served with forcefully imported African labor. In fact, Portugal and Spain dominated the West African slave trade up to 1580. And they also enslaved some native Latin Americans.

In the 17th and 18th centuries, the British, Dutch, and French entered and dominated the West African slave trade. To make Africans readily available to be traded as slaves, the European merchants provided military weapons to the chiefs and instigated intertribal wars by which persons captured in the wars were sold to them as slaves.[8] The enormous European-manufactured goods exported to West Africa gave African chiefs the incentive to get money through slave trade to buy those European goods.

The British and the French exported their West African slaves to their plantations in North America. In the late 18th through the early 19th centuries, the United States dominated West African slave trade far and above Portugal, Spain, Britain, and the Dutch participations at the time.

After over two centuries of slave trade, a movement to abolish it erupted, when in 1772, Lord Mansfield's judgment in the Somerset's case emancipated a slave in England (Blumrosen & Ruth, 2005). In the case, Lord Mansfield ruled that "No master ever was allowed here to take a slave by force to be sold abroad because he deserted from his service, or for any other reason whatever, therefore the man must be discharged" (Walvin, 2001). By 1783, the British people began an antislavery movement to abolish slave trade. Twenty-five years later, in 1808, the British Parliament passed the Slave Trade Act of 1807. This statute abolished slave trade but not slavery. Later, the Parliament of the United Kingdom in the Slavery Abolition Act of 1833 abolished slavery throughout the British Empire. In 1843, the exceptions given to "the Territories in the Possession of the East India Company," the "Island of Ceylon," and "the Island of Saint Helena," by the Act were eliminated.[9]

In 1865, the 13th Amendment to the United States Constitution abolished slavery in the United States. In the same Act of Congress, involuntary servitude was abolished. On March 2, 1867, the United States Congress passed anti-peonage law. However, similar to the ineffectiveness of laws prohibiting importation and use of narcotics drugs, the law against peonage did not eliminate peonage entirely in the southern states of the United States until up the 1940s.

The issues of slave trade, indentured servitude, and peonage are presented here to demonstrate the hypocrisy of the ruling class of every epoch, and how any behavior, no matter how inhuman and brazenness it might be, for as long as it serves the interests of the ruling class, will not be criminalized. As noted in Chapter 1, only when the masses agitate against the objectionable act, the ruling class will not take the right action. All of slavery, indentured servitude, and peonage of the 17th, 18th, and 19th centuries were state crimes and state-motivated crimes.

Looting of Treasuries of Colonial Dependencies

The colonial administrators were not accountable to the people they governed. They were only accountable to their home government. The treasury of a colonial dependency does not belong to her. All of the revenue from exports of natural resources, including raw materials and taxes collected from the natives, were transferred to the treasury of the colonial master in Europe. For instance, there was no central bank in Nigeria's colonial administration.

Unmistakably, when the African dependencies got their independence, the colonial Minister of Finance left little or no money in the national treasury. These former colonial dependencies had to quickly create their own central banking system and change their currency from British Pound Sterling to whatever they chose to handle the situation. This led to another form of state crime in African developing countries in the form of financial fraud during the change of currencies. What is more deviant than leaving a country without money to function?

Neocolonialism and Instigation of Civil Wars

It is very hard to find any country in the world that was a colonial dependency of a European country and has not had a civil war or a coup d'etat. As all African countries were colonized by European nations except Ethiopia, if an African country has not had a civil war, it must have had, at least, a coup d'etat. Why was it so? It was so because the colonial pre-independence constitution was designed to produce that outcome. Many African scholars came up with that conclusion (Osaghae, 1998; Uwechue, 1971).

In addition, the independence granted was half-baked political independence. It was not economic independence. The former colonial dependencies remain poor till this day. The former colonial master still controls the import and export trade of their former dependencies. In fact, the former colonial masters still control who becomes the head of state in those former dependencies, and that is the neocolonialism. The former colonial masters also harbor and protect fugitive, political criminals who embezzled their countries' money entrusted in their care and flew to the former European colonial master. They never allowed these political criminals to be extradited, and they never helped recover the money embezzled. That is a state deviance and a state crime in the nature of abetting and harboring an international fugitive.

Review Questions

1. In today's international humanitarian law, what type of state crime is colonization?
2. What is denial of "self-determination"? Discuss in full.
3. What is Machiavellianism? In what country did the concept originate?
4. What is the Berlin Conference of 1884/1885? Who was the host? What countries were represented?
5. Imperialism was a business enterprise. Explain.
6. What is peonage? What country introduced peonage in the world? Why is it a violation of federal law in the United States today?
7. What are some of the state crimes of colonization?
8. Two countries started trans-Atlantic slave trade. Which are the two countries?
9. Which English judge, and in what judgment of 1772, triggered slavery abolition in England, United Kingdom?
10. What is neocolonialism?

Notes

1. Prester John was a legendary African king whose kingdom was believed to be full of gold.
2. This was a Spanish colonial island now known as Equatorial Guineau.
3. This company was still operating in Nigeria under a new name called United African Company (UAC) until it was nationalized in 2003.
4. Some of these offenses were existing in Nigeria before the soldiers came back from World War II, but they were done in secret and only very few people were involved, but when the soldiers returned from the war, they acted criminally in the open.
5. In 1948, £5 (five Pound Sterling) could give a man a wife among the Ibos of Nigeria. Therefore, £5 in 1948 was about $3,000 (three thousand) U.S. dollars today.
6. Before World War II, Cameroon was a German colony. After the war in 1945, Britain colonized West Cameroon and amalgamated them as part of the Eastern Nigerian regional government, while Eastern Cameroon was colonized by France. That was how Dr. Zik came up with National Council of Nigeria and Cameroon (NCNC) Political Party. In 1959, a year before the Nigerian Independence, Western Cameroon joined Eastern Cameroon by a rigged plebiscite, because the British colonial government did not want Eastern Nigeria (Igbo-controlled region) to be larger in population than Northern Nigeria, but gave North-East Cameroon to Northern Nigeria.

7. See Ebbe, Obi N. Ignatius (2001). Broken Back Axle: Unspeakable Events in Biafra. Bloomington, IN: Xlibris Corporation, p. 13 for what Dr. Zik underestimated.

8. Some African nations had annual skirmishes at their borders, but not the wholesale war that emerged, when the Europeans put a price tag on a captured person during intertribal conflicts. The Europeans' introduction of slave trade, as a money-making enterprise, made interethnic and intertribal conflict inevitable in Africa as a means to make money. Kidnapping of a human being was not a customary feature of Africans south of the Sahara. It was the slave trade that brought such a crime to Africa.

9. "Slavery Abolition Act 1833; Section LXIV" (http://www.pdavis.nl/Legis_07.htm). 1833-08-28. Accessed October 23, 2014.

State Terrorism

Between what is sensible and what seems to be sensible, and between what is reasonable and what seems to be reasonable, how can one cogitate wisely, when a woman's baby is snatched from her and she cries painfully as she pursues the male snatcher. The man turns around and kicks her in the stomach. The woman falls down and dies. The man walks away with the child, while the woman's two other toddlers kneel down around their mother's corpse grieving in anger and indignation, without consolation. The above episode capsulizes the structure of state terrorism that you are going to find in this chapter.

State terrorism is real. Whoever benefits from state terrorism will not see it as terrorism or a crime. In human history, however, state terrorism precedes single and group terrorism, as we shall see later. The terror *cimbricus* of the *Cimbri* tribe in 105 BC and the 1793–1794 "Reign of Terror" (Thompson, 1970; Hugo, 2008) are referred to.

Definition

The definition of terrorism varies according to the actors in terrorism: single, group, or state. When an individual in a traditional society wants another individual not to take any particular action such as not to farm on a piece of land belonging to him, he could post a cultural warning on the land, so that the intruder, seeing it, should back off or face deadly violent consequences.

The deadly cultural sign placed on the piece of land by the person who claims to be the rightful owner, injects "fear," an element in terrorism, in the mind of the intruder. When a

Muslim trader in the City of Kano,[1] Nigeria, who hated *Igbo* business activities in Kano, set his *Igbo* neighbors' trading store ablaze in 1953, he was terrorizing all *Igbo* traders in Kano. He, in fact, was telling Igbo traders in Kano to go back to their homes in Southern Nigeria, else he was going to continue his violent activities against them. In addition, when Timothy James McVeigh bombed the Alfred P. Murrah Federal Building in Oklahoma City, Oklahoma, in the United States, on April 19, 1995, which killed more than 165 people and left over 550 persons injured, he was revenging against the federal government for its attack on Waco[2] in 1993 and the Ruby Ridge[3] incident in 1992. It was concluded that McVeigh felt that his terrorist act would provoke revolt against the U.S. government, which he saw as a tyrannical federal government (Shariat, Mallonee, & Stephens-Stidham, 1998).

The three different episodes narrated above are instances of single terrorist acts. The single terrorist has his motive, aim, goal, and target. He wants to terrorize his target population. He wants to scare his target. He knows that he may not win or accomplish his main goal, or wish, but he wants his target to feel his anger.

Group terrorism is the most terrifying act of violence. The group is angry. It could not achieve its wish by negotiation. The members may have complained to the targeted population to respond to their wishes, but of no avail. They don't have the power to subdue their target. They are grossly frustrated. The group starts to think about what to do to make the targeted population think again, or make the leadership of the target population know that they want to be recognized, respected, and their demands honored. The group begins with identifying crowded occasions, national installations, historic buildings, or cherished properties of the targeted population for violent attack.

There are many instances of group terrorism in world history of the concept. A long-time terrorist group in Nigeria is *Hausa-Fulani* Muslims (the origin of Boko Haram). In 1953, in the Colonial House of Representatives, there were three political parties represented in the House: Action Group (AG) led by Chief Obafemi Awolowo, National Council of Nigeria and Cameroon (NCNC)[4] led by Dr. Nnamdi Azikiwe (Zik), and Northern People's Congress (NPC) led byAlhaji Ahmadu Bello, the Sarduana of Sokoko. In that year, the British colonial administration announced its intention to grant "self-government" in 1956 to any Region that so desired.

Unmistakably, the Southern Nigerian representatives in the House rejoiced over the announcement. Without any further waste of time, a member of the Action Group, Chief Anthony Enahoro, tabled a motion for self-government for all of the three Regions-to-be in 1956. This motion was seconded by a member of the NCNC. Unfortunately, the leader of the NPC made a counter-motion, replacing 1956 with the phrase "as soon as practicable." The members of the two Southern parties (AG and NCNC) were infuriated. When another Northern Nigerian member of the House saw the Southern members' indignation, he moved a motion for adjournment. The AG and NCNC members saw the motion for adjournment as a way to delay the process to self-government and walked out. When the members of the Northern delegation left the House, they were faced with an angry crowd in Lagos. They were booed and called all sorts of insulting names.

Some weeks later, AG and NCNC members, led by Chief Samuel Ladoke Akintola, went to campaign for self-government for all of the three Regions of Nigeria. This campaign was like pouring a gallon of gasoline on a burning house. After that day, the Hausa-Fulani Muslims began attacking *Yourba* and *Igbo* businesses, churches, and persons in the northern ancient cities of Kano, Kaduna, Sokoto, and other major cities in Northern Nigeria with high concentration of Southerners.[5] These *Hausa-Fulani* Muslims attacked individuals, and their businesses from time to time for as long as they were from Southern Nigeria.

At several stages, from the process of self-government to granting of Independence to Nigeria in 1960, the Northern Nigerian *Hausa-Fulani* Muslim oligarchy had agitated for secession from Southern Nigeria. It is the old *Hausa-Fulani* terrorism that emerged as *Boko Haram* terrorism. The Boko Haram members are also in the Nigerian Senate, National Assembly, and the Nigerian Military. That is why the Nigerian government could not wipe out Boko Haram or even weaken them. All the Hausa-Fulani Muslim oligarchy and their Boko Haram want is for all Southerners to leave the north and stop building churches and schools in the north. Western education is unacceptable to them.

Another group described by Britain as a terrorist organization is IRA. They struggle for Irish independence from Great Britain and has been in existence for more than a century. On April 24, 1916, an explosive freedom fighting incident occurred. It was captioned "Easter Rebellion." On that day, members of the Irish Volunteers and Irish Citizens Army besieged Dublin General Post Office and took it along with other buildings around it, and declared the Irish Republic an independent entity (Chaliand, 2007). The leaders of the group were arrested and executed by the British government, but the Irish people recognized them as Irish heroes. These Irish heroes laid the foundation for the emergence of the Irish Republican Army (IRA) under the founding leadership of Michael Collins (Hart, 2007). From 1916 to 1923, the IRA carried out many destructive operations on British principal establishments. It attacked 300 police stations, killed twelve police officers, and set ablaze Liverpool docks and warehouses. Within a space of six years, the IRA had made many lethal attacks on British government civil servants and installations. This culminated in the government signing the 1921 Anglo-Irish treaty that created a free Irish state made up of twenty-six of the island's 32 counties (Coogan, 2002). Of course, the IRA did not see itself as a terrorist organization. Its members saw themselves as freedom fighters. But for the British people, the IRA was a terrorist organization.

There were many freedom fighting terrorist groups before World War II, such as the Irgun in the British Mandate of Palestine that fought against the British, when the latter restricted Jewish immigration to Palestine in 1939. The Irgun agitated against British rule by assassinating a police officer, taking over British government buildings and arms, and sabotaging the British railways (Sachar, 2007). Irgun continued to operate as a defender of the Jewish people and as a terrorist organization in the eyes of the British and the Arabs until the creation of the State of Israel in 1948. In fact, in 1946, Irgun, under the leadership of Menachem Begin bombed the King David Hotel in Jerusalem, which housed the headquarters of the British civil and military administrations. In the bombing, up to ninety people were killed and many others injured (Clarke, 1981).

During the same British Mandate of Palestine, the Black Hand emerged in the 1930s as an anti-Zionist paramilitary group led by Izz ad-Din al-Qassam. The group fought against the Jews and the British in Palestine (Segev, 1999; Lachman, 1982).

After World War II, the anti-colonial rule spread throughout African, Asian, and the Middle Eastern colonial dependencies. When Adolf Hitler and his Nazis warned the British to surrender, Winston Churchill replied that the English people have a right to self-determination. In effect, after the European colonial dependencies helped their masters defeat Hitler, India, a major British colony, under Mahatma Gandhi, appealed to the British government that India should be granted independence, because the Indian people have a right to self-determination. That argument spread fast all over the world like a new song. In the obduracy of the British Crown and Parliament and French arrogance, the appeals from many colonies were rejected and anti-colonial terrorism exploded.

In Asia, the Viet Minh fought against French colonists. In the Middle East, the Muslim Brotherhood fought against British rule in Egypt with bombings and assassinations. They also attacked British soldiers, police stations, and assassinated politicians known to be collaborating with the British rule (Brynjar, 2006). Undeniably, the Muslim Brotherhood was too extreme in their terrorist activities, which included the assassination of the Egyptian Prime Minister Nuqrashi in 1948 (Mitchell, 1993). However, in 1952, a military coup d'etat overthrew the British colonial administration in Egypt.

In French-colonized Algeria, the National Liberation Front (FLN) used guerilla activities and open lethal confrontations to try to achieve independence. Also, in Cyprus, the EOKA, a Greek Cypriot nationalist guerrilla organization fought against the British to end British rule in Cyprus (Hoffman, 2006).

In the United States, there were freedom fighting terrorist organizations that sprang up for certain courses, such as the Weather Underground Organization housed in Chicago as an anti-Vietnam war and anti-American government imperialism, and the KKK (Ku Klux Klan) that is, anti-Jews and anti-African Americans. Both used bombing, burning, and assassinations to promote their courses.

In Africa, Asia, and the Middle East, some freedom fighters in the countries that had struggled and succeeded in obtaining independence from their former European colonial masters decided to provoke the ire of their former colonists, calumniate their agents, and nullify their political and economic systems and moved to embrace communist and socialist ideologies as a system of their newly independent nation. This movement sprang up in Algeria (1963), Congo-Kinsasha (1958/1970), Libya (1969), Madagascar (1975), Somalia (1976), Mozambique (1975), North Korea (1948), Burma (1962), South Yemen (1967), Iraq (1968), North Vietnam (1945), and so forth.

This movement of former colonial dependencies' leanings toward communism and socialism created a new wave of ideological group and state terrorism in the world. The former

European colonial masters (Britain and France) and the United States went after the leaders of the anti-capitalist mode of economic production and decentralized power.

Now, as we have given instances and the nature of individual and group terrorism, we turn to state terrorism. State terrorism occurs when a country uses its secret agents or law enforcement agents to assassinate leaders of freedom fighters, or leaders of socialist or communist parties, or the newly independent country leader leaning toward economic accord with the former Soviet Union, such as the assassination of Patrice Lumumba in 1961 in Congo, because he turned to the Soviet Union for help. In effect, Great Britain and the United States used MI6[6] and the CIA to eliminate him.

Gordon Corera (2013), a BBC News Africa security correspondent writing on "MI6 and the death of Patrice Lumumba" noted:

> In the White House, President Eisenhower held a National Security Council meeting in the summer of 1960 in which at one point he turned to his CIA director and used the word "eliminate" in terms of what he wanted done with Lumumba.

Also, the overthrow of President Kwame Nkruma of Ghana in a coup d'etat on February 24, 1966, when he was on a state official visit to the Soviet Union, has the CIA implicated as backing the coup (Curtis, 1992). Furthermore, the British controlled the Iraq Petroleum Corporation up to 1961. Unfortunately, the British-supported monarchial regime of King Faisal and Prime Minister Nuri El Said, was overthrown in July 1958 by the Arab nationalist revolution (Curtis, 1992). This revolution established a republic under Brigadier Abdul Karim Qasim. Without any waste of time, Prime Minister Said and all of the royal family members were murdered in cold blood, and an angry mob killed a British subject and demolished and obliterated the British embassy.

When the new head of state of Iraq, Qasim, nationalized the Iraq Petroleum Corporation and gave Iraq over 50% of the oil revenue, coupled with the fact that Qasim's government was run by a communist party, Britain and the United States went to work. On February 9, 1963, Qasim's government was overthrown in a coup d'etat backed by both Britain and the CIA (Curtis, 2004). Qasim and his senior officials were killed. General Abdul Arif and the Baath Party leader General Abdul al-Bakr took over power. According to Mark Curtis (2004, p. 83):

> The coup was the result of substantial CIA backing and organization and was masterminded by William Lakeland, stationed as an attaché at the U.S. embassy in Baghdad.

Undeniably, General Qasim and his government officials strongly believed that nationalizing Iraqi oil was doing something good for his own people and not for egotistic reasons. But he did not realize that going communist and nationalizing Britain's bread and butter winner was trying to dance on molten lava. And it turned to be so. According to Aburish (1997) and also cited in Curtis (2004, p. 83):

The U.S. had insisted beforehand on implementing a detailed plan to eliminate the Iraqi Communist Party as a force in Iraqi politics, meaning physical extermination of its members. The CIA provided the February coup leaders with a list of names, around 5,000 of whom were hunted down and murdered. They included senior army officers, as well as lawyers, professors, teachers, and doctors. There were pregnant women and old men among them, many of whom were tortured in front of their children.

In addition, when Saddam Hussein, as President of Iraq (1979–2003), was visiting Dujail, a town 49 miles from Baghdad in 1982, in a motorcade, some youthful Dawa militants booed him and fired at his motorcade. Saddam punished the whole town. About 140 young men were arrested and sent to their untimely death without trial, another 1,486 were imprisoned, tortured, the women raped by Saddam's police, and the whole town was rendered desolate and uninhabitable. That was Saddam's warning to other revolting towns and ethnic groups against his regime. Also, Saddam used assassinations and forced disappearances to terrorize his political opponents (Viorst, 1991; Perazzo, 2002) in the Kurds political leadership long before his army invaded that part of Iraq.

On the African front, after Mobutu Sese Seko and the CIA got rid of Patrice Lumumber, he began to safeguard this regime by publicly executing his political enemies, coup plotters, secessionists, and all individuals and groups that posed threats to his presidency. In fact, he accused three of his cabinet ministers (Alexandre Mahaniba, Mines and Energy; Jerome Anany, Defense; and Emmanuel Bambas, Finance) of having contacted Colonel Bangala and Major Efomi to plan a coup to overthrow him. On May 30, 1966, he executed them before a large crowd of spectators after a biased and manipulated court trial. In the same manner, Mobutu got former Prime Minister Evariste Kimba hanged in public (Young & Turner, 1985; Wrong, 2009 Kelly, 1993).

Mobutu Sese Seko was so ruthless in dealing with his political opponents that in 1968 he lured a self-exiled Pierre Mulele, a Minister of Education under Patrice Lumumber, to come to Congo for a cordial chat. On Mulele's arrival, he was tortured and killed by Mobutu's security guards. In fact, before killing him, they gouged out his eyes, ripped off his genitals, and amputated his legs and hands (Wrong, 2009). Unmistakably, the atrocities of Mobutu Sese Seko's state terrorism cannot be fully enumerated. He and his regime had no cult of good manners.

The last African head of state we want to touch on in explaining state terrorism is President Robert Mugabe of Zimbabwe. Mugabe has been the President of Zimbabwe (formerly known as Southern Rhodesia) since 1980. As soon as he rose to power, he crushed all opposition with his North Korean–trained security force he called Fifth Brigade, and made his country a one-political-party state known as Zimbabwe African National Union-Patriotic Front (ZANU-FP). All those who were loyal to his major political rival, Joshua Nkomo, he either threw in jail without trial, assassinated, or drove them to self-exile. Worst of all, Mugabe engaged in ethnic cleansing. From 1982 to 1985, over 20,000 Ndebele ethnic groups were crushed by Mugabe's security forces in ethnic cleansing, because they happened to be the home and base of his arch rival, Joshua Nkomo. In fact, the illegal and depraved-heart treatments he meted out to white minority settlers are deplorable. Unmistakably, Mugabe is the Saddam Hussein and Adolf Hitler of Africa.

There are so many acts of state terrorism that this volume cannot fully document them. For instance, check the state terrorist acts of the regimes of Muammar al-Gaddafi (Libya, 1969–2011), Charles Taylor (Liberia, 1997–2003), Sani Abacha (Nigeria, 1993–1999), Lauren Kabila (Congo, 1997–2001), Idi Amin (Uganda, 1971–1979), Omar al-Bashir (Sudan, 1993–present), P.W. Botha (South Africa, 1978–1989), Anwar Sadat (Egypt, 1970–1981), Hosni Mubarak (Egypt, 1981–2011), Francois Duvalier-"Papa Doc" (Haiti, 1957–1971), Francisco Franco (Spain, 1939–1975), Slobodan Milosevic (Yugoslavia, 1997–2000), Reza Muhammed Shah Pahlawi (Shah of Iran, 1949–1979), Ferdinand Marcos (Philippines, 1965–1986), Ngo Dinh Diem (South Vietnam, 1955–1963), Chiang Kai-shek (Taiwan, 1949–1975), Syngman Rhee (South Korea, 1948–1960), Park Chung Hee (South Korea, 1960–1979), General Chun Doo Hwan (South Korea, 1980–1988), Marco Vinicio Cerezo Arevalo (Guatemala, 1985–1991) Anastasio Somoza (Nicaragua, 1936–1956) General Suharto (Indonesia 1967–1999), Manuel Antonio Noriega (Panama, 1983–1989), Augusto Ugante Pinnochet (Chile, 1973–1990), and so forth.

All of the above independent state leaders were horrible dictators. Every one of them committed terrorist crimes against their own people, ranging from intimidation at the polls, indefinite detention, illegal search and seizure, torture, and forced exile to assassination and cold-blooded murder of political opponents and their supporters.

Therefore, it stands to reason that state terrorism is an attack by a head of state and his law enforcement officers and the military on individuals, groups, political party opponents, or on other states, who are seen as threats to the government to deter others in the country and beyond from ever challenging its policies or messing with its vital interests. In other words, state terrorism is the use of unlawful violence, intimidation, and lethal force against individuals, groups, or other states that pose threats to the policies and vital interests of the aggressive state.

The aim of the terrorist state is to force its victims to surrender and give up their opposition or line of action or be destroyed. In fact, the terrorist state, in the main, approaches its victim in two ways: first, use the degree of terror that will make the targeted victim to surrender; finally, giving the targeted victim a magnitude of violence fraught with a warning—that failing to surrender means total obliteration from the face of the earth will be an inevitable outcome. This last option very often gives rise to genocide.

There is no consensus in any discipline or anywhere in the world on a single definition of terrorism as well as "state terrorism." Sometimes state terrorism starts like an unprovoked war. What the United Nations calls "war of aggression," or "crime of aggression," which is a military attack waged without justification of self-defense, mainly for acquiring more territories, or the pleasure of defeat (Cryer & Friman, 2010). Unmistakably, war of aggression is a supreme international crime. Unfortunately, the United Nations Security Council and the United Nations General Assembly have no consensus on the definition of "war of aggression"/"crime of aggression."

The United Nations has not been able to arrive at a generally acceptable definition of "war of aggression" because some members of the Security Council can be found guilty of committing crime of aggression. In effect, the only way to circumvent it is to prevent having a generally agreed upon definition of the crime. Otherwise, war of aggression, undeniably, is state terrorism. Notably, war of aggression differs from "war crimes," because it has within itself the accumulated evils of both.

Unlike individual and group terrorism, state terrorism is not a reaction to oppression of another, it is not the weaker in a conflict, and almost always it has unlimited resources to accomplish its political or economic goals. Like individual and group terrorism, its targets/victims can be national or international.

State terrorism can be seen among developed countries, newly developing countries, and underdeveloped countries. This reality is acknowledged by the United Nations' definition of terrorism. In 1992, the United Nations defined terrorism as follows:

> An anxiety-inspiring method or repeated violent action, employed by (semi-) clandestine individual, group or state actors, for idiosyncratic, criminal or political reasons, whereby—in contrast to assassination—the direct targets of violence are not the main targets.[8]

The United Nations' definition makes it clear that a state can be a terrorist. But let us look at three different definitions, two from the United States government and one from Great Britain. The United States Department of Defense defines terrorism as follows:

> "The calculated use of unlawful violence or threat of unlawful violence to inculcate fear, intended to coerce or to intimidate governments or societies in the pursuit of goals that are generally political, religious, or ideological."[9]

In almost similar fashion, the United Stated Federal Bureau of Investigation (FBI) notes:
Terrorism is the unlawful use of force and violence against persons or property to intimidate or coerce a government, the civilian population, or any segment thereof, in furtherance of political or social objectives.[10]

Both definitions coming from the U.S. government units used the three major elements in terrorism: violence, fear, and intimidation. In comparison, in 1974, the British government defined terrorism as:

> ....the use of violence for political ends, and includes any use of violence for the purpose of putting the public, or any section of the public, in fear.[11]

All of the country-based definitions of terrorism above, unlike the United Nations' definition, avoided the characteristics of the terrorist actor. But their definitions can apply to individual, group, and state actors.

There are as many definitions of terrorism as there are different terrorist actors. It is unequivocal that nobody will condemn his own behavior as evil. There is always a technique of neutralization of the evils of the unlawful act (Sykes & Matza, 1957).

State terrorism cannot be well explained and understood without investigating its origin in the ancient and medieval times.

State Terrorism in Ancient and Medieval Times

The use of force, violence and intimidation against others, as a means to achieve an end, is as old as the emergence of society among human groups. Both individuals and groups had used terror to acquire others' resources and territories. The "early man" was a terrorist. He had to invade others' domain as a wanderer as well as a settled farmer. Simple societies (stateless societies) that preceded ancient societies terrorized each other for space and scarce arable land.

Ancient society saw a need for law under a social contract, as noted by Thomas Hobbes and John Locke (Hobbes, 1651; Locke, 1689). In those early times, the term terrorism might not have been used, but concepts that represent "scare," "frighten," "invaders," "terrifying," or "intimidate." It is notable that between 800 B.C. and 500 B.C., city-states had emerged in Archaic Greece. And by 500 B.C., ancient Rome had a government. Unmistakably, both ancient Greece and ancient Rome used what we call "terrorism" today to deal with individuals, groups, and other emerging states who opposed their rule and policies.

From the activities of the "early man" and the savages of the stateless societies, it is undeniable that the concept of terrorism is far older than ancient Greek and Roman civilizations.

The modern concept of "terror" and "terrorism" originated from a warlike *Cimbri* tribe (Germanic people) who waged wars against the Roman Republic between 113 and 101 B.C. (Strauss, 2009).[12] It was in 105 B.C. that the Cimbri defeated the Roman Army at the Battle of Arausio. The Cimbri became a frightening force among the Romans. Instantly, the *"terror cimbricus"* concept became a "panic and state of emergency in Rome indicating that the Cimbri tribe, also known as the Zealots, were coming."[13]

In addition, in the 1st Century CE/A.D. (Common Era/Anno Domini), the *Sicarii* were regarded as the first century terrorists. They were ruthless in fostering revolt against direct Roman rule in 6 CE. The Romans wanted to hold a census of the Jews under the rule of Roman Governor Quirinius in Syria, so that the Jews could pay tax to Rome. But Judas of Galilee charged that the Jews should be ruled only by God, and that they had no obligation to pay tax to anybody. The *Sicarii* fought against the Romans and used terrorist methods in the fight. Also, they used assassinations and murder to fight against Jews who tried to cooperate with the Romans (Horsley, 1979; Smith, 1971; Zeitlin, 1965).

Terrorist acts did not end in the ancient times. In fact, the medieval period laid the foundation for the al-Qaeda and Boko Haram revolutionary terrorism and Maximilien de Robespierre, Mugabe, and Milosevic state terrorisms of the modern times.

The founding father of modern Middle Eastern style of terrorism was born in the medieval times. From the 6th century, Christians were making frequent pilgrimages to Jerusalem—the birthplace of Jesus Christ. But when the Seljuk Turks seized Jerusalem, Christians were prevented from entering the Holy City. When the Turks threatened to invade the Byzantine Empire and capture Constantinople, the Byzantine Emperor Alexius I made a special appeal to Pope Urban II to help him ward off the Turks. Pope Urban had been looking for a way to strengthen the power of the Papacy. Consequently, Pope Urban decided to unite European Christians to fight the Holy War and take back the Holy Land from the Turks. At the Council of Clermont (France), before a large audience of wealthy, noblemen of Christian Europe, Pope Urban delivered a rabble-rousing and motivating speech for the Christians to take up arms against the Turkish Muslims and take back Jerusalem. And the war began. That was the emergence of the First Crusade.

The reaction of the Islamic world about the First Crusade was fury and indignation. Islam had always been militant and radical, because Muslim sects advocated use of force and intolerance. One of the heretical sects that emerged at the time was the Nizaris. It was a "mystical order of warriors founded by a Persian, Hassan Bin Sabah" or Hassan-i-Sabbah (1050s–1124 BCE) known in the Western World as the "Assassins" (Lewis, 2002; Daftary, 2007). He seized Alamut, a mountain fortress, and used it as the headquarters of a decentralized Persian insurrection against the Seljuk Turks.

Hassan inculcated fanatical obedience among the Assassins and made them ignore the fear of capture and death in the face of battle. He instructed them that what they were going to gain by losing their lives in a jihad (Holy War) was more than worldly pleasures. The Assassins' motivation was captured in the stories brought back to Christians in Europe by Marco Polo in 1295 which goes as follows:

> The Old Man of the Mountains fed his followers with hashish before taking them to a secluded garden where they were indulged with forbidden pleasures—principally, the sexual favors of young women. On returning to normal consciousness, the Assassin was told he had experienced the heavenly garden of Paradise and would spend all eternity there, provided he lived in the service of the cult. Assassin cultists would therefore infiltrate enemy courts and army camps, reputedly remaining incognito for years, ready to commit murder upon their master's signal. It was the birth of strategic terrorism (Lewis, 2002).

For Hassan, his Assassin cultists are God's Assassins. He energized the Assassins with his satanic maxim: "Nothing is true. Everything is permitted." The Hassan-i-Sabbah maxim negates Christian beliefs, doctrines, and principles.

Unmistakably, the Assassins' doctrines and Hassan's teachings brought about the modern-day al-Qaeda, Boko Haram, and all of the "jihadists" of our time.

The modern-day use of the concept of terror and terrorism emerged in France during the French Revolution (1789–1799). Growing out of the French Revolution was the Jacobin Club. The Jacobinans, as they were called, commanded a respectable presence in the National Convention. They established the revolutionary dictatorship. The Jacobin dictatorship was led by Maximilien Robespiere, and they enacted the *Reign of Terror*, targeting speculators, monarchists, left-wing agitators, Hebertists,[14] and traitors. This revolutionary state used violence, mass executions by guillotine, assassinations, and intimidation to compel obedience to the revolutionary state.

Undeniably, modern history of terrorism began with state terrorism of the French Revolutionary state dictatorship of the Jacobins in 1793–1994 (the "Reign of Terror"). The Jacobins took extreme measures to achieve their extraordinary situation. They saw that assassinations, executions, and intimidation were instruments to warn whoever wanted to challenge them to be careful of the consequences as Jacques Rene Hebert learned too late on the guillotine.[15] Unmistakably, the Jacobins' type of state terrorism has its followers in the 20th and 21st centuries.

Terrorism in the 20th Century

The terrorism of the 20th century was strongly associated with an unflinching pride of nationalism, anticolonialism, neocolonialism, socialism, communism, fascism, and anarchism. It is irrefutable that state terrorism preceded individual and group terrorisms.

At the Berlin Conference of 1884–1885 of the League of Nations, the seed of political, economic, and religious terrorism was sown. What happened was by 1700 A.D., some Western European nations had explored Africa, Asia, and the Middle East, and calculated the natural resources of the areas. They found that most of the people of these regions of the world were not equal partners in trade but exploitable. They discovered all kinds of natural resources, especially minerals and wildlife in Africa, the second largest continent in the world (30,065,000 sq. km).[16] As a result of the fabulous riches of the African continent, some European nations, throughout the early 1800s, were scrambling to get control of the various kingdoms, and gemeinschafts that covered the whole continent.

The European powers were politically fighting against each other in Africa to get control of different areas of the continent. In the process, they lured some African chiefs and kings into signing fraudulent treaties of land purchases and protection (Pakenham, 1992; Chamberlain, 1974). In fact, it was an unhealthy rivalry among the European nations scrambling for possessions in Africa.

At long last, the European nations tried to settle their differences. In November 1884, in the palace of the German Chancellor, Otto von Bismarck, the Berlin conference was held. The Chancellor invited foreign ministers of fourteen powerful European nations and the United States to hold a meeting to establish ground rules to dissect Africa, like huntsmen dissecting their deer for sharing. Africa, in effect, was sliced like a piece of cake. The pieces went to the most powerful European countries: Great Britain, France, Germany, Italy, Belgium, and Portugal. To demonstrate to the rest of the world and convince themselves that Africans are unpersons and unpeople, not a single African Chief was invited to the conference of partitioning Africa. Sans doute, African nations were not privy to the partition of Africa. The European nations' mindset was, whether African chiefs like it or not, that's the way it is going to be.

The European nations had already given some of the regions of Africa any name that suited their vernacular, because they amalgamated regions of diverse languages and culture. In effect, Africa became a continent of tailor-made countries. For instance, Nigeria was named from the famous River Niger, Gold Coast (Ghana) came from expansive gold deposits in the region, while North Rhodesia and Southern Rhodesia came from Cecil Rhodes who explored the region and exploited, appropriated, and expropriated the natural resources (gold, copper, silver, iron ore, graphite, pig-iron, diamond, etc.) of the region. And at the conference, the League baptized some regions "Crown colonies," "mandated territories," and "protectorates."

The scramble for Africa ended, and the partition of the continent was over. Then each of the seven European powers, including Spain, went to work on merciless exploitation, appropriation, and expropriation of their newly acquired countries.

Resistance to colonial rule led to fierce fighting in every region of Africa. Africans were using bows and arrows, spears, machetes, and stones, and they won a lot of battles. Unfortunately for the Africans, China had invented gunpowder in the 9th century (Partington, 1960; Chase, 2003), and, by the 17th century, England had developed gunpowder firearms (Buchanan, 2006; Cocroft, 2000; Crosby, 2002) and used it to massacre kingdoms in Western Nigeria, emirates in Northern Nigeria, and clans and chiefdoms in Eastern Nigeria in the late 1800s.

Colonial administration in Africa, Asia, and the Middle East was an act of terror. In all of the colonial "dependencies" (as they called them), the colonial masters used their European policemen and some conscripted natives to intimidate the masses. That was state terrorism (Onwudiwe, 2001).

The state terrorism that shocked the collective conscience of some European communities in Europe and America was the reign of terror of King Leopold II of Belgium. During the scramble for Africa, Belgium captured a region in Central Africa and called it Belgium Congo Free State. King Leopold II named the capital in his name, Leopoldville, because he took Belgium Congo as his personal possession. The League of Nations was deceived by the representatives of Belgium to believe that the Congo Free State should be regarded as a "neutral zone" to be administered "by an international association in the interest of bringing science, civilization and Christianity to the indigenes" (Joseph, 1971). The League at the Berlin conference praised the idea, but King Leopold II gave exploitation, appropriation, and expropriation their true meanings in the Congo Free State (Zaire). As he took the whole country as his own with all of its natural resources, he made enormous profits. Leopold II's Belgian soldiers and paramilitary police were trained and ordered to employ Congolese in the king's rubber plantations, chase and kill elephants for their ivory, and construct roads for the export of goods. Individuals and groups who failed to reach production quotas were killed on that same day. In fact, members of a whole community who failed to reach a designated quota were massacred mercilessly (Hochschild, 1999).

There was a world outcry against King Leopold's reign of terror, and it was reported that by the end of his reign more than 10 million Congolese had been murdered in cold blood. He used both starvation and torture to intimidate his subjects (Bourne, 1903; Cauthorne, 1999; Forbath, 1977). In King Leopold II's state terrorism, we could see social, political, and economic terrorism. He had no regard for the value of human life. Of course, he did not see Africans as human beings, and he was not alone. We are going to read more about King Leopold II's atrocities in the chapter on state genocide.

Another country the writer needs to point out in state terrorism in Africa and elsewhere is Germany. Before the 1884 Berlin conference, Germany had colonies in West Africa, East Africa, and Southwest Africa. In West Africa were Cameroons, Togoland (now Togo), and some part of Gold Coast (now Ghana). In the Central African Republic were Congo and Gabon. In German South West Africa was Namibia, and in East Africa were Tanganyika (now part of Tanzania), Burundi, Rwanda, and Ruvumba Triangle (now part of Mozambique in 1919).

The German ruthless process of colonization in Africa was fraught with a reign of terror. Taking events in East Africa as an example, Germany wanted to control the whole of the African Great Lakes region. Like Great Britain's approach in Nigeria in 1861. On February 1885, the German Chancellor Bismarck signed and granted imperial charter to a colonial company led by Carl Peters, who founded the Society for German Colonization. The towns at the African Great Lakes region vigorously resisted the German invasion. After years of battles, some chiefs in the area were lured into signing treaties of peace agreement (Miller, 1974; Bullock, 1939).

Around the same time, 1885, there was a revolt against the German Colonial Company, and the German military was called upon to put down the revolt. The crackdown took many African lives in Tanganyika (Tanzania).

When Carl Peters recruited many Germans to help him explore southwards to Rufiji River and northwards to Witu, located near the coastal lands of the Indian Ocean, to the Sultan of Zanzibar, it was like trying to get him beheaded. In effect, the Sultan protested, because he was the ruler of the mainland. To intimidate the Sultan and all the chiefs in East Africa, Chancellor Otto von Bismarck sent five warships. On the warships' arrival at the coast of Zanzibar, they pointed the guns at the Sultan's palace and threatened to destroy the Sultan and his palace. The Sultan had no other option other than to surrender. Immediately, the British and Germans agreed to divide the mainland between themselves. Germany established its colonial administration over Dar es Salaam, Kilwa, and Bagamoyo.

The German method of exploitation and forced labor led to the Abushiri Revolt of 1888. The Germans, with British help, put down the revolt in 1889. The German military intrepidly continued to expand its area of hegemony in East Africa using inexplicable degree of violence that put the natives on the run. For the natives to come back to their ancestral homes to take care of their ancestral shrines, their chiefs had to sign a treaty of obedience to alien rule.

One town after another was falling into the hands of the Germans. In 1891 to 1894, it was a period of German war between the Hehe tribe (clan) led by the great tribal Chief Mkwawa. The chief wanted the Germans to leave the whole of East Africa. The German military defeated the Hehe tribe in 1894, but Chief Mkwawa resorted to guerrilla warfare against the Germans. When the Germans tried to capture him alive in 1898, he committed suicide (Miller, 1974; Bullock, 1939).

The brutality of the German colonial administration led to the Maji Maji Rebellion or the Maji Maji War in 1905–1907. The Maji Maji War erupted when the ruthless colonial German rule forced the people of Tanganyika to grow cotton for export (Gellately & Kieman, 2003; Pakenham, 1992; Lliffe, 1967). Every community was ordered to produce a certain quota of cotton. In the process, violent repressive strategy was used to control the masses. Torturing and publicly murdering community leaders who refused to carry out the orders was used as a method to intimidate and warn others what could happen to them if they failed to comply. Consequently, the native people of the whole Great Lakes region revolted in the Maji Maji War. The German military was shooting to kill. But the rebels were armed with only spears and arrows. The masses attacked German garrisons located in various parts of the colony. The tribesmen destroyed any colonial establishment on their way. In fact, every tribe in the region formed an army to fight against the colonial German rule.

Colonial Germany found it very difficult to face many columns of native warriors. As a result, they contacted the German government in Germany for reinforcement. Some German soldiers were shipped from a West African colony, and machine guns and other firearms were also shipped to Count Gustav Adolf von Gotzen, Governor of German East Africa. Despite all of the colonial Germany's superior war materials, the rebellion was too much for the colonial German military. Consequently, they decided that the only way to defeat the Maji Maji War was starving the people to death. While some tribes gave up the rebellion, others resisted, and some resorted to guerrilla warfare.

In 1905, Captain Wangenheim, one of the commanding officers of the German troops in the colony, wrote to the German East African colonial Governor, von Gotzen, "Only hunger and want can bring about a final submission. Military actions alone will remain more or less a drop in the ocean" (Pakenham, 1992). The idea worked, but it took more than two years to materialize. It was in August 1907 that the last ferocious war tribe surrendered out of starvation and disease.

The Maji Maji Rebellion took many lives, including the lives of 15 Europeans and five missionaries; among them was the Catholic Bishop of Dar es Salaam, Bishop Spiss (Gellantely, 2003; Pakenham, 1992; Lliffe, 1967).

Colonialism was the beginning of international state terrorism. The modus operandi of setting up colonial rule and exploitation says it all. Germany lost all of her colonies in Africa after World War I to Britain and France.

African resistance to colonization was with fierce indignation and total rejection. The colonial masters obviously wondered why it wasn't easy for them to colonize the people in spite of their machine guns and firearms, while Africans had none. In the face of difficulty in getting Africans to submit to alien rule, the colonial masters resorted to the use of exile and deportation. The use of exile and deportation in the African continent began from the late 1600s and continued to the 1940s. Some chiefs, kings, and other elite were given forced exile. Among traditional rulers sent to exile by the British were Dinuzulu Kacetshwayo for leading the Zulu army against the British rule (Grove, 1995), King Jaja of Opobo (Nigeria), King Kosoko of Lagos (Nigeria), Oba of Benin who was exiled to Calabar (Nigeria), Dr. Nnamdi Azikiwe to Gold Coast, Nze Jomo Kenyata who was incarcerated in prison following his Mau Mau uprising in Kenya, Dr. Kwame Nkruma of the Gold Coast who was incarcerated in prison for agitating for the Independence of the Gold Coast (Ghana), and so forth. Some African chiefs who were exiled were also exiled with hard labor. These chiefs were separated from their ancestral obligations in their towns, their families, and their subjects. All of those exiles and deportations were intended to intimidate and force neighboring territories to submit to colonial rule; else, they would face the same terrible predicament. That is the fact of the colonial state terrorist.

Theories of State Terrorism

The explanation of state terrorism lies in the domestic and international policy of the country, and the ambition of the head of state and his political party. In fact, the ethnic structure of the country plays a significant part in the domestic policy of the country.

State terrorism can be explained by the following factors:

- Ethnic structure and composition of the country,
- The magnitude of natural resources,
- The degree of power struggle in the country,
- The level of education,
- The ambition of the head of state,
- The degree of greediness among the elite,
- Ideology propelling the government,
- Desire to influence what happens in other countries,
- Interest in controlling the economy of other countries, and
- Religious imperialism.

The ten factors listed may overlap. Let us start with "ethnic structure of the country." In a country where there are many ethnic groups, there is a tendency for one ethnic group to assert supremacy or dominate the others. When one becomes a head of state, whether he is from the minority ethnic group or from the majority ethnic groups, others may not countenance his leadership. Such a head of state may be partial in dealing with the affairs affecting other ethnic groups. The other ethnic groups may not like him to be reelected. The head of state may take actions to weaken the political power of any ethnic group that opposes his leadership, such as using his police or security men to intimidate, arrest, and illegally incarcerate the ethnic group's political leader, or threaten the safety of a significant number of political aspirants from the ethnic group, so that they leave the country in self-exile. That was the situation in Zimbabwe under President Mugabe, in Iraq under President Saddam Hussein, in Liberia under Charles Taylor, in Chile under Augusto Pinochet, and so forth.

The amount of natural resources in a Third World country can be a factor in state terrorism, both domestic and international. For instance, in domestic state terrorism, when crude oil is located in a particular region of the country, but the head of state comes from a different region and a different ethnic group, if the oil producing region is ignored in economic development, a rebellion may occur. The President Obasanjo administration in Nigeria (1999–2007) killed more than 1,000 Ogoni people when they revolted against the government and the oil companies that were messing up their environment without compensation. In a political rally in 1994 to condemn the environmental destruction of the Ogoni region, four chiefs were killed in a mob attack. As a result, Ken Saro-Wiwa, a great Nigerian writer and activist, who spoke forcefully against the Nigerian military (Obasanjo) administration and the Anglo-Dutch petroleum company—Royal Dutch/Shell for causing environmental damages to the Ogoni land and people, was arrested along with eight others. He was tried by a special tribunal and found guilty of complicity in the murders of the four chiefs. His trial and subsequent execution provoked international condemnation, and there were calls for economic sanctions against Nigeria.

Other heads of state who used terrorism to deal with ethnic opposition in their regimes include Idi Amin, Saddam Hussein, Muammar Gaddafi, and so forth. Many of their ethnic opposers got assassinated, jailed, or forced into self-exile.

When there are many persons in a Third World country vying for the leadership of a country, unhealthy rivalry emerges in intimidation and use of violence by the incumbent head of state. And his opposers may use assassination to get rid of him, as we saw in the Rwanda-Burundi assassination of President Habyarimana in April 1994. Also, the high degree of power struggle was seen in Mubutu Sese Seko's Zaire (Congo Leopoldville), which shattered the country and moved into genocidal murders.

The higher the level of education of the masses in a country, the less the incidence of domestic state terrorism. Third World countries have less than 50% of their population capable of reading and writing in any of the major languages of the world or even their in their own vernacular. In effect, democracy has no meaning to most of the populace.

Many heads of state and their officers have unquenchable political ambition. Consequently, in Third World countries, the change of leadership becomes a "do or die" venture. This unquenchable ambition goes with a high degree of greediness. Sharing power is unacceptable to many Third World leaders. This was seen in President Mugabe, Muammar Gaddafi, Saddam Hussein, Ferdinand Marcos, Idi Amin, Augusto Pinochet, and so forth.

Another important factor in causing state terrorism is ideological and economic imperialism. During the "Cold War," the Soviet Union and the United States wanted newly independent African and Asian countries to pursue the same political and economic systems as their own. In effect, they created antagonistic divisions in the young African and Asian states: Communist Republics versus Democratic Republics, Socialist democracies versus Capitalist democracies. That situation created the "Cold War." The U.S. military arsenals met Soviet Union's military arsenals in a foreign state conflict. Both domestic and international terrorism took its toll in the in-state political conflict.

Furthermore, when a developing African, Asian, or Middle Eastern country has precious minerals such as uranium, crude oil, gold, diamond, and so forth, powerful European powers and the United States begin to vie for control of the mineral deposits. If the head of state of the young country wants to gain control of his state's natural resources by nationalizing or give the control to another powerful country of his choice, he is either assassinated or overthrown in a bloody coup d'etat. Such was the fate of Prime Minister Patrice Lumumba of Congo[17] (Zaire), President Kwame Nkuuma of Ghana,[18] Qasim regime of Iraq (1963),[19] Prime Minister Mohammad Mosaddegh of Iran (1953),[20] and so forth (Curtis, 2004; Ward, 2009; Gasiorowski & Byrne, 2004; Chomsky & Vltchek, 2013).

The desire to expand and gain control of the territorial integrity of a religious organization can lead to conflicts and terrorist outcomes. In 1095, Pope Urban II proclaimed the First Crusade (1095–1099) with the aim of restoring Christian access to holy places in and around Jerusalem. There were many Crusades called by different Popes in the early and later Middle Ages. In the Crusades, thousands of lives were lost (Riley-Smith, 1995; Setton, 1985).

Mohammedanism (Islam) was designed to use force and violence to gain converts. In the process, throughout the Crusades, Christians and Muslims were at war with each other. Today, we have religious terrorism within the Islamic religion: Sunni Muslims versus Shiite Muslims. In fact, state terrorist activities within the Middle East are based on which Muslim affiliate controls the affairs of the state and wants to support their members in another state.

Domestic/National State Terrorism

This section concentrates on a reign of terror within a state and against its own people. The correlates of domestic state terrorism are multiethnicity (multitribes), religious affiliation, share of economic resources, multipolitical parties, greed, and corruption. In countries in Asia, Africa, and the Middle East, there are many ethnic groups. These ethnic groups, naturally, are concentrated in one part of the geographical area of the country. Each ethnic group (tribe) has its own distinct language and culture, and these are different from that of the other ethnic groups. These ethnic groups happen to be in one country, because European colonization amalgamated them for the convenience of colonial administration. For instance, Nigeria has, at least, 250 distinct ethnic groups, Kenya has over 70 ethnic groups, Malaysia has 3, Cambodia has more than 6, and Burma (Myanmar) has 135 distinct ethnic groups recognized by the Burmese government divided into "eight major national ethnic races: Kachin, Kayah, Kayin, Chin, Mon, Bamar, Rakhine, and Shan" (Naing, 2000). Some of the ethnic groups in each of the countries are very large, and competition for the scarce resources of each country is usually very tense. For instance, in Kenya, the Kikuyu is the largest ethnic group; in Burma, it is the Bamar (68%); in Cambodia, it is the Khmer (90%); Nigeria has 3 major ethnic groups out of its 250; Hausa and Fulani (29%), Yoruba (21%), and Igbo (18%).

Unmistakably, very often the major ethnic group in a country may not be capable of producing a good national leader. The most educated and intelligent persons may come from the minority ethnic groups. The colonial administration deliberately created the territorial and population imbalance. Consequently, political conflict became inevitable after the country gained independence from their former colonial master. Nigeria, Cambodia, Kenya, and many others faced this political instability because of colonial unilateral amalgamation of divergent ethnic groups into one country.

Multiethnicity and unequal Western education among the ethnic groups, pent-up ancestral animosities held against other ethnic groups, in the tailor-made country, build up into political conflicts, assassinations, political murders, and terrorist attacks against some antagonist individuals and ethnic groups.

Domestic state terrorism was unequivocally seen in the governments of President Saddam Hussein of Iraq in his biological warfare against ethnic Kurds. Also, President Robert Mugabe of Zimbabwe's suppression of white minority settlers, and his massacre of Ndebele people who were supporters of Joshua Nkomo, his arch-political opponent. What President Mugabe did in Zimbabwe against Ndebele people is typical of Third World politics in places like Nigeria, Zaire, Kenya, Uganda, Libya, Sudan, Sierra Leone, Cambodia, Malaysia, Burma, Former Yugoslavia, and so forth. It is a politics of one ethnic group domination, or an overly ambitious fascist dictator, who wants to rule the people for life. Fascist leaderships in many countries since the end of European imperialism generated untold state terrorism and other types of terrorism.

Political Party Terrorism

There are 195 countries in the world, and 177 of them are sovereign states. Of the 177 sovereign states, 167 of them are United Nations Organization (UNO) member states. Among the 167 states, 24 are full democracies, 54 flawed democracies, 38 hybrid regimes, and 51 authoritarian regimes.

A full democracy is characterized by free and fair elections, where civil liberties are respected, and there is transparency, a relatively efficient government, and sufficient political participation accompanied by sustained democratic political culture. According to the *Democracy Index* 2012, the following are full democracies: Norway, Sweden, Iceland, Denmark, New Zealand, Australia, Switzerland, Canada, Finland, the Netherlands, Luxembourg, Austria, Ireland, Germany, Malta, the United Kingdom, Czech Republic, Uruguay, South Korea, the United States, Costa Rica, Japan, Belgium, and Spain (see *Economist-Intelligence Unit*, 2013).

A second type of democracy is categorized as "flawed democracy." Flawed democracies may have free and fair elections, transparency, and respect for civil liberties, but have problems of governance, underdeveloped political culture, and low levels of political participation make them flawed. Examples include India, France, Israel, and so forth (see *Economist Intelligence Unit Democracy Index*, 2013).

Hybrid democracies are those that combine the requirements of a representative democracy with those of a direct democracy such as Switzerland, and some states in the United States such as California, where "referendum" and "initiatives" are often employed in elections.

In authoritarian regimes, there is no freedom of the press. Democracy is a coup d'etat of the head of state and his cronies. There may be political parties, but the opposition parties are rendered impotent by intimidation and abject nullification of the rule of law coupled with both manifest and latent nullification of the judiciary. In such regimes, the head of state controls the legislature. Elections, if any, are not free and fair.

In all the types of democracies designed by the *Economist Intelligence Unit*, party politics is fraught with all kinds of conflicts. In some states, it is verbal abuse of opponents and manifest demonstration of absence of a cult of good manners between opponents. In some Third World countries, it is full of violent attacks and street confrontations between supporters of one political party and the other. Very often the party in control of the government, or the party of the head of state will do everything to be reelected. In some places like Nigeria, a strong political opponent known to be on his way to defeat the incumbent head of state may be assassinated by all means, before the election. Such was the fate of M.K.O. Abiola under the General Sani Abacha regime. Unmistakably, state terrorism is endemic and inevitable in multiethnic political party systems of former colonial dependencies because of the nature of the colonial amalgamations.

International State Terrorism

When one country invades another without provocation other than for show of power, to loot and plunder, it is international terrorism. It is a war of aggression. The victim is not prepared for war with any state. All European invasions of Africa, Asia, the Middle East, and South America are all acts of terrorism. To understand international state terrorism, one had to look at anti-capitalist foreign policies of the former Soviet Union, and anti-communist foreign policies of the United States. Both the Soviet Union and the United States fought each other in another country, a newly independent country of the former European colonial master. In that regard, both were terrorists in that former colonial dependency state.

In the former European colonial dependencies, the "Cold War" was terrorism of the super powers against the young sovereign nation for the latter to yield to the political ideology and economic system demands of the former or face total destruction. In fact, an unprovoked attack against one country by another for plunder, capture, or for political and economic hegemony is international terrorism. This is because the motive of the invader is to scare and intimidate the people, and make them run away from their homes and only get back to their homes when they agree to the demands of the terrorist alien nation (e.g., colonial Germany in East and West Africa).

Unmistakably, we saw international state terrorism when, without provocation, President Saddam Hussein of Iraq invaded Kuwait on August 2, 1990. Also, when Libyan state terrorists bombed the Pan Am Flight 103 Boeing 747 jet airliner over Lockerbie, Scotland, on December 21, 1988, killing 243 passengers and 16 crew on board, including 189 Americans; and 35 of the American passengers were students at Syracuse University. President Muammar Gaddafi overtly admitted Libya's responsibility for the Pan Am Flight 103 bombing at Lockerbie and paid compensation to the victims' families in 2003, but he denied that he personally gave the order for the attack. However, during an interview with a Swedish newspaper *Expressen* on February 22, 2011, the Libyan Former Minister of Justice Mustafa Abdul Jalil said that Muammar Gaddafi had personally ordered the bombing of the Pan Am transatlantic flight scheduled from Frankfurt Airport to Detroit Metropolitan Wayne County Airport.[21] That was clearly international state terrorism.

International state terrorism is a crime against humanity.[22] It is a violation of domestic and international law. In addition, international state terrorism is a war of aggression which nullifies the fundamental human rights of the victims.

In the next section, we discuss the issue of state sponsored terrorism. How do they do it?

State-Sponsored Terrorism

Some social media and governments have alleged that some states sponsor individuals or groups to engage in terrorist acts against selected countries or enemies. But what is state-sponsored terrorism? When a sovereign nation covertly or overtly provides means or weapons of violent action to a known terrorist group to perpetrate violent criminal damage to a population among its own citizens, or at a target in another country, for the terrorist group to achieve a certain purpose, that is state-sponsored terrorism. If this type of state complicity and abetting in terrorism is not state-sponsored terrorism, what is it? In this case, a crime is committed. This type of crime is called "terrorism." A state sponsored it. Therefore, it is state-sponsored terrorism.

There are many instances of state-sponsored terrorism. Giving nine examples will suffice. Here are some of the countries that have been accused of being sponsors of terrorism: Iran, Libya, India, Pakistan, United States, Saudi Arabia, Russia, Soviet Union, the United Kingdom, and so forth.

Hezbollah is labeled a terrorist organization by the United States, the Gulf Cooperation Council, Israel, and the European Union. The Republic of Iran is known to be instrumental in the founding, training, and supplying of equipment to Hezbollah. Former U.S. President George W. Bush described Iran as an "axis of evil" and noted that Iran was the "world's primary state sponsor of terror."[23]

In September 1969, Muammar Gaddafi became the head of the Libyan Revolutionary Command Council (RCC) after a bloodless coup d'etat, dethroning King Idris I. The Libyan Arab Republic (1969–1977) was changed into the Great Socialist People's Libyan Arab Jamahiriyar as the government and ideology. This Libyan government trained, accommodated, and supplied weapons and money to a number of armed paramilitary left- and right-wing groups labeled terrorists in some quarters. They include the Palestine Liberation Organization (PLO), the Umkhonto We Sizwe, the Provisional Irish Republican Army, the Polisario Front, the Popular Front for the Liberation of Palestine, the Basque Fatherland and Liberty,[24] and so forth.

India is seen as a sponsor of state terrorism by Pakistan. Pakistan accused the Republic of India of supporting insurgent groups in Pakistan, but the allegation was not confirmed by outside observers.

Pakistan is seen as a sponsor of terrorism by India, Israel, Afghanistan, and Britain. Pakistan is accused of being involved in terrorist activities in Kashmir and Afghanistan. In fact, former Pakistani leader Asif Ali Zardari admitted that Pakistan supported terrorist groups to achieve its foreign policy goals.[25]

Russia has been described as a criminal state (Satter, 2003). But Russia's organized crime activities did not stop there. Russia invaded Ukraine and terrorized the people. That invasion qualifies Russia as engaging in state-sponsored terrorism.

Both Saudi Arabia's friends and foes generally allege that Saudi Arabia is the largest supplier of funds to Salafi jihadist terrorist militant groups like al-Qaeda, the Afghan Taliban, the Pakistan Taliban, ISIS, and the Lashkar-e-Taiba in South Asia. And according to the U.S. Former Secretary of State Hillary Clinton, Saudi Arabia constitutes "the most significant source of funding to Sunni terrorist groups worldwide."[26]

In the Soviet era, Soviet Union's secret service was known to have established a network of terrorist front organizations and was promoting terrorism worldwide (Lunev, 1998; Suvorov, 1984). It has been noted that General Aleksandr Sakharovsky from the First Chief Directorate of the KGB once said: "In today's world, when nuclear arms have made military force obsolete, terrorism should become our main weapon" (Pacepa, 2006). This KGB officer's assertion confirms the high degree of international state terrorism among powerful nations. The more they deny it, the more their postulations and actions betray them.

Nicaragua accused the United States of being a terrorist, and took the United States to the International Court of Justice, but the court refused to take up the case. When it comes to Cuban exiles, the United Sates has been accused of being a state sponsor of terrorism by the socialist Republic of Cuba for supporting Cuban exiles Luis Posada Carriles and Orlando Bosch (Campbell, 2002). It is also claimed that the United States supported Afghan Mujahideen terrorists as part of the Reagan Doctrine.[27]

The last country to discuss its involvement in international state-sponsored terrorism is the United Kingdom. Britain has been accused of supporting Ulster loyalist paramilitaries during "The Troubles," both within Northern Ireland and in cross-border operations into the Republic of Ireland (McLaugh, 2010). Also, Iran has accused the United Kingdom of supporting Arab separatist terrorism in the southern city of Ahwaz in 2006. In addition, in 1967, the United Kingdom openly supported Nigerian military junta to go to war with Eastern Nigeria and supplied the military with most of the weapons they needed to fight the war. Even when Nigeria was not ready to fight Eastern Nigeria (Biafra), the British foreign minister warned the Nigerian leader that, "without the *Igbos* there is no Nigeria." And that warning triggered the Civil War. This warning came when the Nigerian military head of state Yakubu Gowon echoed that "there is no basis for Nigerian Unity." If Nigeria had gone the way General Yakubu Gowon announced, it would have not lost over 3 million lives in the Civil War.

Some aspects of state terrorism feature in Chapter 6. Chapter 5 deals with genocide. What is genocide and who commits it? The answers are provided in the chapter.

Review Questions

1. What is terrorism?
2. What is state terrorism?
3. What is state-sponsored terrorism?
4. Compare and contrast individual terrorism, group terrorism, and state terrorism.
5. Was colonization a state terrorism?
6. What is scramble for Africa?
7. Write a short essay on each of the following:
    - Irish Republican Army (IRA)
    - The Muslim Brotherhood (Egypt)
    - The National Liberation Front (Algeria)
    - Weather Underground Organization (USA)
    - The Ku Klux Klan (USA)
    - Boko Haram (Nigeria).

8. What were the state terrorists acts of the following heads of state?
   • President Muammar al Gaddafi (Libya)
   • President Saddam Hussein (Iraq)
   • President Idi Amin (Uganda)
   • Omar al-Bashir (Sudan)
   • Francisco Franco (Spain)
   • Augusto Pinochet (Chile)
   • Robert Mugabe (Zimbabwe)
   • Mobutu Sese Seko (Zaire/Congo)

9. State terrorism is not a reaction to oppression. What is then the nature of state terrorism?

10. What factors led to the First Crusade? Who was the protagonist of the First Crusade?

11. What is the origin of "jihadism"?

12. What led to the following?
    • The Maji Maji Rebellion of 1905–1907?
    • The Mau Mau Uprising
    • The "Cold War"
    • The Akassa Raid.

Notes

1. Kano is a major city in Northern Nigeria and one of the major homes of Hausa-Fulani Muslims. They are not very industrious business people. But Igbos from Southern Nigeria are Christians, industrious traders in all kinds of merchandise, and they cherish Western education. With being Christians, embraced Western education, and being clever traders, many northern Nigerian Muslims hated them.

2. Waco is a city in McLennan County, Texas, where David Koresh was a leader of the Branch Davidians religious sect who believed himself to be its prophet. In 1993, the U.S. Bureau of Alcohol, Tobacco, Firearms, and Explosives raided the sect and it was later besieged by the FBI, which culminated in the burning of the Branch Davidian ranch. David Koresh and about 75 others died in the fire (see Pitts, William L. "Davidians and Branch Davidians," Handbook of Texas—Texas State Historical Associate. Accessed November 16, 2014).

3. In northern Idaho lived a white separatist, Randy Weaver, who was targeted by the federal government agents after he failed to appear in court to respond to charges for selling two illegal sawed-off shotguns to an undercover Alcohol, Tobacco, Firearms and Explosives (ATFE) agent. On August 21, 1992, U.S. marshals came upon Weaver, his 14-year-old son Sammy , their house guest Harris, and the family dog when they were on a road near Weaver's land. A marshal shot and killed the dog, which made Sammy fire at the marshal. In the gun battle, Sammy and the U.S. Marshal, Michael Degan, were killed. There was a standoff, and the marshal and the FBI besieged Ruby Ridge.

   During the siege, an FBI agent, Lon Horiuchi, who was waiting 200 yards from the position of Harris, Weaver, and his daughter Sarah, by the left of the cabin, opened fire thinking that Harris was armed and intending to fire at a helicopter parked nearby. When Weaver and his family tried to escape, Horiuchi fired again wounding Weaver and Harris, and killing Weaver's wife, Vicki, who he had not known was at the back door of the cabin. Consequently, nine days later, Weaver, Harris, and Weaver's three daughters surrendered to the authorities.

   In 1993, Weaver and Harris were discharged and acquitted by the federal court on murder, conspiracy, and other charges relating to U.S. Marshal Degan's death. But Weaver was convicted of failing to appear for trial on the firearms charge. However, in 1994, Weaver and Harris filed federal civil rights cases against the FBI and the U.S. Marshals emanating from the Ruby Ridge Siege. In 1995, the U.S. government settled Weaver's case for $3.1 million U.S. dollars.

4. NCNC (National Council of Nigeria and Cameroon) was a political party formed by Dr. Nnamdi Azikiwe and Herbert Macaulay in 1944 and remained so until the Nigerian Army overthrew the civilian government in 1966. Cameroon was an administrative part of Eastern Nigeria after World War II in 1945, while East Cameroon was colonized by the French. The structure remained so until the Nigerian Independence in 1960, when West Cameroon joined East Cameroon by a plebiscite. Then NCNC was transformed into the National Council of Nigerian Citizens.

5. Yorubas and Igbos are predominately represented in Action Group and NCNC, respectively. Both are from the south of Nigeria and have members from both ethnic groups and other minorities.

6. A member of the House of Lords, Lord Lea, has written to the London Review of Books saying that shortly before he died, fellow peer and former MI6 officer Daphne Park told him that Britain had been involved in the death of Patrice Lumumba, the elected leader of the Congo, in 1961. When he asked her whether MI6 might have had something to do with it, he recalls her saying: "We did. I organized it." See http://www.bbc/news/world-africa-22006446. Accessed November 18, 2014.

7. Mr. Patrice Lumumba was the first democratically elected Prime Minister of the Congo.

8. What is Terrorism? Terrorism Research. http://www.terrorism_research.com. Accessed November 25, 2014.

9. See http://www.terrorism_research.com. Accessed November 25, 2014.

10. See http://www.terrorism_research.com. Accessed November 25, 2014.

11. See http://www.terrorism_research.com. Accessed November 25, 2014.

12. Also See, "Cimbri People."

    (http://www.britannica.com/EBchecked/topic/117886/Cimbri). Encyclopedia Britannica Online. Encyclopedia Britannica, Inc. Accessed November 25, 2014.

13. Zealots were a political Jewish Party who opposed Roman rule in Judea before the birth of Jesus Christ. Some scholars in both Jewish history and the history of Roman rule in Judea concluded that the Zealots and the Sicarii were totally different forces in present-day Israel/Palestine fighting against the Romans (see Horsley, 1979; Smith, 1971; Zeitlin, 1965).

14. Hebertists and followers of a French political journalist and revolutionary leader during the French Revolution, Jacques Rene Hebert (1757–1794). He and his followers (Hebertists) pressured the Jacobin regime of 1793–1794 into instituting extreme radical measures in the Revolution. When he called for an insurrection of the Commune, his call was a failure. In effect, he was accused of being a counter-revolutionary, and on March 24, 1794, he was arrested and executed by guillotine.

15. See "Hebertists" above.

16. Asia is the largest continent in the world with 44,579,000 sq. km, while North America is the third largest continent with an area of 24,256,000 sq. km (see http://www.7continentslist.com/)

17. Prime Minister Patrice Lumumba was assassinated on January 17, 1961, in a bloody coup d'etat designed by the CIA and the Belgian Government, because they accused him of being a socialist and pro-Soviet Union.

18. President Kwame Nkruma of Ghana was awarded the "Lenin Peace Prize by the Soviet Union in 1963. He made a state visit to Moscow, Soviet Union, in 1966, and he was overthrown in a military coup while he was in Moscow. The coup was designed by the CIA. He died in Bucharest, Romania, in 1972.

19. Qasim regime of Iraq: After the overthrow of the British-backed monarchial regime of King Faisal and Prime Minister Nuri El Said in an Arab nationalist revolution in Iraq, in 1958 Brigadier Abdul Karim Qasim was installed as the executive head of state of Iraq. In 1961, Qasim announced that his government was going to take more than

50% of the profits from oil exports. At that point, the British were in control of the Iraq Petroleum Corporation. Also, Qasim had alleged that the British companies were fixing the oil prices. In 1962 he drafted a law setting up a new Iraqi National Oil Corporation. In short, Qasim wanted to nationalize Iraqi oil industry. Before he could execute his plan, on February 8, 1963, a coup designed by the British Intelligence and the CIA overthrew the Qasim regime, and more than 5,000 Iraqis who were involved in Qasim's government were executed on the basis of a list provided by the CIA (see Curtis, 2004, pp. 80–83).

20. Prime Minister Mohammad Mosaddegh was a democratically elected head of state of Iran. The Anglo-Iranian Oil Company (AIOC) (now known as BP) was in control of Iranian oil production and sales. When it was alleged that AIOC refused to cooperate with the Iranian government, the Iranian parliament voted to nationalize the assets of AIOC and expel their representatives from Iran. Also, Prime Minister Mosaddegh had sought to audit the records of the AIOC and change the terms of the company's access to Iranian oil reserves. In effect, on August 19, 1953, in a coup d'etat orchestrated by Britain (known as *Operation Boot*) and the United States (known as *TPAJAX Project*), Prime Minister Mohammad Mosaddegh was overthrown. Following the coup, a military government was formed under General Fazlollah Zahedi, which allowed Mohammad-Reza Shah Pahlavi, the Shah of Iran, to rule the country as an absolute monarch, who was strongly supported by the United States until he was overthrown by a mass revolt in 1979 (see Ward, 2009; Gasiorowski & Malcolm, 2004).

21. "Muammar Gaddafi ordered Lockerbie bombing, says Libyan minister." News.com.au. 24 February 2011. Accessed December 10, 2014.

22. "Crimes against humanity" are any of the following acts committed as part of a widespread or systematic attack directed against any civilian population, with knowledge of the attack: murder; extermination; enslavement; deportation or forcible transfer of population; imprisonment; torture; rape, sexual slavery, enforced prostitution, forced pregnancy, enforced sterilization, or any other form of sexual violence of comparable gravity; persecution against an identifiable group on political, racial, national, ethnic, cultural, religious, or gender grounds; enforced disappearance of persons; the crime of apartheid; other inhuman acts of a similar character intentionally causing great suffering or serious bodily or mental injury. (see http://www.icc_cpi.int/ Accessed December 11, 2014).

23. "Blair: Iran sponsors terrorism." (http://www.cnn.com/2005/WORLD/meast/02/08/blair.iran/index.html) CNN. Accessed December 12, 2014.

24. "Rescission of Libya's Designation as a State Sponsor of Terrorism" (http://www.web.archive.org/web/20080711101024) (http://www.state.gov/r/pa/prs/ps2006/66244.htm). U.S. Department of State. 2006-05-16. Accessed December 12, 2014.

25. "Pakistan is complicit in killing by Taliban, a Polish official says" (http://www.nytimes.com/2009/02/10/world/asia/10iht10pstan20066897.html). New York Times. February 10, 2009. Accessed December 12, 2014.

26. "US embassy cables: Hillary Clinton says Saudi Arabia's a critical source of terrorist funding" (http://www.guardia.co.uk/world/us_embassy_cables_documents/220186). The Guardian (London). December 5, 2010. Accessed December 12, 2014.

27. "How the CIA created Osama bin Laden" (http://www.greenleft.org.au/2001/465/25199) Green Left Weekly. September 19, 2001. Accessed December 12, 2014.

State Genocide and War Crimes

The crime of genocide is the worst of all crimes. This is a crime, in the main, that kills all men, women, and children in a particular society. The perpetrators have no cult of decency: It is a crime that has no regard for the value of human life. Genocide is one of the *mala in se* crimes that has been in existence from ancient times. The ancient and medieval societies did not coin the term "genocide." While the act was there in ancient and medieval periods, it was not given any term for study. For instance, the most recent genocidal act in ancient times was the destruction of Carthage in Africa in the Third Punic War in 149–146 BC[1] in which an estimated 445,000 inhabitants were killed including 410,000 civilians, 55,000 sold into slavery, and the city-state burned down and left desolate.

The idea of the concept of "genocide" came to the mind of a Polish lawyer of Jewish descent, Raphael Lemkin, in 1943. It was Lemkin who coined the term *genocide* by conjoining the Greek word *genos* (meaning "family," "tribe," or "race") and the Latin suffix *cide* (from the verb *occidere*, meaning "to kill," "to slay," or "to slaughter"). Raphael Lemkin's idea of genocide came to him at a time when he saw concentration camps being established in 1933 by Nazi Germany for the Jews, and from 1941 to 1945, Jews were systematically killed in a genocide of approximately six million.

Today, genocide is universally recognized as a heinous crime against humanity because of a groundwork and campaign of Raphael Lemkin, who sought for the universal acceptance of international laws defining and forbidding genocide. Consequently, in 1946, the first session of the United Nations General Assembly adopted a resolution that "affirmed" that genocide was a crime under international law. However, the UN General Assembly did not provide a legal definition of the crime forthwith. But the UN definition would come some years later.

Definition of Genocide

There have been many definitions of genocide. There are scholarly definitions, media definitions, surviving victims' definition, and the United Nations Genocide Convention definition. The media and surviving victims of genocide see mass killings of a group that lasts for some days or months as genocide, or some killing during interethnic wars as genocide.

A sociological definition of genocide provided by Fein (1993, p. 6) is presented here as a scholarly one. It does not mean that a scholarly definition is the best, or is a universally accepted definition. Instead, a scholarly definition is recognizable, because it carries with it some analytical and intellectual maturity. According to Fein, "Genocide is a sustained purposeful action by a perpetrator to physically destroy a collectivity directly or indirectly, through interdiction of the biological and social reproduction of group members, sustained regardless of the surrender or lack of threat offered by the victim."

There are three weaknesses in Fein's sociological definition: first, it lacks specificity as to what constitutes genocide; second, it includes political groups as likely victims. Including "political parties" as possible victims of genocide is problematic in that in developing countries of the Third World, there are many political parties in each country, and they are always at each other's throat. There is a tendency for street fights, murder, and assassinations during election campaign periods. The killings during a political election campaign period are never sustained. They are eclipsed at the end of the election. Also, in some Third World political parties, membership may be composed of a single ethnic group. In that case, any sustained killing of the members is genocide; but it is not because of their political affiliation, but due to their ethnicity. The third weakness in the claimed sociological definition is the fact that the definition makes proof of a genocidal action very hard in a court of law.

As a writer who saw a pogrom and survived a genocide in Nigerian Civil War (1967–1970), I submit that genocide is a systematic massacre and sporadic killing of members of an ethnic group or a religious group, race, or nation with intent to exterminate a significant number of the leadership and rank and file of the group including nullification of the group's reproductive capacity or transferring their children outside of their ethnic group of orientation. On the basis of my definition, they intend to commit genocide and indicators of genocidal killings can be deduced from the nature of the killings, such as killing babies, children, adults, and pregnant women who have their bowels opened with a knife and the fetus pulled out and smashed on the ground as seen in the Hausa-Fulani Muslims' genocidal murder of the Igbos in Northern Nigeria in 1966–1967 (Ebbe, 2010). Also, more indicators of genocidal killings are a situation in a war, where defending soldiers had run away, leaving in the satellite villages and towns of the fallen city very old persons, disabled individuals, and women and children hiding

#4 by Obe...

in the rooms. Then, the invading soldiers, in a mopping up operation, walked through the city and entered the villages, and began killing the old persons, disabled, women, and children, and raping young and old women and sticking objects in the women's vagina (as in the Khmer Rouge and Nigerian genocides). They are, unequivocally, acts of genocide (Igbo pogrom by Hausa-Fulani Muslims in 1966), Nanking Massacre in 1937 (Wakabayashi, 2008; Chang, 1998; Yamamoto, 2000; Fogel, 2000), Sudan genocide of non-Arab people in Darfur ("Arabs pile into Darfur to take land 'cleansed' by *Janjaweed*).[2] When a targeted group is funneled under a barrage of gunfire into a desert and forced to remain there, so that they die of starvation, that is genocide (Imperial Germany's genocide against Herero in 1904–1907). Also, genocide occurs when an ethnic group and the minorities occupying a region (Biafra), and a country backed by the United Kingdom, designed a strategy of economic blockade by sea, land, and air, so that many people (over 1,000,000), especially children, die of starvation and disease. That is genocide (Nigeria-Britain blockade of Eastern Nigeria [Biafra] July 6, 1967 to January 12, 1970).

There is no all-encompassing, best definition of genocide. What is necessary in the definition of the concept is to make it clear and simple, so that defense lawyers will not have enough room to maneuver in their attempts to exculpate a group or state leader from criminal liability of genocide.

In dealing with state genocide in this book, we rely on the United Nations Genocide Convention definition. It is clearly stated in the introduction to the Convention on the Prevention and Punishment of the Crime of Genocide (CPPCG) that acts of genocide have taken place throughout the history of society, but it was after Lemkin coined the term and the indictment and trial of the perpetrators of the Holocaust at Nuremberg that the United Nations came up with a definition for the crime under international law in the Genocide Convention.

On December 9, 1948, the United Nations General Assembly adopted the "Convention on the Prevention and Punishment of the Crime of Genocide (CPPCG) with effect from January 12, 1951—Resolution 260 (III). Article II of the Convention defines genocide as follows:

> In the present Convention, genocide means any of the following acts committed with intent to destroy, in whole or in part, a national, ethnical, racial or religious group such as:

(a) Killing members of a group;

(b) Causing serious bodily or mental harm to members of the group;

(c) Deliberately inflicting on the group conditions of life calculated to bring about its physical destruction in whole or in part;

(d) Imposing measures intended to prevent births within the group;

(e) Forcibly transferring children of the group to another group.

The above CPPCG definition is an internationally recognized definition of genocide, and it has been incorporated into the national criminal justice system of the 146 to 166 United Nations member states. Also, the CPPCG definition has been adopted by the Rome Statute of the International Criminal Court, which created the International Criminal Court (ICC). Unmistakably, the ICC is the United Nations' judicial agency that hunts down national leaders or states accused of the crime of genocide.

The United Nations definition of the crime of genocide shows that genocide is a crime committed mostly by a state or a group supported by a state. Therefore, it is purely myopic and naïve after studying genocide for anybody to assert that states do not commit crimes. Who commits genocide? It is purely a state crime, and not a crime of an individual. Even when a group or an ethnic group attacks another ethnic group with intent to eliminate them, they are complicitly backed by a government (state). For instance, when the Hausa-Fulani Muslims of Northern Nigeria set out in a prolonged killing of Igbos in 1966–1967, the government of the Northern Region was there and did nothing, because the government was controlled by Muslim Emirs and Sheiks. And the genocidal killings continued up to 1967, when Muslims had taken over the federal government of Nigeria on July 29, 1966. I found no record in history, ancient, medieval, or modern times, where genocide was carried out other than by a state or state-supported force. Undeniably, genocide is a state crime. That is why it had to be defined by the United Nations and it had to be signed by member states.

The fact that genocide is exclusively a state crime is manifest in Kofi Annan's (former Secretary General of the UN, 1997–2006) plea for the establishment of the International Criminal Court:

> "For nearly half a century – almost as long as the United Nations has been in existence – the General Assembly has recognized the need to establish such a court to prosecute and punish persons responsible for crimes such as genocide. Many thought . . . that the horrors of the Second World War – the camps, the cruelty, the exterminations, the Holocaust – could never happen again. And yet they have. In Cambodia, in Bosnia and Herzegovina, in Rwanda. Our time—this decade even— has shown us that man's capacity for evil knows no limits. Genocide . . . is now a word of our time, too, a heinous reality that calls for a historic reponse."[3]

Furthermore, in advocating achievement of "justice for all," Annan postulated:

> "In the prospect of an international criminal court lies the promise of universal justice. That is the simple and soaring hope of this vision. We are close to its realization. We will do our part to see it through till the end. We ask you . . . to do yours in our struggle to ensure that no ruler, no State, no junta and no army anywhere can abuse human rights with impunity. Only then will the innocents of distant wars and conflicts know that they, too, may sleep under the cover of justice; that they, too, have rights, and that those who violate those rights will be punished."[4]

Note in the second citation the assertion, "in our struggle to ensure that no ruler, no state, no junta and no army anywhere can abuse human rights with impunity." Annan was talking about the crime of genocide, and he was not referring to individuals but states. Annan had argued in 2010 that the International Criminal Court (ICC) is the greatest achievement of the United Nations.[5]

Now that we have a guiding definition of genocide, to understand and analyze the degree of involvement of a state in the crime of genocide, let's look at genocide in history before the 20th century.

Genocide in Ancient and Medieval Times

The Convention on Prevention and Punishment of the Crime of Genocide (CPPCG) definition of genocide has given us an index to evaluate atrocities of past centuries to see which ones can be described as genocide. Also, it is expedient to mention here that according to the International Criminal Tribunal for the Former Yugoslavia (ICTY) and the International Criminal Tribunal for Rwanda (ICTR), "No numerical threshold of fatalities had to be crossed for atrocities to count as genocide as long as the mental and physical elements of the crime of genocide are met, and the killing of a targeted group leaders could under certain circumstances constitute genocide." Therefore, on the basis of the CPPCG definition and the ICTY/ICPR guidelines on genocide, there are two very important elements or indicators of the crime of genocide: first a clear "intent" to commit the act, and second, there is unequivocal annihilation of a group or society.

There were many atrocious acts of mass murders in ancient times, but there were two that met the modern definition of genocide. One was the extermination of the Melos in 416 BC, and the other is the destruction and obliteration of Carthage in 146 BC. In both cases, a state invaded another state and eliminated it in a scene of carnage.

Starting with the Greek island city-state of Melos, a state-organized act of genocide was launched by Athenians. What brought the Athenians to attack the Greek island city-state of Melos was fear and uncertainty. The immediate cause of the Athenian invasion of the island city-state was the devastating Peloponnesian War between Athens and Sparta (Sparta being an ancient Greek city-state with dominant military powers), which lasted from 431 BC to 404 BC. The Peloponnesian War was fought all over the Greek World. In that war, the Athenians were defeated in 404 BC (Warner, 1985; Thucydides, 2013).

Throughout the Peloponnesian War, Melos was neutral. After the war, Athens was uncomfortable with Melos' claim of neutrality and its inhabitants claimed to be descendants from a Spartan colony. The Athenians did not want to take a chance. They did not want the presence of any impartial state around the Aegean Sea. Consequently, the Athenians sent representatives to Melos to order them to surrender to the Athenian Empire. According to Thucydides (2013), there was a debate between the Athenians and the Melians called "the Melian Dialogue" (Thucydides & Finley, 1954; Orwin, 1994; Warner, 1985).

In the "Melian Dialogue," the Athenians were clear and precise. They told the Melians to surrender with these words: "Save your city from destruction" (Thucydides, 2013; Warner, 1985). Undeniably, the Melians were aware that they were no match to the military power of the Athenians, but they still adamantly refused to surrender (Constantakopoulou, 2012), when the Athenians besieged the island city-state. The Athenians attacked and defeated Melos. At this point the Melians surrendered unconditionally. Unfortunately, for the Melos, the popular assembly in Athens had approved total destruction of the island city-state despite their surrender. The Athenians, depraved-heartedly killed all Melians of military age without an exception, and sold their women and children as slaves (Leadbetter, 1999; Weier, 1999; Warner 1985).

The intention of the Athenians about Melos was not hidden from the beginning. They wanted to expand their empire; and after losing the Peloponnesian War, they wanted to improve their image before their other Greek allies. The barbaric massacre of the Melos was clearly an act of state crime and genocide.

The second and last of the ancient genocides presented here is the Roman destruction of Carthage, which was briefly discussed in the section on definition of genocide. Why would the great Roman Empire want to destroy a city-state in Africa by the Mediterranean Sea? The answer is simple. Carthage was a Phoenician colony built on commerce and industry as a means to build its empire. In that ambition, Carthage had trading connections with Britain and some other notable states in the north and with traders as far south as Gabon in south-west Central Africa. By so doing, Carthage was booming in wealth, population, and powerful political influence with her neighbors. Rome was only around 400 miles (643,737.6 m) away.

In addition, the military power of Carthage was pronounced. They had Hamilcar Barca (the Lightening) and his son, Hannibal, a Carthaginian military commander regarded as one of the greatest military strategists in history, and one of the greatest generals of antiquity (Cottrell, 1992; Baker, 1929; DeBeer, 1969). Rome did not want any competition in empire building. Among the Romans, there was fear of such an empire in North Africa sharing the Mediterranean Sea with them. Rome did not think it safe to colonize Carthage, because Carthage appeared too powerful to be controlled. But it had to take a series of wars to destroy Carthage. The result of the Roman fears of Carthage led to a series of Punic Wars between Rome and Carthage from 264 BC–146 BC. The word *"Punic"* comes from the word (*Phoinix* in Greek, and *Poenus* from Punicus in Latin). So, Punic applies to the people of Carthage who were an ethnic group of Phoenicia. In effect, Roman writers used a sobriquet *"Punic"* to refer to Carthage; thus, the Punic War.

Records show that Carthage grew in commerce to become the richest and most powerful city in the Mediterranean region before 260 BC. It had a powerful navy, a mercenary army, and a lot of money. But Rome and Carthage had to face each other in a series of battles. The most written about are the First, Second, and Third Punic Wars. At a point, Carthage was on the nerves of Rome to the point that Roman Senator, Cato the Elder, always ended his speeches whether in a right context or not, with "And, further, I think that Carthage should be destroyed."

Like the Athenians to Melos, Rome did not hide her intention. In 149 BC, Rome dispatched an embassy to Carthage and told the Carthaginian government that the city should be moved inland away from the Mediterranean coast. Obviously, Carthage refused and the Third Punic War ensued (149–146 BC). As noted earlier, the Roman general Scipio Aemilianus besieged Carthage for three years. When Carthage fell, it was burned to the ground, and every surviving male was executed and about 50,000 women and children were sold into slavery.[6]

One can see the two common features of state genocide in the destruction of Carthage. Intent was to take action, and the motive to obliterate the targeted group.

A child who would not survive his illness will request his mother that the only thing she had to do for him to survive was for her to use a baseball bat to make a bow for him. This proverb refers to the demands made by Athens and Rome to Melos and Carthage, respectively. Both Athens and Rome had already made up their minds that they were going to destroy their targets even before making their draconian demands.

As noted above, there are many other ancient cases of mass murder that may qualify as genocide such as Sybaris, Skione, Asine, Torone, Askra, Pisatis, the rape of Troy, the razing of Babylon, and so forth. All of them need to be investigated, but there is not enough space for that in this text.

Genocide in Medieval Times

Medieval times (Dark Ages or Middle Ages) in European history pervaded from the 5th to the 15th century. This period started with the demise of the Western Roman Empire and eclipsed with the Fall of Constantinople in 1453 and the emergence of the Renaissance (the beginning of the modern times).

The medieval massacres of groups and states began with the religious institutions and states or monarchies. The Persian Army massacred Christians in Jerusalem, killing an estimated 17,000 to 90,000. In addition, 35,000 people including the Patriarch Zacharias were deported to Mesopotamia (Abrahamson & Katz, 2009). Obviously, there was an intent to attack Christians and destroy Jerusalem, and there was a motive to eliminate Christianity. In effect, the destruction of Jerusalem was an act of genocide.

Presented here are three phases of genocidal massacres and genocides in the medieval period. The three phases are the destruction of the Jews, Muslims, and some Christians in the Crusades (1096–1291), the Mongol invasions (1206–1321), and the persecution of Christians by Arab Islamic Caliphates coupled with Christian persecution of heresy.

In discussing these three phases, some of the massacres may not fit the criteria of genocide provided by the Genocide Convention. However, some scholars have suggested, without a consensus, that some mass killings can be genocidal although it does not constitute genocide as defined in the Genocide Convention (Huttenbach & Esparza, 2011 Fein, 1993). So here are two categories of genocide: One is genocide which meets the Genocide Convention criteria, and "genocidal massacre" as proposed by Kuper (1982 as a second category).

The genocides and the genocidal massacres were committed by states. For instance, the papacy that called for the crusades in 1095 (Pope Urban II) was a state. And the Papacy is still a state up to this day. Also, the Kingdoms or dynasties that were building empires by conquests were states. In addition, the Islamic wars of conversion were backed by Islamic states. Therefore, all of the medieval genocides and genocidal massacres were all state crimes.

The most violent state massacres of the middle stage of the medieval era was the Crusades. The Crusades were a series of European Christian wars against the Muslims to recover Jerusalem and other parts of the Holy Land, which was initiated by Pope Urban II in 1095 BC. Unmistakably, not all of the Crusades were genocides, but those that met the criteria of genocide are identified.

The First Crusade was composed of peasants, European knights, and soldiers led by French nobles. The Crusades were merciless in their killing of people on their way. In 1098, at Antioch, they killed everybody in the city and spent no time in trying to identify who was a Christian, Muslim, or pagan. They killed men, women, and children. In 1099, on the Siege of Jerusalem, with the determination to recover Jerusalem, they spared no human being in front of them. Some scholars noted that the streets of Jerusalem were turned into pools and rivers of blood (Jonassohn & Bjeornson, 1998, Riley-Smith, 1995; Madden, 2005).

The Fourth Crusade (1202–1204), made up of Christians from France, England, and Germany, did not reach the Holy Land, because they did not have the money to get many knights involved. Consequently, they diverted the Crusade to the commercial city of Constantinople to make money in the process by looting and pillage. They first invaded the Christian city of Zara and seized it in 1202. Pope Innocent III was shocked about the invasion of a Christian city by the Crusaders, and he excommunicated the Crusaders (Davis, 1997; Brehier, 1980). In 1204, the Crusades besieged Constantinople and sacked the city, pillaged the churches, and massacred most of the inhabitants. In the end, they divided the empire into "Latin fiefs and Venetian colonies" (Riley-Smith, 1995).

The Fourth Crusade was purely a genocide. The crusaders wanted money and the only way they saw to make it was to attack and eliminate the inhabitants of Zara and Constantinople. The Fourth Crusade started as a moralistic crusade backed by Pope Innocent III, a state, but when he saw that the crusaders had attacked and ransacked the wrong target, he nullified and denied them. The crusaders destroying Constantinople and massacring its inhabitants, men, women, and children, is still a state genocide, because the Pope established the Fourth Crusade. Therefore, Papacy is still liable by the principle of *respondeat superior* (let the Master answer).[7]

The next phase of genocides and genocidal invasions were the Mongol Empire building invasions of 1206–1321, when some of the Crusades were in operation. It is unequivocal that irrefutable genocides were committed in the Mongolian invasions.

Emerging in the early 13th century was a Great Khan (emperor) who founded the Mongol Empire, born with the name *Temujin* (1162–1227). He amalgamated a large number of nomadic tribes of northeastern Asia and conquered the whole of Central Asia. He was proclaimed Genghis Khan (the Great Emperor). In his military campaigns, he engaged in acts of genocide that involved absolute massacres of innocent men, women, and children. By the time he died in 1227 AD., he had brought Central Asia and China under the control of his empire.

After the death of Genghis Khan, his descendants led by Ogodei Khan and Khubilai heartlessly expanded the Mongol Empire. But the grandsons of Genghis Khan, Batu Khan, and Kada commanded forces that set out on the destruction of the East Slavic Kingdoms, and took the Kingdom of Hungary and parts of Poland.

Historians have a consensus that the Mongolian raids and invasions were the most bloody massacres in human history up through that time. According to Landers (2011), "One empire in particular exceeded any that had gone before, and crossed from Asia into Europe in an orgy of violence and destruction. Then Mongols brought terror to Europe on a scale not seen again until the twentieth century." In the same vein, Lary (2012) argues that the Mongol invasions brought about "population displacement on a scale never seen before particularly in central Asia and eastern Europe," and noted that "the impending arrival of the Mongol hordes spread terror and panic." Undeniably, in the course of creating the largest empire the world had ever known up to that period, the Mongols committed so many genocides as each Khan's mindset was focused on the three motives of genocide: eliminate threats to the empire; they had intent to spread terror; and most of the invasions were to acquire fabulous wealth especially from the basal states.[8]

The Persecution of Christians by Arab Islamic Caliphates

In the early 14th century was born Timur, a Turko-Mongol conqueror who founded the Timurid Dynasty in Central Asia. Historically, he was known as Tamerlane and the "Sword of Islam" (Marozzi, 2004; Darwin, 2008). In his ruthless military campaigns, he conquered Asia, Man Luks of Egypt and Syria, the Ottoman Empire, and the Sultanate of Delhi in India. He got Western Chaghatai under his tutelage. From these conquests, he established the Timurid Empire. In his blood-thirsty mania, in 1375–1382 AD., he ordered large-scale massacres of Christians in Mesopotamia, Asia Minor, Syria, and Persia. The Christians were Assyrians, Armenians, and Orthodox churches. His invasions of the Middle East destroyed substantial Christian population and left them desolate (Khanbaghi, 2006; Meri, 2005; Manz, 1989; Chaliand & Blin, 2007; White, 2011). Tamerlene was seen by historians as the most powerful ruler in the Islamic world of the 14th century (Khanbaghi, 2006).

Tamerlane was not after economic advantages; instead, he was after eliminating challenges to Islam such as Assyrian ancient and medieval city of Ashur, and Assyrian churches were destroyed as genocide enterprises.

Medieval Christian and Cather Heresy

Catharism was a Christian dualist organization or movement. Its members were found in many areas of Europe such as Southern Europe, with concentrations in northern Italy and Southern France. They believed in two gods: one good and the other Satan. The problem with their belief was their *"good god"* was the God of the *"New Testament,"* the creator of the spiritual realm, and their *"bad god"* was Satan, the creator of the *"Old Testament."*

The Catholic Church regarded the Cathers as the Church of Satan and denounced all their beliefs and practices. The Roman Catholic Church set out to suppress the Cather heresy.

In July 1209 AD, Pope Innocent III declared the Albigensian Crusade to eliminate Catharism (Cather heresy) in Southern France. The Crusade had knights, professional soldiers, mercenary groups, and pilgrims mostly from northern France. They assembled in Lyon, France. The Crusade was commanded by the Papal legate the Abbot of Citeaux, Arnaud Amalric. The city of Beziers had a cathedral and the churches of Mary Magdalene and St. Jude. While the siege over Beziers was being laid, some mercenary groups caused some confusion in the city without orders. Without taking any chances, the Crusade army broke the city walls and invaded and rampaged the city. Some Catholics, Cathars, and women and children who ran into the churches and the cathedral for safety, were all slaughtered. Very few Christians in the city were left to breathe another day (Oldenbourg, 1961; Costen, 1997).

After the massacres of Beziers, an estimated 100,000 to 1,000,000 lay dead (Lebedel, 2011, Costen, 1997). The situation at the siege of Beziers was so tense that the commander of the Crusade, Papal legate Arnaud Amalric was asked about the danger and risk of killing Christians in the process of the invasion, and he was alleged to have said: "Kill them all, God will know His own" (ExecutedToday.com, 2009). And, in fact, they almost killed them all on that July 22, 1209.

Like Pope Innocent III, on March 17, 1420, Pope Martin V issued a papal bull which ordered a Crusade "for the destruction of the Wycliffites,[9] Hussites,[10] and all other heretics in Bohemia."[11] Most of the medieval Christian persecutions led to genocidal massacres than genocide.

State Genocides in Modern Times

Modern genocides had their footprints in the Dark Ages, otherwise known as the Middle Ages or the medieval times. It is relevant to briefly discuss what brought an end to the medieval times. The Middle Ages came to an end when the Ottoman Empire captured Constantinople, the capital of the Eastern Roman (Byzantine) Empire on May 29, 1453 (Runciman, 1965; Nicolle, 2007). The siege and consequent capture of Constantinople brought the eclipse of the Roman Empire that had seized the world for approximately 1,500 years.

When the Ottoman Empire army invasion of Constantinople was looming, and thereafter, some Greek intellectuals with their texts fled to Italy and other Southern European nations,[12] which spurred the Renaissance in Europe. Most historians agree that the year 1453 marked the end of medieval times and the beginning of modern times (Nicolle, 2003 Runciman, 1965; Crowley, 2006).

The study of the fall of Constantinople is very important in understanding the advances made in arts, sciences, and social change. Without the fall of Constantinople, the Industrial Revolution (1750) and the French Revolution (1789–1799) might have not occurred or occurred when they did, and there wouldn't have been the emergence of Sociology as an academic discipline. The Renaissance that exploded after the fall of Constantinople allowed freedom of writing, arts, scientific explorations, and freedom of expression in Europe.

The early modern times was engulfed in wars of Christianity versus Christianity—that means, Protestant Reformation versus anti-Protestant Reformation. One of the major genocides in the 16th century was the St. Bartholomew's Day massacre in France.

In 1572 AD, there were many assassinations directed against French Calvinist Protestants, otherwise known as the Huguenots. King Charles IX was on the throne of France. His sister Margaret was getting married to a Protestant Henry III of Navarre (later Henry IV of France). The marriage ceremony was being held in Paris. Many Huguenot leaders and wealthy nobles were expected to attend. Five days after the wedding (August 23, 1572), the king ordered the murder of a group of Huguenot leaders including their military and political leader Admiral Gaspard de Coligny. The massacre spread throughout France like a new song or a drought wild fire into the countrysides and other cities.

In the process of the massacres, women and children were not spared. In Paris alone, the massacre lasted for three days. In the heartless killings, it is estimated that 20,000–30,000 Huguenots have been killed, including Admiral Gaspard Coligny (Knecht, 2001; Dyer, 1861; Pearl, 1998; Benedict, 2004).

At the end of the massacres in Paris, it came back to management of spoiled identity. King Charles IX had to say something to the French populace. According to Lincoln (1989), on August 26, 1572, the King and his court tried to express an official version of events by going to the Paris Parliament. "Holding a *lit de justice*, Charles declared that he had ordered the massacre to thwart a Huguenot plot against the royal family." However, at the time of the king's address to the Paris Parliament, the massacre of Protestants was still going on in other cities (Lincoln, 1989).

Undeniably, the St. Bartholomew's Day massacre of Protestants in France was a clear genocide killing of the modern era. In France, under absolute monarchy, church and state were one. Certainly, the St. Bartholomew's Day massacre of the Huguenots was state genocide to eliminate the Protestants or render them impotent in their reformation mania.

There was another genocide during the French Revolution. Vendee, former part of the Province of Poitou by the Atlantic Ocean, had many Catholics because the revocation of the Edict of Nantes in 1685 made many Huguenots leave the city. But the French Revolutionary government of Robespierre created harsh conditions for the Roman Catholic Church. The Catholics revolted against the Revolutionary government in 1793. Many Vendeans were incarcerated. Vendean Catholic parishes were closed and their priests dismissed. Catholic priests were ordered to take oath of allegiance to the Revolutionary government, and there was a penalty of death for failing to take the oath. Crosses, Catholic statues, bells and all signs of religious worship were banned and destroyed (Joes, 2006; Tallet, 1991). The Vendeans had to revolt, and took up arms in what was called "the Catholic Army" (or what was known as "Revolt in the Vendees") fight to restore their religious order. The French Revolutionary government responded with a massacre of 6,000 male and female Vendee prisoners and drowned 3,000 Vendee women at Pont-au-Banx. They also drowned 5,000 Vendee priests, old men, women, and children in the Loire River at Nantes by tying them up in groups, placing them in barges, and then sinking the barges in the river (Jones, 2006).

After the mass killings of the Vendeans, there was forced mass evacuation and deportations, coupled with destruction of crops, and villages and forests were burned to the ground. When all of the killings and atrocities were over, an estimated 117,000 to 500,000 of the Vendee population of around 800,000 was murdered in cold blood (Masson, 2004; Taylor, 1913; Jones, 2006).

The Vendee massacre was a genocide. Many historians call the Vendee massacre the first modern genocide, because "intent to exterminate the Catholic Vendeans was clearly stated" (Jonassohn & Bjeornson, 1998).

After the religion-centered genocides of the modern times came colonization genocides.

Colonization Genocides

The Spaniards started the long chain of colonial genocides in the Caribbean holocaust on Hispaniola (now Haiti and the Dominican Republic). That was the island which Christopher Columbus first landed on and named "Little Spain." This island was the first European settlement in the West Indies. The natives of the island were the Tainos with their Taino language. They were Arawak Indians whose ancestors migrated from South America. The Spaniards did not bring along their women in 1492 when they arrived among the Tainos. So the first conflict between the Spaniards and the Tainos was the kidnapping and rape of Taino women. In time, the Spaniards took Taino women for their common law wives (Whitehead, 1999; Stannard, 1992; Jacobs, 1992).

The struggle for space, land for Spanish settlements, and plantations pushed the Tainos to one edge of the island. The Tainos were angry about their land being forcefully taken away from them. In effect, war broke out between the Spanish settlers and the Tainos. Added to the war, the Spaniards enslaved many Tainos in their sugar plantations, and recalcitrant Tainos were shot and killed instantaneously. The heavily armed Spaniards in the Hispaniola war against Tainos, coupled with ruthless enslavement of the people, caused the death of hundreds of thousands of Taino people. Also, the Spaniards brought some infectious diseases to the island including smallpox, against which the people had no immunity, because their environment did not develop the disease. In effect, many Tainos died of the infectious disease. But the war of aggression by fire-armed Spaniards against a society with bows and arrows, spears, and knives was a mismatch. The Spaniards with their firearms massacred the Taino people to the extinct population today. As far back as 1548, the Taino population had been reduced to less than 500 (Rouse, 1992; Abbot, 2010; Jacobs, 1992; Cook, 1998, 2002). Undeniably, Taino population is today extinct, not because of disease but because the Spaniards wanted Hispaniola Island for sugar plantations. That's why historians call Spanish elimination of Tainos the "Caribbean holocaust."

As Meierhenrich (2014) put it, "the course of colonization has been marked all too often by genocide." Looking at the history of Taino and what happened to them in the hands of uninvited Spaniards, any wanton massacre of a people, in any form, including war of aggression, is genocide. "War of aggression" is genocide, because the attacked nation did not cause it or attacked the aggressor. "War of aggression" is a war of greed, power, ideological mania, and territorial imperialism. That is why the powerful European nations and the United States opposed its definition and including it in the category of "Crimes against Humanity" and in the jurisdictionary powers of the United Nations International Criminal Court (ICC).

Present hereunder are a litany of the worst colonial genocides of the modern times, continent by continent in alphabetical order. We are going to start with the African continent.

Africa

In the cases of genocide committed by the states noted hereunder, some were committed directly by the colonial masters; and some committed because of the type of leadership and problematic constitution they drafted for the colonial dependency which the colonists were forced to give up. In some cases, the state genocide was purely ideological and greed and has nothing to do with a former colonial master.

The Nazi Holocaust was not the first German depraved-heart genocide. Obviously the first German holocaust was the one against Africans in South-West Africa. In 1904, German colonial settlers intentionally destroyed three indigenous ethnic groups in South-West Africa: the Herero, Witbooi (the Hama), and the Damara. The Herero were the largest and most agricultural group among the three ethnic groups. The Herero wanted their land for their farms. The invading Germans wanted the land, too. Who owns the land? The Herero. Why should they perish because they want to farm on their ancestral land? But the Germans regarded the Herero as inferior and an obstacle to German imperial expansion in the area. The Herero, in addition to farming, were also cattle rearers and needed more land for their cattle to graze. At that time, there were over 75,000 Herero in the area (Meierhenrich, 2014).

The Hereros' tenacious holdings on their land painfully bothered the German settlers. Consequently, they informed their home government in Germany about the situation in

South-West Africa. As a result, more than 2,500 German soldiers stationed in West African German colony of Togoland, were moved to South-West Africa. From around August 11–19, 1904, about 2,000 German soldiers were dispatched to Waterberg Mountains, where a little over 62,000 Hereros assembled to discuss how to deal with their invaders. Without any warning, the German soldiers opened fire on the Hereros, funneled them in a horse-shoe formation, and pursued them into the Namib Desert (one of the world's oldest deserts covering over 100,000 sq. miles or 258,998.8 sq. km). The Namib Desert is extremely dry, with sand dunes rising as high as 900 ft. Into this waterless desert, the German drove the Herero to die of starvation and dehydration. But the German soldiers killed most of the Herero before they could reach the desert (Meierhenrich, 2014; Hall, 2006; Kiernan, 2007; Steinmetz, 2007).

The siege of Namibia (South-West Africa)—the Herero, lasted nearly three months, because the German intention was total extermination of the Herero and the other two ethnic groups so that the whole region and all of its natural resources would be theirs, including Herero, Witbooi, and Damara lands. In effect, on October 2, 1904, the commanding officer of the German soldiers, Lieutenant General Lothar von Trotha, gave an "extermination order." The order called for "every male Herero, armed or unarmed" to be shot dead (Kiernan, 2007; Meierhenrich, 2014). About forty-eight hours later, the commanding officer tried to be cogent and specific about his order, and stated: "I believe the (Herero) nation must be destroyed as such" (Kiernan, 2007).

The modus operandi of destroying the Herero was not only by firearms of the Germans. The German commanding officer, von Trotha, had ordered his troops "to seal off western edge of the Sandveld along a cordon stretching about 200 miles (321,868.8 m) and to occupy the water holes, so that no Herero will have water to drink in the very dry season, while they were being pushed toward the Namib Desert. It was absolutely inevitable that the Herero who escaped the German gun fires must die in the scorching heat of dehydration. Unmistakably, the inhumane strategy worked. The entire Herero nation was destroyed. To consummate their genocidal mindset, the German soldiers did not "spare women and children." It was "absolute destruction" (Hull, 2006).

What about the Witbooi and Damara ethnic groups smaller than the Herero in the Namibia region? In 1904–1909, the Germans fraudulently made a treaty of peace with the Witbooi and the Damara. The German settlers employed and killed them, because, to the Germans, they are unpeople (Steinmetz, 2007; Hull, 2006; Meierhenrich, 2014).

From 1886 to 1908, Leopold II of Belgium destroyed, approximately, 8 million Africans in his Congo rubber plantations. He was the founder and sole owner of Congo Free State as a private commercial enterprise. Some writers on African colonization noted that Leopold II was responsible for the death of 2–15 million Congolese (Hochschild, 1998; Forbath, 1977; Weisbord, 2003). While Leopold II wanted the Africans to work for him, he preferred killing them than paying them their wages. Like the Germans in Namibia, the Africans are unpeople.

From 1966–1970, Major General Yakubu Gowon of Nigeria and the British were responsible for the genocide in Eastern Nigeria (the collapsed Republic of Biafra) in which pogrom, genocide, economic blockade, and Civil War in Eastern Nigeria caused the death of more than one million (1,000,000) lives, mostly children who died in refugee camps of *Kwashiorkor* (severe protein-energy malnutrition characterized by edema, irritability, anorexia, ulcerating dermatoses, and an enlarged liver with fatty infiltrates). General Gowon had told the world in a broadcast in 1966, that, "There is no basis for Nigerian unity" after Eastern Nigerian—"*Igbos*"—threatened to secede from Nigeria. The breaking up of Nigeria into three autonomous regions was what the Muslim northern Nigeria had wanted all along, including Western Nigeria. But the moment the British Government heard General Gowon's announcement of "no basis for Nigerian unity," the British Foreign Minister went on the air: "Without the *Igbos* there is no Nigeria." On the next day, General Gowon changed his words and once again announced on the Nigerian radio "To keep Nigeria one is an attack that must be done." With this announcement, Britain provided Nigeria with B-52 bomber jets, rockets, tanks, millions of rifles and 9mm bullets, and military weapons of all types. Britain also provided Nigeria with ships to blockade Biafra from getting imports of food and weapons from any part of the world. It was the blockade that killed the Biafran children and old folks.

I was a Ranger Commander for Biafra in the Civil War, and later a Battalion Commander. I saw with my eyes, driving along Owerri-Okigwe highway, a British jet-bomber hovering very low over a town's open market square that was in session under trees of interlocked canopy.

Figure 5.1 Nigerian Genocide Against the Igbos.
© Bettman/CORBIS

It bombed innocent civilians, men, women, and children, who believed that they were far away from the battlefield, only to be killed in a mass in a hidden market square. The plane dropped more than six bombs, while I parked my Jeep 100 yards (91.44 m) from the market square watching the bomber carnage. Throughout the war, those British planes bombed many civilian market squares, when the market was in session, and the casualties were virtually uncountable. One of the unforgettable British-Nigerian bombings of civilians was the bombing of the city of Aba, because the Igbo saboteurs ("Osu," *untouchables*) informed Gowon that Aba was the Center of Biafran Scientists' Laboratories, where they manufacture grenades and rockets. But all of the casualties in the Aba bombing were civilians. Without the British ideas and aids, there wouldn't be a name "Nigeria" as a country today. We wouldn't be worrying about Boko Haram in Eastern Nigeria today.

The Rwanda genocide was a problem created by Belgium for the Hutu and Tutsi. The Tutsi ethnic group was very enterprising and enthusiastic about Western education. Rwanda Kingdom was traditionally ruled by Tutsi. In effect, the Belgium colonists used the Tutsi to govern the Hutu and everybody else. The Tutsi, like the *Igbos* of Nigeria, the *Kikuyu* of Kenya, and the Bamileke of Cameroon, advocated independence for the states of Rwanda-Burundi.

The Belgium error was that they amalgamated the two countries as one for the convenience of colonial administration. But at independence, the two political entities were separated, whereas there were Hutu and Tutsi in both Rwanda and Burundi. What caused the famous Rwanda genocide was not as a result of a "comedy of errors" but a tragedy of errors. Belgium cannot absorb the whole blame. There was an intrinsic hatred between Hutu and Tutsi. The colonial administration sharpened the hatred. Hutu and Tutsi are relatives (Arab and Israel). But colonial administration brought them under one government. Unfortunately, the Tutsi ethnic group was embraced by Belgium and used in their colonial administration but not the backward Hutu majority. It was a time bomb waiting to explode after the eclipse of colonial administration. And it did. After independence was granted to Rwanda and Burundi in 1962, the trouble began immediately.

At Independence, Rwanda was headed by a Tutsi government, while the Burundi government was led by a Hutu. Again, in both governments, there were Tutsis and Hutus seeking to control the government. From 1962, there were assassinations of political figures of Hutus and Tutsis. Each Hutu or Tutsi regime was a dictatorship. In both Rwanda and Burundi, if a Hutu is in control of the government, Tutsis are targeted for persecution and elimination; and if a Tutsi is in control of the government, every Hutu is in trouble. The result was riots after riots in each regime, which led to many Hutus and Tutsi to fleeing their homes to neighboring countries and becoming refugees there. Some of the refugees in Uganda and elsewhere waged a war against their homeland, which led to loss of a great many lives.

The immediate cause of the Rwanda genocide was when President Jurenal Habyarima of Rwanda (a Hutu) and President Cyprien Ntaryamira of Burundi (a Hutu) were returning home from an overseas travel in President Habyarima's aircraft. They were shot down and both Presidents died on April 6, 1994. A United Nations investigation concluded that a Rwandan presidential guard was responsible. Immediately, the Hutu went on a killing spree hunting down any Tutsi, especially politicians and business elite. And Hutu were in the majority to inflict heavy causalities on the Tutsi. But note that two in every three families among the Hutu have some Tutsi among them. And two in every three families among the Tutsi have some Hutu as a member of the family. Consequently, in the Rwanda genocide, brothers killed brothers, sisters, nephews, cousins, women, and children. It was a tragedy of errors. The whole genocide was caused, in the main, by governments of hate, greed, and economic conditions.

The state genocide in other parts of Africa that need to be discussed in this book are Idi Amin's Uganda, Mobutu Sese Seko of Zaire (Congo), Charles Taylor of Liberia, and Robert Mugabe of Zimbabwe.

Idi Amin overthrew the government of President Milton Obote in 1971 in a coup d'etat, and made himself the President of Uganda. When Obote supporters in exile attempted to invade Uganda to get rid of him in 1972, he decided to purge his own army. All soldiers, officers, and other ranks from Obote's ethnic group, especially *Acholi* and *Lango*, were assembled and killed (Avirgan & Honey, 1982; Kyemba, 1977). During his overthrow of President Obote in 1971, he massacred *Lango* and *Acholi* soldiers in *Jinja* and Mbarara army barracks. In 1972, civilians of *Lango* and *Acholi* citizens were mercilessly killed by Amin's paramilitary guards. After a year in office, his victims included persons from other ethnic groups in Uganda, judges, lawyers, foreign nationals, senior civil servants, journalists, and anybody he felt was an enemy of his government (Gwyn, 1977; Melady & Melady, 1977). In fact, the International Commission of Jurists estimated that Idi Amin killed as many as 80,000 men and women. Other estimates by exiles and Amnesty International range from 300,000 to 500,000 people. Idi Amin was virtually the Adolf Hitler of Africa.

Unmistakably, Idi's genocidal killings was a post-colonial incident, but the British supported Idi Amin's overthrow of President Milton Obote, because Obote had taken actions to nationalize all British and other foreign industries in Uganda. It is absolutely undeniable that the post-colonial genocides (Mobutu Sese Seko's, Charles Taylor's, Robert Mugabe's, etc.) were caused by colonization. Therefore, they fell within the purview of "colonization genocides."

In Zaire (Congo), Mobutu Sese Seko was following the footsteps of his former colonial master, Leopold II of the Congo Free State. The Zairean Army that Mobutu used to overthrow the government of Patrice Lumumba was established by King Leopold II. And throughout President Patrice Lumumba's reign, Mobutu was Lumumba's aide, while at the same time, Mobutu was recruited as Belgian intelligence informer (Wrong, 2009; Edgerton, 2002).

The genocide in Congo (later Zaire in 1971) occurred after Mobutu's assassination of his master, Patrice Lumumba, and Lumumba's followers rebelled against Mobutu. With a combined force of French and Belgian paratroopers and Mobutu's army, Lumumba's followers (socialist group and pro-Soviet Union) and ethnic groups opposed to Mobutu, were massacred in what rose to a civil war from 1960 to 1965. More than 100,000 Congolese among Lumumba's followers were killed before the United Nations' forces intervened (Boulden, 2001; Haskin, 2005; Struelens, 1978).

Mobutu Sese Seko, thereafter, created a "one-man rule," just like his former colonial master, Leopold II. Zaire (Congo) was Mobutu and Mobutu was Zaire. He allowed no opposition party. He killed every political opponent in the country whom he could not bribe with a lucrative position. Even some on self-exile, he lured back to the country, and his paramilitary guards tortured them before gradually killing them (Young & Turner, 1985; Kwitny, 1986; Schatzberg, 1991).

Another post-colonization genocide in Africa is that of Robert Mugabe's Zimbabwe. Robert Mugabe and Joshua Nkomo fought the white minority government of Rhodesia for independence in 1979. They won, and on April 18, 1980, Rhodesia gained independence and changed her name to Zimbabwe. Robert Mugabe became the Prime Minister and later President of Zimbabwe. He was determined to be a dictator and a President of Zimbabwe for life. To achieve his aim, he antagonized his political partner, Joshua Nkomo. He created a one-party system of government, which was his own party—the ZANU-PF (Zimbabwe African National Union-Patriotic Front).

Mugabe's intent was to nullify white minority power in Zimbabwe, eliminate all opposition, and forcefully exile ethnic groups that are his traditional political enemies. To accomplish his aim, he established North Korean–trained Fifth Brigade paramilitary guards. With the Fifth Brigade, Mugabe, like Idi Amin and Mobutu Sese Seko, killed his political enemies, motivated rebellion of ethnic groups opposed to his leadership, and used his paramilitary guards to kill more than 20,000 civilians from Ndebele regions who were supporters of Joshua Nkomo (Norman, 2003; Hill, 2005). Mugabe's killings in Zimbabwe have been described as ethnic cleansing and genocide (Meredith, 2006).

In conclusion, whereas the Rwanda (1993–1994), Nigeria (1966–1970), Zaire (1960–1965), and Zimbabwe (1981–1987) genocides were not carried out directly by their colonial masters, each and every one of them has the fingerprints of their colonial masters in them. Without the colonization, those post-colonization genocides would not have occurred.

Asia

The colonization genocide in Asia was that perpetrated against Aboriginal Australians and Tasmanian Aborigines. In the Island of Tasmania were 5,000 to 10,000 Tasmanian Aborigines at the time of British colonization and occupation in 1803.[13] But by the year 1833, only 300 of them were left. Others were massacred by the colonizers in a war of aggression and persecution, and some died of colonizers' "introduced infectious diseases to which they had no immunity."[14] The last full-blooded Tasmanian Aborigine was a woman called Truganini who was born in 1812 and died in 1876; and another survivor was a woman called Fanny Cochrane

Smith, who was born at Wybalena in 1834 and died in 1905 (see Australian Dictionary of Biography Online, 1994).

The colonization of Aboriginal Australians by Britain began on January 28, 1788. According to Markus (2000), the first stage of colonization of Australia started with a great deal of roving and bottom-up extermination on a relatively small scale. In course of time, across the country, squatters and police in Queensland destroyed Aboriginal communities by shooting down small groups in countless occasions (Moses, 2008).

The Aboriginal Australians were confronted with physical genocide (destruction) and cultural genocide (destruction). There was a policy of child removal which was a *de facto* theft of Aboriginal children by white settlers for the purpose of exploitation or purification, or both. This was an apparent form of cultural genocide or cultural destruction that is estimated to have started around 1840 and became a wide-spread common practice in the early 20th century (Markus, 2000). The practice was condoned and supported by the Australian colonial government. At the time, Aboriginal populations in West Australia, Queensland, and Northern Territory were the largest and estimated to range from 20,000 to 25,000 in each region. But according to *Year Book Australia* (2002), during the pre-European settlement of Australia (1788), the population of the indigenous people (Aborigines) ranged from 750,000 to 1,000,000.

There is no evidence of pure Aboriginal Australians in the 2011 Australian census. What they reported was "Indigenous Australians." By Australian academic and government definition, "indigenous" does not mean being an Aboriginal Australian. In fact, the Aboriginal Australians and Tasmanian Aborigines were regarded as savages by the Australian settlers and were wiped out by war, wilful massacre, and deliberate policy of extermination (Markus, 2000; Moses, 2004, 2008). There are no more Aboriginal Australians or Tasmanian Aborigines. What are found in Australia today are about 520,000 miscegenated Australian Aborigines.

North America

From 1600 to 1800, the French, Dutch, and English invaded North America. From the beginning, the Dutch developed many forts along the Hudson River. The first Dutch (the Netherlands) settlement was founded in 1615. Like the British had the Royal Niger Company to trade and develop Nigeria and the East Indian Company for India, the Dutch established a trading monopoly in North America with the Dutch West Indian Company in 1621 (Israel, 1989; Griffis, 1909). They had the New Amsterdam (now New York City) and Brooklyn, Bronx, and Long Island. By the third Anglo-Dutch War (1673–1674), the Dutch had lost the New Netherland including the New Amsterdam. By treaties and capitulation, the Dutch gave up their provinces in America to the English. And their forts in Acadia to the French in 1674.

At the eclipse of the Dutch in North America, the English and the French fought it out in the upper north of North America, while the Spaniards controlled the southern part of North America.

In the process of building forts and trading posts along the rivers, the native Indians were pushed away. There is no accurate account of the number of native Indians killed between 1622 and 1800. However, the U.S. Census Bureau in 1894 counted over 40 wars with Indians in which 19,000 whites and 45,000 Indians were killed.

Some records show cases of massacre of Native Americans totaling 197 (Churchill, 1997; Heizer, 1993; Thornton, 1987). The massacres do not represent genocides. However, according to some scholars on Native Indian history and records in the American Indian Genocide Museum in Houston, Texas (Stannard, 1992; Thornton, 1987; Norrell, 2004; Melendez, 2012), some Indian villages and communities were exterminated in the army raids from 1700 to 1839.

Furthermore, the United States Indian Removal Act of 1830, which prompted the removal of Cherokee, Muscogee, Seminole, Chickasaw, and Choctaw nations, led to the hideous and infamous "Trail of Tears" in which thousands of Native Americans died "including 2,000–6,000 out of the 16,542 relocated Cherokee" (Anderson, 1991; Bealer, 1996, 1972; Foreman, 1989, 1932), and "the Potawatomi Trail of Death of 1838" in which 859 old men, women, and children had to do more than trekking from September 4 to November 4, 1838, from Indiana to Kansas, a distance at the time of 660 miles (1,062,167 m). And many died on the way of typhoid fever, and exhaustion due to the rigor of the journey (Allison, 1986; Foreman, 1989, 1932; Walkman & Molly, 2009; Anderson, 2005: Remin, 2001; Griske, 1909).

One may look at the Native Americans' wars with early American Settlers and their wars with the United States and conclude that there was no genocide. Be that as it may, any forceful removal of a society, tribe, or nation from its ancestral home to an unfamiliar location within or outside the region is an act of genocide, and it is tantamount to ethnic cleansing. If one thinks that such people removed from their ancestral homes are not dead, think again. They are spiritually dead. Some of them in their late 20s to 40s at the time they were moved, will not reach age 70 or 80 before they get into the land of collective immortality (physical death) and *Zamani* (Mbiti, 1990).

South America

Among the Europeans, the Spaniards started the colonial genocide given their extermination of the "Taino" population on Hispaniola (Meierhenrich, 2014). Spain did not tolerate any resistance from the tribes or nations they invaded. They mercilessly destroyed them so that other tribes would learn not to resist. Spain wanted the land and natural resources of the natives by force. The conquistadors (soldiers for Spain and Portugal) attacked any nation they entered during the Age of Discovery and retained them for Spain or Portugal. There was no negotiation with the natives. It was ruthless invasion (Vanhanen, 1997; Innes, 2002; Kirkpatrick, 1934).

Undeniably, the colonial conquest of Central and South America was fraught with genocidal violence. Such conquests were seen in the destruction of the Indios in Mexico, Guatemala, and Peru. They were all genocides that took thousands of human lives, and towns and villages were decimated (Mann, 2005). To attest to the genocides committed by the Spaniards in Mexico, Peru, Guatemala, and other regions of South and Central America, where are the Incas, the Aztecs, and the Mayas?

The Spaniards conquered the Inca Empire in 1572 and trashed the Inca civilization (Somervill, 2005; McEwan, 2010). In 1521, the Spanish Conquistadores and their allies defeated the Aztecs. The Spaniards committed untold acts of genocide in the Inca and Aztec empires. But the most difficult for the Spanish Conquistadores to conquer were the Mayans. The Mayans had a highly advanced civilization, but were protected from an easy defeat by the Spanish because of two factors. They had no concentrated polity. They had scattered polities, and their lands were very poor in natural resources, unlike Peru and Mexico (Sharer, 1994; Demarest, 2004). As a result of the scattered polities of the Mayas, the Spaniards resorted to eliminating one polity after another. But the Spaniards could not exterminate them all, as they had done the Incas and the Aztecs. In effect, two Maya states survived: the *Itaz* polity of Tayasal and the *Ko'Woj* city of Zacpeten. The two remained occupied and independent of the Spanish until toward the end of the 17th century. It was in 1697 that the Spaniards defeated them (Sharer & Traxler 2006).

Since Spain conquered them in 1697, they have been subjected to humiliation, dehumanization, and unpeople treatments. In the Guatemalan War of 1981–1983, more than 100,000 Guatemalan Maya were killed by the armed forces. Regular and irregular government forces killed, raped, tortured, and forcibly displaced Mayans in the rural mountain regions. In the conflict of the government versus the insurgents, 99.8 percent of the victims were Maya. The conflict ended when the Guatemalan military leaders felt that they had Maya communities under control. The entire conflict was aimed at destruction of Maya population (Meierhenrich, 2014). Leadership elimination intended to weaken the political and economic strength of an ethnic group so that they cannot pose any further threat to the government in power is enough to stand as genocide.

Spain colonized Argentina and ruled it as part of her South American colonial empire. But to understand the genocide committed by colonial Spain in Argentina, at the time of colonization of Argentina, native Indians occupied so many areas and were the largest in population.

There were three categories of native Indians occupying Argentina at the time Spain colonized it in 1512, and the *Viceroyalty* of the *Rio de la Plata* was created with Buenos Aires as its capital in 1776 (Crow, 1992). They were *Selknam* and *Yaghan* in the deep south. Hunting and gathering fruits were their means of survival. The second category were the *Puelche, Querandi, Servanos,* and *Teheuelche*. They were more advanced in hunting and gathering than Selknam and Yaghan. They were conquered and controlled by *Mapuche* from Chile. And the third highly advanced category were the *Charrus, Minuane, Guarani*, Diaguita, *Toconote, Henia, Kamiare,* and the Huarpe. They were all farmers and had developed pottery and other cooking utensils. They occupied the center and center-west of Argentina. They had a sustained culture that raised llama cattle and maintained a relatively modern social structure. They were conquered by the Incas and influenced by Inca civilization (Edwards, 2008; Lewis, 2003).

Why make these calculations of indigenous peoples of Argentina at the time of their colonization? It is because most of the ethnic groups were totally wiped out, especially the advanced agricultural groups. In fact, for more than a century, the population of Argentina has been 97% persons of European origin, with Spain and Italy leading other European countries. Today, only 3% of Argentines are *Mestizo*, whom they call *Amerindian* or nonwhite groups. Think about that. Where are the indigenous peoples? They were the victims of Spanish genocide (massacres) of 1512–1816. The hunting and gathering tribes who ran toward the Patagonian Desert, Monte Desert, and Salinas Grandes Salt Desert were not allowed to remain there long before European ranchers drove them to extinction.

Many Amerindians seen in Argentina today came from Bolivia and Paraguay. In fact, a Complementary Survey authorized by the government of Argentina (first in more than 100 years) of Indigenous Peoples (descendants of American Indians) in 2004 found 1.49% (600,000) of Argentine population of 42 million to be Amerindians (Trinchero, 2006).

What happened to the Amerindians in Argentina is similar to the history of European colonial expansion in other areas of the world. They are genocides that preceded the Nazi genocide of the 1930s and 1940s.

After colonization genocides, there are two more types of genocides to present here. They are ideological genocide and ethnic cleansing genocide. These two types of genocide are also committed by a state or a government.

Colonization Genocides in West Indies

Many Caribbean islands were totally destroyed by Spain, Belgium, France, and Britain in their wars with each other to gain possession of the islands between 1600 and 1800. Take, for instance, how the island of Tobago was crushed over and over again by the four European powers mentioned above. The four European countries fought each other for the control of the Caribbean islands. From 1628 to 1677, each of the four countries massacred each other's colonists and the natives including the slaves. Each country's dialectical invasions culminated in Caribbean genocides,[18] particularly Tobago holocausts.

The most terrible Caribbean genocide was that of General Valeriano Weyler (otherwise known as "butcher Weyler") in Cuba. He is regarded in many circles as the originator of the "concentration camp," made famous by Adolf Hitler in World War II. He was a Spanish Governor General of the Philippines and Cuba in 1897. Cuba rebellion was too much for the Spaniards, because the insurgency was widespread.[19] In addition, the native soldiers were fighting the Spanish soldiers by hit-and-run tactics, and ran back and joined their fellow natives.

General Weyler decided to deal with the situation by separating the civilians loyal to Spain from the freedom fighters. He moved over 300,000 to a new location away from the fighting zone. And whoever was moved to the new location was not allowed to come out to the disputed areas of Cuba.[20] Unfortunately, Weyler neglected the cave of hundreds of thousands of Cubans he had relocated ("re-concentrated"). In effect, many died in the concentration camp, and many who refused to relocate were slaughtered, men, women, and children. He butchered every resistance in the island of Cuba (Tone, 2008). The number of colonists and native Caribbeans massacred in the colonization genocide is inestimable.

Ideological Genocide   *Typology #2*

This type of genocide is committed by a state against ethnic groups or political groups that have socialist or communist views and interests, while the government in power is a capitalist state or vice versa. This type of genocide can be domestic (within the state) or international.

The Cultural Revolution of Chairman Mao Zedong of China from 1966 to 1976 falls under this category. Chairman Mao formed his Chinese Communist Party (CCP), using it to commit acts of genocide unfathomable in Chinese political history. He swept away what he called "traditional class enemies." These traditional class enemies fall into "seven black categories": landlords, rich peasants, counterrevolutionaries, evil-doers, rightists, capitalists, and reactionary intellectuals. In addition, among the traditional class enemies were those individuals who exhibited insufficient revolutionary zeal, such as teachers and intellectuals. In the process, he killed more than 30,000,000 Chinese.

Chairman Mao had "Four Cleanup Movements." The goal of the movement was to cleanse the politics, economy, organization, and ideology of China. This was Mao's Chinese Cultural Revolution (Gao, 2008; Hollingworth, 1985; Carter, 1976). In Mao's Cultural Revolution, his motto was: "Destroy the old world. Forge a new world." In the process, he got more than 30 million people killed. That was purely ideological genocide.

Another example of ideological genocide is that of the Communist Party of Kampuchea (CKP), otherwise known as the Khmer Rouge. This movement emerged from the fighting against French colonization from the 1940s to 1954, when the French were shamefully beaten.

The Khmer Rouge Communist Party was led by Pol Pot, who turned to be one of the most infamous dictators in the world. He and his government were fighting against a pro-American capitalist forces led by Lon Nol. Marshal Lon Nol carried out a coup to remove the Cambodian head of state, Prince Sihanouk. This led to a civil war. Pol Pot allied with the deposed Prince Sihanouk to fight against Marshal Lon Nol's Khmer Republic government.

In the Cambodian civil war, the Khmer Republic government, with U.S. assistance, dropped about half a million tons of bombs on Cambodia which killed about 300,000 people (Jackson, 1992: Vickery, 1984). Some Cambodians who survived the government forces' bombing joined the Khmer Rouge Revolution. Consequently, on April 17, 1975, the Khmer Rouge army captured Phnom Penh, including over 87% of Cambodian territory, and that ended the civil war (Etcheson, 1984; Vickery, 1984).

The genocide in Cambodia occurred at the end of the civil war, when the Khmer Rouge began to rule the country. The Khmer Rouge set out to implement their Maoist and Marxist-Leninist manifesto. They aimed at transforming Cambodia into "a rural, classless society" in which "there were no rich people, no poor people, and no exploitation" (Jackson, 1992; Vickery, 1984; Ung & McElroy, 2011). To achieve their aim, they eliminated the use of money, abolished markets, normal schooling, private property, foreign clothing styles, religious practices, and any form of traditional Khmer culture (Etcheson, 1984; Jackson, 1992). Furthermore, all social institutions such as public or private schools, mosques, pagodas (temples), churches, universities, shops, and government buildings were transformed into prisons, stables, reeducation centers, granaries, and detention centers.[16] The revolutionary black costume was what every Cambodian must wear.

In addition, the Khmer Rouge prohibited three or more persons standing and holding a discussion. Persons who violated the regulation were accused of being enemies of the revolution, and were arrested and executed. To end the old regime, the Khmer Rouge arrested and killed thousands of soldiers, army officers, and civil servants of the Khmer Republic government which was headed by Marshal Lon Nol, because the Communist Khmer Rouge regarded them as "impure" for the revolution. In addition, the Khmer Rouge executed hundreds of thousands of intellectuals, city residents, and ethnic minorities such as the Vietnamese, Cham, and Chinese. They also killed many of their own soldiers and party members who were suspected of being traitors to the revolution. Many Cambodians were arrested, tortured, and executed for appearing to be anti-communist revolution.

When the Khmer Rouge captured Phnon Penh, they ordered every city resident to move to the countryside to engage in farming. During the forceful evacuation, hundreds of thousands of Cambodians died. Before the Khmer Rouge regime was defeated by Vietnamese forces in December 1978, they had killed close to 3 million people (Ung & McElroy, 2011; Etcheson, 1984; Vickery, 1984). At the Vietnamese capture of Phnon Penh in 1978, the Khmer Rouge fled to a Thai territory, where it got disorganized. When Pol Pot died on April 15, 1998, some of the Khmer Rouge surviving leaders defected to the Royal Government of Cambodia, some were arrested, and some died. But two of the surviving leaders, second-in-command of Khmer Rouge Nuon Chea, and another top leader of Khmer Rouge, Khieu Samphan, were indicted by the Extraordinary Chambers of the Courts of Cambodia (ECCC), after Thai and Cambodian Governments reached an agreement to their extradition. Both Chea and Samphan were charged with crimes against humanity, genocide, and war crimes by the ECCC on September 19, 2007. They were convicted as charged and sentenced to life imprisonment on August 7, 2014.

There have been many ideological massacres in European history that may not be described as genocide. However, in the Soviet Union, there was an ideological genocide that needs to be discussed in this text. In Joseph Stalin's Russia, was the Dekulakization of 1929–1931, Ukrainian famine of 1932–1933, the Great Terror of 1937–1938, and the Violent Destruction of non-Russians in the 1930s–1940s.

The dekulakization was Soviet political repression that included arrests, deportations, and executions of millions of wealthy farmers and their families in 1929–1932. The richer peasants were condemned to death, because they were stigmatized as Kulaks and class enemies (Montefiore, 2005; Yakovlov, 2002). In addition, Stalin deported more than 3.3 million groups and ethnic categories to Siberia, where over 43% of them died of disease and malnutrition. The reason Stalin gave for their being deported to Siberia, where he knew that many of them would die of the deadly environment there, was that they posed a resistance to Soviet rule, and they were anti-communist ideology, and separatism was necessary. Also, some ethnic groups such as Soviet Koreans, Volga Germans, Crimean Tatars, Chechens, and Poles were relocated, and some of them died because of the relocation (Parrish, 1999; Yakovlev, 2002; Montefiore, 2005).

The peasants did not want state control, but that was exactly what Stalin wanted. Stalin divided the Kulaks into three categories: (i) those to be shot or imprisoned; (ii) those to be sent to Siberia, North, the Urals, or Kazakhstan after confiscation of their property; and (iii) those to be evicted from their homes and used in labor colonies within their own districts (Conquest, 1986). The chief of the secret police rounded up the peasants for the mass execution (Rayfield, 2004; Carr, 1966).

In the final analysis, Stalin's policy of kulakization and collectivization coupled with other repressive draconian regulations caused mass starvation and the death of more than 15 million peasants plus 5–7.5 million who perished in Ukraine during the Holodomor (a man-made famine—the "Famine-Genocide in Ukraine") under Stalin's reign of terror (Conquest, 1986).

Unmistakably, before the Nazi Holocaust, there was no type of genocide worse than Stalin's genocide in Soviet Russia.

The next section of this chapter deals with ethnic cleansing genocides in Nazi Germany, Former Yugoslavia, and the Armenian genocides.

Ethnic Cleansing Genocides

Among all ethnic cleansing genocides of the 20th century, the worst was the Nazi Holocaust. The Holocaust was the Nazi Government of Germany's premeditated, depraved-hearted, systematic persecution and killing of approximately six million Jews from 1933 to 1945 under the leadership of Adolf Hitler. The Nazi Party was the National Socialist German Workers Party (NSDAP) formed in 1920. From 1920 to 1945, the party practiced *Nazism* (a set of political beliefs of the Nazi Party of Germany).

Adolf Hitler was the engine moving Nazism. He became a member of the German Worker's Party in 1919 before the party became NSDAP. In 1921, Hitler became the leader of NSDAP. And as a veteran of World War I, he hated the Treaty of Versailles, because Germany and her Allies were held liable for causing the war, and Germany was required to pay indemnity. To demonstrate his aversion to the Treaty of Versailles, he began to promote Pan-Germanism, anti-Semitism, and anti-communism coupled with denigrating capitalism as a Jewish scheme

(Bullock, 1999/1952; Bauer, 2000). In effect, he became very popular in the Nazi Party and among a significant population of the German people.

Adolf Hitler's virulent hatred for the Jews became pivotal to the Nazism and the party's ambition to colonize the whole of Europe and other parts of the world. The Nazis, therefore, developed a strong belief that Germans were "racially superior" and that the Jews were "inferior" and should be eliminated to preserve the German "racial superiority" (Bendersky, 2000; Evans, 2005; Fromm, 1977).

The Nazis' intent to colonize all European countries with the exception of those who joined Hitler as allies (to avoid being colonized) did not concentrate on eliminating all Jews only. They wanted to eliminate all those they described as "undesirables." Following the Jews as the Nazis' "undesirables" were the Roma (gypsies), disabled persons, ethnic Poles, Russians, homosexuals, criminals, Jehovah's Witness, Serbs, political prisoners, Catholic clergy and others (Bergen, 2003; Bullock, 1999; Fischer, 1995; Fest, 1974; Dawidowicz, 1975; Furber & Lower, 2010).

The Nazis designed a method to get rid of all of the "undesirables." And the first thing they did was to create concentration camps and extermination camps in all countries under their military control and in "Axis powers" in Europe (Germany, Italy, Hungary, Romania, and Bulgaria).[17] The first Nazi concentration camp was built in Germany in March 1933 after they assumed power in Germany on January 30, 1933. Immediately after Hitler became the Chancellor of Germany (1933), the NSDAP was given control over the police. The rule of law was suspended. The NSDAP and their police arrested political opponents and union organizers, tortured them, and incarcerated them into the concentration camp without trial (Evans, 2005). Heinrich Himmler, who was in command of the Schutzstaffelor Protection Squad (SS), took wholesale control of the police and the concentration camps in Germany from 1934 to 1945. Himmler also took charge of keeping the groups they described as "racially undesirable elements" in various concentration camps (Evans, 2003).

The first concentration camp, however, was opened in Dachau, Germany, for political prisoners. It was designed to accommodate 5,000 politicians. Any politician in Germany in 1933–1934 who was not a member of the Nazi Party was either in the concentration camp in Dachan, or was already killed, or made politically impotent. Also, the general public was under a siege of terror to a point; according to Janowitz (1946), "There were jingles warning as early as 1935," as follows: "Dear God, make me dumb, that I may not come to Dachan." From the time the Nazis rose to power in 1933 to the end of World War II, more than 3.5 million Germans were given the shock of imprisonment by incarcerating them in the concentration camps or prisons for a while by Nazi-controlled Special Courts, courts-martial, and civil justice system (Almond, 1946). In addition, more than 76,000 civil servants, soldiers, and civilians who opposed the Nazi agenda were summarily executed (Hoffman, 1977).

Unmistakably, the intentional systematic killing of political opponents and a mass of civilians, from different works of life, to achieve an absolute fascist dictatorship as the Nazis did in Germany, was genocide. That was how Hitler prepared the ground in Germany for his wholesale extermination of the Jewish population.

When the World War II began in 1939, concentration camps were set up in different places throughout Europe, where the Nazis had control. The concentration camps inside Germany were labor camps, collection camps, Buchenwald subcamps, concentration camps, and labor camps for women. There is no accurate number of concentration camps set up by Nazi Germany. A German Department estimate has it as 1,200 camps and subcamps. While Jewish Virtual Library has it as being, "approximately 15,000 labor, death and concentration camps" (Gilbert, 1986).

Throughout the war period, the Nazis had over 20,000 mobile militia as death squads, whose assignment was to hunt for the Jews everywhere in Europe and take them to the concentration camps. In addition, instead of wasting time taking them alive to the extermination camps, mobile gas vans were used to speed up the killing process. The Jews who were not killed with the poison gas were left in concentration camps to die of premeditated starvation, intentional maltreatment, disease, and overwork. That was the Holocaust process and modus operandi of Nazi and colonial German genocide.

The exact number of persons killed by the Nazis using firearms, poison gas, starvation, deliberate maltreatment, torture, forcible rape, overwork, disease, and criminal negligence, can never be enumerated. In the *Encyclopedia of Camps and Ghettos, 1933–1945* of the United States Holocaust Memorial Museum, Geoffrey Megargee and Martin Dean delineated 42,500 Nazi ghettos and camps in Europe operating from 1933 to 1945 starting from Germany and France to Russia. They came to a conclusion that about 15–20 million people died or were incarcerated in those locations (Lichtblau, 2013).

The Nazi genocide that is always in everybody's mind is their depraved-hearted murder of approximately six million Jews, which was more than wiping out a whole country. But the Nazis committed not just one genocide; they also killed over 76,000 Germans made up of members of opposing German political parties, German civil servants, some German civilian population, hundreds of thousands of Russians, Poles, and Serbs. Apropos of the Genocide Convention and our working definition of genocide, the Nazis intentionally killed those categories (groups) of people with the motive of creating a monolithic race and a fascist dictatorship regime in Germany. Therefore, in Nazi Germany, there were, at least, four genocides. Beyond controversy, ethnic cleansing was the main motive of Nazi genocides.

The Bosnian genocide in Europe is the last case of genocide discussed in this chapter. It is the genocide committed at Srebrenica and Zepa, and includes the ethnic cleansing killing in Bosnia and Herzegovina committed by the Army of the Republika Srpska from 1992 to 1995. Republika Srpska is one of the two political units that made up the State of Bosnia and Herzegovina. In Srebrenica, the forces of Republika Srpska engaged in mass killing of men, women, and children of Bosnian Muslims. Those that they did not kill they drove out of their homes involving 25,000–30,000 Bosniak civilians (Irwin, 2013). The expulsion targeted

Bosnian Serbs, Bosnian Croats, and Bosniaks involving Muslims, Orthodox Christians, and Catholics, and made them refugees in other lands (Mojzes, 2008).

The ethnic cleansing employed such crimes as rape, murder, unlawful confinement, torture, sexual assault, beating, robbery, arson, inhuman treatment of civilians, and destruction of businesses. In addition, the Bosnian elite were specifically targeted, including seizure of real and personal property of the people, unlawful deportation and transfer of civilians, destruction of mosques and churches, and landing artillery shells in predominately civilian neighborhoods (Toal, 2011).

On December 18, 1992, the United Nations General Assembly resolution 47/121 declared in its preamble that ethnic cleansing is a form of genocide. The UN declared as follows:

> Gravely concerned about the deterioration of the situation in the Republic of Bosnia and Herzegovina owing to intensified aggressive acts by the Serbian and Montenegrin forces to acquire more territories by force, characterized by a consistent pattern of gross and systematic violations of human rights, a burgeoning refugee population resulting from mass expulsions of defenceless civilians from their homes and the existence in Serbian and Montenegrin controlled areas of concentration camps and detention centres, in pursuit of the abhorrent policy of "ethnic cleansing", which is a form of genocide, . . .[20]

UN Resolution 47/121 preamble, December 18, 1992. Copyright © 1992 United Nations. Reprinted with the permission of the United Nations.

In further clarifying and certifying that genocide was committed in the Republic of Bosnia and Herzegovina by the Serbian and Montenegrin soldiers, the International Criminal Tribunal for the Former Yugoslavia (ICTY) and the International Court of Justice (ICJ) stated that for atrocities perpetrated on a group to be defined as genocide, physical or biological destruction must have been meted out against a protected group, and there must be a specific intent to commit the atrocious act, and that only the 1995 Srebrenica massacre has been found to be a genocide in 2001 by the ICTY and reaffirmed by the ruling of the International Court of Justice (European Court of Human Rights, 2007; Simons, 2013; ICTY, 2001).(

In addition, the ICTY found that genocide was also committed in Zepa, near Srebrenica. With regard to the Serbian President Slobodan Milosevic and other members of Serbian leadership, the ICTY Trial Chamber concluded that they aimed and intended to destroy a significant part of the Bosnian Muslim population and committed genocide in Sanski Most, Prijedor, Brcko, Srebrenica, Kljuc, Bosanski Novi, and Bijeljina[21] (Mitchel, 2007). In effect, Slobodan Milosevic became the first executive incumbent head of state to be indicted for a crime.

Undeniably, all national leaders who had engaged in ethnic cleansing in their countries have the mind of Adolf Hitler, greed, racism, arrogance, inordinate ambition, sadistic murder, and a depraved mind.

Genocide is a part of "war crimes." War crime is explained in the next section of this chapter, but genocide is the worst of all war crimes.

War Crimes

War crimes have been internationally recognized as being atrocious as far back as the 15th century. In 1474, in Breisach, Germany, was stationed a Dutch mercenary soldier, Peter von Hagenbach. The Duke of Burgundy (France) acquired the city of Breisach in exchange for services he had rendered to the Holy Roman Empire. But he wasn't interested in dealing directly with the city of Breisach.

"They that hazard all do so in hope of fair advantages."[22] So the Duke wanted some rewards for his services to the holy Roman Empire. In effect, he hired Peter to form an army of infantry soldiers to occupy the city and collect exorbitant taxes from the Breisach people. Consequently, the people revolted vehemently. On the spur of the moment, the French Duke ordered Peter von Hagenback "to sack, pillage, rape and burn the city" (Bassiouni, 2010). "Obey the last order" is a common principle in most military organizations. So Peter obeyed his master and carried out the order as was given. But the massacre of Breisach by von Hagenbach's soldiers was extremely unacceptable and beyond pardon. Consequently, there was a general outcry in the whole empire, that the act was a "crime against God and man" (Bassiouni, 2010). As a result, an ad hoc international tribunal, made up of judges from Alsace, Switzerland, and other parts of the Holy Roman Empire, was formed by the leaders of 26 member states of the empire.

Peter von Hagenbach was charged with murder, rape, and other crimes considered to be against the "laws of God and Man." Peter told the ad hoc criminal tribunal, in his defense, that he was following the order of his superior, the French head of state.

The tribunal did not want to go after the French Duke of Burgundy, under the principle of *respondeat superior*. Instead, the court found von Hagenbach guilty as charged, stripped him of his knighthood, and sentenced to be executed in a very brutal method (Bassiouni, 2010).

Unmistakably, the Peter von Hagenbach trial became the First International Criminal Tribunal. The decision of the court became a warning to military officers and men, worldwide, to be careful in obeying unlawful orders; and that vicarious liability (respondeat superior) principle may not hold.

The Statute of the International Criminal Court (ICC) of the United Nations, a treaty-based court, defined war crimes as, inter alia, "serious violations of the law and customs applicable in an armed conflict not of an international character."[24] In other words, customary International Humanitarian Law (IHL), Rule 156, states "serious violations of international humanitarian law constitute war crimes."

The ICC was created for the prosecution of war crimes committed on or after July 1, 2002, when the court came into being. Article 12 of the ICC statute gives ICC jurisdiction over the citizens of noncontracting states in case such states are accused of committing crimes in the territory of any one of the states that signed the treaty.[25]

The Rome Statute of the International Criminal Court's War Crimes includes the following:

1. Grave breaches of the Geneva Convention, such as:

    a. Willful killing, or causing great suffering or serious injury to body or health,

    b. Torture or inhuman treatment,

    c. Unlawful wanton destruction or appropriation of property,

    d. Forcefully making a prisoner of war serve in the forces of a hostile power,

    e. Denial of a fair trial to a prisoner of war,

    f. Unlawful deportation, confinement or transfer.

2. The following acts as part of an international conflict:

    a. Directing attacks against civilians,

    b. Directing attacks against humanitarian workers or UN peacekeepers,

    c. Killing a surrendered combatant,

    d. Misusing a flag of truce,

    e. Making a settlement of occupied territory,

    f. Deporting inhabitants of occupied territory,

    g. Using poison weapons,

    h. Using civilians as shields,

    i. Using child soldiers,

    j. Firing upon a combat medic with clear insignia.

3. The following act as part of a noninternational conflict:

    a. Murder, cruel or degrading treatment and torture,

    b. Attacks against civilians, humanitarian workers, or UN peacekeepers,

    c. Hostage taking,

    d. Summary execution,

    e. Pillage, and

    f. Rape, sexual slavery, forced prostitution, or forced pregnancy.

The Rome Statute, Part II, Article 8, states that the court has jurisdiction over the above crimes only where they are "part of a plan or policy, or as part of a large-scale commission of such crimes."[26]

Persons Charged with War Crimes Since World War II

After World War II, the victorious Allies indicted some of the leading actors among the Axis powers. Many were charged with war crimes. At the Nuremberg trial, some were convicted and sentenced in absentia to death, when they had already committed suicide before the trial, such as Martin Bormann. Some committed suicide before their execution or while serving their sentences in prison such as Hermann Goring and Rudolf Hess, respectively. Also, some Japanese Prime Ministers and Generals were indicted for their war crimes in World War II, such as General Hideki Tojo, General Kenji Doihara, Prime Minister Koki Hirota, General SeishiroItagaki, General Heitaro Kimura, Akira Muto, and so forth. All of the six Japanese leaders in World War II were sentenced to death by the International Military Tribunal for the Far East (IMTFE) in 1946 (Brackman, 1987; Horowitz, 1950; Roling & Ruter, 1977).

This is not an exhaustive list of names of all of those indicted for war crimes in the Nuremberg and Tokyo trials, because there are many of them, but space is limited to have all of them in this text. However, here are the most recent state leaders and government officials indicted for war crimes by the ICC. Only one was court-martialed in the United States.

1. Former Yugoslav President Slobodan Milosevic died in ICC custody in 2006 while awaiting trial.

2. Former Liberian President Charles G. Taylor. He was tried in The Hague for war crimes from 2007 to 2011. He was convicted in April 2012 and sentenced to 50 years of imprisonment.

3. Former Bosnian Serb President Radovan Karadzic ("The Butcher of Bosnia"). He was arrested on July 21, 2008, in Belgrade and brought to The Hague. His trial began in 2010, and it is in progress.

4. Omar al-Bashir is a current head of state of Sudan. He is indicted by ICC for genocide in Darfur. He refused to surrender himself.

5. Former Libyan head of state Muammar Gaddafi was indicted for ordering the killing of protesters and civilians during the Libyan civil war in 2011, but he was killed by a mob before he could stand trial.

6. William Laws Calley, former U.S. Army officer who was convicted at a court-martial by a U.S. military court and found guilty of murdering 22 unarmed South Vietnamese civilians in the My Lai Massacre on March 16, 1968, during the Vietnam War. He was awarded life sentence, but it was later changed to an order of house arrest. Three years later, President Nixon reduced his sentence with a presidential pardon (Anderson, 1998).

7. Ratko Mladic was indicted for war crimes, crimes against humanity, genocide, and violations of other humanitarian laws during the Bosnian War. He was arrested in Serbia in May 2011 and extradited to face trial in The Hague.

8. Joseph Kony, the leader of the Lord's Resistance Army in Uganda. He was indicted by ICC for war crimes and crimes against humanity. He is still at large.

The problem with enforcement of war crimes is that only less powerful heads of state get indicted. But powerful heads of state and heads of state who are close allies of powerful countries hardly get the legal grip of the International Criminal Court.

War of Aggression

This is a medieval war of conquest, a war of show of power, domination, and territorial annexation. In the 20th century, this should be a crime. It is a "war of aggression." Such a war does not make for "international peace and security," which is one of the main purposes for the emergence of the United Nations Organization.

The United Nations has problems getting its key members accept the definition of "war of aggression" as a violation of international law. Most state members of the United Nations support having war of aggression as a violation of international law. In effect, the UN set up a special committee to study and come up with a definition of "Aggression" in Resolution 2330 (XXII) on December 18, 1967. The special committee adopted the definition of Aggression by a consensus in April 1974, and submitted it to the General Assembly of the United Nations.

On December 14, 1974, the General Assembly of the United Nations Resolution 3314 (XXIX) adopted the following Definition of Aggression (Article 1):

> Aggression is the use of armed force by a State against the sovereignty, territorial integrity or political independence of another state, or in any other manner inconsistent with the Charter of the United Nations, as set out in this Defintion.[27]

Article 3 of the Resolution notes that, "Any of the following acts, regardless of a declaration of war, shall, subject to and in accordance with the provisions of article 2, qualify as an act of aggression":[28]

a. The invasion or attack by the armed forces of a State of the territory of another State, or any military occupation, however temporary, resulting from such invasion or attack, or any annexation by the use of force of the territory of another State or part thereof;

b. Bombardment by the armed forces of a State against the territory of another State or the use of any weapons by a State against the territory of another State;

c. The blockade of the ports or coasts of a State by the armed forces of another State;

d. An attack by the armed forces of a State on the land, sea or air forces, or marine and air fleets of another State;

e. The use of armed forces of one State which are within the territory of another State with the agreement of the receiving State, in contravention of the conditions provided for in the agreement or any extension of their presence in such territory beyond the termination of the agreement;

f. The action of a State in allowing its territory, which it has placed at the disposal of another State, to be used by the other State for perpetrating an act of aggression against a third State;

g. The sending by or on behalf of a State of armed bands, groups, irregulars or mercenaries, which carry out acts of armed force against another State of such gravity as to amount to the acts listed above, or its substantial involvement therein.

The General Assembly further specified that the acts outlined above are not exhaustive. This is because, they noted, the Security Council may determine other acts that reach the purview of aggression under the provisions of the UN Charter.

A war of aggression, therefore, is a war waged by one country against another without justification of self-defense, but for territorial gain, ideological expansion, and subjugation. The Rome Statute of the International Criminal Court refers to "war of aggression" as a crime of aggression. According to the ICC, the crime of aggression is one of the "most serious crimes of concern to the international community."

Crime of aggression is one of the crimes within the jurisdiction of the International Criminal Court (ICC). But ICC could not exercise its jurisdiction on crime of aggression until all state parties agree on a definition of the crime and provide conditions under which the crime can be prosecuted. In a Review Conference held on June 11, 2010, the 111 State Parties to the ICC agreed by a consensus to adopt a resolution accepting the definition of the crime of aggression provided above, and conditions for ICC to exercise jurisdiction over the crime.[29] Unfortunately, the definition is not binding on the Security Council, because the General Assembly of the United Nations can only make recommendations to the Security Council, but it cannot dictate to the Security Council. It is unfortunate because war of aggression or crime of aggression is committed in this world mostly by the members of the United Nations Security Council. Crime of aggression has a binding force in international law. Any argument to the contrary is a pure mystification of facts, law, and reason. ICC can only grab poor countries and their leaders to their world court.

War of aggression or crime of aggression is a state crime, which the perpetrators mete out with impunity. It is still a war of conquest; and in the contemporary times, it is an international crime crying to Heaven for vengeance.

Who likes a bully? Who would like to be attacked by somebody they have not offended? Such an attack is an unwarranted aggression. In international relations among countries of the world, such an attack violates the fundamental human rights of the citizens of the attacked State. Undeniably, that is a crime of aggression for which the aggressor should be criminally liable. This is because in the Nuremberg trial, the Allies' judges of the International Military Tribunal charged the leaders of the Axis powers with the crime of aggression among other crimes and found them guilty of the crimes charged. They executed some of them, and others they sentenced for years or life imprisonment. The rule and principles of the Nuremberg trial should not be changed simply because the judges of the Axis powers have become judges in their own case today.

Attack on Refugees

Refugees are meant to be protected by the state in which they reside, whether in war or peace-time. Refugees are civilians made up of men, women, and children. The 1948 Geneva Conventions protect refugees.

Some national dictators, in their power hunger and ethnic cleansing, have attacked refugee camps and killed many men, women, and children. Slobodan Milosevic committed such atrocities against Bosnian Muslims. Mugabe of Zimbabwe targeted Ndebele population, and those of them who escaped his pogrom, torture, and indefinite detention, and hid themselves in north-eastern remote Matabeleland region of Zimbabwe, and those in a refugee camp in a neighboring country, Tanzania, he sent his "Gukurahundi," Fifth Brigade force who slaughtered thousands in the refugee camps[32] (Makambe, 1987).

In Congo (former Zaire), Thomas Lubanga Dyilo, leader of the Union of Congolese Patriots (UPC) and his forces engaged in ethnic cleansing, murder, rape, mutilation, conscripting child soldiers, torture, wholesale human rights violation, and decimation of many refugee camps in the *Ituri* conflict of 1999–2007. On March 17, 2006, Lubanga was arrested by ICC agents and taken to The Hague (Corder, 2009). On March 14, 2012, he was found guilty of war crimes including recruiting children younger than 15 years of age into his army. On July 10, 2012, the International Criminal Court sentenced him to fourteen years of imprisonment.[31]

There is a warrant of arrest for the Sudanese head of State, Omer al-Bashir, issued by the ICC, because of genocide and massacre of refugees in and around Darfur in southern Sudan. He has not been arrested, because China and France are interested in the oil and other natural resources in Darfur.

Many refugees have been attacked in various parts of the world, but they are not always attacked by the government of the country where they reside, but by forces within or from outside of the country. However, refugee camps in every country should be protected by the law enforcement agents of the state in which they reside; otherwise, the state is liable for a crime of omission.

Human Rights Violations

Since the 20th century, human rights violations have become a ubiquitous phenomenon all over the world. However, an effort to protect the human rights of individuals did not start in the 20th century. The recognition of fundamental human rights began, not in the medieval times, but in the ancient times.

The declaration of human rights started in the Achaemenid Empire of Cyrus II of Persia in 539 BC. He was known as "Cyrus the Great," "Cyrus the Elder," the "King of Kings of Persia," "King of Anshan," "King of Media," "King of Babylon," "King of Sumer and Akkad," and the "King of the Four Corners of the World." His Achaemenid Empire was the largest the world had yet seen (Kuhrt, 1995, 2007; Gary & Litt, 1927). He respected the customs and religion of the lands he conquered. He freed slaves, proclaimed that everybody had the right to choose their own religion, and forged racial equality.[32] In addition, Cyrus the Great has been acknowledged by scholars and archaeologists as the oldest known declaration (world's first charter) of human rights, known today as the Cyrus Cylinder.[33] It is presumed that it was transcribed between 539 and 530 BC, the year he was killed in a battle in Syr Darya (Arnold & Michalowski, 2006).

Modern society owes a lot to Cyrus the Great. As a result of his policies in Babylonia, the Jewish religion referred to him in the Jewish Bible as Messiah (Isaiah 44:24, 26-45:3, 13). Cyrus the Great was not a Jewish. So he was the only non-Jew to be called a Messiah (Lendering, 2012).

Today, human rights are a very hot issue in governance. According to the Office of the High Commissioner for Human Rights of the United Nations:

> Human rights are inherent to all human beings, whatever our nationality, place of residence, sex, national or ethnic origin, colour, religion, language, or any other status. We are all equally entitled to our human rights without discrimination. These rights are all interrelated, interdependent and indivisible.
>
> Universal human rights are often expressed and guaranteed by law, in the forms of treaties, customary international law, general principles and other sources of international law. International human rights law lays down obligations of Governments to act in certain ways or to refrain from certain acts, in order to promote and protect human rights and fundamental freedoms of individuals or groups.[34]

The fundamentality and universality of human rights is the cornerstone of international human rights law. The first Universal Declaration of Human Rights was in 1948. That principle of human rights has been reiterated in several "international human rights conventions, declarations, and resolutions."[35] The 1993 Vienna World Conference on Human Rights, for instance, postulated that "it is the duty of States to promote and protect all human rights and fundamental freedoms, regardless of their political, economic, and cultural systems."[36]

But many heads of state, all over the world, whose states are signatories to the adherence to the Universal Declaration of Human Rights, persecute their citizens with impunity, such as the regimes of Augusto Pinochet of Chile, Omer al-Bashir of Sudan, Kim il-Sung and Kim Jong-un of North Korea, Mobutu Sese Seko of Zaire, Idi Amin of Uganda, Robert Mugabe of Zimbabwe, Sani Abacha of Nigeria, Charles Taylor of Liberia, Slobodan Milosevic of the Former Yugoslavia, and so forth.

Looking at the official definition of human rights above, one can see that a state that uses the police and uses tear-gas to disperse peaceful demonstrators, or the police shooting at unarmed person or persons, is in violation of fundamental human rights of the individuals. Unmistakably, ethnic cleansing, recruitment of boys and girls under the age of 17 for military service, torture of prisoners of war, use of chemical weapons in war, prohibition of religious worship, attack on refugees, prohibiting children or adults from having formal education, and so forth are all violations of human rights of the individuals involved. Every country in this world, regardless of dictatorships or democracies, at one point in time, violates the human rights of its citizens. Only the degree of violation varies from developed economies to developing countries.

Controlling State Genocide

The control of the crime of genocide began with the declaration made by the General Assembly of the United Nations in its resolution 96(1) of December 11, 1946, that "genocide is a crime under international law, contrary to the spirit and aims of the United Nations and condemned by the civilized world."[37] The signatories to the Convention on the Prevention and Punishment of the Crime of Genocide (CPPCG), in Article I, confirm that "genocide, whether committed in time of peace or in time of war, is a crime under international law which they undertake to prevent and to punish."[38] The acts punishable under this Convention (Article III) include "genocide, conspiracy to commit genocide, direct and public incitement to commit genocide, attempt to commit genocide, and complicity in genocide."[39] In view of the above, the United Nations had to provide a mechanism for the prosecution of offenders.

The pursuit of perpetrators of genocide was abandoned after the 1945–1946 Nuremberg and Tokyo trials. But the ethnic cleansing atrocities in the territories of the Former Yugoslavia provoked international outrage. In effect, some journalists and nongovernment organizations, especially Amnesty International, spurred the United Nations to action. As a result, the UN created an ad hoc International Criminal Tribunal for the Former Yugoslavia (ICTY) to investigate the atrocities. The ICTY found cases of genocide and indicted the ring leaders. In the same vein, the genocide in Rwanda was detected, and the culprits were prosecuted by another International Criminal Tribunal, referred to as the International Criminal Tribunal for Rwanda (ICTR).

When there was an upsurge of genocidal acts all over the world in the late 20th century and early 21st century, an idea that had been in the United Nations records surfaced. That was to have a permanent international criminal court. That idea, after so many conventions culminated in the emergence of the Rome Statute of the International Criminal Court (ICC). The United Nations Secretary General at the time, Kofi Annan, described the relevance of the emergence of the ICC this way: "The establishment of the Court is . . . a gift of hope to future generations, and a giant step forward in the march towards universal human rights and the rule of law" (Annan, 1998).

There is no more need for an ad hoc tribunal for the trial of state leaders accused of the crime of genocide. A permanent criminal court idea has been achieved. Every head of state, especially those from dictatorship states, is kept on notice that no head of state is beyond incrimination. The creation of the ICC is a very strong mechanism for the prevention and control of genocide.

Another control mechanism in the crime of genocide is imposing sanctions against the state being led by the head of state being sought by the ICC. An example of this situation is the head of state of Sudan, Omer al-Bashir. He was indicted by ICC but refused to go to The Hague, and sanctions have been imposed against him and his government. He could be arrested if he travels to another country that has ratified the Rome Statute of the ICC. There is no deadline for the arrest of such indicted persons. By the International Criminal Court jurisdiction, such state leaders can still be arrested after they leave office.

The ICC has been criticized on the following grounds: That the prosecutor is politically motivated—but there are safeguards against that political motivation; that soldiers are confused about the laws of war—in other words, some soldiers may be afraid to fight the way they should, because they do not know exactly the limits of their military action; that ICC is a barrier to peace and reconciliation. This criticism ignores the situations in ethnic cleansing, where the perpetrators are not ready to settle for anything other than to eliminate the other ethnic group. It is also said that ICC tries to exercise jurisdiction over nonparty nationals. There is nothing wrong about this. No nation should be an outlaw in the committee of world nations. Any exclusionary clause does not make world peace. Another point of criticism against the establishment of the ICC is cost and delay in the prosecution of offenders. Well, that is a truism in all litigations. Finally, ICC has been criticized for focusing on leaders from Africa. This is true. ICC left Augusto Pinochet to go free until he died a natural death. However, which African head of state indicted by the ICC did not deserve being brought to The Hague? The answer is all of them deserve it.

Religious fundamentalism, economic conditions, greed, and despotism are the main causes of genocide. Therefore, the United Nations should watch out for the signs of the above factors among their member states, and warn the leaders of such nations, the way out of their predicament. The UN needs a team of religious, economic, and political experts to advice heads of state of such impending catastrophe.

The economic and political pathologies of greed and despotism are products of moral decay in the individual or in the entire society. Therefore, the only living solution to cure such a head of state is moral revival channeled from a source outside the state.

When a head of state, who is like a glue that holds a whole country or federation or ethnic groups together dies, like Marshal Tito, President of Yugoslavia, from 1953 to 1980, the United Nations should step in, as quickly as possible, to get a successor who would continue the peaceful regime of the predecessor.

In the final analysis, genocide can be eliminated in the world, if the so-called United Nations Security Council members stop their latent alliances with dictators all over the world because of the latter's economic resources. Undeniably, dictatorships breed genocide.

Review Questions

1. What is genocide? Who developed the term "genocide"?

2. The Third Punic War was an act of genocide. What are the causes and course of the Punic Wars?

3. What were the causes and course of the Nazi Germany holocaust of the Jews (1933–1945)?

4. Imperial Germany's genocide against the Herero in 1904–1907 was an indictment of the relevance of European colonization. Discuss in detail.

5. What is the significance of the United Nations Convention on the Prevention and Punishment of the Crime of Genocide (CPPCG)? What is the United Nations definition of genocide?

6. The destruction of Carthage and the Melos were two horrible genocides of the ancient times. Discuss each in detail.

7. What led to St. Bartholonew's Day Massacre in France?

8. The massacre of the Huguenots in France was state genocide. Explain.

9. What is the "Caribbean holocaust"? Who was the mastermind of the "Caribbean holocaust"?

10. Write a short essay on anyone of the following:
    - Nigerian genocide
    - Rwanda genocide
    - Australian genocide
    - Bosnian genocide
    - Colonization genocides.

11. (a) What is the "Trail of Tears"? (b) What is the "Potawatomi Trail of Death of 1838"?

12. The author identified three types of genocide:

- Colonization genocide
- Ethnic cleansing genocide, and
- Ideological genocide. Explain, discuss, and give examples of each that occurred in the 20th or 21st century.

13. According to the Rome Statute of the International Criminal Court (ICC), what are "war crimes"?

14. Name five heads of state and politicians who have been charged with war crimes, genocide, or crimes against humanity.

15. What do you understand by "Fundamental Human Rights"?

Notes

1. Carthage was a powerful African city-state and empire located near the present-day Tunis. General Hasdrubal, one of the two brothers of Hannibal the Great (Hannibal the Great son of Hamicar Barca—a Carthagenian leader) was the commander of the Carthagenian forces. The Roman army under Manius Manilius invaded the Punic City of Carthage (the Third Punic War) in 149 BC. Carthage was highly fortified. The Romans elected the young Scipio Aemilianus as consul to command the Roman army. Scipio defeated the Carthagenians at Nepheris and besieged the city. The Romans were forced to advance slowly, capturing one house after another and one street after another. After three years, in 146 BC, the Carthagenians surrendered. Rome burned down the city-state of Carthage and sold the survivors into slavery.

2. Arabs pile into Darfur to take land 'cleansed' by Janjaweed—a paramilitary force of the Sudanese Islamic government. (http://news.independent.co.ukk/world/africa/article2768232.ece). Accessed December 18, 2014.

3. Kofi Annan's speech as the Secretary General of the United Nations during the UN Diplomatic Conference of Plenipotentiaries on the establishment of an International Criminal Court held in Rome, Italy, from June 15–17, 1998, "to finalize and adopt a convention on the establishment of an international criminal court." (http://legal.un.org/icc/general/overview.htm). Accessed December 18, 2014.

4. Ibid.

5. "Kofi Annan addresses the First Review Conference of the Assembly of States Parties to the Rome Statute of the International Criminal Court." Kampala, Uganda: *Kofi Annan Foundation*, May 2010.

6. After the destruction of Carthage, the area remained desolate for over one hundred years before it was rebuilt following the death of Julius Caesar. During the First Punic War, the city of Carthage was larger than Rome and had a stronger Navy than Rome, but Rome grew from a small city to become the largest and greatest empire of ancient and medieval times.

7. *Respondeat superior* is a legal principle that says let the principal be held responsible. An employer or principal is responsible for the acts of his employee or agents in the course of their services for the employer.

8. The Great Mongol Empire declined because of feuds within the descendants of Genghis Khan. In 1260, the Mongol Empire broke into four smaller empires: the Yuan Dynasty in China, the Golden Horde in Russia and the Pontic Steppes, the Ilkanate in Persia and Middle East, and the Chaghatai in Central Asia. These four Mongol Empires forged ahead in expansion up to the 14th century. However, the Chaghatai Dynasty (Empire) reigned up to the modern times and eclipsed in 1658.

9. Wycliffites were followers of John Wycliffe, an English scholastic philosopher, theologian, lay preacher, translator, reformer and University teacher at Oxford in England. His followers were also known as *Lollards*—a rebellious movement. John Wycliffe was an influential dissident in the Roman Catholic Church.

10. The Hussites were a Christian movement following the teaching of Czech reformer Jan Hus (1369–1415). He was a well-known representative of the Bohemian Reformation, and one of the forerunners of the Protestant Reformation. He was tried for heresy and put to death at the stake on July 6, 1415.

11. Bohemia is a historical country in Central Europe. It is located in the contemporary Czech Republic, with its capital in Prague.

12. Southern European countries are the following: Turkey, Albania, Andorra, Croatia, Bosnia and Herzegovina, Gibralta, Greece, Italy, Macedonia, Malta, Monaco, Montenegro, Portugal, Serbia, Spain, Slovenia, the Holy See, and San Marino.

13. "Tasmanian Aboriginal People and History." *Aboriginal Art Online*. Accessed on December 29, 2014.

14. "Tasmania Embroiled in Dispute over White Tribe of Aborigines." *The Daily Telegraph* July 14, 2005. Accessed December 29, 2014.

15. The first Europeans arrived in Argentina in 1502.

16. See "Life in Cambodia under the Khmer Rouge Regimes" (http://www.cambodiatribunal. org/history/cambodia_hitstory/khmer_rouge_history/). Accessed December 31, 2014.

17. Japan is the only member of the *Axis powers* not in Europe. The *Axis powers* were fighting against the "*Allies*," which are composed of the United States, Britain, France, USSR, Australia, New Zealand, Brazil, Belgium, China, Canada, Greece, Norway,

Denmark, the Netherlands, Yugoslavia, South Africa, and Poland. But the United States, Great Britain, and USSR were the three pillars of the Allies.

18. See Ramerini, Marco (2014). Colonial Voyage Dutch and Courlanders on Tobago: A History of the First Settlements, 1628–1677 (http://www.colonialvoyage.com/eng/America/tobago/du). Accessed January 5, 2015.

19. See "General ValerianoWeyler, Library of Congress" (http://www.loc.gov/rr/hispanic/1898/weyler.htm). Accessed January 6, 2015.

20. See "ValerianoWeyler and Nicolau" (http://www.biolgrafiasyvidas.com/biografia/w/weyler.htm). Accessed January 6, 2015.

21. ECHR Jorgic v. Germany Judgment, July 12, 2001, Section 45 citing Bosnia and Herzegovina v. Serbia and Montenegro ("Case concerning the application of the Convention on the Prevention and Punishment of the Crime of Genocide") the International Court of Justice (ICJ) found under the heading of "intent and 'ethnic cleansing." Section 190. Accessed January 6, 2015.

22. See Milosevic trial, Trial Chamber's "Decision on Motion to Enter Judgment of Acquittal." (http://www.icty.org/x/cases/slobodan_milosevic/tdec/en/040616.pdf).

23. This cited statement came from one of *William Shakespeare's* plays (Twelfth Night or As You Like It, or Julius Caesar).

24. At that time, the States that made up Holy Roman Empire were Austria, Bohemia, Luxembourg, Milan, the Netherlands, and Switzerland.

25. See ICC Statute, Article 8 (cited in Vol. 11, Ch. 44, Section 3.)

26. See "Rome Statute of the ICC. 1998." (http://legal.un.org/icc/STATUTE/00_corr/cstatute.htm).

27. UN Treaty Organization. Accessed January 7, 2015.

28. See "Rome Statute, Part II, Article 8" (http://legal.un.org/icc/statute/romefra.htm) legal un.org. Accessed January 7, 2015.

29. See United Nations General Assembly Resolution 3314 (XXIX), (http://www.umn.edu/humanrts/instree/GAres3314.htm). Accessed January 8, 2015.

30. Ibid.

31. See "Resolution RC/Res. 6!" (http://www2.icc-cpi.int/iccdocs/asp_docs/Resolution/RC-Res6-ENG-pdf). Accessed January 8, 2015.

32. See "Africa Files, Matabeleland Report: A Lot to Hide (http://www.africafiles.org/article.asp?ID=3843). Accessed January 9, 2015.

33. See BBC Staff, "ICC Finds Congo Warlord Thomas Lubanga Guilty (http://www.bbc.co.uk/news/world-africa-17364988).

34. BBC News. Accessed January 9, 2015.

35. See "Cyrus the Great," (http://en.wikipedia.org/wiki/Cyrus_the_Great). Accessed January 9, 2015.

36. See "Cyrus Cylinder, world's oldest human rights charter, returns to Iran on loan" (http://www.theguardian.com/world/2010/sep/10/cyrus-cylinder-returns-iran). The Guardian. Associated Press, September 10, 2010. Accessed January 9, 2015. Also see "Oldest Known Charter of Human Rights Comes to San Francisco" (http://www.kged .org/arts/visualarts/article.jsp?essid=124632). Accessed January 9, 2015.

37. See United Nations Human Rights, Office of the High Commissioner for Human Rights: "What are human rights?" (http://www.ohchr.org/EN/issues/pages/WI). Accessed January 9, 2015.

38. Ibid.

39. Ibid.

40. See United Nations, document A/64/Add. 1. January 31, 1947.

41. See "Convention on the Prevention and Punishment of the Crime of Genocide. Adopted by the U.N. General Assembly on December 9, 1948." (http://www .historyplace.com/worldhistory).

42. Ibid.

Crimes of Dictatorships and Camouflaged Democracies

Introduction

State crimes can easily be exposed by studying states that had been under a dictator and those that are currently under a dictator. The crimes of dictatorships are not hidden from the masses. The dictator carries his despotic actions with impunity. In effect, every adult in the country can see that the normal operations of various organs of the government are not going the way they should. The masses can easily see that normal style of police operations are no more friendly but hostile. The masses may see an emergence of a new security agency to suppress any negative reaction to tyrannical changes.

Dictatorship is a cancer that eats up a society. This is because the sources or means of national development are usually antagonized for the dictatorship to be absolute. The sources antagonized are the intellectuals of the state, the educational institutions, and mass media. The only medium of communication allowed is that owned and controlled by the government. Journalists are shut up by prohibiting freedom of the press.

In a dictatorship, state crime is inevitable. This is because the process of the emergence of a dictatorship is a crime against the people, and may be a violation of the state constitution *ab initio*, which, in itself, is a crime. Some dictatorships emerged fraudulently. That is, what the state leader promised to do that led to his being elected or appointed to lead is not what he decided to do after taking the office. He turned the country into his own property and asset.

This chapter presents the definition of dictatorship, history of dictatorship, types of dictatorship, the methods of turning a country into a dictator state, dictator states since the 20th century by continents or continental regions, the characteristics of dictatorships, the crimes of 15 of the most depraved-hearted dictators, and the negative consequences of dictatorial regimes.

Definition

When people in a country are not free to criticize the policies of their executive head of state and his government, the laws and regulations in the country are only what the head of state feels should be the law of the land, political parties are banned, the law enforcement agencies are under exclusive control of the head of state, the head of state exclusively appoints ministers or secretaries of different departments of the government, the treasury of the country is controlled by the head of state, and freedom of the press is abolished, then you have a dictator state. In addition, the head of state is recognized in the country and beyond as a dictator.

Dictatorship is a despotic type of governance in which the head of state usurps all powers with impunity without the consent of the people, and in spite of all opposition. To highlight the state crimes of dictatorships, here are four types of dictatorships: Inherited traditional dictatorship, camouflaged democratic dictatorship, military dictatorship, and ideological dictatorship.

Inherited Traditional Dictatorship

This is the oldest dictatorship. In ancient and early medieval times, it was seen as normal and accepted by most members of society. The people of that period were meant to believe in the doctrine, "the Divine Right of Kings," and "the King can do no wrong." That means, Kings derived their authority from God and not from man. The assumption was that the governed had no power over the king or monarchy. The monarch, as a head of state, was seen as a messenger of God on earth. In effect, for a person or group at the time to rebel against the monarchy was a serious political crime. Such authority was seen in the absolutism of King Louis XIV of France (1638–1715) and in the arrogance of power of the Stuart Kings of England and King James VI and I (1603–1625).[1] The doctrine of "Divine Right of Kings" was the basis for "absolute monarchies" (unlimited powers). As of 2015, only six countries in the world have absolute monarchy (Brunei, Qatar, Oman, Vatican City State, Saudi Arabia, and Swaziland). With the exception of Vatican City State and Swaziland (Africa), others are Islamic states. With the exception of Vatican City, the last absolute monarch in Europe was Emperor Kaiser Wilhelm II of Germany who abdicated in November 1918 as a result of the German defeat in World War I. Emperor (Kaiser) Wilhelm II was crowned in 1888, dismissed Chancellor Otto von Bismarck, and, in his absolutistic, bombastic, and impetuous dictatorship, he disregarded the opinion of his ministers and ignominiously ended in exile in the Netherlands (Rohl, 1994; Palmer, 1978).

Some traditional dictators like King Abdullah bin Abdulaziz of Saudi Arabia and the Sultan of Brunei, Hassanal Bolkiah, use members of their families as ministers of different government departments. Laws and regulations are those that are in the interest of the monarch and his extended family of ministers to define as being the law of the land. Traditional monarchial dictatorships are acceptable to the people governed, because it is a system that has been in place from time immemorial, and it becomes part of the culture of the people. In addition, inherited traditional dictatorship is more acceptable to the masses when the state and national religion are one, and the monarch is the head of the religious order.

Camouflaged Democracies

Camouflaged democracy is a fraudulent use of democratic principles to get the people's consent to rule, and, after being elected as the head of state, the individual turns the country into a dictatorship regime. This fraudulent system of democracy can be concocted by an ethnic clique like in Ethiopia and Nigeria, or by an ex-military clique, like in Nigeria and some Central and South American countries.

When a single individual turns his country into a camouflaged democracy, he forms a clique of his own, designed by appointing individuals to cabinet positions in his first term in office. He presents to them his surreptitious dictatorial agenda in tete-a-tete meetings. From the dyadic relationship, the head of state discovers whether the particular cabinet minister will support his autocratic agenda. By the end of his first year in office, he identifies those in the cabinet who are totally with him. In the first or second cabinet meeting of his second year in office, he announces his intention to reshuffle the cabinet. He has no obligation to tell any member or the populace why he wants to reshuffle the cabinet. He simply drops some department ministers and replaces them with those he had explored and found that they would follow his camouflaged democracy principles.

When camouflaged democracy is designed by a clique, the execution is easier than when it is by the head of state alone. This is because most members of the clique or junta will be cabinet ministers and others occupy key positions in the government, such as being the director general of police, the director of prisons, the governor of the Central Bank, and so forth.

The establishment of a camouflaged democracy can be very deadly and extremely destructive of careers of some professionals in the country. In the agenda of establishing a camouflaged democracy, there must be a trusted group of clandestine, educated civil servants who are agents of the head of state to continuously watch and find out the opinion of some professionals in the government about the head of state and his policies. These underground agents report back to the head of state or his chief of state about the opinion of the professionals and other important office holders. The professionals whose views about the head of state are negative are quickly removed from office. The removal from office may be preceded by a false accusation of a wrongful act, or the professional may be removed from office without any explanation.

The members of the opposing party are lured into joining the ruling party of the head of state. Those who vehemently oppose the head of state and his policies are either assassinated, or accused of a crime they didn't commit, indicted, and convicted by a judge appointed by the head of state, and incarcerated for many years. In some cases, the head of state made sure that the incarcerated doesn't come out of the prison alive (Examples are President Abacha and President Idi Amin regimes in Nigeria and Uganda, respectively). In addition, some strong opposition members are forced into self-exile. Before the end of the head of state's first term, observers may either see only one weak opposition party that has no chance of defeating the incumbent head of state in the election or the head of state stands unopposed in the next election. (Examples are President Mobutu of Zaire and President Rafael Trujilo of the Dominican Republic). The best examples of this system of camouflaged democracy dictatorship currently in operation are in Ethiopia, Zimbabwe, Sudan, Togo, Yemen, Eritrea, and others can be found in Central and South America.

In the second term of the head of state of a camouflaged democratic dictatorship, he sees his new cabinet as being what he wanted. The real dictatorship agenda starts to come into place. Intellectuals in the country are marginalized. Funding for universities and schools are withdrawn. Many key figures in the government have either been fired or forced to retire. Business is going down, because the purchasing power of the public is low owing to lay-offs in the government service, which trickled down to private businesses. This situation is common in Third World countries, where the government is usually the highest employer of labor. The masses are confused. University students go on strike and other members of the country join them in the demonstration. The dictatorial regime responds with police and army crackdown, torture, killings, and imprisonment of the key leaders in the demonstration. The whole country is intimidated and the students and the masses give up demonstrating because they have seen that peaceful demonstration has become deadly, and the government is not ready to do anything better for the masses.

The Central Bank of the country, at this stage, is under the absolute control of the head of state. The person he appoints to be the governor or director of the Central Bank (Treasury) reports to him. The head of state can change him any time he wants. On the third term, the head of state is reelected in a fraudulent election that has him as the only viable candidate. In some cases, the head of state and his party may allow an impotent opposition party to contest in the election, but the head of state and his political party have already prepared a civil service electoral commission that is working for them. In effect, it does not matter how large the electorate who cast their vote for the opposing party candidate is, the civil service electoral commission will rig the election for the head of state and his party. This is one of the basic principles of camouflaged democracies.

The current heads of state of Zimbabwe, Yemen, Sudan, Eritrea, and Ethiopia have been in office, at least, since the 1990s. Are they the only best national leaders in their countries? In Egypt, since the former President Anwar Sadat was assassinated on October 6, 1981, Hosni

Mubarak has been the president of that country until 2011 (30 years), when he was forced to resign after 18 days of mass demonstration in that year's Egyptian revolution. But Egypt was having presidential elections every four years, and he was always reelected (Kirkpatrick, 2011; Kirpatrick, Shadid, & Cowell, 2011). Mubarak was the president of Egypt for 29 years and 120 days, because Egypt of his time was a camouflage democracy and he was a dictator of that regime.[2]

In a camouflaged democratic dictatorship, the constitution is either suspended or allowed to be dormant. In other words, nobody refers to it. And whoever sues the government for contravening the constitution goes nowhere with it, because the country's judiciary is sucked into the camouflaged democratic dictatorship conspiracy.

Military Dictatorship

This type of dictatorship arises when a clique of army officers conspires to overthrow an elected civilian government in a coup d'etat. Most of the time, the coup d'etat is bloody in which the incumbent head of state and some cabinet ministers are murdered in cold blood, as in the January 15, 1966, coup d'etat of five majors in Nigeria. The January 13, 1972, coup in Ghana led by General Ignatius Acheampong; the military coup in Burma on March 2, 1962, led by General Ne Win; Colonel Muammar Gaddafi's coup d'etat in 1969 that took over the government of Libya; the March 31, 1964, coup d'etat in Brazil that overthrew the government of Joao Goulart; and the May 22, 2014, General Prayuth Chan-ocha's coup d'etat against the caretaker government of Thailand, are other examples.

Some military coups d'etat are bloodless. The armed forces simply force out the head of state such as the 1983 coup led by General Muhammadu Buhari that overthrew the Nigerian federal government of President Shehu Shagari, and the 1985 Nigerian military coup that overthrew the government of General Buhari.

Whenever the military overthrows a civilian or military government, it introduces a military dictatorship. It suspends the constitution, and rules by martial law. There is no senate or House of Representatives. The legislature is replaced with a Supreme Military Council, a Provisional Ruling Council, National Military Council, Provisional Administrative Council, Military Council for National Defense, National Administrative Reform Council, Revolutionary Council, Supreme Revolutionary Council, or a People's Redemption Council. The clique of army officers, who conspired to overthrow the civilian government, may also conspire to overthrow their own military government, so that the key army officers in the clique will have the opportunity to be a head of state of the country. As a result, the country witnesses a series of military regimes (Nigeria, 1966–2000).

Africa has 49 independent countries, but 47 of them have had dictatorships, and 29 of them were military dictatorships. Out of the 29 military dictatorships from 1953[3]–2014,[4] 22 have had a series of military dictatorships, each ranging from two to six regimes. The countries with the largest number of series of military dictatorships, with their numbers in parenthesis, are Nigeria (6), Republic of Benin (4), Ghana (4), Central Africa Republic (4), Mauritania (4), and Sudan (4).

The Americas constitute 62 independent countries including the island territories of the United States, the United Kingdom, and France; while 23 of them have had dictatorial regimes, 21 have experienced military dictatorship regimes, and 14 have experienced multiple military dictatorship regimes each ranging from 2 to 11 times. The countries with the highest frequency of dictatorial regimes are Bolivia (11), Peru (9), Venezuela (7), Argentina (5), and Ecuador and Guatemala (4 each). The Americas dictatorship regimes began in 1839[5]–1994.[6] The Asia-Pacific has 44 countries; out of these, 29 have had dictatorship governments, and 14 of them were military dictatorship regimes. The countries of Iraq and Thailand had the longest series of six regimes, followed by South Korea with four regimes.

Europe is made up of 49 independent countries. Starting with Oliver Cromwell's overthrow of the Rump Parliament in the Commonwealth of England in 1649 to the Alexander Lukashenko regime in Belarus in 1994, European countries have had 39 dictatorship regimes, and 12 of these have had multiple dictatorial governments and were military regimes ranging from two to three times. Turkey is the only European country with three multiple military regimes.

State crimes of military regimes include the following: suspension of the constitution of the country, rule by marital law, denial of due process of law, torture of freedom fighters or student demonstrators, detention of the regime's critics, abolition of freedom of the press, rule by decree, killing of leaders of "civilian government advocates," imprisonment of deposed politicians without trial, engaging in business-organized crime, pilferaging the national treasury, looting of the national treasury especially when they want to leave office, forcible rape of women with impunity, embezzlement, general indulgence in crimes against humanity, human rights violations, and so forth.

Before delineating the general characteristics of all dictatorships, here is the fourth type of dictatorship.

Ideological Dictatorship

Ideological dictatorship is one that emanates from the political and economic ideas and convictions of an individual or a clique. The state had to be built according to the individual's or clique's ideas of national organization. The individual or leader of the clique is the mastermind of the new national direction. It is either his own way or no other. He has his clique behind him. He controls every aspect of the country's political, economic, social, cultural, educational, and religious aspects of society. He builds a totalitarian regime. Most of the time, the old order was a democratic capitalist system. He had to dismantle the old order to create a socialist or a communist order in which he has promised the masses a better society.

On his way to establishing a totalitarian regime, all political parties of the old order are abolished. Most of the key dissidents are not allowed to leave on self-exile. They are either assassinated or imprisoned indefinitely without trial. The dictator works with a clique of like minds in his cabinet. Only intellectuals who support the totalitarian regime are allowed to remain in the country, while others may find a way to leave the country or be assassinated or jailed and starved to death. This ideological dictatorship leads to acts of genocide. Examples of this ideological dictatorship are the regimes of Chairman Mao (Mao Zedong) of China (1949–1976), Joseph Stalin of the Soviet Union (1922–1953), Adolf Hitler in Nazi Germany (1933–1945), Benito Mussolini of Italy (1922–1943), Pol Pot of Cambodian communist Khmer Rouge (1963–1997), and so forth. Every one of the above totalitarian, ideological dictatorships committed genocide before the eclipse of their regimes (see Chapter 5).

Ideological dictatorships had always failed in their economic plans. Their pursuit of egalitarianism has proved to be a myth. In the face of absence of free enterprise, the masses are left with limited resources, while the regime oligarchy lives in clandestine opulence. The ideology only serves the interest of the dictator and his clique. But they have the propaganda to make some of the members of the masses believe that their interests are primary in the pursuit of the mythical egalitarianism. Many citizens of China, Soviet Union, Cambodia, Nazi Germany, and so forth committed suicide after they lost their properties to totalitarian ideas, and saw later that the ideology bounced like a bad check, and they did not know which way to go and where to start all over again.[7] Unmistakably, ideological dictatorship and its concomitant totalitarianism are political and economic frauds of the leadership.

Characteristics of all Dictatorships

Taking the four types of dictatorship developed here (inherited dictatorship, camouflaged democratic dictatorship, military dictatorship, and ideological dictatorship) into account, all dictatorships have the following characteristics.

Single Individual Power Base

There is a single dictator. He has a personality cult. He is an authoritarian. As an authoritarian, he wants every person in the country to obey his orders. He has control of all aspects of government. He appoints persons of his choice to be in charge of various government ministries, statutory corporations, and other government institutions. He can reshuffle his cabinet or junta any time he wants. He develops a cult of personality (worshipful image), a reminiscent of what a German classical sociologist Max Weber called "Charismatic authority" (Weber, 1947). He is feared and respected by every member of his cabinet or junta. He does not, in the main, care about the consequences of his ruthless actions. He is very arrogant. He surrounds himself with paramilitary personal security guards who are independent of his national security guards.

The examples of this type of dictator are Adolf Hitler, Joseph Stalin, Mao Zedong, Mobutu Sese Seko, Juan Peron, Saddam Hussein, Augusto Pinochet, Rafael Trujilo, Muammar Gaddafi, and so forth (Bullock, 1999; Maser, 1973; Kotkin, 2014; Terrill, 1980).

This single dictator is the head of a clique or junta which he formed and controlled. Any piece of advice to him from anybody that is contrary to his mindset is a wild goose chase. To him, nobody in the country is indispensable. He gets his guards to kill whoever needs to be killed for him to keep his regime moving forward.

Formal Security Guards

These guards monitor all aspects of the country's establishments, including government departments. This is a paramilitary force. Within this paramilitary force is a secret service unit monitoring citizens, foreign diplomats, foreign businesses, and immigrants. This secret service unit is used for assassination of government enemies.

Informal Secret Service

This is a counterintelligence secret service unit of the dictator. The role of the informal secret service is to secretly monitor the activities of leaders of all law enforcement agencies and their men, and other government institutional leaders, and report to the head of state (the dictator). This informal unit is set up by the head of state, and its members are also employed in various units of the law enforcement agencies, government departments, and statutory corporations. The dictator, head of state, pays them allowances from the government fund, because he controls the national treasury. The allowance is in addition to their regular salaries from the government department where they work.

Absence of Multiparty System or No Political Party

Most dictatorships abolished multiparty system of government or had no political party at all. Some dictatorships are fascist governments, they allow only one party in power, and prohibit any form of opposition party. You can find this type of government without opposition party in Soviet Union, Nazi Germany, Chairman Mao's China, Kwame Nkruma's Ghana, Mabutu Sese Seko's Zaire, and so forth. Other countries that have been ruled by a single political party and the year of occurrence include the following: North Korea's "Workers Party of Korea" (1948–present), "Communist Party of Vietnam" (1925–present), "Union of National Progress" of Burundi (1966–1992), "Worker's Party of Ethiopia" (1984–1991), "Kenya Africa National Union" (1982–1991), "National Union" of United Arab Republic (1958–1961), "Burma Socialist Programme Party" (Myanmar, 1964–1988), "Romanian Communist Party" (1947–1989), "League of Communist of Yugoslavia/Socialist Alliance of Working People of

Yugoslavia" (1945–1990), "Fatherland's Front" of Austria (1934–1938), "Spanish Patriotic Union" of Spain (1924–1930), "Imperial Rule Assistance Association" of Japan (1940–1945), "Italian Social Republic/Republican Fascist Party" (1943–1945), and so forth.

Any attempt by a body or a group to set up an opposition party is met with utmost violence, arrest, detention, torture, clandestine poisoning, or cold-blooded assassination. And some dissidents are forced to self-exile to save their lives.

In a military government, all political parties are banned. There is no political party in power. The military forms a council to rule by decree. They may maintain the various government departments. They fill the former cabinet structure with senior army, air force, or navy officers. In some cases, they may employ very few civilians of the former civilian administration to run some government departments, but this rarely happens. The author lived through six military regimes that span a period of 33 years. During that time, no military regime employed any civilian, politician or not, to be a minister of any government ministry. They decided to manage the departments by themselves, whether they knew what they were doing or not.

Absence of Representative Legislature

In a civilian dictatorship, the head of state develops a cabinet of his choice based on persons he trusts to support his totalitarian or authoritarian goals. If he came to power through a clique, the clique or junta will form the cabinet, and he is the chairman of the cabinet.

In a military dictatorship, whoever was the leader or mastermind of the coup d'etat that toppled the previous administration becomes the head of state. He then develops the membership of the Military Council to rule the country. He may call it the "Supreme Military Council" or the "Military Ruling Council," or the "Military Revolutionary Council," or the "National Military Redemption Council." Whichever name chosen, that council becomes a law-making organ for the whole country.

The dictatorial regime's cabinet or military council makes laws to protect the regime. The laws, in the main, have no regard for the violation of the fundamental human rights of the citizens and immigrants.

Suspension of the Constitution

One of the first things a civilian dictator does immediately after he takes office is to suspend the constitution of the country. He does this to allow himself to dismantle statutory institutions of the country and establish his own, or to change the composition of those institutions with impunity. He may suspend the constitution under the camouflage that he wants the constitution to be reviewed and a new one put in place. This review may not be completed in two to three years. And a new constitution may not emerge for many years.

The first thing military regimes do in their first national broadcast after seizing power is to tell the masses of citizens that the national constitution stands suspended. This helps them rule by decree. This move puts the masses on notice, that the rule of law is gone.

Absence of Independent Judiciary

When the civilian or military dictator suspends the constitution of the country, it manifestly nullifies the role of the highest court of the land. The civilian dictator may allow the highest court of the country to remain in operation, but he lays off all the judges and appoints those who will carry out his wishes. In fact, the civilian dictator appoints the judges of all the courts in the country. And the judges must rule cases affecting the government according to the interest of the head of state and his political party. That was the case in Adolf Hitler's Nazi Germany, Saddam Hussein's Iraq, Mobutu Sese Seko's Zaire, Mao Zedong's China, and so forth.

In military regimes, most of them abolished the Supreme Court or the highest court of the land, and set up various tribunals for various offenses. The members of the tribunals are their own hand-picked persons. Some of the tribunal members may not have any legal training. This was the case in some military regimes. Whenever a Nigerian military regime allowed the Nigerian Supreme Court to remain in operation, judges from different states of Nigeria were appointed to decide cases according to the military junta's interests. That was the origin of the corrupt judiciary in Nigeria. Some Nigerian lawyers have sued the Nigerian Federal Military Government for damages against some citizens, but the cases were dismissed without offering cogent and meaningful reasons. For instance, on February 18, 1977, during General Obasanjo's military government, a two-story building, a bungalow and appurtenances, equipment including motor vehicles and buses belonging to Chief Mrs. Funmilayo Ransome-Kuti and others were willfully and maliciously set ablaze by agents of the Nigerian Military Government. The plaintiffs sued with a team of high-level lawyers led by Barrister Tunji Braithwaite. The Lagos High Court, after hearing the case, dismissed it. The plaintiffs appealed to the Supreme Court and the Supreme Court also dismissed the case (Braithwaite, 2011). That is exactly what happens in all countries where a dictator is in control of the judiciary. But if a dictatorship government takes a person to court, that defendant is guilty or liable *ab initio*, whether the issue is a criminal or civil matter, respectively.

Absence of Freedom of the Press

Modern democracy demands freedom of speech as an inalienable right of every member of society, with the exception of libelous and slanderous statements and attacks. In addition, in 1948, the United Nations Universal Declaration of Human Rights provided that "Everyone has the right to freedom of opinion and expression; this right includes freedom to hold opinions without interference, and impart information and ideas through any media regardless of frontiers" (Glendon, 2002; Morsink, 1999; Schabas, 1998).

Dictatorships of all types, despite the above provisions of the United Nations for which they are signatories, either totally ban freedom of the press or restrict them to the lowest level. The dictatorships will not allow any newspaper to be established without government approval. Also, when a newspaper is allowed to exist, nothing is allowed to be written about the government and all of its organs without prior approval of the government. Any newspaper that violates that unwritten or written order is banned forthwith. For instance, in September 2013, two Tanzanian newspapers—Mwananchi and Mtanzania—were ordered to suspend publications, because both papers were critical of Tanzanian Government policies. In some cases, when the dictatorship bans a newspaper, it may arrest the editor and his correspondents and incarcerate them without trial. During General Ibrahim Babanquida's military government of Nigeria (1985–1992), a famous journalist, Dele Giwa, was rightfully critical of the military government, and was about to publish a true, but damaging story, with irrefutable data from one Gloria Okon, a Nigerian military government's ally and team player, who had flown to London, United Kingdom, as a means to avoid press interrogation about a criminal issue. Dele Giwa flew to London to get the data from her, which he needed for the story. The next day, after he flew back to Nigeria to publish the story, a letter bomb was mailed to him, which killed him. Since then, the Nigerian journalists have been journalistically shackled, even up to this current camouflaged democratic civilian regime.

In 1993–1998, during General Abacha's military regime in Nigeria, three newspapers were banned, so that they would not continue to publish the fate of imprisoned politicians and senior army officers, when General Obasanjo was among those in prison. Every dictatorship all over the world suspends newspapers, temporarily detains journalists, permanently imprisons some journalists without trial, assassinates some journalists, and bans some or all newspapers. Such media control is recorded in Zimbabwe during Robert Mugabe's rule, the dictatorships of Libya and Nigeria, Chairman Mao's China, Nazi Germany, Soviet Russia, Pinochet's Chile, Sudan's Islamic Republic, Islamic States of Middle East, and so forth.

In fact, between 1993 and 2014, no country in the world recorded as many deaths of journalists on the job as did Russia. Under President Boris Yeltsin (1991–1999), Russia had 170 journalists killed on the job.[8] The highest was under President Putin (2000–2008 and 2012–2014), when Russia had 173 journalists assassinated, and from 1993 to 2014, a total of 243 journalists perished on their jobs.[9]

Colonial dictatorships never allowed indigenous journalists to operate in their own country. When Dr. Nnamdi Azikwe tried it in 1946, he was sent to exile in Ghana by the colonial administration. In all post-colonial governments, like the colonial regimes before them, all media were owned by the government, and they are only allowed to publish whatever the government wants them to publish. Indeed, censorship of the media is the modus operandi of all dictatorships. In addition, in most post-colonial dictatorship governments, radio and television networks are exclusive business of the government. Individuals and groups are not allowed or licensed to own radio and television networks, with the exception of Nigeria and a few other countries that started in the 1990s to allow private ownership of radio and television networks. Fundamental human rights require that individuals and groups in a society should be free to express their views about themselves and about their governments. Any restriction of freedom of speech is a state deviance which is tantamount to a violation of law.

Control of National Police Force

Most dictatorships like to have a national police force. Any suggestion of having a decentralized police system is vigorously resisted. The dictator head of state appoints the Director General of the Police, Inspector General of Police, or Chief of Police Services, whatever name they choose to call him. Why is it so? It is because the head of state can order the Chief of the National Police to arrest anybody in the country, and it is done within a question of hours. He could order the chief to let the police officers shoot and kill the citizen, if he refuses to be arrested. Many Nigerians have been arrested or killed in this way from 1966 to 1999.

Furthermore, the national police in a dictatorship regime have wages that are kept very low, so that they continue to be obedient to the dictatorship for any small remuneration that may come later. In effect, in such a regime, the police do not care for the safety of the citizens. Instead, the police design ways to take bribes from individuals who need their services. And the dictatorial regime allows the police to be corrupt as a form of *quid pro quo* between the head of state and the police force. As a result, successful general and specific law enforcement becomes a wild goose chase. One may think that the police in a dictatorship regime would disobey the head of state, because their salaries are kept low. Not at all, this is because the dictatorship regime's police are not well educated to look for alternative jobs. As a result, they are afraid of being laid off. Their comfort zone to remain on the job of policing becomes wholesale corruption. This method of policing is common throughout post-colonial policing in Africa.

During the 33 years that Nigeria was under military dictatorship, it was common for a police officer to tell a middle class Nigerian, whom he stopped on a highway for an unnecessary road-worthiness check, that the officers have not been paid their monthly salaries for three or four months. And it was true. It was not just in Nigeria alone. It was like that in all military regimes in the African continent. The military government did not care to realize that failing to pay the police force was violation of fundamental human rights of the police. Unmistakably, a dictatorship government that routinely fails to pay the police their monthly salaries was encouraging the police to engage in deviant behaviors of all types including serious crimes.

Absence of Due Process of Law

The idea of due process developed from Clause 39 of the *Magna Carta* in 1215 by King John of England. It was designed to make peace between the King and a group of rebel barons, and proclaimed as follows:

> "No freeman shall be seized or imprisoned, or stripped of his rights or possessions, or outlawed or exiled, or deprived of his standing in any other way, nor will we proceed with force against him, or send others to do so, except by lawful judgment of his equals or by the law of the land" (McKechnie, 1905).

This historical principle means that the state should honor and have some regard for the legal rights that are owed to its members. Due process professes that the individual recognizes and honors the power of the law of the land, while he is protected by it. However, the contemporary English law does not use "due process." Instead, in England and all of its former colonial dependencies, due process is replaced with *natural justice* and *"the rule of law"* as spelled out by a British jurist and constitutional theorist, Albert Venn Dicey (Cosgrove, 1980; Ford, 1985).

While due process was not upheld in England, the United States incorporated it in its constitution. For instance, the Fifth and the Fourteenth Amendments to the United States Constitution contain a due process clause. In the United States, therefore, due process focuses on the administration of justice. Consequently, the due process clause operates as a safeguard from arbitrary denial of life, liberty, or property by the government beyond binding laws. Indeed, the Fourteenth Amendment guarantees that no person shall be deprived of life, liberty, or property without due process of law. These rights include protection against unreasonable searches and seizures (Fourteenth Amendment), protection against self-incrimination (Fifth Amendment), and the right to counsel (Sixth Amendment) (Adler, Mueller, & Laufer, 1991).

The issue of due process of law explained above was addressed by the United Nations under the "Universal Declaration of Human Rights" (UDHR) adopted by the United Nations General Assembly on December 10, 1948, at the Palais de Chaillot, Paris (France). The declaration has 30 articles, which were expounded in subsequent international treaties, regional human rights instruments, national constitutions, and so forth.

The *International Bill of Human Rights* consists of the Universal Declaration of Human Rights, the *International Covenant of Economic, Social, and Cultural Rights*, and the *International Covenant on Civil and Political Rights* and its two Optional Protocols. In 1966, the General Assembly adopted the two detailed Covenants, which complete the International Bill of Human Rights. In 1976, after the Covenants had been ratified by a sufficient number of individual nations, the Bill took on the force of *international law* (Williams, 1981; Morsink, 1999).

All dictatorships are among the 195 member countries of the United Nations that ratified the Universal Declaration of Human Rights bill that has a force of international law, yet they treat their citizens without regard to due process of law covered in the UDHR. That, in itself, is a state violation of law.

Absence of the Rule of Law

Whenever a dictator head of state, his cabinet members, and their law enforcement officers engage in wholesale corruption and all sorts of malfeasance, there is no rule of law. Where there is "rule of law," the behaviors of people who live in the society are controlled by their laws, and their governments respect human rights of the people. Where there is total chaos, anarchy, and social disorganization, there is no rule of law. In such a dictatorial regime, fundamental human rights of the citizens are thrown out the window. People run at cross purposes with one another. Examples of such regimes are post-Soviet Russia, Nigeria, Zimbabwe, Idi Amin's Uganda, some Newly Independent States (NIS) of the former Soviet Union, and so forth.

In 2011, the *World Justice Project's Rule of Law Index* founder, William Neukom, stated[9]: "The rule of law is the cornerstone to improving public health, safe guarding participation, ensuring security, and fighting poverty;" and he added, "without the rule of law, medicines do not reach health facilities due to corruption, women in rural areas remain unaware of their rights, people are killed in criminal violence, and economic growth is stifled." (Stone, 2011). Neukom's assertions about the significance of the rule of law in society show why Third World countries and countries with high frequency of dictatorship regimes have a lower life span than do developed economies.

The World Justice Project Rule of Law Index (2014) identified four general principles of the rule of law. These are (paraphrased):

1. The government and everybody in the country are all under the law. Nobody is beyond incrimination.

2. The laws are clearly defined, made known to the people, stable, and just; applied without discrimination, and protect fundamental rights, life and property of the members of society.

3. The legislative process and administration of justice, must be accessible, fair, and efficient.

4. The administration of justice must be fast and swiftly executed by an adequate number of unbiased, independent individuals who bear the characteristics of the community and have adequate resources to deliver justice.

The above general principles of the rule of law demonstrate why some countries like Nigeria, Russia, Cameroon, North Korea, Saddam Hussein's Iraq, Zimbabwe, Mobutu Sese Seko's Zaire, and so forth, are defined as failed states.

The current regimes of Russia, Nigeria, Zimbabwe, and North Korea are still failed states. In all of those governments, corruption is very high; organized crime is part of the government (predatory state); criminal investigation is a complete farce; administration of justice is a wild goose chase; correctional system is criminogenic; criminal justice is partial; due process of law is marooned; the right to life and security of the individuals is not guaranteed; the health care and sanitary conditions are poor; the checks and balances in the government are weak or absent; there is total absence of accountability in the government; the government and its agencies have limitless power; and so forth.

In the ranking of 99 countries of the world by the World Justice Project Rule of Law Index[10] according to the countries' adherence to the rule of law, the countries that are now dictatorships and those that had been dictatorships rank very low. Take, for instance, among the 99 countries, Zimbabwe ranks 98 and Venezuela 99. Other dictatorial regimes that ranked very low are Nicaragua (96), Cambodia (94), China (92), Ethiopia (91), Iran (90), Russia (89), and Bolivia and Cameroon (88 and 87, respectively).

The five top-ranked countries in adherence to the principles of rule of law in each continent or region of the world, according to World Justice Project 2014, are as follows:

Western Europe: Denmark (1), Norway (2), Sweden (3), Finland (45), and Austria (6);

Russia & NIS: Estonia (12), Czech Republic (23), Slovenia (30), Croatia (40), and Romania (43);

The Americas: Canada (13), Chile (17), Uruguay (18), United States (20), and Colombia (47);

Africa: Botswana (25), Ghana (27), Senegal (33), South Africa (37), and Tunisia (41);

Asia and Asia Pacific: New Zealand (4), Australia (8), Japan (15), South Korea (16), and Singapore (21);

Western Asia (Middle East): United Arab Emirates (42), Lebanon (44), and Iran (90).

The Middle East does not have up to five countries ranked among the 99 countries. According to Irene Khan (2013), "Justice is scarce in Arab countries where the rule of law is absent." Undeniably, dictatorship states, whether military or civilian, are "pathological forms," as Emile Durkheim (1964) would qualify them. They have caused deaths of many of their citizens, and have reduced the life span of their people to the lowest 40s or 30s.

Whenever a dictatorship state suspends the constitution of the country, as often happens, the rule of law is swept into oblivion, and the masses are left in a hopeless state.

It is worthy to note the intellectual and historical significance of the rule of law. The idea of the rule of law is implicitly embedded in Thomas Hobbes' (1588–1679) classical theory of social contract in answering the question, Why is there society or a state? Why didn't humans retain their natural liberty and live and maintain their natural liberty like other animals? Hobbes provided the answer. According to Hobbes (1651), to avoid "a war of all against all," individuals relinquished their natural liberty to the state for the state in return to protect the lives and property of its members. Manifest in Hobbes' assertion of social contract theory is that law is society, and society is law. Also, the rule of law is made preeminent by Aristotle, when he postulated that, "At his best, man is the noblest of all animals; separated from law and justice he is the worst" (Aristotle & McKean, 2001).

Therefore, negation of the rule of law by any state is the worst of all state crimes.

Government by Violence

The emergence of a military or a civilian dictatorship in a country is often resisted by college student demonstrations. Very often nonstudent youths join the college students in a peaceful demonstration. But the military and paramilitary police respond to the peaceful demonstrations with tear gas and firearms. Soldiers and police fire at the crowd of agitators. In the encounter, many youths and college students have been killed and others badly injured. In the 1980s and 1990s in Nigeria, many Nigerian University students were killed by soldiers, some jailed without trial, and some others hospitalized. After many years of protests to let the Federal Military governments fund educational institutions to provide high-quality education were of no avail, coupled with the fact that many students lost their lives, the Nigerian students gave up protesting from 1995 to the present.

In Chile, during the dictatorship of General Augusto Pinochet, many students and members of the opposition party were killed while engaged in peaceful demonstrations, and some opposition leaders were assassinated. In 2014, between February and May, 40 persons were killed in the streets of Venezula in protests against Nicolas Maduro's government (Vyas, 2015).

"Arab Spring"—a revolutionary wave of demonstrations and protests against dictatorships in Tunisia, Egypt, Libya, Yemen, Bahrain, Syria, Algeria, Iraq, Jordan, Kuwait, Morocco, Sudan, and so forth from 2011 to 2014 has led to so many deaths. According to Jessica Retting (2011), the death toll in Arab Spring is estimated to be 3,500 in Syria, 30,000 in Libya, 250 in Yemen, 100 in Bahrain, 300 in Tunisia, and 900 in Egypt.[11] The 3,500 deaths in Syria are not related to the Syrian Civil War.[12]

All dictatorships, especially military regimes, have used violence in the form of murder, assassination, and genocide to consolidate their regimes. "From Stalin to Hitler, to most murderous regimes in the world," killed more than 100,000,000 human beings (Jones, 2014).

The most violent and murderous dictators of the 20th century, including the number of their victims are as follows: Joseph Stalin of Soviet Union (1929–1976) killed 40 million; Adolf Hitler of Nazi Germany (1933–1945) killed 30 million including the Holocaust; Mao Zedong of China (1949–1976) killed 60 million; King Leopold II of Belgium (1886–1908) killed over 8 million Congolese and enslaved millions of them; Hideki Tojo of Japan (1941–1945) killed 5 million in World War II; Ismail Enver Pasha of Ottoman Turkey (1915–1920) killed 2 million Armenians, Greeks, and Assyrians; Pol Pot of Cambodia—"Khmer Rouge" (1975–1979) killed 1.7 million political opponents; Kim Il Sung of North Korea (1948–1994) killed 1.6 million political opponents and civilians through starvation; Mengistu Haile Mariam of Ethiopia (1974–1978) killed 1.5 million Eritreans and political opponents; Yakubu Gowon of Nigeria (1967–1970) killed 1.6 million Biafran children and civilians by starvation and soldiers killed in an avoidable Civil War; Jean Kambanda of Rwanda "Hutu regime" (1994) killed 800,000 Tutsi (Rwanda genocide); Saddam Hussein of Iraq (1979–2003) killed 600,000 Shi-ites, Kurds, Kuwaitis, and political opponents; Josip Broz Tito of Yugoslavia (1945–1966) killed 500,000 communists; Idi Amin of Uganda (1971–1979) killed 500,000 political opponents; General Yahya Khan of Pakistan (1970–1971) killed 300,000 Bengalis in East Pakistan; Benito Mussolini of Italy (1922–1945) killed 250,000 Ethiopians, Libyans, Jews, and political opponents; General Mobutu Sese Seko of Zaire, which is now Congo (1965–1997) killed 230,000 political opponents; Charles Taylor of Liberia (1989–1996) killed 220,000 political and military opponents and civilians; Foday Sankoh of Sierra Leone (1991–2000) killed 210,000 political opponents; Ho Chi Minh of North Vietnam (1945–1969) killed 200,000 political opponents and South Vietnamese; Michel Micombero of Burundi (1966–1976) killed 150,000 Hutus; Hassan Al Turabi of Sudan (1989–1999) killed 100,000 political and religious opponents; Jean Bedel Bokassa of the Central African Republic (1966–1979) killed 90,000 political opponents; Efrain Rios Montt of Guatemala (1982–1983) killed 70,000 peasants and political opponents; Francois Jean Claude Duvalier of Haiti ("Papa Doc," 1957–1971; "Baby Doc," 1971–1986) killed 60,000 political opponents; Rafael Trujilo of the Dominican Republic (1930–1961) killed 50,000 political opponents; Hissene Habre of the Chad Republic (1982–1990) killed 40,000 political opponents; General Francisco Franco of Spain (1939–1975) killed 35,000 political opponents; Fidel Castro of Cuba (1959–2006) killed 30,000 political opponents; Hafez Bashar Alassad of Syria (Hafez 1970–2000 and Bashar 2000–present) killed 25,000–30,000 political and religious opponents; Ayatollah Ruhollah Khomeni of Iran (1979–1989) killed 20,000 political and religious opponents; Robert Mugabe of Zimbabwe (1982–present) killed 20,000 political and tribal opponents; General Jorge Videla of Argentina (1976–1983) killed 13,000 left wing political opponents; and General Augusto Pinochet of Chile (1973–1990) killed 3,000 political opponents (Jones, 2014).

All of the above monstrous state criminals represented pathological forms to society. Their crimes are still felt in many parts of the world.

Negation of Intellectuals and Professionals

In all military dictatorships, civilian professionals and intellectuals are avoided. Civilian dictators do the same, but only embrace those intellectuals and professionals who are willing to promote their totalitarian or authoritarian goals. The negation of intellectuals and professionals in dictatorship regimes is one of the main reasons for economic and financial decline being the correlate of most dictatorships. When professionals and intellectuals are antagonized and frustrated by dictatorship regimes, they leave their countries in self-exile to other countries, where their services are appreciated. That was what happened in Nazi Germany, Chairman Mao's China, Stalin's Soviet Russia, Idi Amin's Uganda, Fidel Castro's Cuba, Robert Mugabe's Zimbabwe, and so forth.

High Unemployment and Discrimination

Dictatorship regimes create a high degree of unemployment. They deal with being employed as a privilege. With the negation of professionals and intellectuals, many people are unemployed, leading to low productivity in the country. Dictators use unemployment as a mass control mechanism. It is more so in military dictatorships than in civilian regimes. Fourteen years after some Nigerians survived military dictatorship, the country has not yet recovered from the extremely high unemployment rate created by a series of military governments. For instance, from the 1980s to 1998, youth unemployment in Nigeria ranged from 24.1% to 26.7%. But a study by Dalhatu and Bagaji (2014) shows youth unemployment in Nigeria from 2006 to 2011 to be as follows: 12.3% (2006), 12.7% (2007), 14.9% (2008), 19.9% (2009), 21.1% (2010), and 23.9% (2011). One can see, as noted above, that youth unemployment in Nigeria is still very high compared to the years of military dictatorship, although lower than in the era of military regimes.

In civilian dictatorships, they give jobs and contracts to persons and companies that support or identify with only their political party. Those who are opposed to the government and single-party government have no chance of getting any jobs.

Head of State for Life Tendency

The head of state in a dictatorship regime wants to rule for life. This atrocious ambition leads the dictator to engage in murders, assassinations, and genocidal massacres to eliminate all persons and groups who pose as obstacles to their goal. Some of them remain in the position of dictatorship until disease, counterrevolution, death, or war ends their regime. Such determined "dictators for life" whose regimes have ended were Adolf Hitler, Joseph Stalin, Mao Zedong, Pol Pot, Kim Il Sung, Saddam Hussein, Mobutu Sese Seko, Idi Amin, Francois Jean Claude Duvalier Papa Doc and Baby Doc, Francisco Franco, Ayatolla Ruhollah Khomeini, Augusto Pinochet, and Muammar Gaddafi.

Dictators who are still on the job as heads of state or stopped by illness are Fidel Castro, Robert Mugabe, Hafez Bashar Alassad, and Kim Il Sung.

The desire to rule for life is the motivation for suspending and, subsequently, changing the constitution of the country.

Looting of State Treasury

The central bank of any country is the economic power house for the society. Unfortunately, one of the first government institutions that a dictator grabs and controls as his personal bank account is the national treasury or central bank of the country. They steal the people's money and hide them in foreign banks in Europe, America, Asia, and so forth. Money laundering is one of the modus operandi of dictatorship governments.

President Duvalier "Baby Doc," looted the treasury of Haiti, "boarded a U.S. Air Force cargo plane and flew to exile in 1986, with truckloads of Louis Vuitton luggage and millions of dollars in Swiss bank accounts," and settled in France until 2011 (Hanes, 2014).

Many Nigerian military dictators have built 10- to 16-story business suites in Lagos, Abuja, and other cities including millions of dollars worth of mansions as their residential homes. They had no business enterprises to make such enormous profits to build those sky-scrapers. Their military salaries could not build them an eight-bedroom two-story house. How then did they get the money to build mighty sky-scrapers and mansions in their villages of orientation? The answer is that during their series of coups d'etat and counter-coup d'etat and dictatorships they looted the Nigerian Central Bank, one regime after another. These series of military dictators made sure that no subsequent regime, military or civilian, will ever probe them. The method which they used to make sure that a civilian regime will never probe them was to retire from the Nigerian army and form a political party to control the Nigerian civilian government. And whoever wants to run to be a Nigerian president must be their puppet. These ex-military dictators used their ill-gotten money to control Nigerian civilian government and the presumed democratic political parties.

Despite the huge Nigerian oil revenue, the dictators and their cronies ignored providing the masses with a stable electric power supply, a fresh water supply system, motorable roads, decent sanitary conditions, and garbage disposal mechanisms. That is why Nigeria is described as a failed state and a camouflaged democracy.

Saddam Hussein of Iraq, Muammar Gaddafi of Libya, Mobutu Sese Seko of Zaire, and Idi Amin of Uganda were in control of their countries' treasuries at the time they were dictators. They lived in aggrandizement of themselves as among the richest men in their countries or in the world. Like Nigerian dictators, Mobutu had more money in foreign banks than the amount of money in circulation in Zaire during his lifetime.

Dictatorships very often change their national currency. Check how many times Third World dictatorships in Africa, South and Central America, and Asia have changed their national currencies since independence. You will find out that they have done so many times. For instance, from 1912 to 1959, Nigerian currency notes were issued by the West African Currency Board controlled by the British colonial administration. On July 1, 1959, the Central Bank of Nigeria issued the Nigerian currency notes and coins, a prelude to the Nigerian independence in 1960, and the West African Currency Board notes and coins were withdrawn. In 1960, Nigeria built what they called the Nigerian Printing and Minting Factory in Onitsha. Nigeria began to print its own currency still in "pound sterling." On July 1, 1962, the legal tender status was changed to indicate Nigeria's new status. In 1968, in almost the third year of the Nigerian military dictatorship, the currency was changed. The claim was that it was done to punish Biafra (Eastern Nigeria) that seceded from the Nigerian federation.

In 1971, almost three years later, the currency was changed again. As they would also give an excuse, this time they said it was to change to decimal currency, but the new currency did not go into circulation until 1973 in a new name as "Naira."

In 1977, they came up with a bank note valued at 20 Naira. And the dictators' reason was to honor General Murtala Muhammued, a Muslim, who committed genocide of massacring innocent old men, women, and children, in Asaba during the Nigerian Civil War.

In 1991–1999, the military regime issued ₦100, ₦200, ₦500, and ₦1,000 Naira notes. What was the need for these frequent changes in national currency notes and the subsequent issuing of totally new ones? It is during the issue of new notes or currencies that heads of state and their cronies commit very costly financial crimes. Every currency withdrawn must be replaced. In Nigeria, the government would tell the masses to return their old currency notes and coins in exchange for the new ones. At this time, dictators, seeking to make millions of money, print millions of counterfeit currencies and dump them in the countries' Central Bank to be exchanged with the new currency notes. When it comes to the time for disposal of the old currency notes, the counterfeit notes would be burned with the old currency after the accomplice Central Bank Governor had credited their bank accounts with millions of Naira claimed to have been exchanged by the head of state and his cronies. There is no accountability in a dictatorship, and that is why this high-class crime is practicable. In fact, the financial crime of leaders of dictatorship governments is a huge field of study.

In summary, state crimes are found in all governments, but they are committed more in dictatorial regimes than in full democracies. This chapter developed four types of dictatorship, namely, inherited dictatorships marked by customary consensus and divine rights; camouflaged democracies marked by deceit, political fraud, and misleading the masses that the single-party governments run for their benefit; military dictatorships marked by coups d'etat and counter-coups d'etat, and negation of due process of law and the rule of law; and finally, ideological dictatorships marked by totalitarianism or communist or socialist ideology.

Furthermore, provided in this chapter are 16 characteristics of dictatorship regimes, namely, a single "cult of personality" dictator; formal security guards, informal secret security services, absence of multiparty system, absence of a representative legislature, suspending or nullification of the national constitution, absence of an independent judiciary, abolition of freedom of the press, total control of the national police in the hands of the head of state, lack of due process of law, absence of rule of law, government by violence, murder, assassination, torture, and imprisonment, negation of intellectuals and professionals, high degree of unemployment and discrimination in employment, and the head of state craves to rule for life.

Crimes of governments, whether in dictatorships or full democracies, are incurable cancers that affect and destroy generations unborn.

Review Questions

1. What is a dictatorship?
2. What are the four types of dictatorship developed in this book? What are the characteristics of each?
3. Six countries in the world today have absolute monarchy. Name them.
4. What are the common characteristics of all dictatorships?
5. What are the four general principles of the rule of law?
6. Name five countries in Western Europe and the Americas ranked very high in adherence to the principles of rule of law.
7. Name seven present and past heads of state known worldwide as dictators.

Notes

1. There were nine Stuart monarchs who ruled only Scotland from 1371 AD until 1603, when King James VI and I was King of Scotland as King James VI and King of England as James I. That was Union of the Crown in English history.
2. Egypt's new constitution since the 2011 revolution that forced President Hosni Mubarak to resign prescribes that an Egyptian president can only be reelected once.
3. The first coup d'etat in the African continent was carried in Egypt by the society of free officers led by Colonel Gamal Abdal Nasser in 1953. They overthrew the government of King Farouk, and gave power to the figurehead leader of the coup, General Muhammad Naguib.
4. The last coup d'etat in Africa as of January 2015 was the 2013–2014 coup in the Central African Republic for military regime change for the fifth time in the country.
5. In the Americas, the first coup d'etat was carried out in 1839 in Bolivia in the regimes of General Jose Miguel de Velasco Franco and Gamarra.
6. The Haitian coup d'etat of September 29, 1991, was the last coup in the Americas up to this 2015 period.
7. See, "Journalists in Russia, An Online Database, 'Deaths possibly linked to work.'" Journalist-in-russia.org. Also see, "Journalist in Russia, An Online database, 'Those missing since 1993.'" Journalists-in-russia.org. Accessed January 23, 2015.
8. The World Justice Project (WJP) is an independent, nonprofit, multidisciplinary organization working to advance the rule of law around the world. It was founded by William H. Neukom in 2006 as a presidential initiative of the American Bar

Association (ABA), and with the initial support of 21 other strategic partners; WJP transitioned into an independent 501(c)(3) nonprofit organization in 2009. Its offices are located in Washington, DC, and Seattle, WA. See (http://worldjusticeproject.org/ who_we_are). Accessed January 24, 2015.

9. "The Index measures the rule of law using 47 indicators organized around 8 themes: constraints on government powers, absence of corruption, open government, fundamental rights, order and security, regulatory enforcement, civil justice, and criminal justice. More than 500 variables are computed to produce these indicators for every country." (http://worldjusticeproject.org/who_we_are). Accessed January 24, 2015.

10. Full estimates of the death toll for other Arab nations involved in the "Arab Spring" protests and demonstrations not provided are not available at the time of this writing.

11. The United Nations estimate on August 22, 2014, of deaths in the Syrian Civil War stood at 191,000, while opposition activist groups put it as between 127,450 and 286,455 (http:www.google.com/?gws_rd=ss/#).

12. "History of Central Bank of Nigeria. See (http://www.cenbank.org/curency/history) Accessed January 26, 2015.

State Crimes of Government

The Emergence of the State

All animals including humans have an inherent natural liberty. This liberty is God's endowment to man of life, free will, and the pursuit of happiness. Other than humans, all other animals have retained and maintained their natural liberty.

What about man? Well, in the "state of nature," the early man retained and maintained his natural liberty. That was a situation without a state or government. In any infringement to the early man's liberty, he was his own police, prosecutor, lawyer, jury, judge, and prison superintendent. This is a situation that Thomas Hobbes (1651) called "the condition of mere nature." There is no authority or power to regulate the individual's actions. Every person is on his/her own, and free to go wherever he/she pleases. There are no boundaries or gate-keepers as to who owns what. And there are no laws, rules, and regulations to control individual excesses. If a person is challenged by another human being, he does one of two things. He runs away in the face of the challenge or danger. Alternatively, he could stand his feet and vanquish the enemy or perish in the quest. Unmistakably, that is what Hobbes calls "the state of nature."

The "state of nature," Hobbes argues, should be avoided. And postulates that man should "submit to the authority of an absolute undivided and unlimited sovereign power," to avoid a "war of all against all." But one of Hobbes' contemporaries, and eminent political philosopher, John Locke (1632–1704), added some stimulus to Hobbes' need for a state or government, when he charged that "the state of nature was preferable to subjection to the arbitrary power of an absolute sovereign" (Locke, 1689).

Undeniably, Locke was one of the flag bearers of democracy that made him detest absolute monarchies and dictatorships. However, Hobbes brought Locke to reason, that (paraphrased):

> Such a dissolute condition of masterless men, without subjection to laws, and a coercive power to tie their hands from plunder and revenge would make impossible all of the basic security upon which comfortable, sociable, civilized life depends. In such a state of nature, no place for industry, because profitability of the venture is uncertain; and consequently no culture of the earth; no navigation, nor use of the commodities that may be imported by sea; no commodious building; no instruments of moving and removing such things as require much force; no account of time; no arts; no letters; and which is worst of all, continual fear, and danger of violent death; and "the life of man, solitary, poor, nasty, brutish, and short." If this is the state of nature, people have strong reasons to avoid it, which can be done by submitting to some mutually recognized public authority, for "so long a man is in the condition of mere nature, (which is a condition of war) as private appetite is the measure of good and evil."

Consequently, the "social contract" theory became inevitable. In effect, to avoid a "war of all against all," individuals relinquished their natural liberty to the state, for the state, in return, to protect the lives and property of its members (Hobbes, 1689).

Unmistakably, the state is an inevitable structure of the Earth. It was a humanitarian gesture to have a government (a state) to maintain law and order, a state had to create laws to control excesses in human behavior. In addition, the state had to create agencies to enforce the laws. To have a stable society or state, there had to be leadership structure in the state or government. Theoretically, both the leader of the state and his subjects are all under the same laws. Unfortunately, some state leaders and their agents violate the social contract with impunity. In many places and cases, the social contract was a fraud.

Undeniably, some states have had fraudulent heads of state, fraudulent state law enforcement agents, and fraudulent civil servants. On the bases of natural law and statutory law, the state is held liable for the occupational crimes and malfeasances and misfeasances of its law enforcement agents and other civil servants. This is the English American law doctrine of "vicarious liability" or *respondeat superior* (let the master answer), which is embraced in international law and jurisprudence of most nations.

Every head of state is sworn in under oath before taking office to uphold the constitution and laws of the state, with the promise of abiding by the laws and customary standards of the state. Unfortunately, after taking office, some heads of state violate the laws and promises they made to the people they govern. That is a fraud. Some state agents commit a similar fraud. Fraud simply means what is promised is not what is delivered. This is what many countries have received from the hands of their state leaders and civil servants.

When people in a country are used to a particular method of economic and political organization, be it capitalism, socialism, or communism and elect their state leader by a consensus of the majority to maintain the contemporary economic and political system, and the new government, without the approval of the masses, changes either from capitalism to socialism or communism and vice versa, that is a fraud, and people and properties destroyed in the process are state crimes of government.

Crimes of Law Enforcement Agencies

The theory of social contract made the institution of the police and other law enforcement agencies inevitable. Undeniably, the police preserved civilization. In modern society, policing is not expendable. The irrefutable, overwhelming, relevance of the police system was demonstrated in two different ground breaking studies of "seriousness of selected criminal offenses."

The major one was conducted in the summer of 1966 by the National Opinion Research Center (NORC) in Washington, DC. (Ennis, 1967). It was commonly referred to as the "Baltimore Survey." On the basis of the Federal Bureau of Investigation's Uniform Crime Reports (UCR) or Part I Crimes and Part 2 Crimes, the Baltimore Survey developed 141 criminal offenses. These 141 criminal offenses were given to 200 randomly selected subjects to rank the seriousness of each offense in a scale of "1" to "9," where "9" is the most serious and "1" is defined as being least serious. The study calculated the mean ratings on each crime.

Here are some of the criminal offenses among the 141 of them and how they were worded:

- Forcible rape after breaking into a home;
- Planned killing of a spouse;
- Planned killing of an acquaintance;
- Killing spouse lover after catching them together;
- Selling secret documents to a foreign government;
- Deliberately starting a fire in an occupied building;
- Planned killing of a person for a fee;
- Assassination of a public official;
- Planned killing of a policeman;
- Assault with a gun on a stranger;
- Armed robbery of a neighborhood druggist;
- Making sexual advance to young children, and so forth.

The 141 criminal offenses covered all of the Part I and Part II crimes of the UCR and were worded as the 12 of them showed above. Guess, among the 141 criminal offenses which one had the highest average rating as being the most serious crime for anybody to commit? The answer was, "planned killing of a policeman" (Ebbe, 1977, 83–87).

In the second groundbreaking study of rating "the seriousness of selected criminal offenses," Ebbe (1977) used the Baltimore Survey as a model to investigate whether cultural differences will impact the subjects' perceptions of seriousness of selected criminal offenses. More specifically, the problem was to ascertain the extent to which a certain group of foreign students from four different countries agree or disagree regarding the "seriousness of criminal offenses" in the United States; and compare their ratings with those of the United States' student sample.

A total of 100 foreign students at Western Michigan University at Kalamazoo was conveniently drawn. Twenty-five (25) students were selected from each country: India, Iran, Malaysia, and Nigeria. In addition, 50 American-born Western Michigan University students were conveniently selected. The overall total sample size was 150 students.

The top 20 most serious criminal offenses as rated in the Baltimore Survey were given to the 150 students at the Western Michigan University survey to rate on the same scale as the Baltimore Survey. Here are some of the results that impact this book, the foreign students' sample (100) and the overall sample (150—U.S. and foreign students), both ranked "planned killing of a policeman" as the most serious crime (Ebbe, 1977) . Unmistakably, the mean seriousness rating of the Western Michigan University study supported the Baltimore Survey with regard to the most serious crimes among the 20 selected offenses.

Therefore, it stands to reason that even young college students are aware of the importance of the police institution. But over the centuries up to the present period, police murder and brutality of innocent individuals around the world have brought the relevance of having the police institution into question.

Police brutality is savage, mindless cruelty to offenders and nonoffenders in situations where a humane approach could accomplish the aim of law enforcement or order maintenance. Police brutality or use of excessive force against innocent citizens as well as against offenders is as old as the institution itself. The first time the concept of "police brutality" appeared in the Oxford English Dictionary was in 1633, but in 1872, The Chicago Daily Tribune of October 12 wrote about a man arrested and beaten up at the Harrison Street Police Station (Chicago Daily Tribune, 1872).

The idea of a nation state establishing the modern police system began in France in 17th century (Johnson, 2004). In the 18th, 19th, and 20th centuries, the idea was embraced by most emerging sovereign states, including the establishment of the famous Sir Robert Peel's London Metropolitan Police in 1829 (Gaunt, 2010). At that same period, there were uncomfortable cases of frequent police use of clubs and attack ropes to bludgeon individuals and groups into submission (Johnson, 2004).

The state has used the police to commit illimitable atrocious acts of brutality right from centuries past. Peaceful labor strikes received violent state responses in the early years of capitalism. State-police brutality was the lynchpin of labor strike control of all government and corporate operations in all centuries. That is reminiscent of the Great Railroad Strike of 1877, otherwise known as the Great Upheaval, which began on July 16, 1877 in Martinsburg, West Virginia, and lasted 45 days. The strike was squashed with a combination of local and state militia and U.S. federal troops (Bruce, 1989; Salvatore, 1980; Yearley 1956). Similar fates faced the Pullam Strike of 1894 (also a railroad strike); the Lawrence Textile Strike of 1912; the Ludlow Massacre of Ludlow; the Colorado Coal Miners' Strike of 1914; the Steel Strike of 1919 which collapsed in January 1920 after state police, local authorities, and the federal troops arrested and jailed some of the strikers in Indiana, Pennsylvania, Delaware, and so forth; and the Hanapepe Massacre of 1924 in which Filipino sugar workers at Kauai, Hawaii, went on strike, because their demand of $2 a day in wages and reduction of the work day to eight hours was rejected. Instead, the company used the plantation armed forces, the U.S. National Guard, and strike breakers, who were paid a higher wage than the strikers demanded, to put down the strike which took 20 lives including the lives of 3 sheriffs (Reinecke, 1997; Beechert, 1985).

Furthermore, the police killings, beatings, using horses to trample down people, and ruthless kicking of black men and women on March 7, 1965, at Edmund Pettus Bridge at Selma during the "Voting Rights" peaceful march from Selma to Montgomery, Alabama, was a terrible dark age in American history. Americans call it a "Bloody Sunday." On the second day of the march, three white Reverend Pastors joined in a sympathy march, and a white policeman shot and killed one of them. That was not law enforcement. Rather, it was a state hate crime.

The American capitalism is based on laissez faire enterprise, and government staying away from profit-making enterprises. When corporations and their employees have disputes regarding wage and conditions of service and the workers go on strike, why should the government provide the police, national guards, and federal troops, to put down the strike by arrests, jail, severe bodily injury, and massacre of the strikers? Is this not a demonstration that the government, in some regimes, is involved in corporate-organized crime? Undeniably, some top government officials have shares in the corporate enterprises. And labor exploitation is the modus operandi of corporate enterprise. The top government officials use their positions to protect their own investments in the corporations by providing government law enforcement agencies to put down peaceful demonstrations for better wages. The government should be a mediator between the workers and the employers, but not to build the dictatorship of corporations. When any government allies with a corporation to put down a peaceful workers' strike, that is deviance, and government–business organized crime.

In the United States, some city councils, state governments, and the federal government, have spent millions of tax-payers' money settling cases of police brutality. In 2014, a federal jury awarded $4.65 million dollars in damages to the family of a homeless street preacher, Marvin Booker (56), whom four police deputies and a sergeant shocked with a Taser, put in a "sleep hold" and then sat on top of him in an attempt to control him in the booking area of Denver, Colorado, jail on July 9, 2010. The coroner ruled the death of Marvin Booker a homicide. Unmistakably, neither the Denver Police Department nor the state government condemned the action or punished the five policemen. Since the Denver incident of July 9, 2010 to December 2014, American society lost 2,050 persons to police killings (see Table 7.1). And bear in mind that police departments report crimes in their jurisdictions to the FBI for the compilation of the Uniform Crime Reports (UCR). The FBI has no control over which crime is reported and which is not reported. Also, the Bureau of Justice Statistics compiles their data from the FBI records, police records, and court records. And victimization record does not apply in homicide for the Bureau of Justice Statistics. Therefore, both the FBI and the Bureau of Justice Statistics recognize that not all justifiable and unjustifiable killings by police are reported.

Table 7.1 Justifiable Homicides by Police Officers in the United States by Months and Years (2010–2014)*

Months	Years				
	2010	**2011**	**2012**	**2013**	**2014****
January	31	33	30	43	52
February	32	30	27	20	13
March	39	31	21	33	16
April	31	29	31	30	11
May	38	36	36	38	20
June	36	32	50	36	40
July	43	39	60	49	24
August	38	33	58	51	105
September	26	35	40	46	78
October	34	42	27	43	56
November	20	34	20	54	92
December	29	30	20	18	82
Total	397	404	420	461	589

Sources: Excerpted and Tallied from the FBI Uniform Crime Reports (2010–2013) and Bureau of Justice Statistics: Justifiable Homicide by Police, 2010–2014. Also see http://www.ojp.usdoj.gov/bjs

**The 2014 data came from BJS records only. The UCR of the FBI for 2014 was not yet out before this tally.

When the police unjustifiable homicide is not punished, such a behavior will likely be repeated (Skinner, 1948). America saw it as a truism when on July 17, 2014, New York City Police killed Eric Garner and medical examiners determined his death as homicide. Less than a month later, an unarmed Michael Brown was gunned down by a police officer in Ferguson, Missouri; and a week or two later, in the same St. Louis, Missouri area, Kajieme Powell was killed by a police officer. Unmistakably, if a behavior, whether good or bad, is complemented, it must be repeated as B.F. Skinner asserted.

Look at the years of 2010, 2011, 2012, 2013, and 2014 of "Justifiable Homicides by police officers in the United States" (Table 7. 1) and see how the number killed increased each year. It is not getting better because local and state governments use the police in their own deviant behaviors. In effect, we have a situation of *quid pro quo*. When the New York City Mayor condemned his policemen's actions in the case of Garner, the police cried "foul," and responded to their boss with anger and indignation. Police brutality is real in the United States as it is all over the world.

In the United States, there are states that are known for high frequency of police brutality. Those states have cities with metropolitan population of over one half of a million people. See Table 7.2 for state-by-state cases of "Justifiable Homicides" from 2010 to 2014.

FIGURE 7.1 New York City, United States, Day of outraged demonstration of police brutality

© Tony Savino/Corbis

Table 7.2 Justifiable Homicides by Police in the United States by State and Years (2010–2014)*

States	2010	2011	2012	2013	2014
AL	0	0	7	9	8
AK	2	0	3	2	1
AR	3	3	6	8	3
AZ	11	15	20	19	26
CA	46	49	61	66	107
CO	21	25	13	18	10
CT	0	0	2	4	2
DE	0	0	2	0	3
FL	14	18	21	26	36
GA	20	42	32	32	16
HI	0	1	1	2	2
IA	0	0	2	3	5
ID	4	2	3	2	4
IL	21	19	20	16	15
IN	8	5	3	7	6
KY	2	2	6	3	11
KS	8	4	6	5	9
LA	9	5	7	10	13
MA	2	2	6	4	2
MD	13	10	10	13	9
ME	2	6	0	0	4
MI	11	9	5	11	10
MN	9	1	4	5	8
MO	10	2	6	9	12
MS	0	0	3	1	7
MT	1	0	3	2	5
NC	0	2	7	8	9

States	2010	2011	2012	2013	2014
ND	0	0	0	0	0
NE	8	2	1	1	3
NH	0	4	2	4	0
NJ	16	8	4	3	10
NM	8	7	5	8	11
NV	11	13	12	5	15
NY	12	17	19	21	18
OH	10	9	12	10	20
OK	9	7	9	8	17
OR	14	8	8	5	8
PA	10	10	19	18	13
RI	0	0	1	0	0
SC	8	10	5	6	8
SD	0	0	0	0	3
TN	13	11	7	4	16
TX	17	22	28	32	54
UT	8	3	5	3	10
VA	8	7	2	4	7
VT	0	0	4	1	1
WA	26	42	12	28	16
WI	2	2	5	5	5
WV	0	0	3	6	6
WY	0	0	0	1	1
DC	0	0	2	3	3
Total	397	404	426	461	589

Source: Tallied from FBI Uniform Crime Reports and Bureau of Justice Statistics 2010–2014. (http://www.ojp
.usdoj.gov/bjs)

States that consistently have a high degree of police killing of persons in their line of duty in the United States during the five-year period include California, Arizona, Colorado, Florida, Georgia, Illinois, Maryland, New York, Ohio, Pennsylvania, Texas, and Washington. Cities like Los Angeles, Denver, Miami, Atlanta, Chicago, New York City, Houston, Dallas, and Seattle catapult the frequency of police homicides of their states. North Dakota is the only state without a police homicide reported in the five-year period. States with less than 10 police homicides reported in the five-year period are Alaska (8), Connecticut (8), Delaware (5), Hawaii (6), Rhode Island (1), South Dakota (3), Vermont (6), and Wyoming (2). During the five-year period, Washington, DC had eight police homicide cases.

Table 7.3 presents "Justifiable Homicides by Law Enforcement Officers in the United States by type of weapon used, 2009–2013" as presented by the FBI—"Expanded Homicide Data[1] Table 14—Crime in the United States 2013" (Uniform Crime Reports, 2013).

It is very shocking and heartrending when one observes on television or reads from newspaper reports or other print media the circumstances that led to persons losing their lives at the hands of the police who are supposed to protect the individuals. In a great deal of the cases, death could have been avoided.

Even in the United Kingdom, where the police do not always carry handguns or rifles when out looking for law violators, police homicides do occur; but the number of people who lose their lives at the hands of the police is not anywhere close as large as in the United States.[2] However, most fatal encounters of the British police and the masses can pass as justifiable.[3] While Great Britain does not have many police homicide cases, police brutality of inflicting severe bodily injury with their truncheons is common. And whenever the police in Britain have shot and killed an unarmed person, riots usually ensued, as in the case of London police (Tottenham, North London) killing Mark Duggan on August 4, 2011. The riot got about 3,100 persons arrested and 1,000 charged with various crimes. In spite of all that violence, on January

Table 7.3 Justifiable Homicides by Law Enforcement Officers in the United States by Type of Weapon Used 2009–2013*

Year	Total	Total Firearms	Handguns	Rifles	Shotguns	Firearms, type not stated	Knives or cutting instruments	Other dangerous weapons	Personal weapons
2009	414	411	326	29	6	50	0	3	0
2010	397	396	323	29	6	38	0	1	0
2011	404	401	305	36	11	49	2	0	1
2012	426	423	339	38	7	39	0	3	0
2013	461	458	332	46	9	71	0	3	0

*Source: FBI Uniform Crime Reports, 2013.

8, 2014, a jury sitting at the Royal Courts of Justice brought a verdict by a majority of 8 to 2 that the killing of Mark Duggan was lawful (Lewis, 2011).

Undeniably, police use of force, with baton or rifle, is an inherent part of British law enforcement system. Back in the 1990s, the United Kingdom used a lot of excessive force in responding to demonstrations and riots. For instance, in April 1967, during a riot between Irish nationalists and the Royal Ulster Constabulary (RUC), the RUC officers forced themselves into the house of a 43-year-old Catholic civilian, Samuel Devenney, who played no part in the riot. He, his daughter, and son were beaten with batons and rendered unconscious. Devenney died in July 1969, and it was believed the police beatings led to his death (Coogan, 2002; BBC News Update, 2014). Samuel Devenney's son, Harry, who survived the beatings said, "it was a 'shocking' night for the family." He further added, "My father was beaten very badly about the head, chest, and face. He was choking when I went into the living room and there was blood everywhere. I had to pull teeth from his mouth" (BBC News Update, 2014).

Four days before Samuel Devenney died, the Royal Ulster Constabulary (July 13, 1969), beat Francis McCloskey, a Catholic in Dungiven, Northern Ireland, very severely with batons during "The Troubles" and he died the next day (Sutton, 1994; McKittrick, Seamus, & Kelters, 2001). In the 1969 itself, in mid-August, the Royal Ulster Constabulary shot and killed five Catholic civilians and opened fire on a crowd of protesting Irish nationalists. The killings of innocent, unarmed demonstrating civilians in Northern Ireland by the Royal Ulster Constabulary were crimes of the government of the United Kingdom, otherwise known as Great Britain. If the government of Britain had ordered the RUC to stop killing unarmed civilians protesting on the streets, they would have stopped.

On April 1, 2009, during the meeting of the G-20 protests in London, one Ian Tomlinson, a bystander, was violently struck down by a police officer, and he died a few minutes later. An inquest determined that he was unlawfully killed. The constable with London Metropolitan Police Service was charged with manslaughter. Unmistakably, he was found not guilty of manslaughter. For a slap on the wrist, he was fired from the police service for gross misconduct (Walker & Lewis, 2012).

Like Great Britain, Canada does not have many police homicides. But it recorded more police homicides from 2009 to 2012 than Britain and far less than the United States. From 2009 to 2012, Canada recorded a total of 36 police homicides (Perreault, 2012). But the number of physical injuries to demonstrators in Canada by the Royal Canadian Mounted Police (RCMP) has not been systematically recorded. There have been many cases of Canadian police beating peaceful demonstrators in Toronto, Vancouver, Montreal, and so forth over the years (see Figure 7.2).

In addition, in Canada, during the Ipperwash crisis over an indigenous land dispute between the government and Ojibwa Indians, the Ontario Provincial Police (OPP) killed an unarmed protester, Dudley George. After an inquiry, an Acting Sergeant was charged and convicted of criminal negligence causing death. He was given community sentence, but he

Figure 7.2 Montreal riot police break up anti-police brutality march in Canada
© Darren Ell/Demotix/Corbis

remained on his job for another five-and-a-half years, before another "discreditable conduct" led to his being forced to resign or be fired (Hedican, 2008; Edwards, 2001).

Furthermore, on October 14, 2007, the Royal Canadian Mounted Police (RCMP) killed a Polish immigrant, Robert Dziekanski, at the Vancouver International Airport, British Columbia, after they tasered him five times. Robert Dziekanski had just arrived at the airport from Poland to join his mother. The Canadian Customs and Immigration Departments at the airport unnecessarily jolted him from one department to another, because he could not speak English. In effect, he rationally got agitated,[4] and they called the police. He was leaning calmly toward an office counter when the police arrived. The police handcuffed him and electroshock-gunned (tasered) him five times, while Dziekanski was not violent. Unfortunately, for the RCMP, they did not know that an eyewitness bystander videoed the whole incident. When the RCMP found out that they were being videoed, they seized the video tape from the man, Paul Pritchard.

Paul Pritchard took RCMP to court to get his tape back. After the tape was given back to him, he gave it to the media, and the case became a shame to the RCMP and their government. According to a retired Vancouver police superintendent, after viewing the video, Robert Dziekanski did not appear to be engaging in violent threats or gestures toward the police, and he could not see how the matter became a police incident (CBC News, 2007; Rolfsen 2007). As it happens in most cases of police brutality and murder, there were no charges against the policemen of the RCMP.

The last unwarranted Canadian police brutality that needs to be discussed here is the merciless beating of an innocent man in his house. On January 22, 2010, some officers of the

Vancouver Police Department wrongly invaded a house while investigating a violent domestic matter. They knocked and busted into the house of an innocent Yao Wei Wu, who could not speak English, pulled him out, and beat him up. Yao told CBC News through an interpreter (CBC News, 2010).

From Canada, let's look at contemporary Russia, France, Italy, Greece, Norway, Spain, Germany, and Turkey. Law enforcement in Russia is as violent as the society itself. The general rate of murder in Russia is high. In comparative analysis, here are the rates of murder in Russia per 100,000 population for a country of 143,300,000 in October 2012:

- 6.3 in 1987
- 21.8 in 1994
- 22.0 in 2001
- 23.0 in 2003

The murder rate increased more than usual after the 1989 collapse of communism. Organized crime, the government, former KGB elements, and the police joined hands to run the country, and the murder rate sky-rocketed. According to Yakov Gilinskiy (2000, 2003, 2013), after the collapse of the Soviet Union, there was an amalgamation of convicts and ex-convicts, organized crime, the government, former KGB officials, and the police to create a "Mafia" state, and Russia became a criminal state. The police became a strong instrument of the criminal state. The country was divided into two: "inclusives" and "exclusives." The "exclusives" face illimitable police repression. The Russian militia, as Russian police are called, operate like a colonial regime's police force in their repressive methods. Persons killed by the militia are unpersons, because they are "exclusives." Russia does not keep an account of the number of persons killed by the militia in their line of law enforcement. Besides, persons killed by the Russian militia (police) while taking over the individuals' businesses by force on false charges of tax evasion, or whatever the organized-crime-controlled government could make up, were "exclusives." The Russian militia are the 007 of the Russian government's organized crime.

In his book, *Darkness at Dawn*, David Satter (2003) describes the government of Russia as follows: "The rise of a business criminal elite and its takeover of the machinery of the Russian state, leading to the impoverishment and demoralization of the great majority of the population." This depiction of present Russia, undeniably, puts Russia in the category of failed states like Zimbabwe, Rwanda-Burundi, Nigeria, Libya, and Equatorial Guinea. The Russian militia are not for the protection of the lives of the masses and their property. Instead, they protect the interests of the "criminal oligarchy" (Satter, 2003) and expedite the corrupt and vice operations of the criminal elite (Gilinskiy, 2013; Shelley, 1995). In the contemporary Russian government are the following law enforcement agencies: militia, customs, immigration, SVR (Foreign Intelligence Service), the FSB (Federal Security Service of the Russian Federation), and FSO (Federal Protective Services). The SVR, FSB, and FSO took over the former role of the KGB, and their leaders are sucked into the criminal oligarchy including GRU (Russia's Main Military Intelligence Directorate) leaders.

The modus operandi of the Russian criminal oligarchy follows the Italian mafian code of operation, which is "manliness." And manliness means to operate without the law. In other words, nullify law enforcement before you operate, before you strike at your criminal target so that you will not be caught. In effect, in Russian organized crime, when the leaders of the state are at the head of the illegal operations, or keep nonchalant attitude toward the vice operations, the sky is the limit for the mafia (Shelley, 1995; Satter, 2003; Gilinskiy, 2003). The government-organized crime in Russia is attested to by the fact that for up to six months, persons on welfare in 2003 had not received any paycheck. This situation was made possible by "collaborations initiated between traditional white-collar criminals, corrupt functionaries, and the criminals, including old 'thieves-in-law'[4] and the new generation of 'bandits' or sportsmen" (Gilinskiy, 2013, p. 141). The new generation of bandits joined some former members of the KGB to form the bulk of Russian organized crime. Therefore, the police (militia) in Russia serve the Russian organized crime oligarchy. The mass of the "exclusives," are the destitute victims without a way out, because the police (militia) have put down every protest with murders, assassinations, torture, imprisonments, and physical injuries (Satter, 2003).

Leaving imperialist Russia, comes another imperialist European country, France. Every imperialistic country is known for running repressive regimes. The French use of the police to oppress its colonial dependences in Africa and Asia is an irrefutable fact. This oppressive treatment was very common during the independence struggles of its former colonies. In France, use of the police to put down peaceful demonstrations and protests is part of French political culture. On November 22, 2014, during a protest in central Nantes, Western France, against construction of a controversial dam, 21-year-old Remi Fraisse was killed during the violent clash with the police.[5]

Furthermore, one cannot forget the French police massacre of large unarmed, peaceful demonstrators of Algerian nationals in Paris on October 17, 1961, in which 100–200 Algerians were killed, excluding those who were drowned in the Paris' Seine River with their hands tied behind them. The Paris massacre was intentional, because attack on the demonstration was forbidden (Swedenburg, 2002; Gordon, 2000; Brunet, 2008). The over 30,000 protesters were unarmed. Why then should an agency that is designed to protect the masses turn around to destroy its subjects? What legitimacy has such a government to remain in power? For Hobbes (1651/2007), Locke (1689/2015), and Rousseau (1762/1968), such a state should not be, because it has failed to provide "peace and defense" for the people.

Given the violence that goes with mafia criminal enterprise, Italian police being hovered by mafian syndicates, have brutality as its method of operation. During the 2001 G-8 27th Summit, the Italian police shot and killed a 23-year-old, Carlo Giuliani, who was protesting against the G-8 in Genoa, Italy. The police officer who killed him was charged, tried, and acquitted on the basis that he killed Giuliani in self-defense. But the death of Carlo Giuliani became a symbol of civil unrest during G-8 Summit in Genoa (Phillips, 2013).

In addition, on September 25, 2005, four Italian police officers killed an 18-year-old student, Federico Aldrovandi. He was beaten to death during an arrest attempt in Ferrara, Italy. The four police officers were tried and found guilty of manslaughter for excessive use of force. They were sentenced to three years and six months of imprisonment, but the sentence was reduced to six months in prison following a controversial pardon issued by the Italian Parliament in 2006 (Alessandri, 2014). This killing of a young Italian by four Italian policemen provoked a mass outrage throughout major cities in Italy.

In Norway, a Nigerian-Norwegian student faced a fate similar to that of Aldrovandi of Italy. On September 7, 2006, Eugene Ejike Obiora, a naturalized Norwegian citizen, was killed by Norwegian police during an arrest. It was alleged that Obiora, who had lived in Norway for over 20 years, was aggressive to the personnel of the social services in Trondheim, Norway. He died while the police was holding "him in a stranglehold." The police were accused of use of unnecessary force and racism. The shameful incident made headlines all over Norway.

Greek police are known for their frequent confrontation with the public. When the citizens of a country are peacefully demonstrating against a war, should the police use guns, batons, or Molotov cocktails to disperse them? No, that is unnecessary. The use of force against such peaceful protesters is state deviance. The masses will see the government as a violent state. But don't say that to the police in Greece. On March 21, 2003, over 150,000 Greek Protesters took to the streets of Athens marching against the U.S.-led war in Iraq. But the Greece Riot Police went into violent action. That was not necessary for such a mammoth crowd. Many people were injured in the stampede caused by police frenzy movements around the crowd.

In the Exarcheia district of central Athens, Greece, a 15-year-old, Alexandros Grigoropoulos, was gunned down by one of two Special Guards of the Greek Police personnel on December 6, 2008. Why? The two Special Guards engaged in a minor verbal clash with a small group of teenagers in one of the streets in Exarcheia area beside a shop premises. The two policemen decided to drive away. On their exit, they met another small group of teenagers at a four-way crossing. A similar clash ensued. At that point, the two Special Guards were ordered by the Greek police at the center of operations to disengage and terminate the confrontation forthwith. Instead of obeying the order, the two Special Guards parked their police car and walked on foot to engage the teenagers face-to-face.

About 9 p.m., the Special Guards and the youngsters faced each other with a torrent of abusive words, which witnesses testified had been started by the Special Guards. In the exchange, one of the Special Guards, Epaminondas Korkoneas, fired his gun killing Alexandros Grigoropoulos.

Hell broke loose on the second day after Alexandros Grigoropoulos was shot and killed. The whole of Athens was engulfed in demonstrations and riots almost unfathomable in Athenian history. This police murder of a 15-year-old boy triggered riots at universities, other workplaces, and cities. The murder, coupled with Greece's poor economic conditions due to 2008 global economic crisis, corruption in the country, and high rate of unemployment, made the demonstrations a kind of an outlet and a safety valve (Glendinning, 2008; Carassava, 2008; Dawar, 2008; Siddique, 2009).

Under the national outcry against police brutality in Greece, the two Special Guards were prosecuted. The police officer who fired the shot, Epaminondas Korkoneas, was charged with murder (which is "intentional homicide" in Greek law), and the other officer, Vasilis Saraliotis, was charged as an accomplice.

The Mixed Jury Court of Amfissa, consisting of three judges and four jurors, found the two policemen guilty as charged. Epaminondas Korkoneas was found guilty of "homicide with direct intention to cause harm," while Vasilis Saraliotis was found guilty as an accomplice. In effect, Korkoneas was sentenced to lifetime[6] and an additional one year and three months behind bars at a vote of 4:3; while Saraliotis was sentenced to ten years of imprisonment by a vote of 6:1 (BBC News, 2010).

The two Special Guards received severe penalties, because they did not know that Alexandros Grigoropoulos came from a very wealthy family. If the 15-year-old boy had hailed from a family of blue-collar workers, this case would have been swept under the rug.

Another European country that has an undying history of government violence using the police is Spain. Spain's colonial hegemony was underpinned by police "crack-head" violence. The colonial type of police violence was brought home to Spain by a Spanish General and Dictator Francisco Franco who ruled Spain for 39 years (1939–1975). Since that dictatorial regime, the Spanish police have not learned to enforce the law without the use of ruthless brutal force.

On February 20, 2012, the police in Valencia, Spain, indiscriminately beat up students who were peacefully demonstrating against police brutality and protesting against budget cuts in education. The bloody police assaults on harmless minors were reminiscent of the dictatorship of the late Francisco Franco's regime. A Spanish newspaper *El Publico* reported that despite "brutal police aggression" and firing rubber bullets at the students, hundreds of the students still took to the streets and surrounded the University of Valencia, protesting in anger and indignation (Roos, 2012). The photographs in Spanish newspapers coming out of Valencia received media and national condemnation, but the government was strongly behind the results of the police brutal actions. Unfortunately, for the police and the government, "Corbis Images" (2012) did not hide the magnitude of the police brutality.

After Spain comes contemporary Germany. Law enforcement in Germany since the end of World War II is the most strictly regulated in the world. Police brutality is not common, as compared to other European countries. There is more harmony between police departments in Germany than in most other industrialized economies. The German police are not trigger-happy guys. Very few cases of shots are fired by the police annually. From 1999 to 2012, only 11 cases of persons killed by German police were reported. The incidents reported

Figure 7.3 Police indiscriminately beat up peacefully demonstrating students in Valencia, Spain, Feburary 20, 2012

© German caballero/Demotix/Corbis

appear justifiable cases (Mendez, 2012). German police are criticized for their mistreatment of immigrants and complemented for its few cases of police brutality. Contemporary Germany exemplifies a state where use of violence and brutality is not the modus operandi of effective law enforcement.

Unlike contemporary Germany, police brutality is a historical method of law enforcement in Turkey. Turkey police are often seen in assault mode. It is a common site to observe 5 to 10 policemen in Turkey beating up a person.[7] As assault weapons, they carry heavy baseball-sized sticks and chase men and women protestors. Also coupled with physical violence, they excessively use tear gas canisters, pepper spray, and water cannon against protesters. The Turkish police, like their Nigerian counterparts, have no accountability. They have no regard for the safety and lives of the citizens. They are after pleasing the government in power. There is no reason to beat peaceful protesters to a point of being half-dead. Protesters alleged that the government had authorized the police to be ruthless with demonstrators. Also, the European Court of Human Rights noted that the Turkish authorities refused to investigate allegations of ill-treatment of peaceful demonstrators by law enforcement officers.[8]

The Turkish authorities are ashamed to investigate Turkish police brutality, because there is no need to investigate facts that are naked and manifest. There are many instances of protesters lying in pools of blood and those admitted to hospitals.

Less brutal in law enforcement than Turkey is Finland. Undeniably, anti-communist police brutality was evident in the 1920s and 1930s upsurge of the Finnish Civil War.

From 2007 to 2013, there were three cases of police misconduct and only two of them involved use of brutal force. All of the three police officers involved were penalized by a fine. Only one received a suspended sentence. While there were only 7,700 police officers in Finland in 2014, their degree of participation in police brutality does not constitute a social problem compared to Turkey.

There are other disturbing and unwarranted police use of brutal force against peaceful demonstrators in other parts of Europe, but the cases presented above of selected European countries, give a significant picture of the magnitude of police brutality in Europe. Next presented here are other countries south of the United States.

Crimes of Law Enforcement in Mexico, Venezuela, Chile, and Argentina

Police brutality in Mexico is as bloody as police brutality in Turkey. Also, Mexican police are like the Russian police. In Mexico, as in Nigeria, the police enforce the law for the highest bidder. Those who try to protest against government policy, government corruption, or question the government about the disappearance of 43 trained teachers who went missing are either jailed until they pay some money to free themselves, or they will go missing, too. It is believed that the drug cartels in Mexico and the police live in symbiosis with each other (Stevenson, 2011).

Police brutality in Mexico is so extreme that it is logical to say that life is safer in Turkey than in Mexico. Mexico demonstrates a society that is in anomie—a state of social disorganization. Mexico is not a police state. It is profoundly in anarchistic mode, because the government is corrupt. In effect, it couldn't enforce its laws because a payoff lets the offender go. Jail in Mexico is an extortionary institution. If an offender or his relatives pay a fee, he is freed. The masses are not protected in Mexico. The rule of law is marooned.[9]

After Mexico comes Chile. Police brutality in Chile is a correlate of Augusto Pinochet's totalitarian regime. It did not stop with the eclipse of General Pinochet. In May 2013, students at the University of Chile were peacefully marching in the streets in protest against the latest education policies of President Sebastian Pinera. The Chilean Police confronted the students with batons, tear gas, and chased them to the campus of the University. According to the official report, 324 students were arrested, 74 persons injured including 24 policemen and 50 students. The police also grabbed two 17-year-olds on the street side and arrested them claiming that they were among the protesters. They beat them up very badly. One of them, Aguilera, lost consciousness, and they left him there in the street, and took the other one, Cesar Reyes, and dumped him stark naked in a police cell. UNICEF and other humanitarian organizations have condemned the police use of violence in the May 2013 student march (Soto, 2013).

Photographs do not lie. The Chilean Police dragged an 80-year-old Mapuche Indian woman by her hands and legs, her clothes brushing the dirty street, to the police station because she could not tell them the whereabouts of her three sons. The Mapuche Indian community has become a subject of frequent arrests, detention, and imprisonment without due process by the Chilean Police in the President Sebastian Pinera and President Michelle Bachelet regimes. According to a Chilean human rights lawyer, Richard Caifal, the law controlling the actions of Mapuche Indians about their claim to their land is "an abomination" and discriminatory.[10]

Wherever there is a dictatorship, there must be police brutality. As a result, Venezuela is not an exception. In a dictatorship, there must be demonstration against the government and its policies. The socialist policies of the late President Chavez did not die with him. The post-Chavez government, led by Nicolas Maduro, continued from where Chavez stopped. Anti-socialist student activists in Venezuela are faced with violent repression. About 500–700 students protesting against the new regime's socialist policies were faced with police brutality. On February 23, 2014, Geraldine Moreno Orozco, a 23-year-old, became the 10th fatal victim of state violence in President Maduro's oppression in Venezuela.

The Venezuelans of the Maduro regime have no freedom of assembly and freedom of the press. The popular "Will Party" leader, Leopoldo Lopez, was incarcerated for organizing a protest. A student, Carlos Tejada, lost an eye to a tear gas bomb. Some other students received beatings, head concussions made by rifle attacks, broken ribs, and burns (Rawlins, 2014). A state that kills some members of its citizenry is not a state but a pirate government or a mercenary government.

Argentina is like Chile in many ways. Both battle with Native Indian populations. And the colonial use of the police to ride roughshod over the indigenous peoples is still alive in post-colonial regimes of Chile and Argentina. After several years of dictatorship, Argentina could not get rid of police brutality. The conception of "the iron fist of the state" is never dead in Argentina. For instance, an eviction at the Argentine Province of Jujuy in July 2011 resulted in the death of four persons. There was no litigation about the incident. It was like nobody died. Like the Mexican and Nigerian police, there is no accountability in Argentine police operations. Worst of all, like in Mexico and Russia, many of the police are for organized crime syndicates.

Negation of fundamental human rights of the people is the method of police operation in Argentina, Mexico, and Chile. There is no rule of law in Argentine police law enforcement procedures. Abuse of suspects is their normal method of law enforcement. In a study at Vanderbilt University, Nashville, Tennessee, Argentina was identified as having one of the worst records of police use of violence and brutality in Latin America. The study noted that 8.7% of the population of Argentina was subjected to a certain degree of violence and abuse in 2009 by the Argentine police force (Cruz, 2009). The number of youths killed by the Argentine police forces from 1991 through 2009 is mind-boggling. Some young adults were disappearing at the hands of the police, just like in the dictatorship years.[11]

Like Argentina, Brazil has a problem of not enforcing the law without ethnic discrimination and brutal violence. However, analyzing data on police violence in Brazil and other countries, Brazil, unequivocally, has the most violent police force in the world. Their basis of law enforcement is ethnic hatred. For the Brazilian military police force, non-white ethnic group teenagers and adolescents are subjects for elimination. According to NPR News (2014), a day before the World Cup began, on June 12, 2014, two Brazilian policemen picked up three black teenagers in Rio de Janeiro—"The three hadn't committed any crime—but they did have a history of petty offenses" (Garcia-Navarro, 2014). The two officers drove the three boys to a wooded hill above the city. They shot one in the head and another in the leg and back. Both died on the spot, while the third boy took to his heels when the first was shot in the head. The boys were about 14 years old. Unfortunately for the police officers, they "left their patrol car cameras on, and the videos surfaced on Brazil's Globo TV" (Garcia-Navarro, 2014). The video had the following statements by the police officers: "We haven't even started beating you yet and you are already crying?" and another officer says, "Stop crying! You are crying too much! Be a man!" And he looked at the other officer and added, "gotta kill the three of them." After their policing crime, one says, "Two less. If we do this every week, we can reach their number. We can reach the goal" (Garcia-Navarro, 2014). According to Garcia-Navarro, the goal they were referring to was a target of crime-reduction quota before the World Cup begins.

The data on police brutality in Brazil show that, on an average, five people are killed in Brazil every day (Wells, 2013). A joint study of Brazil's Forum of Public Security and Open Society Foundation, a U.S.-based NGO, of police killings in Brazil as part of its annual report, found and concluded that:

- 1,890 people were killed in 23 Brazilian states in 2012;
- 1,322 were killed by police in Sao Paulo, Rio de Janeiro, and Bahia in 2012 (Wells, 2013).[12]

There is a culture of violence in the Brazilian police force. Take, for instance, in 1993 in the city of Rio de Janeiro, the police opened fire on a group of about 60 street children, and killed 8 of them[13] (Wells, 2014). In addition, in 2009, Human Rights Watch reported that police in Rio and Sao Paulo had killed more than 11,000 people since 2003 and it represents 1 in every 28 persons arrested in Rio in 2008. They added that Brazilian police routinely use deadly force in their law enforcement operation and are rarely punished for killing innocent persons.[14]

Brazil was under military dictatorship from 1964 to 1985, and that was when military police controlled the streets. Up till today, Brazil uses military police as a method of law enforcement. For the Brazilian police, the non-whites and the non-browns (pardos) are the enemies of the police. Some of the killings are not reported for as long as there are no complainants. Also, those brutally injured by the police are unpeople and hardly included in police crime statistics.

Furthermore, the number of Brazilians killed by the police in the line of duty is unacceptable. For instance, at the time 1,890 people were killed by police in 2013, also killed were 89 police officers. The data show that in Brazil, 21 civilians are killed for every police officer killed. Comparatively, the United States has a population 60% larger than Brazil, and more firearms in circulation and more law enforcement officers than Brazil. But the FBI puts the annual average number of persons killed by the police at 400, and 12 civilians killed for every police officer killed in the line of duty in the United States. The world ratio is 10 civilians killed for every police officer killed in the line of duty[15] (Wells, 2014). Therefore, something is grossly wrong with the government of Brazil and its criminal justice system.

The state of Brazil has an acute problem of malintegration. And a system of malintegration spells "anomic" conditions (Merton, 1968). Unmistakably, the rate of police killings of youths in Brazil and the rate of Brazilian police officers losing their lives in the line of duty show that any claim of racial assimilation in Brazil is a nude myth. In the absence of meaningful integration and assimilation, coupled with high concentration of abject poor majority, high violent crime rate is a proven correlate. In such a society, law enforcement becomes a war of classes.

Following South America come the three major countries in Asia: China, India, and Japan. These three countries have clear systematic records on law enforcement agencies and the public they serve. All of the other Asian countries lack such data. The three countries are among the top 10 most populous countries of the world. Among the three, one is biggest dictatorship in the world (China), another the largest democracy in the world (India), and the last, one of the most industrialized economies in the world (Japan). Therefore, the degree of "crime of law enforcement" in those countries gives a good picture of such crimes in other parts of Asia.

China, with a 2014 population count of 1.3 billion, is the most populous country in the world. The Chinese totalitarian regime of Chairman Mao's period made most Western scholars look at China as a violent country. In reality, China is a very humane society, and that is why it is able to sustain over 1.3 billion people harmoniously over a long time. Take, for instance, with the 2014 population of 1,355,692,576 people, China has only 1.5 people in prison. Compare that with the United States and Russia with 2014 population counts of 318,892,103 and 142,470,272, respectively, and prisoner population of 2,288,424 and 874,161, respectively. What is seen in Chinese law enforcement is that crime does not occur very often. Whenever it occurs, however, the Chinese police have no mercy for the offender in the street. Since crime doesn't occur very often in China, and, as a result, police brutality is seldom.

From 2006 to 2014, China had 25 persons killed by the police in the process of law enforcement. In 2014, there were 13 clearly justifiable killings by Chinese police in the process of enforcing the law, including an innocent bystander who was killed in an exchange of fire with a drug dealer (Wang, 2000). In 2013, there were nine police killings in Xinjiang, in which eight terrorists were the victims.[16] In 2012, there was only one fatal fabricated case by a police officer. The police officer shot and killed a man in Shenzhen and filed a false report that the man was involved in an armed robbery. The police officer was charged with murder and convicted and sentenced to death. But by Chinese criminal justice system, the death sentence was suspended.[17] In Chinese criminal justice system, a death sentence is usually suspended for 365 days. Before the 365th day, if the offender repents, the death sentence is commuted to life imprisonment (Wang & Davidson, 2000).

In 2006 and 2009, only one person was killed by a police officer in each of the two years in China. In 2007, 2008, 2010, and 2011, nobody was reported killed by law enforcement officers. And from 2006 to 2014, only one police officer was killed in the line of duty out of 25 persons justifiably killed by law enforcement officers.

Unmistakably, police brutality happens in China but it is not comparable with Brazil, Mexico, Turkey, and Chile. In 2011, the murder rate in China was 1.0 per 100,000 people, with a total 13,410 murders for a country of 1.2 billion people in that year.

Now let's turn to another country with more than 1 billion population, and that's the Democratic Republic of India. India has many radical religions prone to use of violence to settle their differences and intolerance of other religions. In addition, India was a British colonial dependency with colonial police structure and history. Therefore, police brutality in India is inevitable.

The police in India often severely beat up a suspect who was not caught in the act to get him to confess to the crime. It is a method of law enforcement very common in all former British colonies. The beating of the presumed offender serves as a deterrence to others.

In a peaceful anti-enchroachment drive in Indore, Madhya Pradesh, in September 2014, six persons got the cane very severely, including a woman who sustained an injury. In the same week, a woman was arrested and accused of murder. She was tortured for hours to get her to confess to the crime. She was subjected to inhumane assaults; needles were injected into her fingers, nails, hands, and arms. She was hung upside down and ruthlessly beaten at the same time. The police officers threatened to take obscene photographs of her and publish them in newspapers throughout India, unless she confessed to committing the murder. The woman's daughter compiled the whole police atrocities and threats against her mother and launched a petition before the Madras High Court. The police reacted by threatening the petitioner. But when the police saw that the court was ready to take up the case, they settled the case out of court by offering the woman's daughter a huge amount of money (Neemuchwala, 2014).

The Indian police believe in the use of excessive force. That is the way they were trained, and that is the system of social control their grandfathers, fathers, and they themselves grew up with from the colonial dictatorship. But the Indian civilians do not countenance it. Sometimes the Indian police harassments are for extorting bribe from an innocent civilian, just like in Nigeria. The Indian populace are aware of this police criminal strategy. In 2014, there were three fatal incidents generated by the police in three different places in

India. The police arrested a 28-year-old mechanic for questioning in Chennai. The man did not see any rationale for the police to arrest him for questioning. From previous experience he and other people have had with the police inviting them for questioning, he felt that it was not going to be an hour or two of interrogation. Rather, he would be locked up for any fictitious allegation they could invent, until he paid some bribe. Instead of going through the perceived excruciating embarrassment of those police atrocities, the man committed suicide (Neemuchwala, 2014).

The second incident was that of a taxi driver from Bengaluru, Karnataka, who was arrested by the police for an unspecified legal violation and locked up. He was tortured for hours. After the police left him in the cell, he committed suicide. The third incident was that of a 17-year-old boy from Amritsar, Punjab, who was arrested for an alleged theft. He was taken to the police station, where he was tortured ruthlessly, and left in the cell. Shortly after, he took his own life (Neemuchwala, 2014).

The Indian people are getting increasingly infuriated and concerned about extortionary, unlawful arrests, beatings, and torture of innocent persons by the police. Look at an event of 1987 in India, the 1987 Hashimpura massacre. On May 22, 1987, there was Hindu-Muslim riot in Meerut city in Uttar Pradesh. Nineteen members of the Provincial Armed Constabulary (PAC), allegedly, arrested 42 Muslim youths from the Hashimpura area of the city, drove them in a truck to the outskirts of the city near Murad Nagar in Ghaziadad district, shot and killed them, and dumped their bodies into a canal. A few days later, it was alleged, their dead bodies were found floating on the canal. Similar massacres occurred in 1999 (Tirunelveli massacre), 2003 (the Muthanga killings), and 2011 (the Forbesganj firing, etc.) (*Frontline* 1999; *The Hindu*, 2003; and *Human Rights Watch*, 1999).

The government of India has the duty to reform their colonial police force system. The government calls their police force "National Police Service" (NPS), but they are not doing the type of service the Indian people expect. The India police are still the colonial police force that created it. They violate the law with impunity on behalf of the state of India. Undeniably, the Indian National Police Service beat their suspected civilians black and blue before arresting them, and that is a violation of law.

Japanese police system is a direct contrast to the Indian armed constabulary force. Japanese do not see any reason why a police officer, who is employed to keep the peace, should carry firearms up and down the streets. But their advancements in the manufacturing industry, with the concomitant upsurge of urbanization and immigration, have influenced the prior customary order. Despite all that, Japan has fewer cases of police killings and police brutality than other industrialized nations. And Japan is among the top ten most populous countries of the world.

Japan is not a high crime nation. In effect, whenever a major crime is committed, it disturbs the collective conscience of the people. Not unexpectedly, when a crime is committed and the offender identified, the arrest process can be very traumatizing to the suspect. The police can ruffle the suspect with anger and indignation. To a Western observer, that is brutal. If you are a suspect in Japan and arrested, just like in India, you are already guilty before trial. Do not wait for America's "Miranda doctrine." You are in great trouble. This is how an American musician who was arrested by the police in Tokyo, Japan, described it: "Being arrested is not terribly different from being captured by an enemy force in a military engagement and by that I mean you're fucked" (GaijinAss, 2011).

Among all industrialized countries of the world, Japan has both the lowest murder rate and the lowest overall crime rate. For instance, it is unthinkable for any man to rape a woman in Japan. Wherever such a crime occurred, usually committed by a foreigner, the whole country seemed to be at a standstill. Therefore, if you are arrested in Japan for a crime, not only the police but the whole of the criminal justice system and the masses at large conclude that you are guilty *ab initio* and even before trial begins.

Japan is an industrialized country with an average of two murders by firearms a year. Ownership of firearms is illegal. But one can get a license to own a hunting gun and recreation swords after a whole-day training and passing a very difficult written test. A country of over 127 million people was petrified, when they found out that they had 11 (eleven) murders in one year. In fact, in 1995, when, unknown to Japan, some Chinese "Triad"-organized crime syndicate infiltrated into the west side of the country and committed 25 murders, it prompted inviting 42 experts of the International Police Executive Symposium (IPES) in 1996 to Kanagawa University School of Law, Yokohama, Japan, to find out why there had been 25 murders in one year, and what to do about it. It was a 10-day symposium held partly at Hakoni, Japan, and partly at Yokohama Campus of the University.[18]

The humane and communal method the Japanese use to run their prisons attests to their fervent search for a safe society (Johnson, 2000a, 2000b).

Police brutality is not an issue among the citizens of Japan. The masses and the police are like a team in law enforcement. The Japanese have an ideal police-community relation. The people are intimate with the police. The Japanese police, unlike those in India, Nigeria, Russia, and Mexico, do not want the people to bribe them. That does not mean that there are no deviant police officers among the Japan National Police Agency, because in very 12, there must be a Judas. But the malfeasances of a few police officers are often intra-institutional deviances. And part of the reason the Japanese government has very few law enforcement crimes to deal with is because the National Police Agency is not under the control of the government and the politicians. Instead, the Japanese National Police Agency is under the control of the National Public Safety Commission.

There is an important cultural factor that controls the Japanese and the National Police Agency, and that is the Japanese have altruistic suicide. This means, in Japanese culture, if anyone commits an act that they know is a slur on the reputation of their families, they will immediately commit suicide. This cultural demand has a profound deterrent effect on Japanese and police deviance.

State Crimes of Government in Africa

Listed in this section are the government crimes of law enforcement in Nigeria, South Africa, and Egypt. Nigeria, South Africa, and Egypt are the largest economies in Africa in that order. Nigeria's 2014 GDP is valued at 509 billion dollars, South Africa 350 billion dollars, and Egypt 271 billion dollars.[19] As all countries in Africa, except Ethiopia, were under colonial law and control, choosing these three countries can give us a good picture of law enforcement deviances in other nations of Africa.

To start with Nigeria, it has been consistently shown that one in every five Africans is a Nigerian. That shows how populous Nigeria is as a country. In addition, Nigeria has a little over 250 ethnic groups with distinct languages. This multiple ethnic structure contributes to the problem of law enforcement.

There is no due process of law in the Nigerian Police Force (NPF) law enforcement operations. This is not unique to Nigeria. It is the same in all former colonial dependencies in Africa. But on the exit of colonial dictatorship and ruthless enforcement of their alien laws, the post-independence Nigerian Police Force added more torturous methods of enforcing the law. To understand how colonial law enforcement influenced post-independence law enforcement in Nigeria, here is one incident that happened in Nigeria in 1948 under the British colonial regime.

My father was in a magistrate's court in Orlu (Eastern Nigeria) for a civil case. The magistrate was a British District Officer (popularly described as "D-O") holding in Orlu, the headquarters of Orlu Division. The session was very quiet, as if people were standing in a cemetery. In that context, my father coughed, and the magistrate ordered the police to arrest my father, and ordered the police to collect £5 (five pounds British sterling) immediately. My father was arrested and taken to a police station nearby. He was one of the few men at that period who could enter their bedrooms and bring out £20 (twenty) or more pounds without prior notice. He was a certified "moneylender." Most of the noncommissioned policemen at the Orlu Police Station knew him. Before they put him in a temporary police cell room, they allowed him to send for his daughter who was an elementary school teacher from 1936–1946, who was living with her husband 10 km away in Umuna, Orlu. In less than an hour after his arrest, the £5 was given to the police, my father was released, and he went back to the court. The story of fining a man £5, because he coughed in a colonial magistrate's court spread throughout Orlu Division and Owerri Province like a new song. Undeniably, that was one of the ugly ways the British colonial administration made their money in Nigeria, and the nature of justice system they gave to Nigeria.

The post-independence Nigerian police did not waste any time in applying what they learned from their colonial masters. Corruption is part of the justice system in all former colonial regimes in Africa and beyond. The multiethnicity, poverty, and greed contributed to the wholesale corruption that engulfed the Nigerian Police Force and the government.

The Nigerian police mount roadblocks under the camouflage of checking vehicles for road worthiness. But the road blocks are purely money collection points. For instance, if they find out in the process of checking your vehicle that you have no driver's license or that you are driving with an expired license, or that you have no auto-insurance, or not having all of the above, once you give them a substantial amount of money on the spot, you are free to go. The money they collected at the check points, they share with their senior officers at their district headquarters.

Sometimes, five or six policemen in a patrol car stop at a bus stop and arrest any number of young women there and accuse them of prostitution. They take them to the police station. Those women will not be released until they bribe the policemen. Some of them are raped ever before the bribe is taken. The writer has studied the Nigerian police operations for more than 30 years. The Nigerian police service is "cash and carry." That is, you pay them and then they do the service that you ask to be done.

Commercial vehicle drivers who have all the particulars of their vehicles and their drivers' licenses, and, in effect, refuse to tip the police, may be beaten up by the police until they pay some money. Sometimes the highway police team may seize the vehicle particulars of a private car owner and his driver's license under pretense that there is something they want to investigate. In actuality, there is nothing to investigate. If the car owner gives them some money, they set him free. These Nigerian policemen can stop any private car or commercial vehicle at any point in the street and tell the driver that they want to check the trunk of his vehicle. If there is nothing illegal in the trunk, the good policeman may let him go. But the criminal policeman can cook up any false allegation to get a bribe. From 1993 to 2006, the writer visited Nigeria eight times. On four of the occasions, he was frustrated by the Nigerian police at highway checkpoints and street checkpoints. In a distance of 85 km, he was stopped at three different points.

The civilians who are in a great deal of trouble in Nigeria are those suspected of legal violations or those caught in the act. Suspects who have experienced the torture prefer to die than go through the Nigeria police torture a second time. The Nigerian police brutality is among the top ten in the world. They use torture to extract a confession from the suspect. It is very hard for a compassionate person to watch the Nigerian police beat a suspect with a horse whip. Worst of all, if a suspect is put under detention, he is forgotten. The jail is overcrowded, by over 200% of its capacity.

The Nigerian Police Force (NPF) was functionally destroyed by 33 years of military rule. The military ignored the NPF. Sometimes the Nigerian police were not paid for six months. To survive, the police resorted to taking bribes. In their occupational frustration, they vent their anger on both offenders and nonoffenders.

The most painful part of the Nigerian police operation is the extrajudicial killing of suspects with impunity. Nobody questions the police for the killing. With the emergence of Boko Haram (the Islamic terrorist gang), anybody suspected of being a member of the gang is killed without trial. Consequently, many innocent youths have been killed by the Nigerian police. The Nigerian government is supposed to control the police, but it does not do so. The reason is because the politicians use the police to rig elections (Gambrell, 2010).

The Nigerian government is corrupt. In effect, the politicians and top civil servants need the police to carry out their corrupt activities and to cover up their illegal operations. Consequently, the Nigerian police are free to commit their own crimes with impunity. There is virtually no limit to what the Nigerian police can do to get bribes from the people they are supposed to protect. One can be sure of protection, provided a bribe is paid. That is called "cash and carry."

Because nobody questions the police for killing a suspect, there is no record of persons killed by police in Nigeria. But Boko Haram terrorists have killed some Nigerian policemen. It is because of the corruption of the Nigerian government and the police that Boko Haram survives.

The Nigerian Police Force has developed a systematic culture of brutality in law enforcement. It has become a culture in the police agency, and every Nigerian knows it for a fact. A report by Amnesty International about the Nigerian police system of law enforcement was captioned, "Welcome to Hell Fire: Torture and Other Ill-Treatment in Nigeria." The report delineated the horrors perpetrated in police stations throughout the country: "shooting in the leg, foot or hand; extracting teeth, fingernails, or toenails; water torture or rape" (Maja-Pearce, 2014).

There are some very good police officers in Nigeria, but they are operating in a predatory state, where the government operates like an organized crime syndicate.

The second economically powerful country in Africa the writer wants to discuss is South Africa and its crimes of law enforcement. The degree and nature of police brutality is such that it is as if police brutality was "born and raised" in South Africa. The process of colonizing South Africa and its environs by the Dutch and later the English in the 18th century was fraught with wars and conflicts unfathomable in any other part of the African continent. As a result, the South Africa of the 20th and the 21st centuries could not shelve off the yoke of a police state. Understandably, South Africa's congenital "police state" was exacerbated by a social, economic, and political system of apartheid introduced in the country in 1948. Under the apartheid system of government, by which the white minority ethnic group took over the government and usurped all powers, the police are needed, and the police had to be a paramilitary force. That is the nature of South African police today.

Under the apartheid system of government from 1948 to 1994, black people of South Africa were moved like sheep and cattle from one uninhabitable location to another (The Last Grave at Dimbaza, Chapter 3). South African police brutality under apartheid was a normative standard for the white minority government.

The eclipse of apartheid in 1994 did not end South African police brutality. Instead, the process of integration ignited more forms of police brutality than ever before. The return of self-exiled South African men, women, and the young, coupled with the high degree of immigration of youths from neighboring African countries, created extra social control problems for the South African police. And, *ab initio*, "there is no love lost" between the South African Police Services (SAPS) and the masses. Consequently, the use of violence by the South African police to enforce the law was virtually inevitable.

Over the years, whenever South African coal miners or other workers went on strike, many strikers were killed. For instance, on August 16, 2012, the South African police shot and killed 44 miners and injured 78 of them, when the Markiana miners went on strike against their employer, Lonmin Platinum (McClenaghan, 2012; Poplak, 2012; Laing, 2012).

Reports of South African police brutality have skyrocketed by 313% in 10 years. Unmistakably, the reports show that only 1 in 100 cases of fetal and nonfetal South African police brutality that reached the courts ever led to a conviction (Davis, 2014). One can see again and again that a behavior that is complimented is more likely to be repeated than a behavior that is punished (Skinner, 1948). That is what is seen in South African police behavior, and the behavior of police everywhere, especially Nigeria, Mexico, Brazil, Argentina, Turkey, and so forth.

The degree of police brutality in South Africa is so high and rampant that the local media noted that the people of South Africa are gripped with "fear of both criminals and police officers" (Oneale, 2014).

Unlike the Nigerian government, the South African government settles some cases of police brutality totaling up to 14.8 billion rand (£920 million) in 2 years (Oneale, 2014).

In recent years, both Nigerian and South Africa have charged some police officers of legal violations and convicted and incarcerated them. But no amount of police incarceration in Nigeria and South Africa will stop both countries' police culture of use of excessive force in law enforcement.

Egypt is the last country of investigation in Africa for the crimes of law enforcement. From Egypt's colonial days through the regimes of Abdul Nasser, Anwar Sadat, Mubarak, to the Muslim Brotherhood regimes of President Mohammed Morsi, police use of excessive force

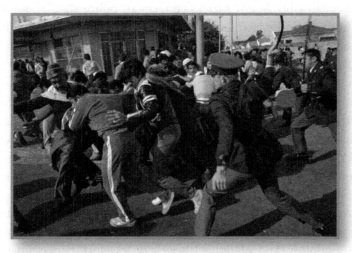

Figure 7.4 South African police quelling a demonstration
© David Turnley/Corbis

against civilians has been a perverted routine. In Egypt, as in Nigeria, Mexico, and Brazil, there is no police accountability. They operate with impunity, because the government is behind them.

Long before the 2011 revolution that ended President Hosni Mubarak's regime, the use of torture to extract confessions from common criminals or teach a lesson to demonstrators, political dissidents, and prisoners was a normative order of police operations in Egypt (Harding, 2011). Like their counterparts in Nigeria and Brazil, Egyptian police frequently carried out extrajudicial killing of armed robbers, burglars, and other serious offense perpetrators with impunity.

Police brutality in Egypt got worse after the democratically elected President of Egypt, Mohammed Morsi, was forced out of office and jailed by the military. The Egyptian police beat, kick, and shoot individuals and groups from streets to squares at random. From the 2011 revolution to after the military overthrow of President Mohammed Morsi, the police killings ranged from 638 (595 civilians and 43 policemen) reported by the Egyptian Health Ministry and 817 reported by Human Rights Watch to 2,600 people reported by the Muslim Brotherhood and the National Coalition for Supporting Legitimacy (NCLS) (Mohsen, 2013; Kirkpatrick, 2013a).

Police brutality in Egypt is exacerbated by the fact that Egypt is an Islamic state which does not tolerate any form of dissent. Use of the police and other security forces to violently put down opposition to government policy, laws, and regulations is the method of governance in all predominantly Islamic countries, such as Sudan, Libya, Algeria, Niger, Morocco, Rwanda, Burundi, Chad, Cameroon, Malaysia, Burma (Myanmar), and Pakistan.

Egypt, like all other Islamic states, is profoundly influenced by Sharia Law in spite of its English legal system experience. And Sharia law prescribes violence in its enforcement.

In the final analysis, police brutality (including murder and assault) and all of the other crimes of law enforcement officers such as rape, embezzlement, drug smuggling, trafficking in human beings, robbery, burglary, and stealing obliterate the sanctity of the state, and the relevance of the theory of "social contract." Undeniably, the crimes of police officers in any country are the failures of the government (state). In addition, where there is a lack of police accountability, the government has inherently failed its people, and the leaders of such a regime should leave the government.

Crimes of Government Omission in Politics, Business, and Professions

The responsibility of the state to protect the lives and property of its members adduced in the social contract theory warrants the state to ensure the lives of its members, protect them from political nonfeasance, business/corporate crimes, and crimes by professionals. These three areas of human activities are pivotal to a society's survival. Unfortunately, many governments, all over the world, are shackled by greed, interest groups, and self-interest to the point that, virtually, these three areas are not adequately controlled, and, in fact, in some countries are not controlled at all. The laws may be there to control them, but the laws are not enforced. When laws are made but are not enforced, or bribes are taken in the process of trying to enforce the laws, that situation leads to Emile Durkheim's anomie or normlessness.

When actors in various enterprises are aware that laws controlling their activities are not going to be enforced, or that agencies who are commissioned to enforce those laws are willing to take bribes in lieu of enforcing the laws, then they will go ahead and violate the laws for as long as violating the laws is more profitable than the penalty for the violation. This is what is happening in both developed and developing countries.

In this section, the writer presents government omissions to act in protecting the masses in political issues, business or corporate deviances, and professional crimes.

In the political arena, the government makes policies assumed to be for the interest of the masses. However, the government leaders are often ruled by self-interest, greed, and power mongering to the point that they fail to develop and invest in electoral districts or states that do not vote for them in an election, or states or regions that stand in active opposition to the government. Such omissions have been seen in President Robert Mugabe's neglect of the Ndebele region in Zimbabwe, because of his "nemesis," (Joshua Nkoumo), the founder of the Zimbabwe African People's Union (ZAPU) opposition party; President Ahmadu Ahidjo's neglect of West Cameroon because of fear of the astute business and political acumen of the Bamileke people of that region; the failure to rebuild the Oji River Power Station in Eastern Nigeria by Presidents Yakubu Gowon, Murtala Mohammed, Olusegun Obasanjo, and Ibrahim Babangida, because they believed that the Oji River Power Station, which was supplying electricity to the whole of Eastern Nigeria, and was deliberately destroyed by the federal forces during the Nigerian Civil War, would economically empower the Igbo ethnic group, and make them recover from the ravages of the war quicker than they would appreciate; and in the ethnic politics in the Newly Independents States of the former Soviet Union. Also, the neglect and slowness in responding to Hurricane Katrina disaster by President W. Bush administration in the United States was seen as both ethnic and political nonfeasance (Thompson, 2008; McQuaid, Marshall, & Schleifstein, 2005).

In government crimes of omission to act where it has a duty to do so, the writer finds government's nonchalant attitude in some countries toward ignoring deliberate exclusions of some segments of the country in voter registration, because the persons being excluded are not likely to vote for the political party in power. They execute this exclusionary strategy by requiring unconscionable qualifications that some people in the targeted area do not have with them. This strategy can be found in many Third World countries, and sometimes in advanced economies.

Furthermore, some governments refuse to prevent and control electoral fraud, knowing that fraudsters are working for them. Similarly, pro-government obstructionist thugs' attempts to prevent supporters of the opposition party from voting are ignored by the government.

In addition, there are occasions when the government in power refuses to take steps to prevent rigging in an election, when they knew that the rigging would be in their favor (Ansari, 2013). This rigging of elections and election vandalism are characteristics of elections in Third World countries. Undeniably, some governments carry out illegal electoral practices with intimidation and impunity.

In the developing countries of Asia, Africa, and the Middle East, multinational corporations and their subsidiaries have a free ride in their deviance and criminal practices. This is because the leaders of those countries accept huge amounts in bribes. Consequently, nobody is interested in checking for the harmful practices of the corporations. Clinard and Yeager (1980) found that corporations engage in a wide range of violations of law in the areas of administrative violations, environmental violations, financial violations, labor violations, manufacturing violations, and unfair trade practices. In those developing countries, the governments ignore such violations because they are heavily bribed to keep quiet. And the victims are the masses.

Even in advanced economies like France, the United States, Great Britain, and Germany, the corporations are not strictly controlled, because some government officials have financial interests in some corporations, and some officials claim that very strict control would slow down productivity and profitability. In effect, many corporations have a free ride in the violation of law. For instance, in the United States, Clinard and Yearger (1979) found that only "1.5 percent of all federal enforcement efforts directed at corporations in 1975 and 1976 produced a conviction of a corporate officer." Clinard and Yeager's findings show that very few corporations are monitored. In those monitored, many violations are detected, very few are indicted, and very few are convicted. And those convicted very often spend less than 30 days in jail (Clinard & Yeager, 2002). If the U.S. Government finds it hard to control the crimes of corporations, you can imagine what is happening in Third World countries and small developing countries of Europe.

In many countries, both advanced and developing economies, governments ignore false advertising. In developing countries, nobody officially complains; if you do, it goes nowhere, so why waste your time writing about it. In advanced countries, there has to be an avalanche of complaints to many departments of the government before the company making the false advertising is questioned. In the United States, investigative journalists save the day for the masses, when complaints about false advertising reach their ears.

Furthermore, in both developed and developing countries, the governments systematically ignore informing their people about the dangerousness of a by-product of a manufacturing company being established in their neighborhoods until some people fall sick or die of the fatal by-products of the company. Most of the time, the people in the neighborhood or country may never know.

The most serious failure or omission of governments, world-wide, is a gross inaction in some countries and inadequate action in others about control of offshore banking. An offshore bank is a bank located outside the territorial integrity of the country of the depositor. Offshore banks are tax havens. In some cases, there is very low tax requirement. The depositor has wonderful financial and even legal advantages.

You are meticulously protecting your assets, when you have them offshore through a business instrument in a foreign jurisdiction with more lucrative business and tax laws. An offshore bank account is outside the reach of your creditors and court judgments against you.

Where do big organized crime syndicates and heavy transnational drug smugglers hide their million and billions? They are in offshore banks. Crooked politicians and top crooked civil servants who took millions of dollars in bribes from contractors, where do they put the money so that national strategic intelligence law enforcement agencies like the U.S. FBI, British Scotland Yard, MI6, Canadian SIU, German BND, or Italian AISIS will not find it? In the freezer of your refrigerator or under the floor of your toilet? No, those locations are the most likely locations an intelligence agency will go to when they come to your house or hotel to investigate your financial manipulations. The offshore bank is the answer.

Here is another important question. Why is it that most countries don't care to find a way out in controlling offshore bank deposits? And a great complicated country like the United States did not seriously start to investigate offshore banking until the 1990s? The answer is simple for a seasoned political criminologist.

The unexpected illegal money of top politicians and top civil servants, and the excess profits from foreign operations of multinational corporations and their agents in the governments, all over the world, are hidden in offshore banks located in many island countries around the world. So why would any government come up with a meaningful legislation to crush offshore banking, which is where their retirement paradises are based? No man will destroy a mansion he built for himself, when he cannot afford an alternative. The United States has been negotiating with Swiss banks (UBS) to reveal names of Americans who have accounts in their banks. But that is just a tip of the iceberg. Offshore bank is money laundering underground. You can't catch them all. Multinational corporations scattered their billions of dollars all over the offshore banks. For you to see the picture of the enormousness and clandestine nature of offshore banks, these are the places where they are located: Bahamas; British Virgin Islands, Cayman Islands; Cook Islands; Barbados; Belize; Antigua and Barbuda; Channel Islands (Jersey, Guernsey, Alderney, Sark, and Hern); Bermuda; Dominica; Cyprus; Ghana; Curacao; Labuan Territory; Malaysia; Liechtenstein; Isle of Man; Malta; Luxembourg; Mauritius; Macau; Monaco; Montserrat; Nauru; New York; Panama; Singapore; Switzerland; Seychelles; Turks and Caicos Islands; Saint Kitts and Nevis; and so forth.

Other than New York, Ghana, and Switzerland, most of the offshore banks are located in small island states in the Atlantic, Indian, and Pacific Oceans. Most of the islands like Seychelles, Montserrat, Bermuda, Saint Kitts and Nevis, Turks and Caicos Islands, Cayman Islands have populations in 2013 ranging as small as 5,900 (Montserrat) to as high as 1,261,208 (Mauritius). Some of them are autonomous independent states, while others are dependencies or overseas territories of the United Kingdom. Some have per capita income higher than those of the United States, Japan, or United Kingdom (Bermuda $85,747; Macau $88,700; United States $52,800; United Kingdom $37,300, and Japan $37,100).

The question one needs to ask is who owns these offshore banks? Unmistakably, offshore banking system, in the main, is a colonial government's conspiracy with the leaders of their former dependencies. Switzerland, New York, Monaco, and Liechtenstein may be exceptions, but all of the other offshore banking centers are small island colonies and peninsulars founded by colonial masters. Some very rich individuals and multinational corporations, in the process of time, joined in the ownership. Rich and poor countries' top government leaders, individual multimillionaires and billionaires, and multinational corporations dump their hidden money from taxation in offshore banks. Economic and financial experts strongly assert that as much as half the world's capital flows through offshore banks around the world. Those offshore banking centers that are tax havens for their clients are inhabited by only 1.2% of the world's population, but holds 26% of the world's wealth, including 31% of the net profits of the U.S. multinational corporations (Komisar, 2001). To further substantiate, according to *The Guardian* (UK) (2012), "an estimated £13–20 trillion is hoarded away in offshore accounts."[21]

Also, experts argue that assuming the lower estimate of £13 trillion on deposit in offshore accounts earn an average of 3% a year in income for their owners and taxable at 30%, the offshore deposits would generate £121 billion in tax revenues[22] (*The Guardian*). But nobody pays any tax on those.

The leaders of the governments of developing countries have no interest in talking about offshore banks. It is a secret they keep to themselves. It is not a social problem to them, because they are the offenders. For the far advanced economies like the United States, Great Britain, Russia, France, Germany, China, and Australia they try to wake up to talk about offshore banking recently because of attacks from the International Consortium of Investigative Journalists (ICIJ). The ICIJ collaborated with reports around the world and came up with a number of investigative reports that ICIJ called "The Global Muckraker" (ICIJ, 2013). The ICIJ found 2.5 million secret records about offshore assets of people from 170 countries and territories out of the 195 countries and territories of the world. The investigation yielded what ICIJ called "Offshore Leaks," which disclosed 130,000 offshore accounts in April 2013. Some powerful governments' attempts to try to control offshore banking are just a mystification of the truth, because they run with the hare and hunt with the hounds.

In the professions, there is virtually no control of malpractices of medical doctors, dentists, accountants, engineers, nurses, contractors, civil servants, and others in Third World countries. Any laws enacted to control these professionals are nullified by corruption. In far advanced countries, some do not have well-trained agencies to monitor the deviant acts of some professionals. For those countries, it is their failure. The masses should be protected from the avariciousness of some professionals.

State Negligence

The state emerged, it not only had to protect the lives and property of its members but it also had an inherent responsibility to perform some essential services to its people. Every country needs food, water, shelter, and roads. It is incumbent upon a country to provide these basic essential needs for its people's survival.

Some countries like Nigeria, Sudan, Chad, and Sierra Leone, do not care about the quality of water available to its members. Most of their people still drink stream or river water that is highly polluted. In effect, dysentery kills many children every year in those countries.

Good sanitation rules and principles save many lives in any country where they are applied. In other words, there is a strong positive correlation between good sanitation and high life expectancy. Countries like Sierra Leone (38), Chad (51), Democratic Republic of Congo (49.5), Central Africa Republic (48.5) and Nigerian (53), have very low overall life expectancy by WHO 2012 estimates. In fact, 29 countries with overall life expectancy less than 60 years come from Africa. To my estimation, the major cause of low life expectancy in those African countries is poor sanitation. There are mountains of garbage heaped by the sides of the streets in Nigerian cities, and empty cans, bottles, and orange and banana peels left on the street-sides. Airborne diseases, germinating from the garbage, kill many people. It is the responsibility of every government to provide garbage disposal mechanisms, and make enforceable rules and regulations about refuse disposal.

Some Third World countries still dispose of their human excreta in open grounds in the woods, while the government could provide pit-latrines in the rural towns and toilet facilities in the urban centers. Bucket latrines should be eliminated in countries like Nigeria, but they are still found in some small cities. Good sanitary conditions are affordable to the Third World countries, but greed, corruption, ignorance, and setting poor priorities destroy the well-being of the masses.

As a result of corruption, discrimination, racism, and poor management, some governments will not provide roads, bridges, or fast access-roads to some parts of their countries. Some of these countries have the means to provide the roads and bridges, but the factors mentioned above prevent them from executing their responsibilities. In countries in Africa, the reasons for not providing the necessary roads, bridges, good water systems, and electricity supply are corruption and tribalism. Tribalism is almost like racism. As tribes or ethnic groups occupy a particular area of the country as their base of existence, a tribal leader as a head of state may not like to provide the needed roads and bridges that are very seriously needed by the people of a tribe, that he hates, or his own tribe hates to see prosper. When a government discriminates against some ethnic groups in the country, in rendering services, that is a serious deviance and criminal.

Civil Service Pilferage

In some governments, the tax payers lose a lot of money to top civil servants who pay salaries to ghost employees. On the payroll list, which is submitted to their department's accountant are names of persons who do not exist. This type of crime is organized in the government department involving three key figures: the chief executive officer of the department, the chief accountant of the department, and the government auditor. This type of pilferage occurs in countries where corruption is endemic, for example, Nigeria, Mexico, Russia, Zimbabwe, and so forth.

The head of state may know about this type of corruption, but will not take action to control it. Also, while civil servants are supposed to turn in receipts of their expenses when they travel on official duty, nobody checks whether the receipts are genuine or not, because the boss who should check the authenticity of the receipts is doing the same whenever he travels. In effect, stealing from the state (the people) becomes a norm and a culture. This is a common practice in most of the Third World countries. The government official who traveled on official duty to another city might have spent two, three, or four nights in a friend's or relative's house, but he will turn in receipts from a hotel that will receive a bribe and issue him such a receipt. Alternatively, he lodged in a hotel but made the hotel give him a receipt priced higher than what he actually paid. This is how Third World countries continue to be poor states. The Third World governments are aware of the corrupt practices but refuse to design mechanisms for their control.

Review Questions

1. What is natural liberty?
2. What is meant by "crimes of law enforcement"?
3. In the National Opinion Research Center (NORC)'s Baltimore Survey (1966) and Ebbe's (1977) Western Michigan University Survey, "Planned killing of a policeman" was rated "the most serious crime" for anybody to commit. Why is it the most serious offense among "Part 1 and Part 2 Crimes" of the FBI's Uniform Crime Reports?
4. What is police brutality? Why is the state liable in police brutality cases?
5. Which five states in the United States have the highest "justifiable homicides by police" from 2010 to 2014?
6. What is meant by "Russian criminal oligarchy"?
7. Describe in detail the crimes of law enforcement in the following countries: India, Nigeria, Argentina, Mexico, Venezuela, and Chile.
8. What is the "Last Grave at Dimbaza"? What country is connected with it? What is apartheid?
9. How can a state omission to act be a crime?
10. What is Hanapepe massacre?

Notes

1. The killing of a felon by a law enforcement officer in the line of duty.

2. "First Fatal Police Shooting Since 2011 Report in London." (http://www.slate.com/blogs/the_slatest/2014/09/05 Slate.com). Accessed February 21, 2015.

3. "Man shot by police outside Guildford Cathedral lawfully killed," (http://www.telegraph.co.uk/news/uknews/law_and_order/6067562/Man-shot-by-police-outside-Guildford-Cathedral-lawfully-killed.html), *The Telegraph* (newspaper article). Accessed February 21, 2015.

4. According to Toronto *Globe and Mail*, "He spent 10 hours frustrated by airport bureaucracy. Just 24 seconds later, police shot him with tasers," Toronto: *The Globe and Mail*, October 26, 2007. See http://www.theglobeandmail.com/servlet/story/RTGA.20071025.wtaser1026/BNStory/National/home. Accessed February 25, 2015.

5. See "France_Police_Environmental_Demo." Georges Gobet/AFP/Getty Images, November 8, 2014. (http://www.gettyimages.com/search/2/im). Accessed February 25, 2015.

6. Lifetime sentence means life imprisonment. A life imprisonment in Greek penal code does not mean that the person will remain in prison until he dies. Instead, a life imprisonment in Greek law means that the offender is eligible for parole after serving 16 years. If the prisoner received more than one life sentence, they can become eligible for parole after serving 20 years. Parole is not compulsory or required by law. If parole is rejected, the prisoner can reapply every 2 years.

7. See "Turkish Police Brutality" (http://tumblr.com/register/follow/turkishpolicebrutality). Accessed February 26, 2015.

8. See *The Economist*, "Tear Gas as a Dangerous Weapon." (http://www.economist.com/blogs/charlemgne/2013/07/aftermath_unrest_turkey). Accessed February 26, 2015.

9. See "Missing Mexico Teachers: Protests Organized by union Quashed in Violent Police Crackdown," (http://www.huffingtonpost.come/2011/08/1). Accessed February 26, 2015.

10. See "Prosperous Chile's Troubling Indigenous Uprising," *Time Magazine*, December 12, 2009.

11. See "Buenos Aires Tragedy," (http://paperspast.natlib.govt.nz/cgi-bin/paperspast?a=d&d=EP19091116.2.64). Evening Post, November 16, 1909, p. 7.

12. Also see http://www2.forumseguranca.org.br/novo/storage/download/anuario2013.pdf. Accessed February 27, 2015.

13. Also see http://www.ibtimes.com/candelaria_church_massacre_brazil_marks_20th_ anniversary_police_murders_homeless_street_children. Accessed February 27, 2015.

14. See "Insight Crime Analysis." http://www.insighterme.org/news_analysis/why_do_ brazilian_police_kill. Also see http://www.hrw.org/news/2009/12/08/brazil/curb-police-violence-rio-s-o-paolo. Accessed February 27, 2015.

15. See also http://www.insightcrime.org/new-analysis/why-do-brazilian-police-kill. Accessed February 27, 2015.

16. "Police probe fatal shooting of 21-year-old by officers" (http://www.scmp.com/news/ hong-kong/article/1504833/knife-wielding-man-who-threaten-wife-and-security-guards-shot-dead?pape=all), South China Morning Post. Accessed February 28, 2015.

17. "Shootings rise after China gives its police guns," (http://bigstory.ap.org/article/ shootings-rise-after-china-gives-its-police-guns), Associated Press. Accessed February 28, 2015.

18. I was the Coordinator of the November–December 1996 International Police Executive Symposium (IPES) held in Hakoni and Yokohama, Japan, Campuses of Kanagawa University. I presented "Organized Crime in Africa," and was detailed at the symposium to deliver a short lecture titled: "Organized Crime and Politics in Contemporary Society" to 300 Kanagawa University School of Law students and their faculty.

19. See "Top 10 Largest Economies in Africa." (http://answersafrica.com/largest-economies/). Answers Africa. Accessed February 28, 2015.

20. The per capita income figures of the countries are based on IMF Data for 2013 GDP.

21. See *The Guardian* (UK), July 21, 2012, "£13tn: Hoard Hidden from Taxman by Global Elite," (http://www.guardian.co.uk/business/2012/jul/21/global-elite-tax-offshore-economy). Accessed March 6, 2015.

22. Ibid.

State Negligence and Environmental Pollution Deviances: Domestic and International

The state has an inherent duty to preserve the environment. A clean environment is a healthy environment. Raising children in a clean environment is an insurance to longevity of subsequent generations. The low life expectancy recorded in most developing countries is a result of very unhealthy environments. The five major factors that make for high life expectancy are (1) increased food supplies and distribution, (2) better nutrition, (3) improvements in medical and public health technology (such as immunizations and antibiotics), (4) improved sanitation and personal hygiene, and (5) safer water supplies.

Among the five factors that increase life expectancy of a country, the last two are grossly lacking in Third World countries and other developing countries. It is incumbent upon the state to provide good water supply and lead the people in sanitary practices by providing garbage disposal mechanisms, making sound sanitary rules and regulations, and ensuring sanitary facilities in every urban residence. Many countries in South and Central America, Asia, and Africa are deviants in their neglect of sanitary policies and their enforcement. Undeniably, good water supply and excellent sanitary conditions make for good environment, and vice versa.

The countries with very high infant mortality rates are the ones with unsafe water supply and very poor sanitary conditions. Infant mortality rate refers to the number of babies out of 1,000 born who die before their first birthday. In countries with poor water supply or where 60% or more of the residents still drink and cook with stream (creek) or river water, and have

Table 8.1 Infant Mortality Rates per 1,000 Births in Selected Developed and Developing Countries

Developed countries	Rates	Developing countries	Rates
Australia	4.49	Afghanistan	187.5
Canada	4.78	Angola	81.75
China	7.20	Burkina Faso	78.30
Germany	3.48	Central Africa Republic	94.05
Italy	3.33	Chad	91.94
Russia	7.19	Democratic Republic of Congo	74.87
Spain	3.35	Mali	106.49
Switzerland	3.8	Niger	87.98
United Kingdom	4.5	Nigeria	72.97
United States	5.2	Rwanda	61.3

Source: United Nations World Population Prospects: 2013 Estimates.

very poor sanitary conditions, are the countries with very high infant mortality rates. A comparison of infant mortality rates in selected 10 developed countries and 10 developing or Third World countries will shed some light on the effect of poor water supply and poor sanitation on a population.

Table 8.1 shows that among the 10 developed countries, only China and Russia have up to 7.20 and 7.19 infant mortality deaths per 1,000 live births, respectively. All of the others have less than 5.3 per 1,000 live births. Look at developing countries, all of them have above 72.0 deaths per 1,000 live births except Rwanda with 61.3. Six of the 10 developing countries have above 81.0 deaths per 1,000 live births. Unmistakably, poor sanitation and poor water resource management are the major causes of the high infant mortality in developing countries.

State Violation of Fundamental Human Rights of its Citizens

In about 92% of the countries (states) of the world, their governments violate the human rights of the people with impunity. By the social contract theory, every state owes its members provision of the basic needs of man, namely, food, shelter, water, heath care, and security of life and property. It is absolutely a deviant act, and in some cases criminal, if a state fails to provide the above five factors adequately to its members. Undoubtedly, over 92% of the states in the world do not adequately provide those basic needs for their members to survive.

Human rights are natural rights fundamental to every human being irrespective of one's nationality, place of residence, sex, tribal or ethnic origin, language, creed, race, or any other social status. All humans are equally entitled to human rights without discrimination or clannishness. These human rights are adduced to be interrelated, interdependent, and indivisible.[1]

These rights are inherent in human existence. In effect, universal human rights are commonly expressed and guaranteed by law, in the form of treaties, customary international law, general principles, and other sources of international law. In fact, international human rights law explicitly laid down obligations of governments to act in certain ways and desist from certain acts, in order to promote and protect human rights and fundamental freedoms of individuals or groups.[2]

From the standpoint of the United Nations General Assembly, human rights are "universal and inalienable" rights. The principle of universality of human rights is the cornerstone of international human rights law. This principle was pivotal in the Universal Declaration on Human Rights in 1948, and has further been reiterated in many international human rights conventions, declarations, and resolutions. For instance, the 1993 Vienna World Conference on Human Rights emphasized that it is the responsibility of the state to promote and protect all human rights and fundamental freedoms, irrespective of their political, economic, and cultural systems.[3] Undeniably, the United Nations General Assembly's forge of human rights is apropos of the social contract theory.

Understandably, fundamental human right spells "social justice." From the standpoint of American Federation of Labor and Congress of Industrial Organizations (AFL-CIO), social justice is the "fair and proper administration of laws conforming to the natural law that all persons, irrespective of ethnic origin, gender, possessions, race, religion, and so forth are to be treated equally and without prejudice."[4] Furthermore, social justice is "justice in terms of the distribution of wealth, opportunities, and privileges within a society" (Flexner, 2010). In addition, social justice assigns rights and duties to the institutions of society, which warrants individuals to receive the basic benefits and burdens of cooperation (Rawls, 1971). The significant institutions in social justice include education, health care, labor rights, social security, public services, progressive taxation, regulation of markets, fair distribution of wealth, equal opportunity, and absence of social injustice (Paine, 1797; Rawls, 1971). Implicitly, social justice is central to the theory or philosophy of social contract.

State Negation of Universal Health Care

Who would like to live alone in what used to be a city or society? Nobody. Robinson Crusoe did not like it. Things changed for the better for him when Man "Friday" joined him. Think about that, think about being marooned in an uninhabited island. Think about a city left desolate by cholera epidemic, or a city or society debilitated by hunger and disease. None of these is a pretty sight or evokes a wonderful environment. But we have some parts of a country or city decimated by hunger and disease all over the countries of the world, because of the state's neglect and premeditated nonfeasance. Unfortunately, you can find such areas in both developed and developing countries. But countries with Universal Health Care (UHC) system are less deviants in the health care of their citizens than those without Universal Health Care (UHC) systems.

According to an economist, Ghanta (2009), countries with Universal Health Care (UHC) with their year of adoption in parenthesis are Norway (1912), New Zealand (1938), Japan (1938), Germany (1941), Belgium (1945), United Kingdom (1948), Kuwait (1950), Sweden (1955), Bahrain (1957), Brunei (1958), Canada (1966), the Netherlands (1966), Austria (1967), United Arab Emirates (1971), Finland (1972), Slovenia (1972), Denmark (1973), Luxembourg (1973), France (1974), Australia (1975), Ireland (1977), Italy (1978), Portugal (1979), Cyprus (1980), Greece (1983), Spain (1986), South Korea (1988), Iceland (1990), Hong Kong (1993), Singapore (1993), Switzerland (1994), and Israel (1995).

Undeniably, the United States is the only industrialized country without Universal Health Care (UHC) system. Besides, in health care, in general, the United States is ranked dead last compared to the selected 10 industrialized nations (Munro, 2014).

In the United Sates, we have what is called Selective Health Coverage (SHC) instead of Universal Health Care (UHC). Universal health care or universal health coverage is a health-care system which provides health care and financial protection to every citizen of the country. The government implements this through legislation, regulation, and taxation. Legislation and regulation can direct providers what care must be provided to whom, and on what basis. In some countries, government involvement includes directly managing the health-care system, and some countries utilize mixed public-private systems to deliver universal health care (WHO, 2004). In selective health coverage, government does not provide health care to its citizens. Employers are required to provide basic health care for its employees. Unemployed are not insured. Children and other dependents are on their parents' or guardian's insurance, if they are employed. If the dependents' guardians or parents are not employed, they are not insured by government or anybody. Individuals may be on "Medicaid," which is a social health-care program for families and individuals with low income and limited resources. But this "Medicaid" depends on if one is qualified, and it is nowhere close to Universal health-care system.

The Commonwealth Fund (2014), after the 2014 survey on overall health care, ranks 11 industrialized countries as follows:

1. United Kingdom
2. Switzerland
3. Sweden
4. Australia
5. Germany and Netherlands (tied)
6. New Zealand and Norway (tied)

7. France

8. Canada

9. United States (Commonwealthfund.org 2014)

According to Munro (2013), the lack of Universal health Care (UHC) in the United Sates has unwelcomed consequences:

a. The United States is the only country where medical expenses are one of the major factors that causes personal bankruptcies, and sometimes a major leading factor.

b. The United States is the only country where an employer had to consider the cost of health care before making an employment.

c. The United States is the only country where there are 84 million nonelderly Americans are either uninsured or underinsured.

The First Global Symposium on Health System Research (2010) summarized its findings as follows: "Out of 194 countries in the analysis, 75 countries had legislation that provided a mandate for UHC. Of these, a further 58 met access, quality, and outcome criteria for UHC in the years 2006–2008." The U.S. was not among the 58 countries.

The developing countries have a worse health-care picture than developed countries. Most of the developing countries of Africa, Asia, the Middle East, South and Central America, and the Caribbean Islands were colonial dependencies. They inherited their colonial masters' system of health care, which was highly cost-minded. Unfortunately, colonial medical services were urban-based curative care system. The rural towns and villages, which inhabited more than 80% of the population of the countries, were ignored. At the few urban centers, the colonial masters built what they called "General Hospitals." It was accessible to all of the inhabitants of the city. Those who were living 40–50 miles from the city could go to the General hospital for treatment. What was required of the patient was to register at the hospital for a small amount of an affordable fee. But over 75% of the population, at the time (1940s–1960s), either had no transportation or could not afford transportation to the city to see a doctor.

In addition, some people in the rural towns and villages in the 1940s in Nigeria had no idea of a hospital. They relied on traditional medicine. But traditional medicine could not cure all ailments. For instance, in 1946, a 30-year-old man, James Urigwe, could not empty his bowel for 4 days. His parents tried all traditional medicine from traditional medicine men, but none worked. There was no general hospital located within a 50-mile (80-km) radius of their village. The only hospital close to them was Okigwe General Hospital. There were no motorable roads. James had to be taken to Okigwe General Hospital, about 60 miles (96 km) away, on a bicycle. Whatever treatment he was given at the hospital as an out-patient individual did not help. His parents and relatives brought him back the next day. He died two months after he was brought back from the hospital, because he could neither urinate nor empty his bowel for a long time. In 1947, James' younger brother, Godwin Urigwe (27-year-old), died of the same inability to urinate and empty his bowel.

The post-independence states of Africa and Asia are still far behind in universal health care for their citizens. In a recent study titled, "Moving Towards Universal Health Coverage: Health Reforms in Nine Developing Countries in Africa and Asia," the nine countries are Ghana, Rwanda, Nigerian, Mali, Kenya, India, Indonesia, the Philippines, and Vietnam (Eagle, 2012). According to Margaret Chan, Director General of the World Health Organization, "Universal Health Coverage is the single most powerful concept that public health has to offer" (Chan, 2012). The study shows that more than 75% of the Rwandan and Philippine citizens are not enrolled in health insurance programs; Ghana, Vietnam, and Indonesia have 50% of the citizens covered; while Mali, Kenya, India, and Nigeria, at the early stage of the health reform, have less than 20% covered (Eagle, 2012).

The study confirms the writer's assertion, based on his personal knowledge of African countries, that they are still far away from the universal health-care system. Unmistakably, a healthy population makes for high economic productivity. Most of the developing countries have natural resources to provide universal health-care coverage. Their problem is corruption. The money to provide universal health care is siphoned off in criminal conspiracy of overvalued contracts, organized looting of the national treasury, setting salaries of members of the legislature extremely high as in Nigeria, deliberate system of absence of accountability, and so forth. Take, for instance, some Nigerian politicians, ex-military officers, ex-police officers, former judges, present and retired civil servants set up seven- to 10-story buildings that their monthly salaries multiplied by 100 years could not afford to build 25% of the skyscrapers, but nobody will question them about how they got the money. This manifest absence of accountability is endemic in all former colonial dependencies of African and Asian developing countries.

Failure by any country in this 21st century to provide universal health care for its citizens is a very serious deviance. This is because the failure by any developed or developing country to provide universal health care is a result of greed, hatred of the poor, primitive accumulation or Third World pathologies, and the arrogance of power.

Poverty is like a disease that can be cured. If a disease can be cured, and nothing is being done about it, then it is going to proliferate. Undeniably, that is the nature of poverty. Poverty is created by society. Most capitalist societies believe that any attempt to eliminate poverty creates socialism or communism. But this is not true. Starting with developed countries, some far advanced countries or developed economies try to manage the poor instead of helping them get out of poverty level. For instance, giving the poor food stamps or money to buy food in the United Kingdom, Medicaid, disability money, housing allowance in the United Kingdom, and Section 8 Voucher in the United States are all managing the poor. Those programs cannot get them out of poverty. Those programs perpetuate poverty. Not only perpetuating poverty of the existing adults, those poor adults raise children who become poor persons in future. Sociologists correctly believe that behavior is learned. It is learned through constant communication with relatives and friends (Sutherland, 1947). Therefore, children learn to stay idle like their parent or parents who stay home every day doing nothing just waiting for welfare check every month.

Poverty cannot be completely eliminated, because it is a cultural universal. But poverty can be reduced to the minimum. Instead of managing poverty, as obtained in some developed economies, the poor who are under the age of 65 should be given free vocational education to get them out of welfare. Some incentives should be given to them to start vocational schools. If you continue to give more to somebody every month to buy whatever he or she wants to keep body and soul together, the person will run out of money before the end of the month, and he/she will come back again to you for help. Therefore, as Donald Trump (2007) put it "the best education is financial education" (Trump, 2006). Give the poor vocational training and teach them how to make and manage money. That is the financial education. You cannot reduce the population of the poor in any country without the government spending some money to refocus the mind of the poor toward economic independence from government welfare fund.

There are women who were on welfare who are now dentists, nurses, school teachers, and so forth, because of some incentives given to them in job training during President Bill Clinton years (1992–2000). The program to reduce the poor population should be pursued in every country.

The idea of managing poverty in the United States and giving young single women with children a certain amount of money per child—Temporary Assistance for Needy Children (TANF) or Aid to Family with Dependent Children (AFDC)—has created a new structural career, which is having children as an occupation. The five-year limit imposed by the 1996 *Personal Responsibility and Work Opportunity Act*, which replaced AFDC with TANF, has not deterred some young women from engaging in having a bunch of children as an occupation. The five-year limit of receiving TANF has led to high infant mortality among lower class women, and their babies weigh less compared to middle class newly born babies, especially among poor African-American women on the TANF program. The AFDC remained in operation for a very long time from 1935 to 1996. So the AFDC became a culture as it was costing $24 billion a year (1996 figure). So the change to TANF with the five-year limit of receiving the assistance did not stop young, single women from getting pregnant and not worrying about how to get money to raise the child after five years.

While developed countries have a problem of managing the poor, most developing countries ignore them. More than 80% of Africans in each African country have no health insurance. There are no payments to the poor and disabled, and there is nothing like TANF or AFDC. In those countries, if you are a young, single woman and get pregnant, you are on your own. Nigeria provides free health care for pregnant women, but she had to be married to get it. In effect, single women in Nigeria and the whole of African countries do not jump into getting children. Besides, it is a taboo in most of the African countries for a single woman to have a child. They regard such a child as not having a lineage—a bastard.

South Africa is the only country in Africa that has some form of social welfare. According to Haroon Bhorat and Aalia Cassim of Brookings Institute—*Africa in Focus* (2014), the South African government committed itself in 1980 to removing racial barriers in its social benefits programs. In 1993, every person in South Africa in need was receiving the same grant level of benefits. "South Africa's social grant network has since grown to be among the largest in the developing world and, for the first financial year, the program's expenditure is projected to reach $12 billion" (Bhorat & Cassin, 2014).

The poor in developing countries, especially, those of Africa, have learned to farm the land and survive on the land from generation to generation without the welfare system. Fortunately for them, they do not suffer, in the main, from relative deprivation, at least to the degree as the poor in developed countries. The African poor persons have no television nor are they exposed to premises of the rich. This is because, for instance, most Nigerian poor persons live in their houses, for which they do not pay any rent. Those who live in the cities are the ones who experience relative deprivation, but 80% of African poor, including the Nigerian poor, live in the rural towns and villages.

The most serious problems of the African poor are lack of pure water supply, poor or absence of health-care services, poor sanitation, and inadequate security of life and property for those who live in urban areas.

The deviancy of developed countries in the area of inequality is pursuit of policies that expand the gap between the rich and poor and increasing the population of people in poverty. For the developing countries, over 80% of them totally ignore the poor. One would wonder why it is so. It is so because, taking the African continent as an example, Muslims dominate the African population. The percentage of Muslim population in Africa is 53.04%. Look at Table 8.2 for 24 countries in Africa with Muslim populations ranging from 50% to 100%. The high controlling population of Muslims is a major explanation for African poverty. There are two major reasons for this fact and this is not an assumption. First, the African Muslims transmute poverty and begging as virtues of grace. Therefore, hard work and pursuit of wealth, like investing for more income, is not a correlate of Islamism in Africa. The Muslim attire for men and women, worldwide, is not for hard work and long hours of tedious work. The Muslim men's *thobe*, mostly white, ankle-length and loose coupled with *ghutra* covering the head and tied in place with *egal*, is not for farm and factory work. In addition, high productivity of Muslim women is hampered by their attire too. The Muslim women's *hijab, khimar, abaya, Chador, Nigab,* and *Burqua,* which cover the entire body with little space on the face to see, are not for farm work or tedious factory work.

Second, Islam is a religion based on feudalism. The overlord (the Imam, Grand Imam, Grand Mufti, the Sheik, etc.), traditionally, has a large population that he feeds from his accumulated wealth built by his servants. His subjects had no ambition of their own other than to engage in subsistent work that will not hinder their hourly prayers. The emergence of capitalism through European colonization was hateful to the Muslims. The Muslims have not forgiven Europeans for bringing this cut-throat capitalism to them. The Muslims prefer a simple life devoid of this stressful capitalist mode of production and economic domination. In the European colonization of predominately Muslim countries and introduced capitalist economy, the Muslims adjusted to engaging in some nonstressful and in non-time-consuming occupations, while most of them continued with services to the *Imam* or *Sheik* as a means of subsistence.

Table 8.2 Percentage of Muslim Population in 24 African Countries in 2014

Country	Percentage of Muslim population
Algeria	99.7
Burkina Faso	60.5
Chad	50
Comoros	98
Djibouti	96
Egypt	95
Eretria	50
Ethiopia	50
Gambia	90
Guinea	85
Guinea Bissau	50
Libya	99
Mali	90
Mauritania	100
Mauritius Mayotte	97
Morocco	99
Niger	95
Nigeria	47.9
Senegal	94
Sierra Leone	60
Sudan	97
Tanzania	55
Togo	50
Tunisia	99

Source: Muslim population in the world (http://www.muslimpopulation.com/africa/). Accessed March 14, 2015.

Unmistakably, finding lucrative natural resources like oil, gold, uranium, or other minerals in a Muslim-controlled country reinforces the prior feudal economic order, and mass poverty proliferates in the contemporary world capitalist order.

Out of the 24 African countries listed in Table 8.2, Nigeria, Tanzania, Burkina Faso, and Sierra Leone have Muslim populations ranging from 47.9% to 60.5%. All of the other 16 countries have above 84% Muslim population. And out of the 16 countries, 14 of them have 90–100% Muslim population. With a laidback Muslim culture, Africa, Asia, and the Middle East will continue to have many poor states for a long time. This is because whenever a

Muslim-dominated country finds oil and other minerals in their domain, the money therefrom is squandered in conspicuous consumption. They do not invest in their youth and in new industries to provide jobs for the youth. The money freezes as it comes into their hands. At worst, they stock them in foreign banks. The high degree of youth unemployment means nothing to the leadership. Very often, their states fall into a "failed state" status without their knowing it. The 2011 Arab Spring revolution attests to the neglect of the youth.

Nigeria, with a Muslim population of 47.9%, is a good example of a country ran down by Muslim leadership. Nigeria has oil revenue from 1970 through 2004, that if well invested, no Nigerian worker would be bothered to pay income tax or pay tuition at public universities. Instead, the Nigerian oil money was partly hidden in foreign banks and squandered in building skyscrapers that have 85% empty suites, and partly hundreds of thousands of dollars given to women in Nigeria and around the world for a night of sexual gratification. Take, for instance, in 1981, my department had a picnic by Tennessee River in Chattanooga. An African-American female journalist based in New York City, visiting her family in Chattanooga, joined us in the picnic. In the process of our conversation, she learned that I was born and raised in Nigeria. She said to me, "You guys have a lot of money in that country." I asked why she came to that conclusion. She replied: "A Nigerian whose name starts with 'Alhaji' gave my friend $350,000.00 (three hundred and fifty thousand dollars) after my friend passed a night with him in his hotel." "Yaaaaooh!!!" I exclaimed. I had never heard something like that about Nigerian leaders with women before. I only knew that in Nigeria, a Hausa Muslim would give any *Igbo* woman a large amount of money for sex, but not in hundreds of thousands of dollars.

In 1994, I saw with my eyes, that what the African-American female journalist told me in 1981, was a tip of the iceberg. It was June 1994. I went to Nigeria on vacation, to gather some data, and see my mom and other relatives. I landed at Enugu Airport, and took a taxi to Modotel Hotel, Enugu. When I entered the hotel reception area, the person standing by a check-in clerk was one of my soldiers in the Biafran Military Counter-Intelligence Operations Ranger Regiment. He saluted before giving me a hug, and said, "Happy survival," because we hadn't seen each other since the end of the Nigerian Civil War. He was the hotel manager. As I was checked-in at the desk, I could see aggregates of beautiful young women scattered all over the large lounge and other corners of the hotel. I entered the elevator to go to my room on the fifth floor. There were six young women riding the elevator with me. They knew, from my physical outlook, that I am an *Igbo*, so they did not say anything to me, and I kept quiet too. I knew they were all *Igbo*. After I entered my room, I got ready to go to the lounge to chat with the hotel manager. In the elevator going down to the lounge, I saw another aggregate of young women, all *Igbo*, riding the elevator to the lounge with me.

"What conference are these Igbo women having at this hotel," I asked the hotel manager when I got to the lounge. Conference??? No! They are not here for a conference. They are lodged here by one Alhaji Brigadier . . . " the hotel manager replied in a deplorable tone. "The Alhaji Brigadier...lodged them here for what?" I inquired. "They are his comforters, troop comfort." He replied. "How many are they?" I asked. "Thirty-five of them; he employed two civilians to guard them here," the manger explained. Modotel Hotel was the most costly hotel in Enugu at that time. Each woman was occupying a suite in the hotel at $400 a night. For 35 women (ages 19–29), the Alhaji Brigadier was paying to the hotel $14,000 per night. That did not include tax, meals, and the cost of lodging two security guards at the hotel. And who knows how much he was paying each woman a night.

Nigeria was under military rule (dictatorship) at that time of the Modotel Hotel incident. My subsequent inquiry about Nigerian Muslims in positions of power in Nigeria and their degree of reckless chasing of women showed that the lodging of many Igbo women in a hotel by military officers and their top civilians in the federal government was an irrefutable pattern. Undeniably, the Muslims in positions of power do not know how to make money, but they know how to squander it in conspicuous consumption. That is why Africa is a poor continent. The colonial masters, especially the British and French, can attest to that.

In the colonial days of Nigeria, we had the "groundnut (peanut) pyramid" in Kano. The British colonial farmers had peanut farms (groundnut) throughout Northern Nigeria with people from Southern Nigeria (especially Igbos) as the major workers in the farms. The groundnut pyramid was a huge export raw material that was yielding millions of dollars in foreign exchange. It constituted 70% of the export earning of the region. When the British left following independence, the Hausa Muslims of Northern Nigeria did not allow the *Igbos* to continue working in the groundnut farms. As a result, the groundnut production disappeared and that was the eclipse of groundnut farms pyramid in Kano City.[5] The groundnut farms were a gold mine given to the Hausa Muslims of Northern Nigeria, but they left it to disappear, because they hate to settle down and work for hours on the farms, and they didn't want the non-Muslims to take over the farms. They prefer roaming the streets and woods in the company of their cattle, and hate Western education more than dogs hate cow poopoo.

All of the money embezzled by the Nigerian military government officials and other senior civil servants, and squandered in sexual gratifications and conspicuous consumption, are state crimes of omission to enforce the law. Corruption in Muslim leadership is always very high in a country where the Muslim population is almost half of the whole country.

The Muslim states have a practice of giving civil service jobs to Muslims than to non-Muslims, even when the Muslim applicant is not a citizen of the country and does not have a permit to work in the country. My study shows the same pattern in Senegal, Gambia, Nigeria, and Sierra Leone. For instance, out of the 36 states of the Federal Republic of Nigeria, 19 are located in Muslim-dominated Northern Nigeria. In Borno, Yobe, Sokoto, Jigawa, Kano, and Katsina states, the writer found many non-Nigerians working as civil servants. A University Lecturer at the University of Sokoto from Bendel state told the writer that some of the non-Nigerian Muslim foreigners, who are working in the states' civil service and some as staffs at the University, had no Nigerian immigration papers to work. He added that those non-Nigerian Muslims came from India, Pakistan, Bangladesh, Ethiopia, and Eretria. The writer saw this situation in Borno state in 1980, when he was gathering data from Maidugri Prison, and saw it again when he visited Sokoto, Kano, Yobe, Katsina, and Jigawa in 2006. There are so many unemployed university graduates from Southern Nigerian states, but since they're not Muslim, they are seen as unqualified by Northern Nigerian Muslim leaders. This type of discrimination is a deviant behavior of both the Nigerian Federal Government and the state governments of Northern Nigeria.

In Asia, a small minority of non-Muslims in Indonesia, Pakistan, Bangladesh, and Malaysia suffer the same discrimination at the hands of their Muslim majority leaders (Pressly, 2006; Parry, 2010; Ariffin 2014). There is a strong solidarity among Muslims. They shield embezzlements and other corrupt activities of their Muslim members for as long as a Muslim is a head of state. Nigerians call them "Kaduna Mafia." In Nigeria, there is no limit to the crimes they commit with impunity especially when they constituted a military junta. It is the same in all Islamic military dictatorships worldwide. In any country where there is tribalism, racism, ethnocentrism, religious discrimination, and employment discrimination in government operations, as found in such countries as Nigeria, Indonesia, United States, Malaysia, Pakistan, India, Russia, United Kingdom, Australia, Rwanda, Japan, Germany, and Israel , that country is guilty of deviance and of a crime of omission to enforce the rightful behaviors among its people.

Undeniably, it is due to racism, clannishness, ethnocentrism, and prejudice that there are shanty houses in Rio de Janeiro, Brazil; Buenos Aires, Argentina; Mexico City, Mexico; New Delhi, India; Pretoria and Cape Town, South Africa; Santiago, Chile; North London, United Kingdom; and the slums of Los Angeles, New York City, Chicago, in the United States, and so forth. Those shanty houses and slums should not be associated with very wealthy countries like the United States, Great Britain, Russia, France, and Germany, but those cities are correlated with shanty towns. In fact, those shanty houses and slums are indicators of pathologies of economic and political power. They are demonstrations of the capitalist elite war on the poor (Farmer, 2005).

The Prison Industry and Prison Inmate Annihilation

Very few countries in the world treat prison inmates as human beings. The countries that treat prisoners as human beings are Scandinavian countries—Norway, Denmark, and Sweden; followed by Japan, China, and Finland. Then there are countries with mixed good and bad prisons: United States, Spain, England (United Kingdom), Morocco, the Philippines, Indonesia, Germany, Austria, Uganda, Chile, Australia, Switzerland, and Venezuela.

In the United States, Federal Correctional Institutions are good examples of how a prison should look like and be administered. Most state prisons in the United States give the country a bad name in dehumanization of prisoners. But some states set examples of good prison structures and humane administration. They are Jessup Correctional Institution, Maryland, where inmates are taught skills that they could use after prison life; Richmond City Jail, Virginia, where they have family-oriented activities that make the inmates behave well and abide by jail rules; and Taft Correctional Institution in California, where inmates' cells and bathrooms look like decent hotel rooms.

It is true that some prisoners have committed very heinous crimes. The very violent and dangerous ones should be locked up, but at the same time, they should be taught humaneness. Prisoners are not for butchery. Some countries have realized that, and redesigned their prisons and retrained their prison guards. Unfortunately, out of 195 countries in the world, less than 60 of them have taken note, that torturing and keeping criminals in subhuman environment does not correct. Here are some prisons in 15 different countries that show reduction in recidivism rates because of good housing and excellent treatment of criminals: Halden Prison in Halden, Norway; Otago Corrections Facility in Milton, New Zealand; Burner Federal Correctional Institution, North Carolina, United States; Suomenlinna Prison in China; San Pedro Prison in La Paz, Bolivia; Her Majesty's Prison Addiewell, Addiewell, Scotland; Dublin Federal Correctional Institution, California, United States; Her Majesty's Prison Forest Bank, Manchester, England (United Kingdom); Cebu Provincial Detention and Rehabilitation Center, Cebu, the Philippines; Justice Center Leoben, Styria, Austria; Cordillera Jail, Santiago, Chile; Luzira Upper Prison, Kampala, Uganda; Alexander Maconochie Centre, Hume, Australia; Santa Ana Jail, California, United States; and San Antonio Prison, San Antonio, Venezuela.

The characteristics common to all of these prisons are structural designs that make the prisons look like a university, a clean geographic location, spacious rooms that look like three-to four-star hotel rooms, excellent bathroom and toilet facilities, good educational programs, libraries for the inmates, conjugal and nonconjugal visitations, provision of meaningful paid jobs for the inmates inside the prisons, good meals; emphasis on rehabilitation and not punishment, very limited need for prison guards, and so forth.

Furthermore, some of the prisons listed above have some unique features; for example, in Halden Prison in Norway, the cells are fully furnished which include refrigerators and televisions, and some of the prison guards walk around without any firearms. Suomenlinna Prison in Helsinki, Finland, is an "open prison." There are no cells or locked doors. The inmates live in shared houses with private rooms. San Pedro Prison in La Paz, Bolivia, is among the most unique prisons in the world. It is its own functional community with its own leadership structure. Inside the prison are the inmate families, businesses, cafes, and an ideal community life of a free society. Her Majesty's Prison Addiewell, Scotland, is like a bed-and-breakfast business environment than a prison. In this prison, one sees clean, colorful rooms, and the inmates are holding full-time jobs.[6]

Unmistakably, at Her Majesty's Prison Forest Bank, Manchester, England, inmates are given five "luxury meals" every day, "with menus offering many choices in meats, drinks, and desserts."[7] Cebu Provincial Detention and Rehabilitation Center, in the Philippines, is a maximum-security prison holding most of the violent criminals in the country, but has a unique rehabilitation program. The inmates are allowed to get together and choreograph elaborate dance numbers to hits like "Thriller" and "Gangnam Style."[8] The inmates of the Justice Center Leoben in Austria get a leisure time. It is like a "well-chaperoned vacation."[9] It is common knowledge that African prisons, like the Brazilian ones, have no regard for human rights, but not at Luzira Upper Prison in Kampala, Uganda. The prison is strongly focused on education and meaningful rehabilitation programs. Some prison inmates earn their bachelor's degree while in prison, and acquire lucrative job skills through vocational education. In effect, like other prisons mentioned above, the recidivism rate is among the lowest in the world.

Australia's 'Alexander Maconochia Center' is a luxuriously designed prison with luminous open cells and a rich library teeming with books. San Antonio Prison, Venezuela, is more a night club than a prison. They have pools, barbeque pits, and dancing groups here and there; families and overnight visitors are allowed. The only thing that makes San Antonio Prison (Venezuela) look like a prison is the presence of armed guards.

There are prisons that are not for human beings, but human beings are incarcerated in them, and you find them in most countries of the world. You find them in every country except Norway, Sweden, Denmark, Japan, and Finland.

Before analyzing the state crimes of inhuman incarcerations, here are some selected worst and brutal prisons of the world: Camp 22, North Korea; Carandiru Penitentiary, Brazil; Diyarbakir Prison, Turkey; Bang Kwang Central Prison, Thailand; Rikers Island Prison, New York City, United States; La Sabaneta Prison, Venezuela; El Rodeo, Guatire, Prison, Venezuela; Tadmor Prison, Syria; Gitarama Central Prison, Rwanda; ADX Florence Supermax Prison, Colorado, United States; La Sante, Paris, France; Gldani Prison, Tbilisi, Georgia; San Quentin Prison, California, United States; San Juan de Lurigancho, Lima, Peru; Petak Island Prison, White Lake, Russia; Black Beach Prison, Malabo, Equatorial Guinea; Butyrka Prison, Russia; Kamiti Maximum Security Prison, Nairobi, Kenya; Vladimir Central Prison, Russia; Camp 1391, Northern Israel; Montelupich Prison, Cracow, Germany; Attica Correctional Facility, New York, United States; and Stanley Prison, Hong Kong.

The characteristics common to these 22 prisons are as follows: absence of rehabilitation programs, absence of goal-oriented vocational education or liberal arts education, absence of open-field recreational facilities, housing less dangerous and most dangerous criminals in the same facility and the same block, inmates in narrow cells, prison staff abuse of the prisoners, poor meals, restricted freedom of movement within the prisons, high degree of inmate versus inmate physical fights, highly restricted communication with the outside world, very high degree of overcrowding, inmates torture inmates and prison guards torture inmates, absence of social harmony between the inmates and the guards, and all of the prisons have had at least one inmate riot.

Atrocities committed in some of the prisons, not mentioned above, include being on death row for more than 5 years, guards murdering inmates, inmates murdering fellow inmates, torture as a daily routine, merciless beating that sometimes results in death of the inmate, letting inmates beat each other, rampant malnutrition and disease, epidemic of AIDS and tuberculosis, cells for 10 inmates housing 100, inmate cells reek of toilet stench that hangs in the air around the prison halls, constant presence of rats and lice in the filthy cells, prison staff and inmates living in criminal symbiosis as inmates sell drugs to fellow inmates supplied by some prison staff, a hot bed of violence and aggression, cruel treatment meted out to inmates causing mental illness, and hell-hole torture chambers of cruel and inhuman brutality causing many inmates to drink drain cleaner or other lethal cleaning substance to terminate their misery in suicide. Many of the prisons are cited by Amnesty International for human rights violations, unlivable conditions, sexual abuse of inmates, psychological torture by keeping the inmates locked up for weeks or months, allowing gangs in prison, incarcerating rival gangs in the same prison, insufficient food, inadequate health care, allowing inmates access to design their own weapons to kill each other, deplorable living conditions, and mass execution of inmates by the guards leading to closure of such prisons because of press and Amnesty International intervention.

All of these atrocities committed in various prisons are state crimes. The state built the prisons and employed the prison staff. The criminal atrocities committed in those prisons by the prison staff and by the inmates are all state liabilities. The way the prison guards treat the prisoners is the standard of treatment approved by the state. This study found that in the United States, there is no single United States Federal Correctional Institution that does not meet the United States Standard Minimum Rules for the Treatment of Offenders, unless there is anyone they privatized. In fact, the United States Federal Penitentiary Institutions are designed and administered excellently, far and beyond the Standard Minimum Rules for the Treatment of Offenders, held at Geneva in 1955, and approved by the Economic and Social Council by its resolutions 663C (XXIV) of July 31, 1957 and 2076 (LXII) of May 1977.[10]

Any crime or harm committed against an inmate in a U.S. Federal Penitentiary Center by a prison's guard is a U.S. liability. And that is true in all states of the world. All the good prisons of the world identified in this study are owned by the state and operated by state employees. And those states took good care of the prisons. The states of Norway, Sweden, Denmark, Finland, Japan, and so forth gave us a good example of how prisons should be designed and administered so as to have less criminals in the streets. The same way the state is answerable for the crimes of law enforcement officers, similarly, the state is liable for the crimes of prison officials. In addition, the state is liable for the violent crimes committed inside the prison by the prison inmates, because prisons where every inmate is assigned a productive self-enriching role, vocational education programs, liberal arts education programs, well-paid work program inside the prison and outside, humanely designed prison structure, inmate and prison guards in harmony, conjugal and friends visitation rights, open field recreational facilities, social hours of inmates and staff, and so forth, have low recidivism rates, and little or no acts of violence.

The draconian prisons of torture, starvation, and murder located all over the world are designed and administered the way they are due to either ignorance, sadism, or greediness of the government leaders. In some countries, individuals are contracted to run prisons. The private prison is a profit-oriented enterprise. In private prisons, offenders are physically confined by a third party under a contract with a state agency. The state pays the contractor based on the number of offenders incarcerated in the private prison. England and Wales in the United Kingdom have at least 14 private prisons under contract with private companies involving 13,500 prisoners (Bates, 1998; Zito, 2003).

Private prisons are not new in the United States, but went into obsolescence in the early 20th century. However, hell broke loose in 1983 when Corrections Corporation of America (CCA) emerged to own and manage private prisons and detention centers in 20 states in the United States. CCA has at least 60 facilities with a capacity of 89,500 beds, but has approximately 90,000 inmates. Their revenue is $1.736 billion, with operating income and net income at $332.06 million and $162.51 million, respectively. They have a total asset of $3.020 billion.[11]

Unmistakably, privatization of prisons, jails, and detention centers is part of state-organized crime. Private prisons do not correct or rehabilitate the offender. Instead, private prison owners and their managers want the prisoners to be reincarcerated shortly after they are released from the present incarceration. There will be no huge profits if recidivism is not high. Therefore, private prison system is for incapacitation and destruction of the prisoner; and, therefore, focused on temporary specific deterrence and retribution. Unmistakably, incapacitation-, deterrence-, or retribution-focused prison systems do not reduce recidivism.

The private prison system is a state criminal enterprise. Here are the facts, in the "kids for cash scandal," Mid-Atlantic Youth Services Corp, a private prison company that operates juvenile offenders' corrections, was found guilty of paying two court judges, Mark Ciavarella and Michael Conahan, a fabulous amount of $2.8 million to incarcerate 2,000 children to their prisons. And the two judges sentenced the children to their prisons for such misdemeanor offenses as "trespassing in vacant buildings," and "stealing DVD from Wal-Mart Store" (Monbiot, 2009; Pilkington, 2009). Furthermore, groups hired by Corrections Corporations of America to lobby for them lobbied in many states including New York, Tennessee, Texas, and Illinois, to pass or defeat private prison legislations (Pulle, 2009). On the U.S. federal front, between 2002 and 2012, Corrections Corporation of America spent $17.4 million lobbying the Department of Homeland Security, U.S. Immigration and Customs Enforcement (ICE), the Office of Management and Budget, the Bureau of Prisons, both houses of Congress, and in campaign contributions to states and federal politicians (Sanchez, 2011; Shen, 2012).

According to the Justice Policy Institute (JPI) report, the private prison industry utilizes three methods to influence public policy: lobbying, direct campaign contributions, and networking (Sanchez, 2011). The three major private prison companies in the United States (Corrections Corporation of America, the Geo Group, and Wackenhut Correctional Corporations) have corrupted state and federal politicians, county sheriffs, court judges, and police officers in big cities to a point of no return. These private prisons contract with state (government) officials to supply their prisons with a certain number of offenders to be incarcerated in their facilities. Take for instance, in 2012, Corrections Corporation of America dispatched a letter to prison officials in 48 states, offering to purchase their prisons in exchange for a 20-year management contract and a guaranteed 90% occupancy rate.[12] It is undeniably criminal for a state to engage in a contractual obligation to fill the prisons to 90% occupancy which would make the community, the police, and courts to create more criminals (Kirkham, 2012). In effect, many innocent persons would be arrested by the police, dragged to court, and found guilty for a crime they didn't commit, or a crime that should be handled safely and less costly in the community as done in China, Japan, Norway, and many other countries.

The Associated Press (AP) noted that the private prison corporations make remarkable profits emanating from their making remarkable lobbying campaign (Shen, 2012). Also, it is observed that the three major private prison corporations, within the past decade, spent $45 million on campaign donations and lobbyists to engineer and expedite legislations favorable to private prison industry at the state and federal levels. At that same period, the private prison corporations rake in over $5.1 billion (Sanchez, 2011; Shen, 2012).

Lobbying has been turned into bribery. Nobody calls it bribery. Lobbying seeks to influence a cause of action, or to get members of congress or state legislature to support one's cause. But American business law says, "You don't get something for nothing." In lobbying, dollars exchange hands, from the lobbyist to the politician or government official who will execute the policy. In other countries, it is called bribery. In America, we are ashamed to call it bribery. So we call it lobbying. But it is a crime against the taxpayer. In this case, the state is complicit in the violation of the laws it created.

State prisons and private prisons in the United States have more recidivism rates than any country in Third World nations. This is because most of the U.S. state prisons and all of the private prisons in the United States are not designed for rehabilitation. The private prisons even lease some prisoners to county jails for a fee to deal with their own overcrowding. The inmates are there for incapacitation and retribution. They follow little or no program of corrections in private prisons and some state facilities. Furthermore, the fundamental human rights of prisoners are violated with impunity in private prisons. That is why private prison corporations have had a lot of riots, homicides, and lawsuits (Boone, 2012, 2013).

The United States is not alone in the private prison industry. As already noted, the United Kingdom (England and Wales) is among the countries with private prison contracts, the others being Australia, New Zealand, Scotland, South Africa, Canada, Oceania, and some countries in South America. Some of the other notable private prison corporations are G4S and Serco of Great Britain, and Correctional Corporation of Australia, an international venture of Corrections Corporation of America (Mattera, Khan, & Nathan, 2003).

The lobbying to sell national prisons to domestic and foreign private prison corporations is nothing short of state-organized crime, and also a transnational organized criminal scheme (Nwebo & Ubah, 2015; Ubah, Nwebo, & Ezeanyikan, 2015). G4S, CCA, and the Geo Group lobby and contract with other countries to manage their prisons. This sale of state or national correctional institutions to domestic or foreign private prison corporations is a vagrant violation of international law, because the fundamental human rights of the individuals are trashed. There is no humanity in private prison administration. Studies in the United States have shown that the profit motives of prison privatization led to inadequate services, gangs controlling other inmates, unsafe environment, frequent assaults and murder, and very few staff workers (Mason, 2013; Austin & Coventry, 2001).

The writer taught inside the notorious Attica Correctional Facility (maximum security prison), New York, for 11 years, from Fall 1989 through Spring 2000, for the Consortium of Niagara Frontier (Daemen College). It is identified as one of the most brutal prisons in the world, but Attica Correctional Facility is like a clean university compared to any private prison or jail in the United States. Undeniably, there is nothing good about privatization of prisons and jails. While some states privatized their prisons and jails under the camouflage that it is cheaper in private companies, unfortunately, that is a fraud. Privatization of prisons cost more in every measure, financially and humanely. Both the politicians (states) and the private prison owners are searching for money in a pool of blood. They have ruined so many lives. Private prison system is state-organized crime.

The failure of the state to its people can easily be seen in telephone, electricity, gas, and cable service bills in the United States. There are so many taxes added almost every month. For instance, the writer started with one of the popular Cable Companies in 2005 with cable, Internet, and telephone services at $75 a month. In March 2015, his bills in the past 3 months ranged from $177 to $200 a month. This is because there are too many additions that the state failed to monitor. The service companies know that the state may not catch them. As Jimmy Carter put it when he was American President, "America is over-lawyered and under-represented." Similarly, citizens of various countries are overtaxed and "under protected."

Now let's see another aspect of state deviancy and crime which disturbs the collective conscience of communities around the world. That is environmental pollution.

Dumping of Nuclear and Industrial Wastes and Garbage

This is a crime committed by almost every state in the world. Yes, most countries do not have nuclear wastes. But both developed and developing countries of the world have industrial wastes and garbage that need to be carefully disposed of, where they will never pose any harm to the present and future generations.

Let's start with nuclear wastes. This is a crime of developed countries. Undeniably, countries with nuclear reactors to generate electricity produce radioactive wastes. In other words, radioactive wastes represent wastes that have radioactive material. Put succinctly, radioactive wastes are by-products of nuclear power generators and other applications of nuclear fission or nuclear technology. Beyond controversy, radioactive wastes are lethally hazardous to humans, other life forms, and the environment. Countries that generate a lot of radioactive wastes have agencies that regulate their safe disposal to protect the health of people and the environment. The length of time radioactive waste must be safely stored depends on the type of waste and radioactive isotopes. This could range from a small number of days for very short-lived isotopes to millions of years, if one chooses to waste the unspent portions of "spent nuclear fuel" (Marshall, 2005, 2008). Over 400 million metric tons of hazardous wastes are generated worldwide, and they originated mostly from countries belonging to the Organization for Economic Cooperation and Development (OECD).[13] About 50% of the members of the OECD are industrialized countries, and generate nuclear radioactive wastes.

In recent decades, disposal facilities for hazardous wastes have become scarcer than ever before, and costly in the originating industrialized countries. The industrialized countries that created the radioactive toxic wastes promulgated safety laws to protect their own people in Europe and the United States. In effect, the toxic disposal costs became very exorbitant, as high as $2,500 per ton. Consequently, European countries, the United States, and their manufacturing corporations began to look for "the closest, poorest, and most unprotected shores— West Africa" became the answer (Brooke, 1988). From the shores of Casablanca, Morocco, to Boma and Matadi of the Democratic Republic of the Congo, every country in between the West African Atlantic Coast received offers from European and American companies looking for inexpensive locations to dump their toxic wastes (Brooke, 1988; Walsh, 1992; Vir, 1989; Porterfield & Weir, 1989).

It is unequivocal that lesser developed countries were targeted as dumping grounds for the deadly toxic wastes. The developed countries, undeniably, knew that West African countries had no idea about how to dispose of nuclear waste materials, but they still went to these poor countries. In fact, without a second thought, they offered some Africans $3 a ton to take their deadly toxic waste (Brooke, 1988).

Here is a journey of tons of toxic wastes whose story featured on the front page of every major newspaper and headline news of every television network around the globe. The journey began in Italy in 1987. The destination was Nigeria in West Africa. An Italian businessman, Gian Franco Rafaelli, negotiated with a 67-year-old Nigerian businessman, Sunday Nana of Koko, Delta State of Nigeria, for the Italian to ship toxic waste from several Italian industries to Nigeria for storage in the backyard of Sunday Nana. The Nigerian signed an illegal contract with the Italian for the latter to store 18,000 drums of the hazardous waste in his property at a fee of $100 per day. The toxic wastes were exported from the Italian port of Pisa to the receiving firm in Nigeria, the Iruekpen Construction Company owned by Sunday Nana. The toxic wastes were imported as miscellaneous construction material substances "relating to the building trade and as residual and allied chemicals" (Abu, 1988a, 1988b).

The 18,000 drums of over 3,500 tons of toxic waste arrived, and Nana stored them in his backyard without knowing the hazardous nature of his import. The drums were filled with polychlorinated biphenyl sulfate (PCBS),[14] methyl melamine, dimethyl ethyl-acetate formal-dehyde, and so forth, which are the world's most hazardous wastes (Onwumere, 2007). Nana emptied some of the drums and used them to store rainwater and drank from them without knowing that he was drinking poison.

The story about the scam first broke in Italy that some toxic wastes had been dumped in Koko City in Nigeria. The Nigerian Embassy did not alert the Nigerian Government. Instead, some Nigerian students in Italy telephoned *The Nigerian Guardian* newspaper. And the Nigerian government and its Federal Environmental Protection Agency (FEPA) began running helter skelter to exculpate themselves from blame. This is because the Nigerian public wondered how such a cargo could arrive in a Nigerian seaport, be off-loaded, and hidden in a small town of Koko without some government agencies not being aware of its arrival. The Nigerian government quickly reacted and found out in the process, that not only PCB but asbestos fiber and dioxins were also dumped.[15] More than 100 employees of the Nigerian Ports Authority (NPA) were deployed to remove the dangerous waste. The Nigerian government gave the workers some equipment, including gas masks and protective clothing. But the protective clothing were not enough. Worst of all, some of the workers had no hand gloves.

Furthermore, the hazardous wastes were more toxic than the government and the workers realized. Consequently, many of the workers ended in Koko General Hospital with multifarious ailments including chemical burns, nausea, paralysis, and vomiting of blood .

As these events were happening in Koko, the Nigerian government recalled its Ambassador to Italy, and gave the Italian government an ultimatum to take back their toxic wastes; else, it would file a lawsuit at the International Court of Justice (ICJ) in The Hague, the Netherlands. Without any delay, the Italian government agreed to pay all costs of cleaning and returning the toxic wastes to Italy, and that they would later determine the guilty parties. In effect, in July 1988, two ships, the *Karin B* and the *Deep Sea Carrier*, began to carry the toxic wastes from Nigeria to Italy (Ekeocha, 1993). While the toxic wastes were en route to Italy, there were demonstrations in Italy about the port where the wastes were to arrive, after the Italian Environmental Minister, Giorgio Ruffolo, announced the Italian ports designated to accept the toxic wastes as the Tuscan Port of Livorno, and either Ravenna or Manfredonia Harbour in the South Adriatic. The ships assigned were *Karin B* for Livorno and *Deep Sea Carrier* for Ravenna or Manfredonia. In a very cordial manner, Nigeria and Italy settled their differences.

The European countries' dumping of toxic wastes in West African countries did not start with Nigeria. Such dumping started in the mid-1970s, when France used its special relations with Francophone Africa as a means of disposing of its toxic wastes (Anaclet, 1988; Schissel, 1988; Vir, 1989). The Benin Republic, Ivory Coast, Guinea Bissau, Mali, Senegal, Burkina Faso, Mauritania, and Niger are former French colonies in West Africa. Some of them have been French waste dumping destinations.

Poverty, greed, and poor leadership are Africans' political and economic nightmare. The president of the Benin Republic, despite the danger posed by toxic wastes, and strong opposition of Benin's neighboring states of Nigeria and Togo, determined to import the toxic wastes as a means of his small country's economic survival. He didn't care about the toxic wastes speeding up the death of his own people. He wants to get the money and build his mansion hundreds of miles away from the dump site. He is a typical African head of state. That is brainless greed.

European countries are not the only ones terrorizing Africa with toxic wastes dumping. In 1979, an American Company, Nedlog Technology Group, Inc., offered the English-speaking West African country, Sierra Leone, a sum of $25 million a year to use the country for toxic wastes processing and disposal. The president of Sierra Leone at the time, Siaka Stevens, saw the offer as being very attractive. However, owing to popular opposition, he backed out of the deal. Also, a ship called Kian Sea carried 2,000,000 tons of Philadelphia Ash from Panama to Guinea-Bissau in West Africa.

In Ivory Coast (Cote d'Ivoire), according to Onwumere (2007), the Netherlands dumped some tons of toxic wastes. In actual fact, a Dutch company, Trafigura Beheer BV, which owns the ship Probo Koala tried through Amsterdam Port Services to handle the disposal, but the workers refused because of the foul smell of the cargo. To handle the toxic waste cargo, an alternative service cost was offered by Afvalstoffen Terminal Moerdijk at 500,000 euros. But Trafigura felt that the cost was too high, and they resolved to turn to West Africa. Cote d'Ivoire was chosen, because an Ivory Coast (Cote d'Ivoire)-based company, Compagnie Tommy, in Abidjan agreed to take the toxic waste and dispose of it at a pittance of 18,500 euros. Compagnie Tommy secured a landfill in Abidjan area and buried the hazardous chemicals.

The fatal consequences of the landfill disposal was terrible. Over 30,000 people were badly injured, with 17 fatalities. This has been called the Trafigura "2006 Cote d'Ivoire toxic waste dump" and "Trafigura scandal." In fact, after a nongovernment agency sued Trafigura in a Dutch Court, for the international dumping, the court found Trafigura Beheer guilty of orchestrating the dumping of toxic waste in Cote d'Ivoire during the month of August 2006, which subjected "thousands of Ivoirian citizens at the receiving end of chemical warfare" (Evans, 2010).

There have been so many contracts rammed through some other West African countries by the Western world and their companies. The Italo-Swiss Intercontract-Jelly Wax Group tried to negotiate toxic waste dumping with Guinea-Bissau, Djibouti, and Senegal. In 1987, Djibouti rejected a shipment of 2,100 tons of chemical waste from the Port of Marina di Carrara after they found out that the shipment was toxic waste. Also, Guinea-Bissau was to receive 500,000 tons of pharmaceutical and industrial wastes from Switzerland's Intercontract firm at a price of $40 per ton. They turned down the deal after they found out the hazardous nature of the cargo. Unmistakably, Africa has become a dumping continent for Western nuclear wastes.

Despite the Basel Convention, which calls for the management, "in an environmentally sound manner,"[16] of all transboundary shipments of hazardous wastes as well as household wastes (Murphy, 1993), state signatories to the Convention began to violate the international rules and regulations concerning the disposal of the toxic wastes domestically and internationally with impunity. This is because Africans are regarded as unpeople, and they are too poor. And the United Nations is a toothless bulldog. It does not have strong enforcement mechanism for its international laws, unless those laws are violated by a poor country (a factor that killed the League of Nations). When the developed countries violate those international laws, it appears nothing wrong has been perpetrated, and that is one of the reasons the world today is at war with itself.

The Western world selecting the underdeveloped countries as a dumping ground for their toxic wastes has been described by some journalists as Western terrorism, and Africa as "the waste basket of the West" (Ruffins, 1988).

African countries are not the only destinations of Western wastes. Some Asian and Central and South American countries are also victims. It is documented that some electronic wastes from Western European countries end up in China, India, and West African countries (Selva, 2006).

Nigeria has made it a capital offense for anybody to import toxic wastes into Nigeria. In fact, it developed a list of items that no ship should carry to Nigerian ports and no individual or business should import. Some other African countries have followed Nigeria's legal code on waste dumping.

Undeniably, states (governments) commit too many crimes domestically and internationally. Because there are no police to enforce the international laws, the world body is in an anomic condition. Sanctions as a mechanism to enforce international law are ineffective for two main reasons: first, some members of the United Nations Security Council may oppose the sanctions against their political or business ally; second, if the sanctions are unanimously approved, there are countries, individuals, or businesses that are enthusiastic to make a profit out of the situation by smuggling the prohibited goods to the sanctioned country. In effect, the underdeveloped countries of the world are at the mercy of the developed economies.

Now, let's look at goods that may or may not be deadly, but are exported anyway.

Export of Inferior Goods

The export of inferior goods from industrialized countries to nonindustrialized nations has been in vogue for centuries. The deviance of exporting inferior goods is not an exclusive practice of Western countries. The industrialized Asian countries (Japan, China, and South Korea) are among them. There are no international standards of production of export products. Each country sets its own quality standards of the quality of products it is going to import. As a result, nonindustrialized countries, especially Third World countries, are victimized. Some Third World countries may have Bureaus of Standard to determine the quality of what should be imported and what should not enter the country, but corruption from head to toe obliterates the effectiveness of the regulation.

Inferior textile materials, batteries, electronic equipment, agricultural materials, and household items that can't sell in the origination country, are exported to Third World countries for as long as they have the money in their foreign reserve to pay. The worst area of inferior export to developing countries is the area of medicine. Some pharmaceutical companies in the West export medicines already rejected by their governments to Third World countries. The governments may be aware of such exports, but remain silent.

Think about automobiles recalled by the origination or manufacturing country, but hundreds of those have been shipped to underdeveloped countries. Did anybody recall those vehicles that have been found faulty from developing countries where they have been shipped? No, that is a developing country's misfortune. A good example of what I am talking about in this section is the fact that asbestos sheets are banned in Western countries in building construction, homes, ships, boats, and so forth; but go to Nigeria and other West African countries, and you will see, on streetsides of shopping plazas, piles of asbestos sheets from some European countries and the United States for sale. Nigerians use them as ceiling boards for homes, partitioning offices, and special partitions in small-scale factories. But it is well documented that exposure to asbestos fiber causes cancer of the lungs and the linings around the lungs (mesothelioma cancer).

The export of inferior goods to consumer countries may not be criminal, but it is deviance. However, when products such as asbestos sheets or tiles, or deadly pharmaceutical drugs, are deliberately exported in spite of the impurity of the drug, that constitutes a criminal intent to kill, and a serious deviance. If it is illegal to sell such a product in the manufacturing country because of its deadly composition, it should also be a crime to export such a product. But the state of origin allows such inferior and deadly products to be exported. That, in itself, is a serious deviance.

Differential Law Enforcement of Environmental Laws

This is a state malfeasance. When state officials blindfold their eyes to environmental pollution by a company, in spite of public outrage, it amounts to a serious deviance. Why would state officials do that? It is because the owner of the company has bribed the environmental protection agency officials, or the leaders in the government have their shares in the company, and any effort by the company to comply with the pollution control law would lead to a very high cost of production, which reduces the company's profit.

However, some governments enforce pollution laws against some companies, because such companies do not have any "godfather" in the government or in the environmental protection agency. In effect, the agency had to use them to show that they are doing their job. This differential law enforcement in environmental pollution is seen more in developing countries where foreign manufacturing companies bribe their way out of obeying environmental regulations. This is a common feature of foreign manufacturing companies in Nigeria and the Nigerian Federal Environmental Protection Agency (FEPA). If a company does not tip the FEPA agents, then FEPA agents will always keep a watch on the company's adherence to pollution standards.

Review Questions

1. Poor environmental preservation is a state deviance. Explain.
2. What are the five major factors that make for high life expectancy?
3. What is "social justice"?
4. According to Munro (2013), what are the consequences of lack of Universal Health Care (UHC)?
5. Why is it that developed countries have problems of managing the poor?
6. What are the two factors the author gave as to why Africa is a poor continent?
7. The state is liable for crimes committed against prison inmates by the prison's staff. Why is it so?
8. Private prison system is a state-organized crime. Discuss.
9. According to the "Justice Policy Institute" (JPI) report, what are the three methods the private prison industry uses to influence public policy?
10. How is nuclear waste disposal a state transnational crime?
11. What do you understand by "Basel Convention"?
12. Why is nuclear waste dumping in some developing countries described by some journalists as an act of terrorism?

Notes

1. "What are Human Rights?" (see http://www.ohchr.org/EN/Issues?pages/Whatare HumanRights.aspx). Accessed March 12, 2015.
2. Ibid.
3. Ibid
4. "Social Justice" definition (AFL-CIO). (http://www.businessdictionary.com/defintion/ social-justice.htm/#ixzz3UE00F891). Accessed March 13, 2015.
5. Groundnut pyramids were bags of peanut (groundnut) without the shells, packed in big twine bags and heaped like the Egyptian pyramids.

6. "The 50 Most Comfortable Prisons in the World." (http://blog.arrestrecords.com/the-50-most-comfortable-prisons-in-the-world/). Accessed March 17, 2015.

7. Ibid.

8. Ibid.

9. Ibid.

10. See "Standard Minimum Rules for the Treatment of Offenders." United Nations Human Rights, Office of the High Commissioner for Human Rights. (http://www.ohchr.org/EN/HRBodies/Pages/HumanRightsBodies.aspx). Accessed March 18, 2015.

11. See Corrections Corporation of America (www.cca.com).

12. "CCA Letter" (http://big.assets.huffingtonpost.com/ccaletter.pdf) (PDF). Huffington Post. Accessed March 20, 2015.

13. Organization for Economic Cooperation and Development (OECD) began on December 14, 1960, with 20 countries at a Convention on OECD. Today, there are a total of 34 countries, mostly Europeans. The foundation members signed in 1961. Non-European member countries (with the year they joined in parenthesis) are: Australia (1971), Canada (1961), Chile (2010), Israel (2010), Japan (1964), Korea (1996), Mexico (1994), and New Zealand (1973). There are five newest European member countries of the Newly Independent States (NIS) of the former Soviet Union. These are Czech Republic (1995), Estonia (2010), Poland (1996), Slovak Republic (2000), and Slovenia (2010). (http://www.oecd.org/about/membersandpartners/list-oecd-member-countries.thm). Accessed March 20, 2015.

14. Polychlorinated biphenyls (PCBs) is a group of organic compounds used in the manufacture of plastics, as lubricants, and dielectric fluids in transformers, in the protective coating for wood, metal, and concrete, and in adhesives, wire coating, and so forth. PCBs have been demonstrated to cause many types of diseases, and have been shown to cause cancer in animals. PCBs have also been shown to cause non-cancer health problems in animals, including effects on the immune system, reproductive system, nervous system, endocrine system, and other health effects. Studies in humans generate strong evidence for potential carcinogenic and noncarcinogenic effects of PCBs. Available data strongly point to the fact the PCBs are a probable cause of cancer in humans. (PCBs are probably human carcinogens). (http://www.epa.gov/wastes/hazard/tsd/pcbs/pubs/aroclor.htm). Accessed March 22, 2015.

15. Polychlorinated dibenzodioxins (PCDDs), or simply called "dioxins," are a group of polyhalogenated organic compounds that are significant environmental pollutants. Members of the PCDD family bioaccumulate in humans and wildlife because of their lipophilic properties, and may cause developmental problems and cancer. Also see Beychok, Milton R. (1987). "A Database for Dioxin and Furan Emissions from

Refuse Incinerators." *Atmospheric Environment 21*(1), 29–36. Also see Schechter, A; L. Binbaum; J.J. Ryan; and J.D. Constable (2006). "Dioxins: An Overview." *Environmental Research, 101*(3), 419–428.

16. The Basel Convention on the Control of Transboundary Movements of Hazardous Wastes and Their Disposal, usually known as the Basel Convention, is an international treaty that was designed to reduce the movements of hazardous waste between nations, and specifically to prevent transfer of hazardous waste from developed to poor countries of the world.

State-Organized Crime: Political-Criminal Nexus

State-organized crime and political-criminal nexus go hand in hand. So, as the left hand and the right hand wash each other, similarly criminal syndicates and some politicians help each other in their endeavors to amass wealth, including the latter's political survival. However, before delving into the analysis of this symbiotic existence, the terms organized crime and "state organized crime" must be explained. Undeniably, there are as many definitions of organized crime as there are many researchers on the subject, and a common ground is lacking.[1]

Almost every criminal event is organized, but not every organized criminal activity is organized crime.

Definition of Organized Crime

The definition of organized crime even varies among individual states in the United States. Taking two as an example, Mississippi law defines organized crimes as "two or more persons conspiring together to commit crime for profit on a continuing basis." By contrast, California law states:

> Organized crime consists of two or more persons who, with continuity of purpose, engage in one or more of the following: (a) the supply of illegal goods and services, i.e., vice, loansharking, etc., (b) predatory crime, i.e., theft, assault, etc. Several distinct types of criminal activity fall within the definition of organized crime. These

types may be grouped into five general categories: (1) Racketeering—criminal activities organized. (2) Vice operations—continuing business or providing illegal goods and services, i.e., narcotics, prostitution, loansharking, gambling. (3) Theft/ fence ring—groups organize and engage in a particular type of theft on a continuing basis such as fraud and bunco schemes, fraudulent documents, burglary, car theft and truck hijackings, and purchasing stolen goods. (4) Gangs—groups who band together to engage in unlawful acts. (5) Terrorists—groups of individuals who combine to commit spectacular criminal acts, example, assassination, kidnapping of public figures to undermine public confidence in established government for political reason or to avenge some grievance.[2]

California's definition emphasizes the types of illegal activities that fall within the generic term "organized crime," and is therefore very relevant in the investigation of state-organized crime and political-criminal nexus. All the illegal activities that fall under organized crime in California are also crimes in most countries.

Furthermore, to be an organized crime, it must be a formation of two or more individuals strongly united to execute some criminal enterprises in an ongoing mode.

The above definitions are traditional and contemporary definitions of organized crime in business and professions. The legitimate state organization fights to control them, and they try to avoid state control. Well, hell breaks loose when the legitimate state organization becomes a coopted partner or a lead partner in contemporary criminal enterprise. The definition of state-organized crime below will alert the reader to the structure and forms of the concept in some developed and developing countries.

Definition of State-Organized Crime

State-organized crime is when the legitimate leadership of a state and syndicated gangsters or organized crime groups exploit the entire national population of its natural resources and gross national product (GNP). The state leaders are the "political criminal upper world, while the gangster-state is the criminal underworld" (Hirschfeld, 2015).

Therefore, in state-organized crime, the state is the political-criminal upper world, while the gagster-state is the criminal underworld. The state-organized crime enterprise can emerge in one of four ways:

First, the state leadership initiates the criminal relationship in a multiparty charged dictatorship or camouflaged democracy with its law enforcement agencies as instruments of mass exploitation, repression, appropriation, assassination, predatory taxation, and wholesale corruption; and the police and the military are allowed to make money on their own by all means. Examples are Haiti under the "Papa Doc" Duvalier (1957–1971), and "Baby Doc" Duvalier (1971–1986) regimes, Mobutu Sese Seko's Zaire, Rafael Trujillo's Dominican Republic, and so forth.

Second, a head of state and his government collude with the gangster-state for the latter to continue in its line of criminal enterprise for as long as it gives a large amount of money to the government or the political party in power.

Third, the gangster-state is too powerful for the government and too violent to be controlled. The government operators, to safeguard themselves, cooperate and allow the gangster-state to remain in operation, because "best safety lies in fear" (Shakespeare, 1596/1988).

Fourth, open-ended state-organized crime is found in advanced, democratic economies. In such regimes, the state allows multinational corporations to operate in any way they want, however, in violation of existing national laws for as long as they are giving substantial contributions to the powerful political parties.

These four ways of the emergence of state-organized crime will be expatiated below.

Causes of State-Organized Crime

State-organized crime emerges out of fear of a loss of political power. The political leadership aspirant promises gangster-state leaders of giving them opportunity to continue in their criminal enterprises of drug smuggling, illegal arms trafficking, trafficking in human beings, loan sharking, gambling, and all types of racketeering if they finance and fight for the political party leader be elected, or reelected.

Another factor that causes state-organized crime is the fervent desire for financial security. The aspiring head of state wants huge amounts of money under his control, and conspiracy with the gangster-state will make it possible.

Organized crime syndicates or gangster-states' code of operation is manliness. Manliness is to operate without the law. In a formal-state, law-abiding economy, the gangster-state must nullify the law before any criminal operation. Therefore, when the head of state promises the gangster-state that his law enforcement agencies will not be in their way, then the sky is the limit in their racketeering operations. And they are going to work for the criminal head of state to the last sweat.

In addition, the gangster-state, like the criminal head of state, wants money and power. In effect, the four ways listed above by which state-organized crime could emerge come into play.

Head of State–Initiated Organized Crime with Security Forces

After gaining political power as a head of state either by democratic election or by a coup d'etat, the newly installed head of state decides to enshrine his power base. He is afraid that if he doesn't do something drastic, he would lose that position. He sees the only way out of his fears is to control the national treasury, control the national foreign reserves, and have foreign bank savings accounts. Therefore, the way to do it is to get the national police, strategic intelligence agency, the customs and excise, and the military to work for him. Also, all those he appointed as ministers of various government departments must be working for him. Any minister who fails to bring him money out of his department's annual budget is dropped in the next cabinet reshuffle, including any minister who questions his criminal policies and political and economic agenda (Ebbe, 2003).

The next venture is predatory taxation. It is used to fight against businesses and professionals who are members of an opposing political party, or who do not make campaign contributions to the head of state's political party (Hirschfeld, 2015; Scott, 1972). Natural resources such as oil, gold mines, and all mineral processing operations are under his control. The national treasury, to which he appoints the governor or director, is like his personal bank account. The states that fit this structure are Nigerian military regimes (1966–1999), Haiti under the Duvaliers (1957–1986) regimes, Zaire under Mobutu Sese Seko (1965–1997), Zimbabwe under Robert Mugabe (1987–present), the Dominican Republic under Rafael Trujillo (1930–1961), Chile under Augusto Pinochet (1973–1990), the Philippines under Ferdinand Marcos (1965–1986), and so forth.

The regimes of Papa Doc Francois Duvalier and Baby Doc Claude Duvalier in the Republic of Haiti exemplify "head of state–initiated organized crime with its security forces." Papa Doc nullified his military after an abortive coup to overthrow him. Instead, he set up a paramilitary force called Tonton Macoute who were allowed to be ruthless in dealing with the Haitian people. He was known for the use of a personality cult and voodoo. In the process, more than 30,000 Haitians were murdered and many others were sent into exile.[3] The Duvaliers authorized the Tontons Macoutes to perpetrate systematic violence and all sorts of human rights violations just to suppress political opposition. Some political opponents disappeared and were never seen again, and some were overtly attacked with impunity. Like the Mexican drug cartels, they killed some people and displayed their corpses for the public to see as a warning against any organized opposition (Abbott, 1988a, 1988b; Burt & Diederich, 1969).

Both Papa Doc and Baby Doc monopolized control of the tobacco industry, flour mills, gambling operations, insurance and state lottery businesses (Ezrow & Frantz, 2013; Hirschfeld, 2015). They designed governance of the state in such a way that the state is almost the only employer of labor (Scott, 1972; Hirschfeld, 2015). In other words, during the two regimes, it was virtually only from the Duvaliers that Haitians could "suck reviving blood." To compensate the Tontons Macoutes, the Duvaliers authorized them to extort whatever they could from the masses (Scott, 1972). In effect, the Haitians became a besieged and exploited population throughout the years of 1957 through 1986.

This type of regime is a gangster-state itself, and there are still many of them in the world today. As Hirschfeld (2015, p. 95) put it, in a normal democratic government, if a person is robbed, he calls the police to apprehend the robber and recover the property. However, "in a kleptocratic gangster-state, if you are robbed, it is likely to be by the police, who will use their powers to arrest competing thieves and thus secure a monopoly on thievery for themselves."

Undeniably, this is the same strategy that organized crime drug cartels use when they have the state law enforcement agencies on their payrolls, and get the state agencies to crush their competitors, so that they gain monopoly of the narcotics drug market.

The Duvaliers were a mafia of their own. They had nobody to fear. The sky was their limit in executing criminal schemes. For instance, under the Duvaliers, as narrated by Timothy Schwartz (2008), a state cooperative bank was created to help peasant farmers save and borrow money for their businesses. The state cooperative bank was highly advertised, and the people were promised that their savings deposits would yield 23% return every month. Some farmers joined the state cooperative bank. In a few months, some substantial increases appeared in the customers' deposits. The participating farmers were happy about the increases in their savings deposits. As a result, they encouraged their friends and relatives to join in the lucrative banking service. Consequently, many rich and poor farmers in Haiti not only deposited the cash they had at hand into the state cooperative bank but some also sold their land and other valuable items and deposited the money in the bank. According to Schwartz (2008), a farmer took his life savings of US $5,000 and deposited it into the bank. And in less than 3 months, some "government officials absconded with all the funds—US $250 million." The cooperative bank collapsed, and many Haitians lost their means of survival.[4]

The establishment of a state cooperative bank and the officials' absconding with the poor peoples' money give an example of how state-organized crime can ruin a whole nation. This book will provide more instances of some governments stealing their people's money through running down a state statutory corporation.

Can this type of state-organized crime survive for a long time in a camouflaged democracy? Yes. This is because one of the modus operandi of a camouflaged democracy is election rigging. For instance, in both the Duvaliers' regimes, the Tontons Macoutes were found everywhere at the polls during the 1961 and 1964 elections that got Papa Doc reelected despite atrocities he perpetrated to the masses. Baby Doc saw that the elections would not favor him all of the time, so he used assassination of potential challengers at the polls.[5]

The engineer and promoter of state-initiated organized crime in the Caribbean and Latin America was Rafael Trujillo of the Dominican Republic. Trujillo was one of those individuals who was a known criminal before becoming an executive President or a head of state. Born and raised in the Dominican Republic, he got a job as a telephone operator at the age of 16. After holding the job for a short period, he set out to get engulfed in a life of crime. He counterfeited checks, stole cattle, and engaged in postal robbery. In effect, he spent some time in prison for his criminal onslaught against the public. During the time he was incarcerated, he designed a violent criminal gang of armed robbers, and nicknamed it "42" (Diederich, 1978, 1999).

Trujillo wanted to be at the top of the Dominican Republic by all means from his early youth. When the United States occupied the Dominican Republic in 1916 and established a Dominican army constabulary to impose order, Trujillo joined the National Guard in 1918, and trained with the U.S. Marines (Diederich, 1978). To reach his ultimate goal, he joined the

Dominican politics. By some political and strategic maneuvers, Trujillo rose up in rank from Lieutenant to General, and in a twinkling of an eye, he became the Commander-in-Chief of the Dominican Army. The "ex-con" knew what he wanted from the Dominican Republic. Consequently, there was a rebellion against an incumbent President of the Dominican Republic, Horacio Vasquez. While the rebels were marching toward the capital city of Santo Damingo, Trujillo knew that President Vasquez was going to order him to use his soldiers to fight against the rebels. In effect, he made a deal with the rebel leader, Rafael Estrella Ureña. The deal was for Trujillo to allow the rebel leader to seize presidential power, and in return, Rafael Estrella Ureña would let Trujillo run for the presidency in a forthcoming election.

When the rebels were still on their way marching toward Santo Damingo, President Vasquez ordered General Trujillo to go after the rebels and dislodge them. Instead of obeying his head of state's order, General Trujillo left his soldiers in their barracks. Consequently, Rafael Estrella Ureña and his rebels marched into Santo Damingo and took the city. The incumbent president went into exile.

Rafael Estrella Ureña was installed as the acting President, while General Trujillo became the head of both the police and the army. A political party was formed captioned *Patriotic Coalition of Citizens*. Rafael Trujillo was the new party's presidential nominee, while Rafael Estrella Ureña was his running mate (Galindez, 1973). There were other presidential candidates in the election. Trujillo used his soldiers to harass and intimidate them. As a result, most of the other candidates gave up and dropped out of the race. Trujillo and his presidential running mate got up to 99% of the votes. According to Galindez (1973), quoting the American Ambassador, "Trujillo received more votes than actual votes."

On June 16, 1930, Rafael Trujillo was sworn in as the President of the Dominican Republic. The ex-con was now a President, and did not waste any time in throwing his opponents and potential future aspirants to the presidency into prison, some even before he was sworn in as the President (Galindez, 1973; Crassweller, 1966; Turits, 2004, Lopez-Calvo, 2005).

He set aside the constitution of the Dominican Republic. Trujillo was the constitution and Trujillo was the Dominican Republic. His dictatorial power was like no other in the Western Hemisphere. He had a high cult of personality, more even than that of Adolf Hitler. He destroyed all other political parties, and made the Patriotic Coalition of Citizens the only party in the country. As an avaricious criminal head of state, he required that every civil servant in his government donate 10% of their salaries to the national treasury (Block, 1941; Diamond, 2005). He forced all adult citizens to join the Patriotic Coalition of Citizens party, and required every member to carry a badge of membership all the time. It is reported that not carrying the badge could get a person arrested for vagrancy law violation (Block, 1941). It was considered a very risky venture for anybody to fail to join the party, because opponents of the party routinely disappeared without a trace.

As a personality cult monger, he got the capital city of "Santo Damingo" renamed to Ciudad Trujillo to reflect his name; the province of "San Cristobal" renamed to Trujillo; "Pico Duarte" (the country's highest peak) renamed Pico Trujillo; his statues "El Jefe" (the Chief) were built all over the Republic; bridges and public building answered his name; vehicle license plates bore praises of Trujillo such as "Viva Trujillo;" "Year of the Benefactor of the Nation;" and "Dios y Trujillo," an electric light sign shinning day and night, was erected in the city of his name, Ciudad Trujillo. Churches were required to post signs that read "Trujillo on Earth, God in Heaven" (Block, 1941; Diamond, 2005). Besides, in 1934, he promoted himself to the rank of generalissimo of the army (Galindez, 1973).

Throughout his 30-year regime, Trujillo maintained his leadership of the army and the Dominican Party. In addition, while Miguel Angel Paulino was the leader of "the 42" criminal gang, President Trujillo was still the director of operations of "the 42." All Trujillo's clandestine assassinations and disruption of businesses competing against his enterprises were carried out by "the 42." While SIM (the Military Intelligence Service) secret police were everywhere committing all sorts of political crimes and rackets for President Trujillo, "the 42" personal criminal gang of Trujillo operated as a counterintelligence unit as well as racketeering for the boss. In their counterintelligence operations, they monitored the activities of the SIM and secretly eliminated those found to be working against Trujillo, the boss.

Trujillo committed so many assassinations in the Dominican Republic, using is secret police (SIM). The elimination of his enemies or suspected enemies, who disappeared without a trace, was carried out by the "42." Even Trujillo's international attempts to assassinate foreign national leaders who opposed his criminal state organization such as President of Venezuela, Romulo Betacourt, Cuban President Fidel Castro, and so forth were carried out by both SIM and "the 42" (Crassweller, 1966).

Like traditional organized crime bosses, Trujillo had a fervent greed for money and power. In such a devil-incarnate frame of mind and ambition, destroying any human being on his way was a task that must be executed by all means. To get the supreme power (Trujillo on Earth, God in Heaven), he must usurp all economic opportunities in the Dominican Republic. And anybody who was in his way in controlling the economic opportunities in the Dominican Republic must be eliminated. So not only were his political opponents being clandestinely and overtly eliminated but also his business competitors.

As an avaricious criminal head of state, Trujillo amassed fabulous wealth by monopolizing cattle lands, meat and milk production, sugar, tobacco, salt, coffee, cocoa, and beer industries.

In his efforts to control the entire economy of the Dominican Republic, Trujillo owned 111 companies. In addition to his ownership and control of many industries, Trujillo controlled all government sources of revenue, customs and excise duties, all kinds of taxes, coupled with grabbing and sale of government lands. He received kickbacks for all public works contracts. To avoid anger and indignation among persons of his inner circle, he increased economic prosperity of his family supporters, members of his secret police network of spies, and military personnel.

When opposition to his regime was mounting underground, Trujillo allowed opposition parties to be formed to challenge his Patriotic Coalition of Citizens party. But that was a bait to identify leaders of such opposition parties and kill them. And that was exactly what happened. Some members and leaders of emerging opposition parties came out, and he killed some and tortured and expelled others (Crassweller, 1966).

Of all of the atrocities of Trujillo, the one that profoundly touched the Dominicans and the whole Western world was his assassination of the three Mirabal sisters. The three Mirabal sisters: Minerva,[6] Patria, and Maria Teresa, joined a political movement against Trujillo, after one of them observed the massacre of 20,000 to 30,000 Haitians by Trujillo. The three sisters were incarcerated because of their antidictatorship views and being against Trujillo's reign of terror. They were released, jailed again, and released. Then their husbands were jailed. It was when the three sisters visited the jail to see their husbands that Trujillo committed one of the satanic atrocities of his regime. As they were returning from the jail, on November 25, 1960, Trujillo's hitmen stopped their car and killed them. They left them in the car, moved the car up a hill slope, and pushed the car down to the edge of the road to make the brutal murder look like an accident. Unfortunately for Trujillo, the Dominicans and the Western world were not fooled. It was clear and unequivocal that President Trujillo masterminded the assassinations, and his own days were numbered.[7] The assassination of the three sisters touched the nerves of the world. Trujillo's criminal fame began to sink. The assassination was an attack on women's rights, a feminist resistance (Rohter, 1997). And the whole world paid attention[8] and reacted to the atrocities (Farrington, 2013).

All in all, Trujillo violated fundamental human rights of people as if there were no such international laws in existence. Unmistakably, he gave many subsequent Latin American national leaders and some of those beyond the Americas a model of how to run a "criminal state" or a predatory state with gangsters, and the head of state being the supreme boss of the criminal state.

In Latin America, following the examples of Trujillo in running a dictatorship/authoritarian criminal state were President Fulgencio Batista of Cuba (1952–1959), Anastasio Somoza Garcia of Nicaragua (1937–1947 and 1950–1958), Anastasio Somoza Debayle of Nicaragua (1967–1972), Jorge Ubico of Guatemala (1931–1944), Carlos Castillo Armas of Guatemala (1954–1957), Maximiliano Hernandez Martinez of El Salvador (1931–1944), Tiburcio Carias Andino of Honduras (1933–1949), Gustavo Rojas Pinilla of Columbia (1953–1957), Francois Duvalier of Haiti (1957–1971), and so forth. Every one of these criminal state dictators, with the exception of President Duvalier, was a military general. All of them, without an exception, ran their government as an organized crime enterprise. They governed their people by total exploitation, and those who escaped assassination looted their countries' treasuries. Consequently, they were either assassinated, or they flew into exile except Francois Duvalier (Papa Doc), whose son (Baby Doc) continued with the criminal state regimes style of governance until 1986.

Like many of those national leaders that he corrupted, Trujillo was assassinated on May 30, 1961, while he was driving home to his capital, Ciudad Trujillo (Santo Damingo). That was six months after he assassinated the Mirabal sisters (Harris, 2011). The seven assassins who killed him included some members of his armed forces.

There have been many presidents who masterminded state-organized crime; however, due to space limitations, only a few are presented in this text.

Second Example of Head of State–Initiated Organized Crime

Mobutu Sese Seko of Zaire is another example of head of state–initiated organized crime. In 1960, Belgium granted independence to Congo. The writer was a student at a teacher training college, and had been reading in newspapers about the events in Congo, because the Independence was followed by a Civil War (1960–1964). Nigerian soldiers were sent to Congo under the banner of the United Nations forces. It was a heavy war in Katanga Province of Congo. The writer studied Congo's political and economic history under African political history in the teacher training college.

In 1960, Patrice Lumumba was elected the first Prime Minister of Congo, and Joseph Kasavubu became the first ceremonial President of Congo Kinshasa (former Leopoldville). In 1964, Moise Tshombe became the Prime Minister after Cyrille Adoula's (1961–1964) regime as the Prime Minister of Congo. In 1965, President Kasavubu forced Prime Minister Tshombe to resign. The assassination of Patrice Lumumba in 1961 in a coup masterminded by the CIA, because the former was pro-Soviet Union, was still causing a lot of rivalry within the Congolese political structure.

Under the political charade that surrounded the Congolese players, there was a latent anarchy. The violence that followed the assassination of Patrice Lumumba took over one million Congolese lives, and there were still some skirmishes along ethnic borders. Under this state of affairs, Colonel Joseph-Desire Mobutu, carried out a military coup and assumed power.

Congo is a country of four major ethnic groups and over 200 smaller ones with distinctive languages. During the independence election in 1960, there were 15 political parties. This was because in African politics, there is tribalism. That means, whichever ethnic group produces an executive head of state will occupy key positions in the government of the country. And the natural resources of the country are regarded as a national cake, which each ethnic group had to scramble for and try to get as much of the lion's share as possible. Consequently, the moment Joseph-Desire Mobutu seized power from Kasavubu, he engaged in oppression, repression, assassination, and violent alienation of all opposing ethnic groups, and against those he had a personal hatred. He wanted no peace with anybody that he didn't trust, and he trusted nobody. He used people to achieve his aim, and then he dropped them or killed them after reaching his goal.

Congo has a great deal of natural resources, which the Americans and Europeans were after. They have uranium, diamonds, gold, copper, cobalt, oil reserves, and all sorts of minerals for aerospace technology. In effect, among all revolts by Congolese people, including the 1991–1992 students' revolt in which 100 students of the Lubumbashi University were murdered, France and Belgium sent in their troops to help Mobutu.

Before the various riots could die down, Joseph-Desire Mobutu changed his name to Mobutu Sese Seko. Then, he changed the name of the country from Congo-(Kinshasa) to Zaire. At this point, he wanted to design Zaire as his own personal property. He was afraid that the only group of people who could overthrow him was his military. To destroy that fear, he accused four top generals of his army of treason. And after a trial by his hand-picked judges, the four generals were found guilty and publicly executed before thousands of Congolese. Even some ministers of government departments during the short-lived Patrice Lumumba's regime and Moise Tshombe's regime, were invited individually under the camouflage of a friendly chat at his palace. They never came back alive. He got his presidential guards to kill them. In fact, one of them, who had gone on self-exile, was invited back. When the man visited him, he made his presidential guards torture him, cut his joints and disfigured his face and dumped him in the street far away from the palace. The atrocities of Mobutu Sese Seko were more than those of Nazi Germany, but his Western allies kept their ears and eyes closed. Mobutu was a devil's incarnate.

Unmistakably, the ultimate goal of Mobutu Sese Seko was to control all the state revenue of Zaire, and he did. The moment he seized power and saw that the Western world depended on him for Congo's uranium for their nuclear energy, he nationalized some mining industries. Then he created a state-owned mining company called *Gecamines*. The main purpose of creating a state mining company was to have a source of illegal diversion of public revenue to his personal bank accounts. That was at the early state of his regime. After he got rid of all opposing parties, weakened all opposing ethnic groups, gave key positions to trusted members of his Ngbandi ethnic group, he created a one-party state (Popular Movement of the Revolution or MPR).

Between 1980 and 1988, President Mobutu was siphoning, on an average, $400 million of public money each year and hiding it in various European and American banks (Berkeley, 2002; MacGaffey & Gould, 1980; MacGaffey, 2014; Acemoglu et al., 2004). Before 1990, Mobutu had made himself an absolute dictator. He made himself the King of Zaire and an executive president for life. He was a kleptocrat-in-chief.

He created gangs of racketeers who were funneling illegal money to his coffers. In addition, he created gangster warlords in the areas of uranium, gold, diamond, coffee, timber, cobalt, and illegal arms trafficking. All money realized from all these natural resources and illegal trades went directly to his personal accounts, and not to the national treasury that had already been personalized. While he was in absolute control of the national treasury, less amount of public funds were deposited in it. At the same time, American and European mining companies were complicit to Mobutu's kleptocracy, because they bribed him huge amounts to get the mining and processing of various minerals and export and import endeavors (Acemoglu et al., 2004; Gould, 1980; MacGaffey & Mukohya, 1991; Reno, 1999; French, 1997).

As avaricious as Mobutu was, he hardly paid salaries to his civil servants and soldiers on time. He expected them to subsist by sale of services, extortion, theft, and bribery. Many government institutions were ignored. In the wake of his nonchalant attitude toward social services, there emerged "shadow states" in which an individual in charge of a province or a local government usurped all positions and services of the local authority, leaving services unperformed, and pockets the money allocated to the local government. This was because there was no accountability, reminiscent of the Nigerian government, and many others in Africa, Caribbean, and Central and South American states.

Mobutu got so much drunk with money and power that he ignored maintaining roads and bridges, hospitals, public buildings, and the overall infrastructure of a normal national government. In addition, he could not even build up the economy of Zaire. From 1993, strong and overt opposition to his dictatorship began to mount. The last straw that broke the camel's back was when he ordered Rwandan-Burundi Tutsi refugees to leave Zaire on a penalty of death (Atzill, 2012). The rebellion that followed was too much for Mobutu do deal with, coupled with the fact that he had already burned his bridges badly. He rose to power, using soldiers faithful to him. After arising to the top, he "scorned the base degrees by which he did ascend," (Shakespeare, 1596/1988). He mistreated his soldiers and weakened his entire army. In effect, when he needed them, many of them had already joined the rebel forces. And his nemesis, prostate cancer, had no mercy for him. He had to fly away in 1997 when the rebels and foreign government forces from Uganda and Rwanda were marching very close to his capital city of Kinshasa.

For 32 years of Mobutu's bloody authoritarian regime, he escaped assassination and a coup d'etat. But all of the alleged $8–$10 billion that he stored in European and American banks could not purchase him freedom from cancer on September 7, 1997.

Head of State's Selective Alliance with Gangsters

The second type of state-organized crime is where a head of state identifies some criminal groups in certain areas of economic activities, including those in the areas of illegal import and export businesses. Also, he uses his ministers and top civil servants as members of the organized crime scheme. His aim, like the traditional "Mafia," is to amass fabulous wealth to ensure his political survival, power, and honor that come with such huge opulence. This type of state-organized crime is common in a multiethnic, Third World country. Nigeria is used in this text to exemplify how this type of state-organized crime works, because it has a lot of natural resources and multiethnic struggles that make political-criminal nexus inevitable.

The Nigerian Case

Nigeria has been a "predatory state" since the military counter-coup d'etat of July 29, 1966, through 1999. Even when the civilians were allowed to experiment with democracy in 1979–1985, the military was still running the show. The predatory structure was still there, when

General Muhammadu Buhari overthrew the civilian government in 1983. The military continued with the state-organized crime governance. It got worse when from General Ibrahim Badamasi Babangida, the predatory criminal state went into the hands of General Sani Abacha. General Abacha's dictatorship lasted from 1993 to 1998.

Strategies of Nigeria's Predatory State

A predatory state is a government that resorts to wholesale abuse of governmental power, and where the head of state rules and decrees much like the head of an organized crime "family," using criminal individuals and syndicates to loot his country's treasury. To that end, he uses government agencies, cabinet ministers, and directors of statutory corporations as bribe-collection agencies. In such a predatory regime, administrative checks and balances are rendered null and void. A cabinet minister or a chief executive of a statutory corporation in such a regime remains in his position only as long as he continues to funnel substantial sums of money budgeted for his department or corporation and kickbacks from contractors to the predatory head of state. It can be argued that Mobutu's Zaire (Congo), Duvalier's Haiti, Somoza's Nicaragua, Stroessner's Paraguay, Ferdinand Marcos's Philippines, and all military regimes of Nigeria, had indicators of a predatory state, given the amount of money found to have been illegally laundered in foreign banks by the above leaders.

Among the Nigerian military heads of state, it was only in the case of General Sani Abacha that the billions of U.S. dollars he had laundered in foreign banks was being gradually returned to Nigeria, and that was because of the intervention by the United Nations and the United States. This repatriation of the money stolen from the Nigerian people was made possible because he died in 1998. If he were still alive, nobody would touch his ill-gotten money. General Babangida and General Obasanjo looted larger amounts from the Nigerian treasury, more than General Abacha had done. Besides, there are other retired Nigerian generals who siphoned larger amounts of the Nigerian people's money. This was during the regimes of Generals Gowon, Murtala Mohammed, Buhari, Babangida, Obasanjo, and Abacha. They had hidden the money in foreign banks, including in off-shore banks.

Only some of the money that General Sani Abacha had laundered in European and American banks is being recovered. But those deposited in Saudi Arabian banks are still buried in controversy. As a result of the combined efforts of the Mutual Legal Assistance of the United Nations Convention on Corruption, the World Bank, the United States, and President Jonathan's Federal Government of Nigeria, three locations of General Abacha's stolen money have been identified. One in the United States and two in Europe: Switzerland and the Principality of Liechtenstein.

In the United States, the ex-dictator, Sani Abacha, left millions of U.S. dollars in the hands of Nigerian Liquefied Natural Gas (NLNG) contractors as bribe money to keep for him. The companies are based in the United States. But bribing a foreign government in order to get a contract is a violation of the U.S. Foreign Corrupt Practices Act, which carries heavy fines as a means of deterrence. It was over $6 billion for the Nigerian Liquefied Natural Gas contract. The United States Justice Department has decided to "keep $917 million bribe settlement" (Alike, 2010). "Techip agreed to pay the sum of $338 (million) to the U.S. government for scheming to bribe Nigerian Government officials to get the contract" (Alike, 2010). In the same manner, "KBR . . . agreed to pay $579 million, when it was discovered that it also bribed Nigerian officials to get the contract" (Alike, 2010).

We are going to see below strategies with which the Nigeria military dictators and their ministers and senior civil servants collect and share the money. General Abacha did not start it. It all began from the second military head of state, General Yakubu Gowon, and through all of the 33-year Nigerian military dictatorships to all of the regimes thereafter.

Nigerians lost a lot of money in the whole NLNG contracts. The contractors made away with some millions of dollars, and General Abacha hid away a lot of irrecoverable amounts worth millions of dollars all over Europe and America.

In 2005, Switzerland repatriated $505 million stolen from Nigeria by General Abacha. The repatriated amounts were returned to Nigeria in tranches of $461.3 million and $46.1 million (Alike, 2010). In June 2014, the Government of the Principality of Liechtenstein repatriated $227 million to Nigeria as money hidden in their banks by the ex-military dictator. The money stolen by General Abacha is coming back to Nigeria, in the main, because the Nigerian Federal Government of Goodluck Jonathan filed a case against General Abacha's son to return all of the money siphoned from the Nigerian treasury by his late father and hidden in foreign banks. As a result of the Nigerian government promise to drop all charges against him, on March 23, 2015, the Swiss prosecutors "announced that another $380 million is to be returned to Nigeria as funds linked to the ex-dictator Sani Abacha" (Clark, 2015).

A symbiotic relationship of varying degree exists among some Nigerian politicians and criminals. General Abacha's case is a good example. General Abacha did not make any overseas travels throughout the 6 years in which he was in office as the head of state of Nigeria. But he was able to deposit his stolen money all over Europe, America, and the Middle East. That is the job of his criminal syndicates. There is no doubt that totalitarianism leads to a predatory state; and a predatory state facilitates a political-criminal nexus, because military dictatorships lack the checks and balances found in full democracies.

The Multiethnic Factor in Nigerian State-Organized Crime

Political conditions

Nigeria is not a single national entity, but an amalgam of nations designed by a colonial power to serve the latter's own interests. Even during the colonial administration (1849–1960), especially when the British administered Nigeria directly (1900–1960), the three major ethnic groups (Hausa, Ibo [Igbo], and Yoruba) did not unanimously consent to the idea of "one Nigeria" as a united country. Each occupies a particular region of Nigeria: the Hausa-Fulani in the north, the Ibo in the east, and the Yoruba in the west. There are clearly defined natural boundaries. The colonial administration redefined the boundaries of the three regions, effectively remaking Nigeria.

Nigeria's natural resources, which were controlled by the colonial administration, and later by the federal government following independence in 1960, are often referred to as "the national cake." Throughout the colonial administration, the three regional representatives were competing and struggling with each other to get a larger share for their regions or ethnic group. What happened after independence was predictable.

Once the administration of the Nigerian federal government was handed over to Nigeria on October 1, 1960, and all the British colonial administrators in government agencies departed, the struggle by each ethnic group for its share of the "national cake" intensified. Each politician representing his own region/ethnic group in the federal administration resorted, with impunity, to embezzlement of federal property entrusted to his care.[8] In effect, expropriation and appropriation of the "national cake" became the sport of every federal government office holder. The politicians led the way, and the civil servants followed. Effective law enforcement was impossible, because the centralized Nigerian Police Force (NPF) was also ethnically divided. In effect, despite the laws against bribery and stealing from the government, there was no sense of guilt in graft, pilferage, and wanton malfeasance among some politicians and top civil servants.[9] Consequently, corrupt activities went unchecked.[10] The inability of the government to control the wholesale criminal activities of the politicians and top civil servants led to public agitation for a change of government. Consequently, the military overthrew the elected government of Nigeria's first Prime Minister, Abubaka Tafawa Balewa, in a bloody coup d'etat on January 15, 1966.

The overthrow of the Balewa administration on charges of wholesale corruption, and hostilities against the Ibos of Eastern Nigeria, led to the collapse of "one Nigeria" on May 30, 1967, and to the secession of the Eastern Region of Nigeria, which declared itself the Republic of Biafra. The secession of Eastern Nigeria led to the Nigerian Civil War (July 6, 1967 to January 12, 1970). With the combined forces of Great Britain, the United States, Soviet Union, the Nigerian Military, and Igbo ("Osu") saboteurs, Biafra lost the war and Eastern Nigeria was brought back to the fold of "one Nigeria."

The ostensible reason for the Nigerian military's overthrow of the Balewa regime was to erase corruption. Unfortunately, the military themselves, once in power, became even more corrupt than the civilian regime before them. The same extreme ethnic allegiances that fueled corruption in the Balewa administration also haunted the military regimes.[10]

The overthrow of the Balewa administration was led by an Ibo army major, Chukwuma Kaduna Nzeogwu. In the coup, many top politicians of Hausa and Yoruba origins were killed, but not a single Ibo politician lost his life. Many Hausa and Yoruba people, therefore, perceived it as an "Ibo coup" to take over leadership of Nigeria. In addition, after the January 15, 1966, coup, the most senior army officer in the Nigerian army at the time, Major General Thomas Umunnakwe Aguiyi-Ironsi (an Ibo), was installed as military head of state. On July 29, 1966, a company of Hausa army officers attacked and killed him and installed their own man, Major General Yakubu Gowon, in August 1966. It was the cold-blooded assassination of Major General Ironsi by the Hausa soldiers, the genocidal massacre of the Ibos living in the north and west of Nigeria in August 1966, and the consequent failure of the Aburi accord that led to the secession of Eastern Nigerian and the consequent Nigerian Civil War.

From August 1966 through December 1998, Nigeria has had seven military regimes and only one democratically elected civilian regime, which was the Second Republic (October 1, 1979 to October 1983). Everyone of the seven military regimes (Gowon, 1966–1975; Mohammed, 1975–1976; Obasanjo, 1976–1979; Buhari, 1984–1985; Babangida, 1985–1993; Abacha, 1993–June 1998); and General Abubakar, June 1998–1999), behaved like an organized crime family. They nullified the role of the Nigerian Police Force, ruled by martial law, and consigned the rule of law to oblivion. What would have constituted a Third Republic was overthrown by General Buhari in December 1983. Each regime appointed its own Inspector General of Police who would not check, monitor, or investigate malfeasances and syndicated criminal connections in the government.[11]

The "national cake," controlled by the federal government, was seen by every politician and top civil servant as something "up for grabs." The various ethnic groups devised criminal techniques to secure their own share. The military head of state represents his own personal interests and the interests of his ethnic affiliation. Patriotism has been forsaken. The concept of Nigeria as a nation, of a people with a destiny, faded, and became an increasingly distant memory. Many Nigerians seeking outlets for their talents, found none, and instead experienced mounting feelings of hopelessness. On the other hand, for past and present military heads of state, their cabinet members and military warlords, the politicians chosen on the basis of their ethnic status, and the members of the criminal syndicates, every day was pay day.

Ethnic rivalries in both colonial and post-colonial regimes prevented the rise of nationalism and loyalty to the state. A study of the short-lived democracy of the years 1960–1964 may reveal that political-criminal nexus was not common, because opposition parties and ethnic watchdogs controlled it. Corruption did exist then, but it did not rise to the high level of political-criminal nexus. The Second Republic was corrupted by the military that preceded it, because they continued to exert a great deal of influence on the leaders and ministers.

Every military regime in Nigeria suspended the Constitution and ruled by martial law. The first six Nigerian military regimes also suspended the rule of law.[12] In other words, martial power was used to overthrow the rule of law. Like an organized crime family, each regime ruled by intimidation, threats, and murder. Journalists and politicians who criticized the military leaders' policies and flagrant criminal activities were either assassinated, detained, imprisoned after trial on trumped-up charges, or driven to self-exile. Some regimes have been referred to as "Bida Mafia" and "Kaduna Mafia" of Hausa-Fulani enclave by Nigerian journalists and the southern Nigerian elite.[13] The assassination of the famous Nigerian journalist, Dele Giwa, is frequently remembered by many Nigerians. A letter bomb was dispatched to him by top army politicians, because he exposed their illegal narcotics trafficking, which they operated through organized criminal groups.[14] The military regimes had no need to obey the laws, because the decrees in existence were their own and were enforced by them. They were judges in their own cases. Nobody had either the courage or the will to charge them with legal violations. The judiciary was not independent of the military warlords either. In effect, the judiciary was intimidated and rendered incapable of performing its legal duties. The population, in general, lacked social and moral controls. This had a profound effect on Nigerians in general and especially on young people of both sexes, who resort to the criminal lifestyle of their national leaders. In effect, Nigeria became a disorganized society, where law had little meaning. The laws were not enforced because of bribery and corruption among the national leaders and the law enforcement agencies.

The Nigerian Police Force became impotent, because it was controlled by the military and used by them to realize their criminal and noncriminal interests. The successive military regimes failed to attend to the welfare and interests of the junior police officers and other ranks. Consequently, some resorted to begging for money in the streets and on highways. Others used extortion and robbery to get by. The military turned the newly formed, strategic law enforcement units into witch-hunting units for their own political advantage.[15]

Even the only elected civilian government of Shehu Shagari (October 1979–December 1983) collapsed because the predatory state of the previous military regimes swept into the civilian government.[16] This was not surprising because some of the top politicians in the Shagari administration were accomplices in the criminal enterprises of the previous military regimes. During the civilian government of Shehu Shagari, the political-criminal nexus reached epidemic proportions, because the seeds of a wholesale predatory state of organized crime had been sown by the military regimes. Under the civilian regime, the top military warlords had nothing to fear by continuing their organized criminal ventures. The military and the top politicians became allies in wholesale organized crime.

The political upheavals in Nigeria have shown that the British colonial administration had imposed some degree of order in the country, which the post-independence governments, even the military ones, were unable to accomplish. There were criminal groups in the colonial days, but they were not connected to the colonial government. The links between the government and the criminals were forged when the military took over the government.

Economic conditions

Another factor that has contributed to the emergence of state-organized crime and the political-criminal nexus in Nigeria is the neglect of the agricultural sector. Most Nigerians are engaged in subsistence agriculture, using tools that are local and almost primitive. They produce very little for the market beyond subsistence. Mechanized agriculture is too removed for most farmers. Even so, before the mid-1970s, Nigerian farmers were producing enough for the Nigeria population at the time. All of the traditional export crops, cocoa, palm produce, groundnut, cotton, soya beans, copra, and so forth were being produced and exported throughout the

1950s and up to the mid-1960s when the military seized power. In fact, throughout the 1960s, Nigeria was still exporting agricultural products, such as palm produce and cocoa, and competing internationally. But the irrational economic and political policies of the military regimes coupled with the appearance of the "oil boom," destroyed the Nigerian agricultural economy.

When the military regime failed to develop the agricultural economy, the young and the old left the rural towns in large numbers and migrated to the urban areas in search of jobs that were not there.

The oil boom

The sudden discovery of many oil wells in the delta region in the early 1970s, and a sharp increase in worldwide oil prices at the same time, boosted Nigeria out of the ranks of poor nations. The military regime, however, did not invest this surplus wealth in the traditional agricultural base that had long sustained Nigeria, nor in building small-scale industries that could produce basic needs for the people, but instead resorted to personal enrichment and conspicuous consumption through graft, embezzlement, and blatant malfeasance.[17]

Every top army, navy, or air force officer in Nigeria was also a politician. Each established his own criminal gangs to secure some of the federal government revenue through one or more of the federal government corporations, agencies, or departments.[18] The military head of state was involved in the mass expropriation of the "national cake," and it was he who appointed the senior military officers who accepted bribes from contractors and embezzled money entrusted to their care.[19] He demanded his own share of their booty, and, of course, they obliged in order to retain their lucrative appointments. When the head of state leads the way in corruption and malfeasance, who will control the law breakers? Top police officers, too, were drawn into the criminal conspiracy.[20] Former civilian politicians without federal or state offices allied themselves with top army officers, and became registered contractors without any obvious expertise for the work, as a way to steal Nigerian people's money.

Before the Nigerian Civil War, the military regimes, and the emergence of the oil boom, organized crime in Nigeria was at an elementary stage, or almost unknown. The end of the Civil War and the emergence of the oil boom brought about a high degree of sophistication to domestic and international organized crime in Nigeria.[21] When the war ended, the Ibos returned to Nigeria. It was an uncomfortable reunion with the Ibos for the Yorubas and Hausas, because the Ibos had the reputation of amassing huge wealth from little capital. Consequently, the Yorubas and Hausas, who were in control of the Nigerian economy and who also had the political power, resorted to intensified expropriation of federal properties before the Ibos had a chance to assert themselves. In the process, the Yorubas and Hausas became enemies and remain so. The Ibos were observers until 1975, when General Murtala Mohammed overthrew the government of General Yakubu Gowon and gave some Ibo politicians political offices. The old three-way, inter-ethnic struggle for the "national cake" began again in earnest. At this stage, in the mid-1970s, the military politicians and their cronies developed various forms of organized crime strategies to amass wealth. These went far beyond the "national cake," which nevertheless remained a target.

Military-Politicians and State-Organized Crime

In the wake of the oil boom, state-organized crime activities developed in the context of various relationships and enterprises that can be summarized as follows:

1. Governor/minister–domestic contractors, and organized crime.[22]

2. Governor/minister–foreign contractors, and organized crime.[23]

3. Minister–federal agencies graft gangs:[24]

   Passport Office, Citizenship Office, Immigrant Visa Office, Customs and Excise Office;

   Nigerian National Petroleum Corporation (NNPC); Nigerian External Telecommunication (NET), and so forth.

4. Military/politicians–vice operations:[25]

   Brothels, gambling casinos.

5. Illegitimate Enterprises:[26]

   Child trafficking and slave labor, trading body parts, narcotics trafficking, illegal importation of certain goods, counterfeit currency dealing.

6. Legitimate Enterprises:[27]

   Illegal diversion of government property, illegal contracts, and ghost contractors.

Among the above activities, numbers four to six involve career or professional criminals who were already engaged in criminal enterprises before allying themselves with politicians. The activities in categories one, two, and three involve mostly career civil servants. Most of the civil servants belong to the same ethnic group with the politician-boss who masterminded the graft and criminal conspiracy.

The following examples illustrate how the military-politician organized crime syndicates operate.

Ministers and domestic contractors

The minister is a career army, navy, or air force officer appointed by the military head of state to direct a federal government department or a department of the army, air force, or navy. The department may have a director general (Permanent Secretary) who is under the minister. Both the minister and the director general work hand in hand in every large project in the department, including in criminal schemes.[28] They select building and other project contractors, as well as supplies and service contractors. Before bids are even invited, they will have already made an agreement with other contractors, usually members of the same ethnic group as the minister or the director general.[29] The project costs are always overestimated.[30] The contractor, the minister, and the director general all know what the real amounts are, and they share the difference among themselves, with a designated amount going to the military head of state.[31] There is no fear of government audit because the Federal Audit Department is like a toothless bulldog. It operates in fear of the top military officials,[32] as does the Nigerian Supreme Court.

Some of the contractors in this organized crime enterprise may even be nonexistent, "ghost contractors,"[33] who are "awarded" contracts by the minister and the director general. On behalf of the federal government, the minster and the director general sign false papers certifying that the job has been completed, paying the "contractor"—themselves —for this fraudulent scheme. According to some self-exiled ex-ministers, the military head of state takes up to 50% of ghost contractor payments.

Minister-foreign contractor

Contract awards to foreign construction or service companies work in much the same way. The foreign contractor is informed of the conditions under which the contract will be awarded. These include signing over a certain amount above the true cost of the project, often millions of dollars or British pounds, to all the top officials involved in the illegal contract award. This money is then deposited in the officials' Swiss or British bank accounts. Many foreign contractors willingly participate in such criminal conspiracies.[35] That is the reason the amount of money left in foreign banks by Nigerians living in Nigeria today is more than the amount of money in circulation in Nigeria.[36]

In situations in which the minister awarded a contract without involving the director general, the native or foreign contractor must pay the director general 10% to 15% of the value of the contract before the director general will sign a check for payment on the contract work completed. Such practices make some foreign contractors understandably nervous.

Minister-federal agencies graft gangs

Every one of the nine federal agencies listed in item three above has a director appointed by the military head of state. The director is answerable to a federal department minister under which the agency operates.

a. Passport Office, License Office, Citizenship Office, and Immigrant Visa Office

On the writer's personal observations during his 1973, 1979, 1984, 1986, 1988, and 1993–1997 visits to Nigeria, the directors in each of these agencies employed young men and women as agents. These agents who were not federal government employees, accost visitors to the Passport, Citizenship, and Immigrant Visa Offices to find out why they are there. If they are seeking a passport, business license, citizenship certificate, or visa, the agents take the individual aside and explain how much it will cost. The agents emphasize that there is no other way to get the documents. Once the applicant hands over the money demanded by the agent, the document applied for arrives, often in less than an hour. Applicants who refuse to pay never get their documents. Sometimes they are told that their application files are missing and to reapply; then, a bribe must be paid to obtain the forms. To get the actual documents will cost more. To understand the scale of the graft, one would have to imagine that Americans paid one hundred and fifty dollars ($150) for a passport. A Nigerian passport costs around 150,000 to 250,000 Naira. Two-thirds of Nigerian workers do not make 150,000 Naira in a year. For foreign nationals or those who have dollars or pounds, the Nigerian passports are cheap because of the weak Naira. Nigerian passports are easy to get, because nobody investigates the real nationality of an applicant once the bribe has been paid.[37]

Every Nigerian knows that it is impossible to get federal documents without bribing the agents. Many Nigerians already know who the agents are and even go to their homes or offices to deliver the bribe money. The agent simply obtains the data needed for the application, and takes the information and the money to the federal agency concerned. Two to three hours later the document is handed over to the applicant.

There are other rackets in all four federal offices that deal with passports, immigrant visas, import licenses, business licenses, and citizenship certificates. The federal government issues only a certain number of official documents to each state office, and most of the time, it is less than the number of applicants.

b. Customs and Excise Office

The minister, other politicians, and top military officials employ gangs of smugglers who are guaranteed free passage at the Nigerian Customs check-points.[38] These privileged smugglers are not checked at the ports of entry. The writer witnessed these gangs on several occasions arriving at the Nigerian Murtala Mohammed International Airport with loads of heavy cartons and boxes of contraband goods. A senior army officer or Customs official was standing nearby, and raised his baton swerving it to his left or right side as a sign to let the smuggler pass without being checked. Sometimes the goods are piled up on one side of the luggage claim area, until other passengers have left. Then the smuggling agents move the contraband goods without anybody asking any questions.[39]

Direct bribes to customs officials at ports of entry are paid by individual smugglers not affiliated with a politician or military or customs officer. These smugglers pay bribes, because it is easier than going through the process of assessment to determine how much duty is to be paid (Mabaku, 1994). The only smugglers who get arrested by customs officials are those who are unaffiliated or who refuse to pay bribes.[40] All bribes received by Customs officials are shared with the officers at the port, as well as the director of Customs and the minister of Internal Affairs.[41]

c. Nigerian National Petroleum Corporation, and Nigerian External Telecommunications

In all three federal corporations, the directors engage in embezzlement, contract fraud, overvalued contract awards to domestic and foreign contractors, and pilferage through intermediate and subordinate employees (Chambliss, 1976). The proceeds are shared with whoever is the military head of state.

Today, every Nigerian who has been a director of the Nigerian Airways Corporation owns either an airline enterprise or is a partner in a private airline. The Nigerian Airways Corporation was led to bankruptcy, obliterated, and its assets shared among the Nigerian military warlords. And there was no probe into the activities of the former directors, because the military heads of state were a party to the conspiracy to bankrupt the statutory corporation (Whiteman, 1986).

Nigerians in all walks of life know that all federal statutory corporations are sources of illegal money for the military head of state and his cronies. The federal government pumps oil money into the corporations every year to support them, but the public and the federal government get nothing back in return. Where, then, do the profits of these corporations go? The money given to the corporations each year by the federal government to support operating costs, as well as the annual profits, are embezzled by the directors, the head of state, and the minister under whom the corporation is administered. No one looks out for the interests of the Nigerian people, and the nation deteriorates further.[42]

d. The Judiciary

As the members of the judiciary at the federal courts are handpicked by the military head of state, they are not prepared to cite the illegality of his actions and decrees. Instead, the judiciary's response has been to resort to wholesale corruption.[43] Whoever pays the larger kickback wins the case. Almost every judge at the federal and state courts has agents who offer financial propositions to the parties in a case.[44] In June 1996 and January 1997, the writer observed these agents at work at the Nigerian court buildings. Every land case has its price. Even child adoption has its price, and nobody adopts any child at a State Court without paying a specified bribe to the agent of the judge.

Military/politicians–vice operations

The vice operations involve brothels, casinos, and bootlegging. From the writer's own investigations, the illegal import and sale of alcohol are not enterprises run exclusively by top politicians and military officials, but casinos and brothels are. These politicians and military officers are the real heads of the criminal enterprise, but like organized crime bosses, they stay away from the everyday activities of the enterprise. When politicians are partners in vice operations, the other partner is not a politician. The politician partner uses his position to protect the illegal enterprise from police harassment and law enforcement. This manifestation of the political-criminal nexus is widespread, although not as highly integrated with the upper echelons of government. The ties to the head of state and to the inspector general of the Nigerian Police Force may not be very strong. For this reason, this kind of criminal enterprise is vulnerable to action by the police or any other federal law enforcement agency.

Prostitution is illegal in Nigeria, but many politicians and top military officials own brothels in various cities, including so-called "call-girl" brothels. These are prestigious hotels, but call girls are permitted to frequent the premises. In some hotels, only call girls who are working for the politician-owner are allowed. Occasionally, in cities like Onitsha, Aba, Jos, Kano, Abuja, Port Harcourt, Lagos, Enugu, Ibadan, and Benin, the police raid brothels owned by lower class businessmen who refuse to pay bribes. They arrest both the prostitutes and the owner. On the other hand, brothels owned by politicians and businessmen who pay are never raided or harassed. Similarly, casino and liquor businesses owned by politicians and military officials are left alone, despite the fact that it is illegal to operate casinos in Nigeria.

Unlike in the United States and other industrialized nations of Europe and Asia, vice operations in Nigeria are masterminded by the individuals who supposedly make policies for their control. This corruption of the Nigerian leadership is rooted in an obsessive desire to amass wealth, to be superior to all other entities in the country, and also to gain ethnic domination of the political and economic sectors of Nigerian society. In effect, customs and police officials do not see any reason for stringent enforcement of the law as long as the smuggler or bootlegger is willing to give them a bribe. Five customs officials that the writer interviewed in Lagos in 1997 said that "the leaders of the nation violate the laws with impunity, why then should a small man be prosecuted for the same offense? Unless the small man refuses to offer a bribe, then we get him arrested, and he will end up in prison."

Illegitimate enterprises

Only a few Nigerians without political and military connections were involved in illegal business activities during the oil boom. However, in the mid-1980s, when the oil industry collapsed, many Nigerians got into illegal arms smuggling, narcotics trafficking, counterfeit currency trafficking, smuggling of all sorts of prohibited textiles and foods, trading in body parts, and trafficking in children for slave labor and prostitution.

Several developments led to this growth in illegal activities. By 1985, the Babangida administration had devalued the currency and introduced the Structural Adjustment Program (SAP), which gave Nigeria easy access to foreign currencies. The politicians and military officials, who were already in the illegal enterprises, were forced to lure some unaffiliated smugglers to run their illegal activities for them, with guarantees of protection from prosecution, if they get caught crossing the Nigerian borders. It was during this period that new organized crime groups emerged and came to be known as the "419" syndicates. The name, pronounced "four-one-nine" came from a government decree that prohibited, among other things, illegal transfer of money to foreign banks. The "419" syndicates, under the camouflage of legitimate business, built their own banks, hotels, and other enterprises. The banks were more like loansharking operations, lending money at a rate of interest 25% higher than government regulation. This underground banking system also facilitated money laundering. The bankers "maintain ledgers in code so that no official paper trail is created" (Beare, 1990). The speed, simplicity, and confidentiality of these transactions made them attractive and safe. The trusted brokers at the receiving end know that the money is from an illegal source. Some senior police officers, politicians, and military officials are friends of the "419" syndicates and guarantee them protection against criminal prosecution, in exchange for money and personal security from time to time. Others have established regular business alliances with the "419" syndicates (Chizea, 1991).

The syndicates also run illegal casinos. With friends or partners in high places, the casinos operate without license or interference from the police. According to unsolicited statements of some associates of "419" elements, some politicians, top military officials, and contractors provide the money for the illegal enterprises of "419" syndicates.

Some of the joint activities by politicians and the "419" organized crime syndicates are associated with high levels of violence and/or do profound harm to innocent Nigerians. These include narcotics drug trafficking in cocaine, heroin, and marijuana; theft and distribution of stolen property; child stealing; kidnapping; trading in body parts; illegal manufacture of drugs for medical use; production of counterfeit medicines; forging foreign trademarks for Nigerian-made goods that are later sold as "foreign made imports," and racketeering.[45]

There are three principal types of Nigeria state-organized crime syndicates: the traditional criminal syndicates of the 1960s to the present, the "419" syndicates of the 1980s to the present, and the secret societies of the past and present. Each type of organized crime syndicate has its own specialty. Unlike organized crime operations in the United States, there is no division of territory, nor is there a common bond among them. This is partly because the head of state is a participant in the illegal enterprises and no Nigerian head of state remains in that position for a very long time. When a regime is toppled, it spells the end of the associated criminal enterprises.

Both the traditional organized crime groups in Nigeria and the "419" syndicates engage in the same kinds of criminal enterprises. Both are involved in drug smuggling and both have female members. Unlike the traditional Nigerian organized crime groups, the "419" syndicates also have branches in London and Paris, and in major cities of the United States, India, Pakistan, Bangkok, Thailand, Brazil, Colombia, Ethiopia, Italy, Ghana, Cameroon, Kenya, South Africa, Namibia, and Zimbabwe, while they maintain their base of operations in Nigeria.[46]

The traditional organized crime and "419" syndicates have rings specializing in stealing cars, artworks, and valuable domestic and office items. They distribute the stolen items across Nigerian borders in Africa, and smuggle the artwork overseas.[47] Both engage in "the sale of children into bonded labor, prostitution, and domestic slavery" (Tortein, 1996). According to a leading Nigerian human rights group and the Constitutional Rights Project Report:

> Middlemen go out scouting for families with more children than they can care for.
>
> They convince such families of the juicy employment opportunities for their wards in the city, inside Nigeria and outside Nigeria.
>
> Ten-year-old Chukwudi Joseph was recruited and shipped to Gabon to work for a logging company. After three years, Gabonese authorities deported him to Nigeria. He had never been paid.
>
> Thirteen-year-old Tope came from neighboring Benin (Republic) on the promise of work, but when she arrived in Lagos (Nigeria) found that work was in a brothel. When she became pregnant she was abandoned on the street (Eke 1997).

An even more horrific fate awaited those children and adults killed by "419" syndicates for their "body parts" (Modupe, 1997; Anueyiagu, 1997). In fall 1996, in the city of Owerri (Imo state of Nigeria), the police found body parts in a freezer at the Otokoto Hotel. The hotel owner,Otokoto, a local government official from the Ikeduru area, was arrested after being implicated by a tip-off from other "419" syndicates. The investigation had been triggered by the disappearance of the son of a very wealthy Owerri citizen. The police also forced Otokoto to show them where the bodies of the persons whose heads, liver, kidney, penis, and genitals, were found in the freezer, had been buried. Sixteen human bodies without heads were exhumed near Otokoto's home and he later confessed to selling body parts since 1976. Nigerian newspapers reported that some politicians were involved with the "419" criminal activities and in the selling of the body parts (Jenrola, 1990).

Immediately after the arrest of Otokoto, unemployed youths, some of them university graduates, known as "area boys," went on the rampage and burnt the Otokoto Hotel to the ground. Next they torched all residential buildings, hotels, and businesses known to be owned by "419" syndicates. Whether or not they were related to Otokoto, the "area boys" knew that every "419" group is an organized crime group. The relatives of Otokoto were subsequently excommunicated by the people of Imo state.

Trading in body parts went unnoticed by the public in Nigeria for many years, because some politicians and some very wealthy persons were said to be involved. Because those elites also control the police, there were no investigations.

There are some "exclusives" even in Nigeria. Eighty-five percent of the "area boys" interviewed in Owerri said that the "419" syndicates are not in the bootlegging business. Bootlegging is the exclusive business of the traditional Nigerian organized crime groups and their political affiliates. They supply contraband liquor and distill and sell it without a license. However, both "419" and traditional syndicates are racketeers. Fraud is the most lucrative business of "419" syndicates, and the federal government of Nigeria is most often the victim. Some politicians, executives of statutory corporations, and top civil servants are privy to these fraudulent schemes (Jenrola, 1990). Other "419" fraud victims include other governments in Africa, foreign companies, and individuals and businesses in the United States, Canada, Britain, France, Germany, Japan, India, and Pakistan (Okpa, 1995).

The "419" syndicates are also deeply involved in document fraud and currency counterfeiting, especially Nairas, U.S. dollars, and British pounds. They use their own banks and corrupt bank managers in other commercial banks to put the counterfeit money into circulation. They operate in collaboration with some top federal government officials to fake business certificates and Nigerian passports as well as those of other countries.[48]

State-Organized Crime in Legitimate Enterprises

Organized crime elements pose as legitimate business in the construction industry, banking, and manufacturing. Activities in these areas are also masterminded by politicians and military officials. In the construction industry, organized crime groups including "419" syndicates register themselves as contractors. Some "419" companies are registered as legitimate companies, but they use illegal methods in the contracts awarded to them. They either perform the contract fraudulently or do not carry it out at all, but still collect their money in full from the government as if they had satisfied all the terms. Either the head of state is a member of the conspiracy or a top politician is privy to the fraud, so the syndicates get away with it. In some situations, both the head of state and a minister of a government department are part of the fraudulent deal. All of them share the millions of dollars usually involved. In operating the legitimate enterprise, the "419" syndicates resort to assassination of competitors, terrorism, and tax evasion. They also underpay or even never pay their workers, knowing that because a politician is a partner in the enterprise nobody will do anything.

There are cases of "419" contractors who ally with politicians and directors general and receive contracts on a continuing basis. As noted earlier, some of the contracts are performed and some are not, but are still paid by the federal government or state government. The politicians and the directors general get their share of the money and nobody questions the contract nonperformance or poor performances.

The scale of bribery in private and statutory corporations and the manufacturing industry demonstrates that the traditional organized crime groups have effectively nullified government regulation by bribing the federal agencies assigned to enforce the regulations. If the head of state is the owner of the enterprise, no police officer or regulatory agency will enforce the law against him. If the enterprise is owned by a politician and his criminal partners, the influence of the politician on the inspector general of police or on the individual police officers in the area will accomplish the same end. These organized crime manufacturing enterprises avoid paying taxes by keeping two sets of books, one for government inspection which determines the taxes to be paid, and another for the company's own use to evaluate productivity and overall profit. Government inspectors are bribed not to ask for production records (Oroh, 1990; Gahia, 1990).

In Nigeria, banks fail frequently because of wholesale fraud by "419" groups and bank managers and their collaborators outside the bank. As of June 15, 1997, more than 2,000 bank managers and their chief accountants have been in detention for over 6 months without trial. And between January 1995 and January 1996, over 188 bank managers and accountants were sentenced to prison terms ranging from 7 years to 21 years. The bank managers' conspiracies include some military officials, politicians, "419" syndicates, and big businessmen.[50] The bank managers were jailed and detained indefinitely for giving fraudulent loans or for embezzlement. However, most of them came from commercial banks that were not in the head of state's personal "portfolio." His were largely untouched.

Sociocultural Factors in Nigerian State-Organized Crime

Three important sociocultural factors facilitated the development of the political-criminal nexus in Nigeria and led some Nigerians to use all means available to "make it" economically. They are, first, the interethnic scramble for a share of the "national cake"; second, the concept of extended families, of being one's brother's keeper, and the expectations thus raised; and, finally, a culture that honors conspicuous consumption.

The expectations of the extended family system and the cultural requirement of sons to take care of aged parents create enormous pressures. Public opinion holds that "what belongs to the government also belongs to everybody." To steal from the government is a minor abuse of power, at best. So a son with a government position who fails to expropriate from the government that which belongs to the government to help his relatives and members of his constituency is regarded as weak and wicked. Government workers who try to live by the rules are worthless to the community. They may be nick-named "Holy Nweje," a colloquialism that means a false holy person in the eyes of God. Similar expectations about government service can be found in all ethnic groups in Nigeria, and in all African societies south of the Sahara.

The pressure of these cultural expectations and the desire to succeed economically led some to join secret societies that guarantee members opulence and prosperity. There are many secret societies in Nigeria, but only two types are directly involved in organized crime: "wealth-oriented secret societies" and "Untouchable (osu)-sorcery societies."

The "wealth-oriented secret society" resembles a satanic cult in certain respects whose adherents will do anything to amass wealth in their business enterprises. Members must be willing to sacrifice their nearest and dearest to the satanic entity who, in return, will make them fabulously rich. This might mean a wife, son, daughter, mother, father, or a friend, whoever is held most dear and is acceptable to the entity. Demands might also extend to the member's own body, anything short of life-threatening such as an eye, a hand, or a leg. Once a member had confronted the satanic oracle, there is no going back. The principles, rules, and missions of the cult are secret. From time to time however, members attempt to leave and enter spiritual churches in an attempt to protect themselves. It is then that some of the secrets are revealed. The existence of this type of cult is general knowledge in Nigeria and throughout African societies, and is well documented in African law and literature about Nigerian customs. Although some members of the wealth-oriented secret society belong to the Untouchable (osu) caste, others have joined since Christianity emerged in Nigeria in the 1860s. If a cult member becomes a politician, he is protected by the cult through its chief priest. This protection may increase motivation to engage in the activities of organized crime (Elias, 1956; Forde, 1965).

This wealth-oriented secret society is the oldest type of traditional organized crime in Nigeria. Its members run all kinds of businesses, both legitimate and illegitimate, without any government intervention. Like organized crime groups in the United States, they support political candidates who can protect their enterprises. Politicians know them and respect them for their fabulous wealth.

The Untouchable sorcery society has its roots in Eastern Nigeria, especially among the Igbos, and has since grown to embrace others with similar life experiences in various parts of Nigeria. Individuals become members by virtue of their status as outcastes or osu, an ascribed status. They are not freeborn by birth. Their ancestors committed an abomination and were dedicated to the gods. They worship the holy shrine (god) to which they were dedicated

(Achebe, 1959). Their descendants also became outcastes or untouchables simply by being born into such a family, and were treated accordingly (Ebbe, 1996). There is a certain injustice in the culture which punishes someone for the crimes of one's ancestors.

Unfortunately, forming a secret society became a kind of coping mechanism for the untouchables. Today, they claim to use witchcraft to fight against the freeborn, even those who had not wronged them in any way. In Eastern Nigeria, some people believe that untouchable sorcery society members also use witchcraft to destroy the businesses of the freeborn and that their gangs of murderers assassinate the men and women who segregated them, or freeborn politicians who opposed their members in their constituencies. Politicians who are from untouchable families are more likely to engage in state-organized crime syndicates and in money making opportunities associated with it, because they believe that wealth and opulence will lead to general acceptance and positions of authority in the country (Osifo-Whiskey, 1988; Balebo et al., 1994).

The untouchable sorcery societies are known to engage in assassinations, and since the 1970s, they have killed many prominent Igbos and non-Igbos in Eastern Nigeria, whom they claimed had segregated them. Their methods are well-known, but nothing can be done because many of them are in political leadership of Nigeria, some in the topmost echelons.[51] Their members in the media prevent adverse reporting on their illegal activities. Some are highly educated, because they were the first to go to church and school when the Europeans came to Nigeria (Achebe, 1959). Among their ranks are lawyers, judges, medical doctors, professors, engineers, and other professionals. They identify their own through a "password" or sign that acknowledges membership of the outcaste (osu) institution, even if they are meeting for the first time.

External Forces in Nigerian State-Organized Crime

The oil boom of the 1970s attracted many foreign industrialists to Nigeria, and with their arrival a large market for Western-manufactured goods sprang up. Some foreign companies and foreign contractors who were prepared to launder illegal money in overseas banks amassed fabulous wealth through illegal business deals with Nigerian politicians and military war lords. Some specialized in carrying out illegal and fraudulent business transactions with Nigerian politicians as part of Nigerian state-organized crime partnership operating across the Atlantic and Indian Oceans (Gahia, 1990). Throughout the 1970s and 1980s, every major bank in Western Europe, Japan, and China had Nigerians as customers in both legal and illegal bank accounts. There are laws against money laundering in Nigeria, but like most Nigerian business laws, they are not enforced, and the "419" leader may be the director general. In other cases, it is a top businessman who happens to be a friend of the politician. The negotiations about the division of the illegal profits and the modus operandi of the illegal scheme take place between the politician, the director general, and the "419" leader.

Patterns of Exchange Between the Politicians and the "419" Syndicates

The "419" syndicates are sources of income for some politicians. Their connections involve defrauding national and foreign governments, banks, and businesses, money laundering for the politicians and the military officials, and running illegal businesses such as brothels and casinos for the politicians. The "419" groups often register hotels and other forms of businesses under fictitious ownership names for the politicians or military officials. The latter, in return, provide the "419" syndicates immunity from police harassment and prosecution (Ubani, 1989, 1990a).

Some "419" syndicates specialize in providing personal security to the politicians. Politicians with strong influence in the Customs and Excise Department secure easy and uninterrupted passage across Nigerian borders with contraband good for the "419" syndicates. In all cases, both financial and nonfinancial favors are exchanged in an atmosphere of mutual respect. When "419" members are prosecuted, their protectors come to their aid and the case may die down without any further court action.

Other "419" organized crime syndicates also engage in terrorism. Politicians who want to be rid of their political opponents or business competitors pay the "419" syndicates and guarantee them immunity from prosecution. The assassination of Senator Chief Obi Nwali in Port Hacourt (River State) in 1994, and Kudirat Abiola, the wife of Chief M.K.O. Abiola, in Lagos (1996), have been described by some Nigerian newspapers as the work of "419" state-organized crime syndicates (Ubani, 1990b).

During 1996, many politicians escaped assassination attempts. In the case of the former minister of justice, Onagoruwa, the "419" state-organized crime gangs killed his son instead. In January 1997, Chief Abraham Adesanya, the deputy chairman of the National Democratic Coalition (NADECO), a pro-democracy movement in Nigeria that is against military rule in Nigeria, escaped an assassination attempt while driving to work in Lagos. The last assassination attempt in Nigeria in 1997 was on General Oladipo Diya, the Nigerian vice president. A bomb killed his security officer. The attacks were said to be the work of the "419" political-criminal-nexus-organized crime gangs hired by some politicians excluded from the current military regime and by top military officials seeking to secure their own positions by eliminating their fellow officers. The political assassinations and assassination attempts in Nigeria are somewhat reminiscent of the ancient Roman Senate (Proal, 1898).

Perpetuating Nigerian Military Dictatorship State Organized Crime

Since 1966, the Nigerian military generals have been overthrowing themselves, as if it were an accident. All of the coup d'etat and counter coups d'etat after their overthrow of Major General Aguiyi-Ironsi were premeditated conspiratorial coups. Unsuccessful coups were not in with the order of succession or conspiratorial order of succession. From General Buhari, who overthrew a democratically elected civilian government, to General Abacha were premeditatedly designed. There was a lot of money to be made by being a dictator of a Nigerian government. General Buhari, General Babangida, and General Abacha agreed on the coups they carried out.

General Babangida overthrew the dictatorship of Buhari, in 1985, now Babangida is backing General Buhari to head the 2015–2019 Nigerian civilian government in this year's presidential election. The coup of General Abacha was masterminded by General Babangida. It should not surprise anybody that at the end of the two-term presidential limit of the Nigerian political system of Buhari leadership, that another retired Nigerian General will come up to contest for the Nigerian Presidency. The Hausa-Fulani Muslims, who do not want to work, and do not want to invest the stolen money in businesses, which could offer jobs to millions of unemployed Nigerians, saw being a head of state of Nigeria as an occupation. And using gangsters in Nigeria and around the world to deposit the stolen money in foreign banks is their governing specialty.

A report shows that during the five years General Abacha was the head of state of Nigeria, "he was estimated to have stolen up to $5 billion" (Clarke, 2015). The amount due to General Abacha in the NLNG deal that got stuck with the contractors based in the United States is said to be "over $1.2 billion", which is said, that "Nigeria may have lost to bribes" (Alike, 2010). But take note of this, Abacha did not steal Nigeria's money as much as those generals who ruled Nigeria before him. How would one prove this? Both Babangida and Obasanjo ruled Nigeria longer than Abacha. But neither General Babangida nor General Obasanjo reduced Nigerian foreign debts. Instead, the two leaders continued to multiply Nigeria's foreign debts, and Nigerian foreign reserve plummeted.

Undeniably, records show,

> The Abacha administration become the first to record unprecedented economic achievement: he oversaw an increase in the country's foreign exchange reserves from $494 million in 1993 to $9.6 billion by the middle of 1997, reduced the external debt of Nigeria from $36 billion in 1993 to $27 billion by 1997, brought all the controversial privatization programs of the Babangida administration to a halt, reduced an inflation rate of 54% inherited from Ibrahim Badamasi Babangida to 8.5% between 1993 and 1998, all while the nations primary commodity, oil, was at an average of $15 per barrel (see *Premium Times Nigeria*,[52] also *Vanguard News*,(http://vanguardngr.com/2011/06/sani-abacha-legacy-of-a-great-leader).[53]

It's a normal strategy of a "mafia boss" to do great services to his community, and make charitable donations to various community events to present himself as a nice guy. Such benevolent gestures are very often seen among other criminal gang leaders. That is exactly what General Abacha did to Nigeria. He worked hard for Nigeria, but at the same time stole a lot of their money. He was better than those who stole more than he did and still perpetrated irrecoverable damages to the Nigerian people. Where is Nigerian Airways (2004–present)? It was sold to European and the United States Airlines; and Asian and other African countries' airlines share the booty.

The former Nigerian military leaders shared the Nigerian oil wells among themselves, and gave some to their friends and relatives, according to Obinna Akukwe (2012) of the *Nigerian Master Web Citizen News*. This same avaricious military dictators came up with the idea of privatizing Nigerian statutory corporations, and took some of the industries for themselves without paying a fee to the Nigerian people.

When a head of state is a criminal, like Rafael Trujillo, then he had to ally with known criminals. That is the case for Nigeria. General Abacha told the whole world by his kleptocracy that all of the Nigerian military regimes were criminal state regimes. This is because the average price of crude oil was far higher than $15 per barrel in both General Obasanjo and General Babangida regimes. But where is the surplus compared to General Abacha's regime? Nigeria is not alone in the world. You are going to see Zaire, Russia, and Mexico later in this text, as criminal states.

Powerful Organized Crime Groups and a Weak Government

This is a situation where the organized crime syndicates are too powerful for the state to control. It occurs, in the main, in a country in transition. Such a state is not used to dealing with controlling organized crime. It can also emerge in a country in a state of anomie (Durkheim, 1964). In an anomic situation, people work at cross-purposes with each other. There is virtually an absence of regulation. The law enforcement agencies are weak and have no motivation to enforce the law, unless in a situation where they have something to gain by enforcing the law. In such a state of affairs, organized crime thrives. Any attempt to enforce the law against them results in cold-blooded murder of the law enforcement officer. Any politician who tries to exercise his political power is gunned down to scare others. And when they kill a very powerful law enforcement officer or politician, they make sure that the masses are aware that they did it. Any journalist who tries to show his or her talent in investigative journalism pays the price with his blood.

When a head of state finds himself in such a situation, he seeks a compromise with the leaders of the organized crime syndicates. In this type of state-organized crime, Russia and Mexico are the current best examples.

Russia State-Organized Crime

The sudden collapse of the Soviet Union left the masses of Russian people like five under-age children whose both parents died in an automobile accident, and they are the only survivors. And they did not have any known uncle, nephew, aunt, or cousins. Unfortunately, Boris

Nikoayevich Yeltsin grabbed a disorganized Russia like a man who is having a hangover every second of the day. A powerful nation became a toothless bulldog overnight.

Russia has always had men of the underworld as far back as the Stalin period, but the Communist Party did not give them a chance. Many were in Soviet Gulag, and some were free on the outside subsisting with communist black market. Communism was their major headache. They watched Western movies of Sicilian and Italian mafia, and American organized crime families. They had no opportunity to experiment on what they watched. Those who left Soviet Russia for the Western world kept in touch with the men of the underworld they left behind.

Mikhail Gorbachev's perestroika gave the Russian underworld a little breathing space. It was a preparatory period for what they believed would later happen. They found their "new haven" after the 1991 Soviet abortive coup attempt to overthrow Soviet President Mikhail Gorbachev by a group of Soviet Union hardliners who hated the President's perestroika reform policy.

Immediately after the abortive coup, the Soviet Republic began to secede and declared their independence from the Soviet Union. Boris Yeltsin became both the President and Prime Minister of Russia. On December 25, 1991, Mikhail Gorbachev resigned as the Soviet President, and the Soviet Union officially came to an end on December 26, 1991.

The Russian underworld criminals heaved a sigh of relief. The masses of the Russian people were happy that Soviet dictatorship had come to an end, and celebrated it. They anticipated wonderful freedom that democracy would afford them. But it turned out to be a hopeless euphoria.

The Russian underground criminals had been tied down in prisons and frustrating corners of Russian cities for decades of communist totalitarianism. At the eclipse of the Soviet Union in December 1991, the next year was a new moon and the beginning of a new economic (capitalism) and political order (democracy). On that first year of capitalism and democracy, the natural resources, statutory corporations, communist central planning institutions, state buildings, state service businesses, import and export license controls, and so forth were all up for grabs. There was no prior, smooth planning in place for a gradual transition from central planning to capitalist mode of private ownership of property. The central planning that was in place was disorganized by the aftermath of the abortive coup attempt. Before Boris Yeltsin could be authorized to rule by decrees, the Russian criminal underworld, who have been languishing in silence of unfulfilled criminal aspirations, exploded into the streets of Moscow and other cities. They began with robbery, burglary, scaring owners of businesses with extortion, fraud, and all sorts of rackets. There were many gangs trying to take control of different parts of Moscow. "Almost every day, corpses are found in Moscow with bound hands and feet, sometimes even parts of bodies," Moskovsky Komsomolets reported to a Moscow bureau chief for *The Toronto Star* in July 1992 (Handelman, 1995).

The Russian gangsters have their super hotels and all sorts of businesses. They began with killing some top business owners who were in competition with them. The worst of all, they make huge amounts of money by extortion. Many business tycoons lost their lives, because they did not pay off.

According to Handelman (1995), in his interview in a hotel with a Moscow young man, asked him, "If he would describe himself as a businessman?" The young man replied: "I don't have a job. I don't need to work, but I make very good money. This is a country where you can make a lot of money without doing anything." In the process of the interview, Handelman found out from him that he was a hit man. From the interview, any business establishment that is in a Russian city that does not pay protection money is closed. If the owner of the business intrepidly operates, he is killed in cold blood within 48 hours of his obduracy. Some former Soviet state food warehouse employees, who engaged in illegally supplying "shadow markets" (black market) dealers with state food items during the central planning system, already knew the "Mafiya" (Russian term for "Mafia") lords over 10 years before 1992. In effect, those former Soviet state food warehouse employees, who opened grocery stores in various Russian cities, found it easier to protect their stores from young emerging Mafiya gangs, by hiring the older crime lords to protect their businesses. When some Mafiya gangs struck at the protected stores, their blood was flowing on the sidewalks of Moscow streets (Handelman, 1995; Satter, 2003).

In 1992, it was like Russia was at war with itself. Professional businesses like medical clinics, law firms, owners of newly acquired or leased former Soviet State service industrial centers, and hotels were forced to hire Mafiya protection gangs after the latter fired incendiary grenades into some professional businesses at midnight. Some Mafiya gangs walked into professional businesses and other business establishments and demanded routine protection money or else (Satter, 2003; Handelman, 1995; Hirschfeld, 2015).

The Russian Grand-Mafiya (the rich and powerful notorious criminal underworld) acquired some Soviet state corporations and service companies for peanuts or free leases through their publicly presumed decent oligarchic (member of Russian business elite) executives. Those Soviet state corporations and service companies not acquired by the grand Mafiya syndicates became subjected to violent take over by the grand Mafiya.

There are two groups of Mafiya in Russia. "Grand Mafiya" and "Street Mafiya." Grand Mafiya control Russian economy today. They are rich. They protect the well-known traditional oligarchs for a fee. Those oligarchs who appeared arrogant and refused to have anything to do with the Grand Mafia were either assassinated or they ran away from Russia into self-exile. This Russian Grand Mafiya have more deadly firearms and other explosives than do many countries in Western Europe. In 1993, they used those weapons against pro-Soviet Union politicians who posed obstacles to their wholesale criminal mission to take over Russian economy. In effect, when the pro-Soviet Union politicians wanted to impeach Boris Yeltsin, they became Yeltsin's defenders, using their agents to bribe members of the Federal Council of Russia (the Upper House) and members of the State Duma (the Lower House). As a result, Yeltsin was incapacitated in controlling organized crime (Mafiya) in that early stage of Russian capitalism and democracy.

The Street Mafiya gangsters are clusters of consolidated ex-convicts and unemployed young men in their 20 and 30s controlling some areas of large cities. They subsist by extortionary protection fees from non-Mafiya businesses, narcotics drug smuggling and peddling, hired killing, robbery, burglary, running prostitution rings, and racketeering of all types. Each Street Mafiya syndicate controls its territory. It is always bloody if one syndicate penetrates into another's area of operation or attacks a syndicate's client's protected business venture. Unaffiliated street robbers, drug addicts, alcoholics, and street prostitutes lose their lives when they criminally or recklessly stray into the Street Mafiya areas of operation (Gilinskiy, 2000; Handelman, 1995).

The combined operations of the Grand Mafiya and the Street Mafiya throughout Russian cities, coupled with ruthless control of the members of the Federal Council of Russia, the State Duma, and the poor civil servants in the ministries, through inescapable bribes and murder, brought the former super power into the category of a predatory criminal state.

From the opportunities offered by Gorbachev's perestroika to the demise of the Soviet state in December 1991, some politicians in Russia made themselves both members of the upperworld and the underworld at the same time. In 1991, such politicians were already oligarchs before the 1992 emergence of capitalism and democracy in Russia. In effect, they used their money and political connections to acquire Soviet state companies at giveaway prices (Klebnikov, 2001). Boris Berezovsky is an excellent example of such a double-faced politician in Russia from 1989 through the present. Some of them blended into the Grand Mafiya solidarity, while others, as noted above, went into self-exile.

When the battle of how to control the Russian masses, and the over 2,000 Grand Mafiya and Street Mafiya syndicates came upon how to go about it in the Russian upper and lower houses without a consensus, the Russian militia (police) were in a dilemma. Besides, they were not prepared to deal with capitalist system of law enforcement. The Grand Mafiya and Street Mafiya explosion, and their ruthless violence, overwhelmed the Russian militia (from now on referred to as the Russian police or the police). In fact, the Russian police in the streets were not as heavily armed, from 1991 to 1999, as the Russia Mafiya. Controlling the Mafiya, in effect, became a wild goose chase (Shelley, 1996; Gilinskiy, 2000; Satter, 2003).

The way Boris Berezovsky made his money under President Boris Yeltsin, along with other oligarchs of Yeltsin's regime, who flew away after Vladimir Putin became President of post-Soviet Russia, has a lot to tell. And those of them who did not escape dropped from being billionaire and millionaire statuses they acquired from Yeltsin's privatization auction of Soviet state properties. Many of them were new political-business oligarchs, who turned themselves into new Mafiya but not cooperative with the Grand Mafiya of the traditional "Thieves' World" of the Bolshevik Revolution. As a result, some of them were being hunted by the Grand Mafiya. Whoever was not ready to cooperate with the Grand Mafiya control had to leave Russia or perish in the quest. As noted above, the Grand Mafiya are in control of over 75% of the Russian economy, and absolute overt racketeering is their modus operandi.

The characteristics and domination of Russian society by Mafiya are succinctly delineated by Louise Shelley (1996) (paraphrased) as authoritarian domination of the economy and the ruling structure of Russia, intimidation of the masses, privatization of state coercion (usurp police control), intimidation and obstructing investigative journalism world-wide, privatization of state resources exclusively to Mafiya syndicates, and subversion of an evolving new Russia.

The Mafiya took over Russia, because they intimidated the new president of the emerging capitalist mode of production and democracy, Boris Yeltsin, and scared the hell out of him with killing of powerful pro-Soviet state politicians. At the same time, Yeltsin was under fire with pro-Soviet Union politicians who could not believe that communism was freezing overnight in their hands. Consequently, Yeltsin had to go it easy with the Grand Mafiya, who posed to bail him out of the looming impeachment. By the time Yeltsin left office for Vladimir Putin, Russia was too legally, morally, socially, politically, and economically broken. Not only was Russia broken, it became a very deadly environment for every Russian politician including Putin, the former KGB agents, and the Russian military. It is a saying that "where ignorance is bliss, it is folly to be wise." And a surviving coward is better than a dead brave soldier. Also, as Chairman Mao (1966) put it, "the basic principle of war is to preserve oneself and destroy the enemy." This is the line President Putin and his government decided to take, to follow the line of easy resistance. They had to let the criminals rule, because before the emergence of capitalism on January 1, 1992, they had no capitalist-system-trained police, no FBI, no *Guardia di Finanza* of Italy, no Scotland Yard and MI5 of the United Kingdom, and so forth, specialized in law enforcement in a cutthroat capitalism. In effect, the masses of Russia were thrown into a selfish world of capitalism. It is absolutely a rational reasoning to leave it to the criminals in such a terrible situation. In addition, in Russia, there were absolutely no business laws including contract laws in place before the emergence of the capitalist mode of production, distribution, and consumption.

Unmistakably, it is not unexpected that when some people in Russia opened investments and cooperative bank accounts that some Mafiya who own and opened the banks would run away with the savings deposits and the shares of the poor and rich. It is not unexpected, because we have seen such criminal bank operations in states that have capitalist law enforcement agencies such as Trujillo's Dominican Republic, Duvalier's Haiti, and Nigeria in the 1980s of Generals Buhari and Babangida regimes, and so forth.

Undeniably, Russia is an example of a state where the mobs say, "Our way or no way." President Putin did not start the Mafiya in Russia. Mafiya was there underground as far back as the 1700s as bandits and thieves of the period (Gilinskiy, 2003; Satter, 2003). Neither Vladimir Lenin nor Joseph Stalin could wipe them out (Molly, 2001).

The opportunity came gradually to the Mafiya during the perestroika, and they exploded in President Yeltsin's regime. By the time Putin came to power, some members of the police and KGB had already joined the Grand Mafiya including friends he had among the former KGB. He didn't want to die controlling the Mafiya. Rather, being their referee gives him all the political, social, and economic successes that he desired. Consequently, the Mafiya took control and undermined reform (Handelman, 1994). Obviously, to many inside and outside of Russia, it appears that President Putin is part of the Mafiya. The writer estimates to the contrary. Putin saw the savage attacks and murders of great men including court judges in Russia by Mafiya, that no one had ever seen in Russia before, and decided to save the day to fight tomorrow. In Putin's hands-off diplomacy, the Grand Mafiya responded to him in a seeming quid pro quo symbiosis. But, in reality, he is not for them.

Another state similar to Russia in some ways is Mexico, especially in organized crime power control.

The Dialectics of Mexican State-Organized Crime

The political experience of Mexico is like that of Russia. When a colonial master ruled a country in an authoritarian, dictatorship model for 115 years, and all of a sudden decided, unwillingly, to leave their dependency with a democratic system that the people had never experienced, it is bound to fail. Such dependencies are African countries. Nigeria was colonized by the British in 1849 and granted her independence in 1960, a period of 111 years. But think about Mexico which was ruled by Spain for approximately three centuries (291 years). F. Hernandez de Cordoba landed on the Mexican Peninsula Yucatan, on January 1, 1517. Two years later (January 1, 1519), Hernan Cortes had begun conquering the Aztec empire which formed the beginning of Spanish colonization of Mexico[56] (Young, 2007; Bethel, 1987; Benson, 1992; Archer, 2007).

Mexico, like many other former colonial dependencies and contemporary Russia, had no idea of democracy. All they lived through was a dictatorship of a few Western oligarchies. And Mexico was buried in that colonial dictatorship for a long time. After the Mexican independence in 1810, freedom jumped out of the window as fast as it came in. Besides, colonial Mexico, like the British and French subjects of the late 19th and 20th centuries, was exploited and neglected by Spain longer than their African counterparts (Pimentel, 2000). After independence, Mexico endured "a century of local dictatorship by revolutionary leaders" (Pimentel, 2000). Undeniably, such combined four centuries of dictatorship in modern times, in the words of Stanley A. Pimentel, "could not then allow a democratic civil society to evolve overnight."[57]

Throughout the early 1900s to 1929, there were many political groups, and that favored organized crime groups. As organized crime likes a weak government, the multiplicity of opposed parties made the dictatorships of military and civilian ones a fertile ground for organized crime. For instance, from 1822 to 1914, there were three military dictatorships and four civilian dictatorships in Mexico. Such unstable governments are where organized crime breeds. In effect, in Mexico of the period, the Mexican drug cartels were in control. The politicians were not sure of how long they were to remain in power. In effect, many of them were on the pay checks of organized crime. The law enforcement agencies: the police, military, and internal security agencies, were also neutralized with bribes they could not refuse.

In 1929, however, the various political factions came together under one umbrella to form *Partido Revolucionario Institucional* (PRI). This political party became something like a savior of the people. But it had a monopoly of political power. And it remained authoritarian for many years. It fought to get power back from the criminal organizations by reorganizing its internal security forces, the military, and the police to crack down on organized crime. The government used taxation and stringent enforcement of the law to control organized crime. Some of the organized crime lords were given long terms of sentences. The Mexican government built up its treasury with heavy taxation against the organized crime groups and confiscation of drug money seized from the smugglers (Curzio, 2000).

At this stage, the political authorities were exploiting organized crime groups. There were groups they allowed to carry out their illegal drug smuggling for as long as they paid their taxes, made substantial campaign contributions to the ruling party (PRI). According to Pimentel (2000), "the political authorities provided immunity from prosecution for the criminal groups while obtaining money for development, investment, and campaign funding for the party, as well as for personal enrichment."

In a process of time, the criminal groups revolted because of the changing times. It was in the 1980s. Social change began to bring in new directions in the economy, politics, and the emergence of more educated middle class; the concern for human rights violations, the demands of the North American Free Trade Agreement (NAFTA), and opposition parties winning important positions, made it very hard for the PRI political authorities to continue to manipulate and control organized crime (Hirschfeld, 2015; Pimentel, 2000; Curzio, 2000).

The social changes that gripped Mexico in the 1980s and 1990s destroyed the symbiotic existence between the political authorities and the criminal groups. The criminal drug cartels want all of the money they earned smuggling narcotics drugs across the U.S.-Mexican borders and elsewhere. In effect, they fought against the old authoritarian regime, because new sources of political power in the emerging democracy armed the drug cartels with new alliances at less cost.

To take over control of their territories without interference, they began with assassination of well-known political figures, tough law enforcement officials, and nullifying the Mexican military with bribes (Manaut, 2000; Pimentel, 2000). Overall, the criminal groups knew from past experience that party politics needs organized crime money. As a result, drug cartels in Mexico decided to use it to their advantage, but not to continue to be a "cash cow" for a single dictatorship. The killings in government security agencies, prisons, court officials, including prosecutors, drove Mexican state authorities to a surrender mode, just like in present-day Russia. By the turn of the 21st century, the drug cartels had built a lot of stores of hidden cash in dollars and pesos for nullifying law enforcement.

In 2000, the cartels' control of lives and needs of the Mexican people at the Mexican-U.S. border areas was too much to bear to a point, that the Mexican President, Vincent Fox, dispatched his military men to Neuvo Laredo to crush the cartels. It was a fight between the Gulf and Sinaloa Cartels and the government troops. It was between January and August 2005 in which 110 people were killed (Marshall, 2005). As older cartels got weak and collapsed, new cartels emerged, especially when the *La Familia Michoacana* drug cartel dug in at Michoacan in 2005, which sparked a new wave of uncontrollable violence.

Mexican drug wars today are as a result of the following reasons:

- The eclipse of the Colombian Cali and Medellin Cartels in the 1990s, and Mexican drug cartels had to dominate the market to fill the void created by the absence of the Colombian drug lords (Vulliamy, 2010; Longmire, 2013).
- Mexico is a major drug-producing country, a great producer of cannabis.
- Mexico is a major drug transit and an entry point of South American cocaine and Asian methamphetamines to the United States.
- The draw in Mexico drug market are Cannabis, cocaine, heroin, and methamphetamine.
- Extreme poverty forced lower class youths to be readily available for recruitment into criminal groups. For instance, between 2006 and 2010, there were 52 million Mexicans living in extreme or moderate poverty,[58] and the "youth assassins" are paid 12,000 pesos a month, which is more than three times what most Mexicans earn at that same time (Ramsey 2011).
- The failure of the Mexican government to provide well-paid jobs for the youths.
- Of 90% of Mexican children who attended primary school, only 62% proceeded to secondary school, and of those who attended secondary school, only 25% passed on to higher education (Agren, 2012; Alba, 1982).
- The amount of money involved in the narcotics drug trade ranges from $13.6 billion to $49.4 billion annually. That is the enticement.
- The drug cartels raped the government to near death by corrupting and intimidating law enforcement officials. In effect, the Mexican local government, state, and federal government officials, including police forces, at some points, had to work with the drug cartels, like in Russia, in an organized chain and network of corruption (symbiosis).

In Russia, it is "*pax Mafiya*;" in Mexico, it is "pax cartel" (Mafioso), a quid pro quo form of "corruption which guarantees a politician votes and a following in exchange for turning a 'blind eye' toward a particular cartel" (Vulliamy, 2010).

What has been happening in Mexico disturbs the collective conscience of the people. There have been many wars happening inside Mexico at the same time. As Paul Kan (2012) noted:

> Cartels battle one another, cartels suffer violence within their own organization, cartels fight against the Mexican state, cartels and gangs wage war against the Mexican people, and gangs combat gangs. The war has killed more than 60,000 people since President Felipe Calderón began cracking down on the cartels in December

2006. The targets of the violence have been wide ranging—from police officers to journalists, from clinics to discos.

Unmistakably, the drug cartels are a threat to Mexican democracy, just as the "Mafiya" has, in the main, taken over Russian democracy. The bloodshed of young children, teenagers, young adults, and middle-aged men and women in Mexico, has gone beyond epidemic proportions. According to Grillo (2012), since 2006, 40,000 people have been murdered; "police chiefs shot within hours of taking office; mass graves comparable to those of civil wars; car bombs shattering storefronts; and headless corpses heaped in town squares." Longmire (2013), a security expert, stepped into the world of the Mexican cartels and saw a complicated, risky underground method of drug delivery, where the recruits will do whatever it takes to deliver the narcotics to willing American consumers. And observed a network of secret tunnels used for smuggling the drugs, and armies of submarines that transport narcotics along Central American coasts. The riskiness of this illegal drug trade is what makes it too bloody a venture. And in the presence of Mexico's economic, social, educational, and political problems, the cartels will reign supreme over the government for a long time.

The cartels have a strategy with which they terrorize everybody, including the politicians and the government authorities. Hirschfeld (2015) noted, "in 2009, over 5000 people were killed in drug related violence in Mexico, and journalists have noted a shift in recent years from hidden or private killings (corpses displayed in places visible only to underworld rivals) to public displays intended to terrorize all onlookers into submission."

The Mexican cartels' drug wars are like Rwandan genocide. All kinds of persons of all ages are killed in an assembly in hotels, prisons, cafes, bars, and so forth, like they are not human beings. The Mexican government doesn't even have enough willing police and army personnel to fight them. For the Mexican government to be on top again over the cartels, it will require a cooperative, coordinated, international military intervention.

With the Mexican government experience in capitalist economic system, one can see that blaming President Putin, or regarding him as an ally of the Mafiya, is an unfair judgment. This is because Mexico has been a capitalist economy and democratic system of government longer than Russia, and has trained its police force for a capitalist economy than Russia. But see how the masses of Mexicans are defenseless, just like in Russia.

Open-Ended State-Organized Crime

This type of state-organized crime is prevalent in more advanced economies of Europe and North America, where full democracy and capitalism operate at their highest pitch. In those jurisdictions, the literacy rate is 99%. The governments in those countries are committed to nationalism and underpinned by checks and balances.

The state in "open-ended state-organized crime" does not participate or condone traditional mafia. Instead, it fights against the La Cosa Nostra type of organized crime. The state in those regimes has the strategic intelligence agencies to control mafia operations. Its well-trained law enforcement agencies seek to dislodge the operation of criminal syndicates every day.

These advanced economies get into the business of organized crime when they fail to enforce the laws intended to control multinational corporations for purely quid pro quo reasons; when they give tax breaks to some of the corporations who do not need any tax exemption or tax break just to catapult their profits to billions of dollars, which is "corporate welfare;" when they turn a "blind eye" to deadly environmental pollution; and when they illegally compromise on the amount of profit a foreign corporate investor should repatriate to its country of origin.

Undeniably, the quid pro quo is embedded in the corporations giving substantial campaign contributions to the major political parties of the state and making some huge contributions to state courses. In addition, some state authorities have shares in stocks of such corporations which were never divested, when they got into political power.

Kickbacks: Political-Criminal Nexus

In national and local government contract awards, one may find the grand quid pro quo called kickback. A kickback is bribery, and it is illegal in all jurisdictions. There are two parties in a kickback taking: the person awarding the contract and the company or individual executing the contract. Both parties may not be directly involved in the negotiations. Both or one party may be represented by a broker. The negotiation in a government contract involves the amount of money the government (state) is willing to pay for the contract, the extra amount of money the government should add (illegally) far and above the actual or equitable value of the service to be rendered, the amount of money to be paid to the broker or brokers, and the amount to be given to the government official awarding the contract. Kickback is an illegal scheme to which both parties willingly cooperated (Wrage, 2007, 2010).

Kickback is an endemic corruption in virtually all states of the world. It is almost a cultural universal. Both rich and poor nations are parties to it. In some developing countries, such as India, Nigeria, Indonesia, Argentina, Brazil, Kenya, it is like a culture. Nigeria calls it "10 percent" (Ebbe, 1999, 2003). In Indonesia, President Suharto, who ruled the country from 1967 to 1998, was nicknamed in the country as *Mr. 25 percent.* This is because he required every contractor for a major contract award to give him 25% of the amount of the contract before it gets his approval (Campos, 2007; Elson, 2001). As in Nigeria, the President of Pakistan from 2008 to 2013, Asif Ali Zardari, was also known as *Mr. 10 percent,* because he required contractors to pay 10% of the value of the contract before appending his signature to the contract agreement (Wrage, 2007).

The 10% to 25% extortionary kickbacks in Nigeria, Pakistan, Indonesia, and so forth are a reminiscent of the illegal activities of some U.S. state governors such as Spiro Agnew of Maryland (President Richard Nixon's Vice President), was indicted by the FBI for tax fraud arising from receiving kickbacks from contractors, when he was governor of the State of Maryland (1967–1968). He responded to the FBI charges with *"nolo contendere."* He received a 3-year unsupervised probation and a fine of $10,000. A federal court judge ordered him to repay the state of Maryland $147,500 he received in kickbacks with interest of $101,235 totaling $248,735 (Franklin, 1981). In fact, before and after the Agnew case, many U.S. State governors have been convicted of various crimes of bribery, mail fraud, extortion, money laundering, racketeering, and so forth. Most of the state governors served time in prison for their crimes. In all of the above kickback crimes of the state governors, the national government created loopholes in the law for the political-criminal nexus to emerge. The number of state governors caught in those kickbacks and all sorts of racketeering crimes is just a tip of the iceberg. In every type of crime committed in a society, only a fraction of it is detected. There are more hidden crimes than known crimes.

Undeniably, in all contemporary regimes, democracies and dictatorships, industrial and nonindustrial nations, developed and underdeveloped societies, and capitalist and socialist economies, political-criminal collaboration is a truism.

Review Questions

1. What is organized crime?
2. What is state-organized crime?
3. Why would some heads of state engage in organized crime?
4. What is political-criminal nexus?
5. (a) What is a predatory state? (b) What is predatory taxation?
6. Write a brief account of each of the following:
   - Tontons Macoutes (Haiti)
   - The "42" (Dominican Republic)
   - The "Mirabal Sisters" (Dominican Republic)
   - The "419" (Nigeria)
   - Soviet Gulag
7. What are the cultural factors of Nigerian state-organized crime?
8. Compare and contrast the Russian Mafiya and the Mexican drug cartels.
9. What are the two Mafiya groups identified in Russia by the author. What are their differences?
10. There are dialectics in Mexican state-organized crime. Describe them.
11. What does the author mean by "open-ended state-organized crime"?
12. What is "kickback political-criminal nexus"?

Notes

1. Howard Abadinsky. *Organized Crime*, 3rd ed. (Chicago: Nelson-Hall 1990). Also see Jay Albanese, *Organized Crime in America* (Cincinnati, OH: Anderson Publishing Company, 1985); also, Jay Albanese, ed., *Contemporary Issues in Organized Crime*, (Monsey, NY: Criminal Justice Press, 1995); Rufus Schatzberg and Robert J. Kelly, *African-American organized Crime: A Social history* (New York: Garland Publishing, Inc., 1973); and Gary W. Potter, *Criminal Organizations: Vice, Racketeering, and Politics in an American City* (Prospect Heights, IL: Waveland Press, 1994).

2. Abadinsky, op. cit. pp. 2–4.

3. Papa Doc Duvalier was a physician by profession, known for successfully fighting disease, which gave him the nickname, "Papa Doc." He was given the title of "President for Life" in 1964. He continued to be President of Haiti until he died in 1971. He was succeeded by his son Jean Claude, as "Baby Doc."

4. The Duvaliers sowed a seed of organized crime in Haiti. In July 2002, "Government-endorsed cooperative banks collapsed across Haiti, losing the life savings of thousands, amid allegations the accounts were used to launder drug money. Violent protests ensue and more Haitians try to reach U.S. shores" (Associated Press 2/11/04). (See http://www.timelines.ws/countries/HAITI/HTML). Accessed March 31, 2015.

5. The Tontons Macoutes: "The Central Nervous System of Haiti's Reign of Terror" (httop://www.coha.org/tonton-macoutes/), Council on Hemispheric Affairs (COHA). Accessed March 31, 2015.

6. Trujillo was a womanizer, and made several romantic advances to Minerva in 1949, which Minerva refused. As wicked as Trujillo was, after Minerva studied law and became a lawyer, he made sure that Minerva didn't get a license to practice law in Dominican Republic. See "The Mirabal Sisters" (http://www.learntoquestion.com/seevak/groups/2000/sites/mirabal/English/assassination_fs.html). LearnToQuestion. com. Accessed April 3, 2015.

7. In his nemesis, six months after the assassinations of the Mirabal sisters, President Rafael Leonidas Trujillo was assassinated on a road outside of Ciudad Trujillo (Santo Damingo) Capital City.

8. The three "Mirabal Sisters" received deserved recognition, on December 17, 1999, from the United Nations General Assembly by designating November 25 as the "International Day for the Elimination of Violence against Women" in commemoration of the sisters. (http://www.un.org/womenwatch/daw/news/vawd.html). United Nations. Accessed April 3, 2015.

9. Other Nigerian Generals who had headed the Nigerian military government had taken the title, "Chairman" or "Head" of the Supreme Military Council.

10. See "Jobs for Sale" in the Nigerian Government. *The African Guardian* (January 15, 1990), 17. Also see "Corrupt Politicians List Out Soon." *The African Guardian* (February 6, 1989, 17. This refers to Nigerian politicians who have accounts in Swiss Banks: Chukwuemeka Gahia, Emenike Okorie, Ray Echebiri, and Tunde Oguntoyibo. "Changing Tidal Waves: Nigeria-Britain Brace up for New Ties – Special Report," *The African Guardian* (May 15, 1989), 11–14.

11. See "Why Oyakhilome Was Removed," *New Breed* (April 1, 1991), 5–26. The Nigerian head of state, Babangida and his wife were implicated in a narcotics deal by the only non-Hausa senior police officer, Deputy Inspector General (DIG) Oyakhilome. Oyakhilome was removed so that the Inspector General of Police and his other senior police officers could suppress evidence already exhumed by Oyakhilome.

12. A journalist and individuals who criticized the military regime were arrested and thrown into jail without trial for months and years. See "Detained journalist in Court," *West Africa* (June 11, 1984), 1239–1240; "Press Decree Published" and "Journalist Held," *West Africa* (April 23,1984), 900; "Sword Against the Pen," and "Why Five Journalists Are Held," *West Africa* (May 7, 1984), 960 and 964, respectively.

13. See "Who Killed Dele Giwa?" *West Africa* (Ocotober 19, 1987), 2089; "Fawehinmi in Dele Giwa Court Battle," *West Africa* (March 2,1987), 436. Also see "Senator Obi Wali Murdered," *Nigerian News Update* (May 13–16, 1993), 2. See also "Assassins on the Prowl Again in Lagos: Gunmen Attack NADECO Chief" *Daily Times* (January 15, 1977); and an attempt to assassinate the Chief Justice of Nigeria, Mr. Onagoruwa, which led to an assassination of his son. See "General Abacha Comforts Onagoruwa," *Daily Times* (January 14, 1997), 1.

14. Onome Osifo-Whiskey and Kola Ikori, "Deaths That Defy Defection: Mysterious Killings Send Shock Waves into a Hitherto Peaceful Community," *Newsweek* (June 13, 1988), 8–15. Also see Mike Ubani, "War Against Drugs," *The African Guardian* (April 16, 1990), 15.

15. Tim Whiteman, "Nigeria: Red Alert on Oil Fraud," West Africa (April 10–16, 1989), 546–547.

16. See Onyema Ugochukwu, "Nigeria: And Now for the IMF," *West Africa* (April 23, 1984d), 866–867; see "Bank Summons on JMB Scandal," *West Africa* (January 30 to February 5, 1989), 158, where some Nigerian politicians and their Nigerian business friends conspired to defraud the Nigerian government using a British company, Johnson Mathey Bankers (JMB), in falsification of import documents. See "184 NET (Nigerian External Telecommunication) Officials Sacked," *West Africa* (April 30, 1984), 950. Also see overvalued contracts in "Banchi" *West Africa* (December 14, 1981), 3013.

17. Enukora Joe Okoli, "Opening up Tender," *West Africa* (June 12, 1982), 1812–1815; Ugochukwu, op. cit., p. 53 (1984a), p. 1056 (1984b); Bentsi-Enchill, op. cit., p. 3018;

Whiteman, op. cit., p. 3012. Also see Onyema Ugochukwu "Nigeria: A Parade of Gubernatorial Convicts," *West Africa* (July 2, 1984c), 1349–1351.

18. See "Tribunals Move Center State" and "Illegal Importation of Goods" and "Illegal Transfer of Money by Politicians" in *West Africa* (June 11, 1984), 1204–1205.

19. Chukwuemeka Gahia, Emenike Okorie, Ray Echebiri, and Tunde Oguntoyibo, "Changing Tidal Waves: Nigeria-Britain Brace up for New Ties – Special Report." *The African Guardian* (May 15, 1989), 11–14. Also see "Extradition Bid Fails," *West Africa* (February 20–26, 1989), 289; and "Extra Misled: Iwuanyanwu to Government," *Thisday* (December 31, 1997), 1.

20. Gahia et al., op cit. See "Buhari's New Year Broadcast" West Africa (March 9, 1984), 56–57. Also see "Towards 1992 Corruption and Indiscipline," *West Africa* (August 31, 1987), 1688–1690; and "Kaduna, Police Corruption in the State," *West Africa* (March 2, 1987), 438.

21. Okoli, op. cit., pp. 1812–1815.

22. Ugochukwu, op. cit., pp. 53–56, (1984a), pp. 1056–1057 (1984b), pp. 1349–1351 (1984c); Okoli, op. cit., p. 1812; Gahia et al., pp. 12–17. Also see Janet Mba-Afolabi, "Haven for Fraudsters," *Newswatch* (December 4, 1957), 17–18; see "Public Fund Recovery Panels Findings: Contract Awarded Twice, Different Letter-head Paper Used," *Nigerian International Times* (January 15, 1997), 5. Also see where the head of state was involved in illegal contract deal – "The Panoco Connection," *West Africa* (December 7, 1987), 2410. Also see "Extradition Bid Fails," *West Africa* (February 20–26, 1989), 289. Also see "Ex-governor Jailed for 21 Years," *West Africa* (June 25, 1984), 1329.

    See Onyema Ugochukwu, "Nigeria: And Now for the IMF," *West Africa* (April 23, 1984d), 866–867; see "Bank Summons on JMB Scandal," *West Africa* (January 30 to February 5, 1989), 158, where some Nigerian politicians and their Nigerian business friends conspired to defraud the Nigerian government using a British company, Johnson Mathey Bankers (JMB), in falsification of import documents. See "184 NET (Nigerian External Telecommunication) Officials Sacked," *West Africa* (April 30, 1984), 950. Also see overvalued contracts in "Banchi" *West Africa* (December 14, 1981), 3013.

23. Ugochukwu, op. cit., pp. 53–56 (*1984); Tim Whiteman, "Nigeria: Red Alert on Oil Fraud," West Africa (April 10–16, 1989), 546–547.

24. Okoli, op. cit. p. 1813; Mike Ubani, "The Aba Ring," *The African Guardian* (February 13,1989), 25–26; Alain Adesokan, "A Horrifying Miasma," *Newswatch* (January 10, 1994), 13–16; see "Passport Office Minister hits out," involving middlemen in Nigerian passport visa racket, *West Africa* (July 4, 1983), 1579. Also see "Gongola Audit Reveals Embezzlements," *West Africa* (November 23, 1981), 2807. "Immigration Department Fights Passport Rackets," *Nigerian News Update* (January 15, 1993), 6; "Audu Ogbe Indicated," *The African Guardian* (May 1, 1989), 14; "Fraud Probe at NEC" (Nigerian Electoral Commission). *West Africa* (February 20–26, 1989), 289.

25. Tim Whiteman, op. cit.; Oladipo Adamolekun, "Sense and Nonsense," *West Africa* (May 12, 1986), 992–994; see the following: "Politicians Not Mentally Healthy," in *West Africa* (April 23, 1984), 900; "Crude Oil Racket," in *West Africa* (August 22, 1988), 1547; Toxic (nuclear) waste imported from Italy – "Mysterious Exits from the Country," *West Africa* (January 23–29, 1989); "Last Batch of Toxic Waste Removed," *West Africa* (August 29 to September 1, 1988); and "Police to Try Pornographic Violent Films Dealers," *The Guardian* (January 15, 1997), 6.

26. Oladipo Adamolekun, op. cit.; Kunle Jenrole and Felix Obanya, "Deals . . . Dirty Deals: Sharp Practices Rob Nigeria of Invaluable petroleum Revenue," *The African Guardian* (March 5, 1990), 19–25; John Nwaobi, Paul Nwachukwn, Debo Adesina, Abdul Oroh, Wale Akin Aina, and Ben Akaranta, "Hitting a Dangerous High: Hard Drugs Threaten Menacingly Society Looks on Helplessly," *The African Guardian* (September 25, 1989), 12–15: Mike Ubani and Billy Okonedo, "Furor Over Frisking: Nigeria Airways, Customs Find No Alternative to Crude Searching Methods," *The African Guardian* (March 13, 1989), 15; Wale Akin Aina, "The Quandary of the judiciary," *The African Guardian* (July 10, 1989), 18; Mike Ubani and Adegbe Onu Adegbe, "Worms in the Apple, Smugglers Smile, the Nation Bleeds," *The African Guardian* (February 13, 1989), 19–23; Chukwuemeka Gahia, "The Making of a Scandal; Nuclear Waste Dumped in Nigeria," *The African Guardian* (June 28, 1988), 12–17; Mike Ubani, "In the Pangs of Crisis: Awka-Etiti Communal Feud Deepens Following another Murder," *The African Guardian* (May 7, 1990): 8–11; Stephen Agwudagwu, "Jail Bonanza," *Newswatch* (June 13, 1988), 37; Olaniyi Ola., "Smugglers Paradise," *West Africa* (March 27 to April 2, 1989), 468; Seye Kehinde, "Guilty as Charged," *African Concord* (November 4, 1991), 42; see the following: "Ex-Commissioner Denies Drug Deal," *West Africa* (June 11, 1984), 1240. Over-invoicing by licensed importers – "Smuggling problems," *West Africa* (January 4, 1982), 19; "Illegal Miners Arrested," in *West Africa* (January 16–22, 1989), 80; Illegal drug trafficking – "Kenyan and Three Nigerians Sentenced to 28 Years for Drug Trafficking" in *Nigerian Times* (September 15–30, 1995), 8; Currency trafficking – "Nigeria Impounded a large Amount of Cash at Airport," *Nigerian Times* (September 1–14, 1995), 23; Smuggling Contrabands: "Billy EKO Panel to Report," *West Africa* (May 11, 1987), 935; "N.A. Acts Against Drug Smuggling," *West Africa* (April 27, 1987), 840; "Diplomat Held over Drug Smuggling," *West Africa* (September 19, 1983), 2204; "Trouble at High Commission" (drug smuggling), *West Africa* (December 14, 1981), 3012; Licensed importers smuggling – "Smuggling Problem," in West Africa (January 4, 1982), 19; "Smugglers to Face Life Jail," *West Africa* (January 4, 1989), 2459; "Nigeria's Illegal Gems Behind the precious Stones Boom," *West Africa* (January 23–29, 1989), 96–97; "Timber Smuggling," in *West Africa* (January 23–29, 1989), 122; Cocoa smuggling – "Anti-Smuggling Task Force," in *West Africa* (January 11, 1988), 53; "Renewed Effort to Combat Smuggling" in *Africa Report* (March–April 1982), 35; "Customs Seize

Petroleum products from Smugglers," in *Nigerian News Update* (December 14–27, 1993), 10; "Customs Seize 130,000 Liters of Petroleum Products at Seme," *Nigerian News Update* (November 2–15, 1993), 8; "NDLEA (Nigerian Drug Law Enforcement Agency) Arrested 243 Traffickers," in *Nigerian News Update* (November 2–15, 1993), 11; "Alleged Drug Baron Appears in Court over $20 Billion Heroin Import," *Nigerian News Update* (February 7–20, 1994), 2; "NDLEA Arrest 20 for Drug Offenses," in *Nigerian News Update* (January 24 to February 6, 1994), 3; "Nigeria Loses $50 Million Daily to Oil Smuggling," in *Nigerian News Update* (March 15–30, 1993), 9; "Former Army Major Arrested with Drugs," in *Nigerian News Update* (December 14–28, 1992), 4; "Drug Agency Prosecutes 1,285," *Nigerian News Update* (December 14–28, 1992), 4; and Counterfeiting currency – "Nigeians Gaoled in Taiwan," *West Africa* (April 30, 1984), 951.

27. Kunle Jenrola and Felix Obanya, op. cit.; Okoli, op. cit., pp. 1812–1815.

28. Ugochukwu, op. cit., p. 1056 (1984b) and p. 1349 (1984c); Adamolekun, op. cit., p. 992.

29. Kaye Whiteman, "475 Detainees – Idiagbon," *West Africa* (March 19, 1984), 638.

30. See "Bank Summons on JMB Scandal," note 24.

31. Ugochukwu, op. cit., pp. 53–56.

32. Sunny Biaghere and MazinoIkime, "The Wig and the Gun," *The African Guardian* (November 20, 1989), 8–9.

33. See "Vast Probe" for ghost workers and ghost contractors, *West Africa* (March 19, 1984), 637.

34. Gahia et al., op. cit., pp. 11–14. See the following: "Ex-military Governor Restricted," in *West Africa* (June 11, 1984), 1239; "Extradition Bid Fails," *West Africa* (February 20–26, 1989), 289.

35. See "Bank Summons on JMB Scandal," *West Africa* (January 30 to February 5, 1989), 158; a British financial institution, Johnson Mathey Bankers, was implicated in falsification of import documents that led to millions of British Pound sterling losses to the Nigerian government. A total of 86 percent of all present and ex-government officials interviewed testified to this in an interview.

36. Uzoma Onyemaechi, "Fraud in Nigeria," Internet News (UZO@alumni.sil.umich.edu), 1996.

37. Mazino Ikime, "Still Walking on Crutches: NIPOST Remains Unreliable in Spite of Public Criticism," *The African Guardian* (March 5, 1990), 12.

38. Jenrola and Obanya, op. cit., pp. 19–25; See Nigerian passport rackets, note 25. Also see "3,000 Civil Servants Dismissed," *West Africa* (April 23, 1984), 900.

39. See "Customs Men Questioned," *West Africa* (January 30 to February 5, 1989), 162.

40. See note 27. Also see "Customs Seize 18 Drums of Petrol," in *West Africa* (November 30 to December 13, 1993), 9.

41. See note 24. Also see "*Farewell Nigerian Air Waste*," *West Africa* (February 27 to March 5, 1989), 304.

42. All of the ex-cabinet ministers interviewed agreed on this point.

43. Pedder, op.cit., pp. 3–14; Tignor, op. cit., p. 175.

44. See "*£5bn (5 billion pounds) Racket, Government Steps-in*," *West Africa* (September 19, 1983), 2204. Also see "National Seminar on Corruption," in *West Africa* (May 2, 1983), 1089. The money stolen by the politicians including the Head of state are smuggled out of Nigeria by their agents. See "*Illegal Dealing in Naira*," in *West Africa* (May 2, 1983), 1093; "Nigeria's Foreign Exchange Crisis," in *West Africa* (May 10, 1982), 1274.

45. See "Nigeria Loses $50 Million Daily to Oil Smuggling," *Nigeria News Update*, (March 15–30, 1993), 9; "Notes for Nigerian Creditor," in *West Africa* (April 6, 1987), 677, and "Plateau, N5-6m Rice deal," *West Africa* (April 30, 1984), 951.

46. See "Police Recover Computers Worth N40 Million," in *Nigerian News Update* (February 7–20, 1994), 13. Also see "Robbery by Military Personnel on the Rise," *Nigerian Records* (January 1995), 12.

47. See the following "419" cases of fraud: "FIIB Arrested Three Who Tried to Dupe a German of $141,000," *Nigerian News Update* (February 7–20, 1994), 13; "Colombian and Six Nigerians Arrest over Diversion of NITEL's N26 million," *Nigerian News Update* (February 7–20, 1994), 14; "Maritime Fraud Cost Nigerian N5 Billion in 5 Years – Insurance Association Boss Says," *Nigerian News Update* (January 10–23, 1994), 8; "Fraud Suspects Face Tribunal," *Punch* (January 10, 1997), 7, "NITEL duped of N2.5 billion," *Daily Times* (January 14, 1997), 1; "Two Arraigned over N3 M Fraud," *Daily Times* (January 10, 1997), 4; and "N2.9 Billion Lost to Bank Fraud," *Nigerian Times* (October 1–14, 1995), 4. "Kaduna: 26 Officials Sacked over N38.83 Million Fraud," *Nigerian News Update* (February 7–20, 1994), 7; "Ministry Investigates Fraud-ulent Practices of Officer," *Nigerian News Update* (January 24 to February 6, 1994), 4; "Adamaw Administrator Orders Arrest of Auditor-General," *Nigerian News Update* (February 7–20, 1994), 6; "Ondo: Government Recovers N4 Million from Former Commissioner," *Nigerian News Update* January 24 to February 6, 1994), 6; "17 Workers in Trouble over Fraud," *Nigerian News Update* (November 30 to December 12, 1993), 5; "Ex-accountant General Charged with Fraud," *Nigerian Times International* (December 16–31, 1995), 11.

48. See "Nigeria's Currency Change," in *West Africa* (May 28, 1984), 1103. Also see note 27.

49. Also see *Thisday* (November 30, 1998). General Abacha illegally withdrew $832 million (N71.6 billion) from the Nigerian Central Bank.

50. See "Nigeria recovers assets from detained bank chiefs" which amounted to $8.75 million (N700 million) in *Nigerian Times* (September 1–14, 1995), 8; "Bosses of failed banks on trial for fraud," involving $3 million (N242 million) *Nigerian Times* (September 1–14, 1995), 29; "New Law against Money Laundering Underway," *Nigerian News Update* (January 15, 1993), 8.

51. There may be other persons charged or dismissed that were not reported by *West Africa* and other Nigerian publications.

52. "Why We Honored Abacha – Nigerian government." *Premium Times Nigeria.* (http://www.premiumtimesng.com/news/156004-why-we-honoured-abacha-nigerian-government.html). *Premium Times Nigeria.*

53. "Sani Abacha Legacy of a Great Leader," (http://vanguardngr.com/2011/06/sani-abacha-legacy-of-a-great-leader/). *Vanguard News.*

54. "Under Mobutu, Theft Was State Industry Zaire's Mines and Factories Were Systematically Plundered. Foreign Aid Vanished." (http://articles-philly.com/1997-05-09/news/25562451_1_president-mobutu-sese-seko-cobalt-gecamines). *The Inquirer*, May 9, 1997. Accessed April 8, 2015.

55. See "Plundering politicians and bribing Multinational undermine International Development, Say TI." *Transparency International*, March 25, 2004.

56. See, "The History of Mexican Independence," (http://www.mexonline.com/mexican-independence.htm). Accessed April 8, 2015.

57. Stanley A. Pimentel was a Senior Career FBI official who worked in Latin and Central America for many years and served two tours as legal attaché in Mexico before retiring in the late 1990s.

58. See, "Violence and Crime in Mexico at the Crossroads of Misgovernance, Poverty and Inequality" (http://web.archive.org/web/20121020160702) (http://blogs.worldbank.org/governance/violence-and-crime-in-mexico-at-the-crossroads-of-misgovernance-poverty-and-inequality). World Bank blog. Accessed April 9, 2015.

Mechanisms for Controlling State Crimes and Conclusion

The state is a very powerful institution. When state authorities violate their own laws, it is very hard to get them to be answerable to the violation. Some individuals and groups have tried and sued the state in an issue of a general nature. Most of the time, the state was found not liable, because the courts are controlled by the state authorities. In individual and group cases of torts, some individuals and groups have won. But it takes a lot of strength and courage to sue a state. Undeniably, the state is a legal entity. It can sue individuals, groups, and corporations and vice versa.

This text has highlighted the various crimes of the state which individuals or groups do not have the authority, power, or avenue to sue the state. For that reason, countries (states) of the world knew that a state could commit a crime against its citizens, citizens of other countries, or violate the sovereignty of other nations. As a result, states band together to form the League of Nations, which was obliterated by World War II, and the United Nations inherited some of its agencies.

The birth of the United Nations was in the Charter adopted and signed on June 26, 1945. The essence of the formation of the United Nations Charter was as a result of a perceived necessity to provide a better means of arbitrating international conflicts and negotiating peace than was provided by the obliterated League of Nations. The UN Charter emerged to "save succeeding generations from the scourge of war, . . . to reaffirm faith in fundamental human rights, . . . to establish conditions under which justice and respect for the obligations arising from treaties and other sources of international law can be maintained, and to promote social progress and better standards of life in larger freedom," (http://www.history.com/this-day-in-history/) (Accessed April 9, 2015).

State crimes, as have been presented here, are many. And there are state crimes that only an international body or bodies can bring the deviant state to justice. To achieve that aim, the United Nations, since its inception, has held so many conventions that created international laws for controlling various state crimes of both national and international effects.

In this last chapter, we are going to analyze the various steps that the United Nations has taken to control state crimes. These steps are the international humanitarian laws, the United Nations Conventions in justice related issues, the International Court of Justice, the International Military Tribunals, the International Criminal Tribunals, the International Criminal Court, the Nature of United Nations Sanctions, and the victimology and future of state crimes.

The United Nations International Humanitarian Law

There is a commonsense knowledge that without some international constraints, some states can go to excesses in trying to perpetrate damage against their enemies. Consequently, the United Nations saw that it was fit to set boundaries during an act of war between or among nations. This concern gave rise to the international humanitarian law.

International humanitarian law is a set of rules and regulations enacted for humanitarian purposes to guide parties at war or in armed conflict about the limits of their aggression. International humanitarian law is a part of international law, which tries to protect persons who are no more participating in a conflict or hostilities. "It comprises of a set of rules, established by treaty or custom, that seeks to protect persons and property/objects that are (or may be) afflicted by armed conflict, and limit the rights of parties to a conflict to use methods and means of warfare of their choice" (GSDRC, 2013). This includes "*the Geneva Conventions* and the *Hague Conventions*, as well as subsequent treaties, case law, and *Customary International Law*" (Stewart, 2003).

The international humanitarian law is based on humane, rational, common sense reasoning. This rational reasoning realizes "the heart of man," in the words of a humanistic philosopher, Erick Fromm, (1964), "its genius for good and evil." If societies are not held in check, by some international humanitarian laws, when they wage wars against one another, they could go to the extreme as to obliterate innocent persons from the face of the earth. The international humanitarian law is intended to control and limit states pugnacity. The international humanitarian law is saying that once individuals have given up hostilities, or resigned from fighting, they should be left alone. Any pursuit of such people and killing them constitute a war crime. You do not kill a person who is not a threat to your life. That is a key notion of international humanitarian law.

The Various United Nations Conventions

The United Nations legislations are enacted in the form of conventions. The UN Conventions are agreements among nations on various issues that have a force of international law. They are treaties whose violations are violations of international law for which the United Nations may impose sanctions.

In this section are presented those United Nations Conventions that are related to states' treatment of human subjects in time of war or conflict, treatment of offenders, disabled, and destitute; conventions on genocide and transnational organized crimes, and so forth. The offspring of all conventions concerning the protection of human beings are the Geneva Conventions.

Geneva Conventions

The Geneva Conventions are a series of international agreements (treaties) entered in Geneva, Switzerland, between 1864 and 1949, to alleviate the pains of war on soldiers and civilian subjects, and provided for the humane treatment of prisoners of war (POWs), the sick, wounded, and the dead in the battlefield.

The emergence of the Geneva Convention

The Geneva Convention was masterminded by the founder of the *Red Cross*, Henri Dunant. He started international negotiations that led to the "Convention for Amelioration of the Wounded in Time of War in 1864." The 1864 Convention provided the following:[1]

a. Respect and remain untouched all items and equipments for the treatment of the wounded, sick soldiers, and their caregivers;

b. Kind, and unconditional treatment of all fighting forces;

c. Protection of civilians who are helping the wounded; and

d. Respect for the Red Cross symbols and those wearing them as a means of identifying individuals and equipment covered by the agreement.

The second Geneva Convention was in 1906. Its provisions applied to maritime warfare through the Hague Convention of 1899 and 1907.

The Third Geneva Convention was the "Convention of War (1929), which required that nations at war should treat each other's prisoners of war humanely, provide information about them, and allow neutral individuals or groups to visit the prison camps or detention camps.

The Fourth Geneva Convention (GCIV) was the 1949 convention which produced four treaties:

1. The Convention for the Amelioration of the Condition of the Wounded and Sick in Armed Forces in the Field;
2. The Convention for the Amelioration of the Condition of the Wounded, Sick, and Shipwrecked Members of Armed Forces at Sea;
3. The Convention Relative to the Treatment of Prisoners of War; and
4. The Convention Relative to the Protection of Civilian Persons in Time of War.

The Fourth Geneva Convention of August 12, 1949, was necessitated by abuse of the principles of the earlier conventions by some combatants in World War II. As a result of the abuses in World War II, the International Red Cross conference in Stockholm, Sweden, in 1948, elaborated and codified the existing provision, and developed the four conventions or treaties of the 1949 Geneva Convention.

The first treaty of the Fourth Geneva Convention specifies that soldiers of the enemy armed forces who are wounded or found sick in the battlefield should be helped to survive as if they were own troops.

Treaty number two provides that enemy soldiers or naval forces who are shipwrecked at sea should be rescued and treated humanely.

Treaty number three specifies that prisoners of war (POWs) should not be tortured but treated humanely.

And the fourth treaty of the Fourth Geneva Convention provides that civilians should be respected and treated kindly without molestation or torture in time of war.

The Fourth Geneva Convention was also coupled with two "*Protocols.*" A Protocol is an agreement among nations that are less formal than a "Convention" or a "Treaty."

The protocols to the 1949 Geneva Convention were necessitated by anti-colonial hegemony after World War II. Adolf Hitler ordered the British to surrender, else he would reduce Britain into a sand dune. And the British Prime Minister, Winston Churchill, replied that the British people have a right to self-determination, and will not surrender to Nazi Germany. When the World War II began, Hitler attacked two most colonial masters of the world, Britain and France. To defeat Hitler's Nazi Germany, Britain and France conscripted able-bodied men of their colonies in African and Asian continents to fight against the Nazi Germany.

At the end of World War II in 1945, both Britain and France allowed the soldiers of the colonial dependencies, who survived the war, to go back to their respective countries. Unmistakably, World War II opened the eyes of most the colonies' soldiers. The soldiers from the colonies saw the relevance of freedom, which the British and French fought for their own self-determination. Consequently, Mahatma Gandhi of India requested the British Parliament that the Indian people helped the British defeat the Nazi because the "British people have a right to self-determination. Therefore, it is time for the British to grant Independence to India, because the Indian people have a right to self-determination" (paraphrased). Gandhi's idea was strongly supported by the United States. In effect, in 1947 India and Egypt received their independence from Great Britain.

However, independence for some British and French colonies had to be achieved by war. There were so many wars of independence, especially in former French colonies such as Algeria and Vietnam. The 1949 Geneva Convention did not foresee the anti-colonial wars. Consequently, the 1949 Geneva Convention was followed by two Protocols to cover issues not addressed by the original conventions.

Protocol I. The first, (Protocol I),[2] extended protection under the Geneva and Hague Conventions to individuals involved in wars of "self-determination." These were redefined as international conflicts. The protocol led to the United Nations establishing fact-finding commissions in cases of alleged violations of the convention (ICRC, 1977).

Protocol II. The second, (Protocol II), provides *human rights* protections to individuals involved in deadly *civil conflicts*, which were not covered by the 1949 agreements. This protocol prohibited collective punishment, torture, the taking of hostages, acts of terrorism, slavery, and "outrages on the personal dignity, in particular humiliating and degrading treatment, rape, enforced prostitution and any form of indecent assault" (ICRC, 1977).

The granting of political independence to former colonial dependencies created civil wars in some continents (Africa and Asia), coupled with the collapse of the Soviet Union giving rise to 15 newly independent states (NIS) and its concomitant civil wars, such as in Yugoslavia. As a result, the United Nations Security Council proclaimed that the internal conflicts in Yugoslavia, Rwanda, Somalia, and so forth amounted to a threat to or a breach of international peace and security, and made resolutions on the conflicts binding on the fighting groups. Since the Security Council's expansion of the definition of international armed conflicts in the intrastate and interethnic conflicts, an increasing number of rules outlined in the Geneva Convention and their protocols have come to be regarded as binding on all states. The rules include humane treatment of civilians and prisoners of war (Bothe & Partsch, 1982).

The 1949 Geneva Conventions have more than 180 states as parties to them. About 150 states are parties to Protocol I, and 145 states are parties to Protocol II. The United States became a party to the 1949 Geneva Convention in 1955, but not yet a party to Protocol I and II; although it has signed both protocols, it has not ratified them. However, in 2007, the United States became a party to Protocol III.[3] Under Protocol III, all persons wearing the protective sign of the Red Crystal, whether medical or religious personnel at times of war, instead of the traditional Red Cross, Star of David, or Red Crescent symbols are doing *humanitarian* service and must be protected by all combatant parties.

Undeniably, the relevance of the Geneva Conventions and their protocols was featured in the establishment of more state control mechanisms discussed below such as the war crimes tribunals for the former Yugoslavia (ICTY) (1993) and Rwanda (ICTR) (1994), the Rome

Statute (1998), which established the International Criminal Court (ICC), and the Special Court for Sierra Leone (SCSL) (2000).

Other United Nations Conventions to Control State Deviances

After the Geneva Conventions of 1949 and their protocols, the United Nations concluded many other conventions. As noted above, the conventions the writer wants to address here are those concerning safety of human beings that may be perpetrated by state authorizes or their agencies and groups.

There are many examples of the United Nations Conventions and Protocols to control state deviances.

The Convention on the Prevention and Punishment of the Crime of Genocide (CPPCG)

This convention was adopted by the United Nations General Assembly on December 9, 1948, as General Assembly Resolution 260. The convention entered into force on January 12, 1951[4] (Schabas, 2009). Details of the genocide convention are covered in Chapter 5.

International Convention for the Protection of all Persons from Enforced Disappearance (ICCPED)

The ICCPED is an international human rights instrument of the United Nations promulgated to prevent forced disappearance defined in international law and crimes against humanity. It was adopted by the United Nations General Assembly on December 20, 2006. It entered into force on December 23, 2010. Most of the UN member states have signed the convention (UN Resolution 133).[5]

United Nations Convention against Torture

The Convention against Torture and other Cruel, Inhuman or Degrading Treatment or Punishment (simply called the *United Nations* Convention against Torture) is an international human rights treaty intended to prevent torture and other acts of cruel, inhuman, or degrading treatments or punishments meted out to people in various states in the world. This convention requires states to take action that nobody is tortured in territories under their jurisdiction, and that nobody should be transported to any other country, where there is reason that they will be subjects to torture (Sifris, 2013).

The convention was adopted by the United Nations General Assembly on December 10, 1984. This convention came into force on June 26, 1987. The convention against torture has been accepted as a principle of customary international law.[6] Also, the convention has been signed and ratified by 157 state parties.[7]

Convention for the Suppression of the Traffic in Persons and of the Exploitation of the Prostitution of Others

This convention is a resolution of the United Nations General Assembly. Its preamble states as follows:

> "Whereas prostitution and the accompanying evil of the traffic in persons for the purpose of prostitution are incompatible with the dignity and worth of the human person and endanger the welfare of the individual, the family and the community."

The convention requires member states to punish any person who "procures, entices or leads away, for purposes of prostitution, another person, even with the consent of that person," "exploits the prostitution of another person even with the consent of that person" (Article 1), or runs a brothel or rents accommodations for prostitution purposes (Article 2). In addition, the convention prescribes procedures for combating international traffic for the purpose of prostitution, including extradition of offenders. Also, member states are required to abolish all rules and regulations or to the possession of a special document or to any exceptional requirements for supervision or notification (Article 6). And member states also are required to take measures for the supervision of employment agencies to prevent persons applying for jobs, especially women and children, from being exposed to the danger of prostitution (Article 20).

This convention was approved by the UN General Assembly on December 2, 1949, and came into effect on July 25, 1951. The convention has 82 member states as parties to it in December 2013. There are an additional 13 member states who have signed it, but have not ratified it.[8]

International Convention on the Suppression and Punishment of the Crime of Apartheid

The 2002 Rome Statute of the International Criminal Court (ICC) defined the crime of *Apartheid* as inhumane acts of a character similar to other crimes against humanity "committed in the context of an institutionalized regime of systematic oppression and domination by one racial group over any other racial group or groups and committed with the intention of maintaining that regime" (Bassiouni & Derby, 1981).

On November 30, 1973, the United Nations General Assembly opened for signature and ratification the International Convention on the Suppression and Punishment of the Crime of Apartheid. It defined the crime of apartheid as "inhuman acts committed for the purpose of establishing and maintaining domination by one racial group of persons over any other racial group of persons and systematically oppressing them."

After the UN opened the floor for signatures and ratification on November 30, 1973, there were 91 votes in favor, 4 against (Portugal, South Africa, the United Kingdom, and United States), and 26 abstentions (Dugard, 1973). The crime of apartheid convention came into force on July 18, 1976. So far, as of August 2008, it has been signed and ratified by 107 member states of the United Nations.

Convention on Certain Conventional Weapons.

The United Nations Convention on certain Conventional Weapons (CCW) consummated in Geneva on October 10, 1980, and came into force on December 2, 1983, prohibits the use of certain conventional weapons which are deemed extremely harmful or whose effects are undeniably indiscriminate. The convention is fully titled as "Convention on Prohibitions or Restrictions on the Use of Certain Conventional Weapons which may Be Excessively Injurious to or Have Indiscriminate Effects." This convention covers landmines, booby traps, incendiary weapons, blinding laser weapons, and clearance of explosive remnants of war (Matthews, 2001).

The convention was signed and ratified by 120 member states in January 2015.

United Nations Convention against Corruption.

This convention is the first legally binding international anticorruption instrument concluded by the United Nations. The United Nations Convention against Corruption (UNCAC) requires that member states of the UN take anticorruption measures. The measures should be intended to prevent corruption, criminalize certain conducts, strengthen international law enforcement and judicial cooperation, provide effective legal mechanisms for asset recovery, technical assistance and information exchange, and mechanisms for implementation of the convention, including the Conference of the State Parties of the United Nations Convention against Corruption (UNCAC).

This convention was approved by the United Nations General Assembly on October 30, 2003, by Resolution 58/4. It was opened for signature in December of that year with 140 states committed.[9] In April 2015, as many as 175 states have signed of which 172 are member states.[10]

Convention on the Elimination of All Forms of Discrimination against Women.

Discrimination against women is almost a cultural universal. It is so widespread among nations that both developed and developing countries are deviants in that regard. Consequently, the United Nations came up with a convention to eliminate it.

The Convention on the Elimination of All Forms of Discrimination against Women (CEDAW) was adopted in 1979 by the United Nations General Assembly. The CEDAW is often referred to as "international bill of right for women." The convention defines discrimination against women as:

> . . . any distinction, exclusion or restriction made on the basis of sex which has the effect or purpose of impairing or nullifying the recognition, enjoyment or exercise by women, irrespective of their marital status, on the basis of equality of men and women, of human rights and fundamental freedoms in the political, economic, social, cultural, civil or any other field."[11]

The United Nations General Assembly spurred member states to accept the convention and by accepting the convention, states must commit themselves to taking drastic measures to end discrimination against women in all forms, including the following:

1. To incorporate the principle of equality of men and women in their legal system, abolish all discriminatory laws and adopt appropriate ones prohibiting discrimination against women;

2. To establish tribunals and other public institutions to ensure the effective protection of women against discrimination; and

3. To ensure elimination of all acts of discrimination against women by persons, organizations or enterprises.[12]

Member states that have ratified the convention are legally bound to put its provisions into practice, and are required to submit, at least once every 4 years, reports they have taken to comply with their treaty obligations.

United Nations Convention against Transnational Organized Crime (UNTOC).

Organized crime is a worldwide problem. It is a crime that crosses international borders. In 2000, the United Nations sponsored an international treaty against transnational organized crime. The UN Convention against Transnational Organized Crime was adopted by the UN General Assembly on November 15, 2000, by a resolution. This convention is also referred to as the *Palermo Convention* (Italy). The Palermo Convention was accompanied by three protocols,[13] which are as follows:

a. Protocol to Prevent, Suppress and Punish Trafficking in Persons, especially Women and Children;

b. Protocol against the Smuggling of Migrants by Land, Sea and Air; and

c. Protocol against the Illicit Manufacturing and Trafficking in Firearms.

On September 29, 2003, the convention came into force as an international law. As of January 2015, 185 parties have signed it, including 180 United Nations member states.

In addition to the various Geneva Conventions and the concomitant protocols, there are other very relevant conventions that the United Nations uses to control the deviances and excesses of some states in international relations and dealing with their own subjects. All of the United Nations Conventions and Protocols cannot be addressed in this text, because there are too many of them. The writer wants to demonstrate that states violate the law, criminal and noncriminal acts, and that there is an agency (UN) that controls state crimes.

The international criminal laws, including the international humanitarian law, are created, in the main, to control states' excesses.[14] The same spirit and principles govern the way sovereign nations promulgate laws for control of their own people, yet some of their subjects violate the laws and suffer the consequences; similarly, the United Nations, by conventions and protocols, promulgate laws, signed and ratified by member states, yet some member states, with impunity, violate the laws and treaties. Well, the great French sociologist, Emile Durkheim (1964), saw it more than one hundred years ago, that deviance is functional, because it marks the boundaries of acceptable and unacceptable behaviors. In other words, laws are made to be violated, because if they are not going to be violated, it would be unnecessary to enact them in the first place. As noted above, even governments (states) violate the laws which they created. This is because governments are selfish entities because they are always run by egoistic individuals (political animals).

United Nations' Realization of Possibilities of State Crimes and Deviances

Even before the emergence of the League of Nations on January 10, 1920, European, Asian, African, American, and Middle Eastern nations had known that states invade states and loot and destroy a weaker state's precious properties, which are contemporary societies' acts of terrorism. In effect, the United Nations learned from the failures of the League of Nations, and refined the League's 1922 Permanent Court of International Justice (PCIJ) and came up with an international court of its own, the *International Court of Justice* (ICJ).

See below why the United Nations came up with the International Court of Justice, the International Military Tribunal (IMT), the emergence of the International Criminal Tribunal for the former Yugoslavia (ICTY), the International Criminal Tribunal for Rwanda (ICTR), the International Criminal Court (ICC), and the "Special Court" for Sierra Leone. You can see how all of the United Nations' listed courts targeted states and their leaders.

Preamble to the Emergence of the United Nations' Courts to Control State Deviances and Crime

"No independent states, large or small, shall come under the domination of another state by inheritance, exchange, purchase, or donation." *Immanuel Kant*, 1795.

Why "World Courts of Justice"? Every sovereign nation or traditional society has a court or courts of justice. But why should the whole world have a court of justice? Well, the world of the medieval period to the modern times, of 1453 to the 1800s was a world of one society against another. It was like Thomas Hobbes (1588–1679) stated, "war of all against all." The Western European countries were engulfed in empire-building. Great Britain, France, Spain, Portugal, Germany, Belgium, and the Netherlands invaded kingdoms and autonomous nations in Africa, Asia, the Middle East, South and North America, the Oceanic Islands, and Australasia, conquered, dominated, exploited, and expropriated them (see Chapter 3). The consequent partition of the African continent is a living testimony. In today's world, all of those unprovoked invasions of nations would tantamount to acts of terrorism, crimes against humanity, genocide in some cases, violations of human rights, and wars of aggression, which are all violations of international criminal law (Ebbe, 2013).

Some of the 17th and 18th century social and moral philosophers, such as Immanuel Kant (1724–1804), saw the world as going to be in a deeper mess than it was in their time, if there was no system of global peaceful community. As far back as 1795, in one of his great writings (*Perpetual Peace: A Philosophical Sketch*), Kant, like a prophet, prescribed "the establishment of a peaceful world community" (Kant, 1795). It was not long until 1914, when the Central Powers, Germany and Austria-Hungary, soon, engaged in what came to be known as the World War I (1914–1918). At the end of the war, there had to be a mutual agreement not to wage any more wars. An attempt to end the war gave rise to the League of Nations.

Before the League of Nations, Kant had warned the world leaders of his time thus, "no treaty of peace shall be held valid which there is tacitly reserved matter for a future war." This warning was violated in the League of Nations. The major purpose of the League of Nations, referred to as the Paris Peace Conference, was to prevent wars through negotiation and arbitration.

Consequently, the League of Nations established a Permanent Court of International Justice in 1922 to deal with conflicts between its member states. But, the League of Nations could not deal with violations of its covenants by powerful European nations. It could only deal with violations by poor weak countries. Besides, the League did not have its own military force and did not provide in its covenant how the member states should provide such a military enforcement. In effect, some key members of the League withdrew their membership, because the League could not do anything before, and when, Italy invaded Abyssinia (now Ethiopia).

In addition, the League could not prevent World War II. Besides, Germany attacked Austria in 1928 and annexed it, and the League showed itself as being weaker than a toothless bulldog. Consequently, in 1939, Adolf Hitler set the World War II in motion. At the end of World War II, in 1945, victorious Allies determined that there will be no more World Wars. They dismantled the League of Nations and set up the United Nations (UN) at a conference in San Francisco, California (United States) in 1945 to promote world peace and security, maintain treaty obligations, respect the dictates of international law, and cooperate in furthering social progress.

International Court of Justice (ICJ)

The UN inherited some of the agencies of the League of Nations, such as the International Labor Organization, World Health Organization, the Permanent Court of International Justice (PCIJ), and so forth. In 1945, the UN dismantled the Permanent Court of International Justice and set up the International Court of Justice (ICJ) by a statute.

The statute of the ICJ is annexed to the UN Charter. In other words, the ICJ is an integral part of the UN Charter. The ICJ is one of the six principal organs of the UN. And, the ICJ is the only one of the six principal organs not located in New York. This court is not a criminal court. It is a civil court. It is a court for settling disputes between member states of the UN if both parties agree to bring their case to the court.

The court is composed of 15 highly qualified judges. They are elected by the General Assembly of the UN and the Security Council from a list provided by the Secretary General of the UN. The list is compiled by the Registrar of the ICJ, based on nominations from member states of their most qualified judges. Both the General Assembly and the Security Council hold their elections independent of each other. Two persons from the same country cannot serve in the court at the same period. If it happens that the General Assembly elects one judge from Japan, for example, and the Security Council elects another Japanese judge from the list, only the older of the two Japanese Judges will serve and the other is dropped.

The decision of the ICJ judges is based on majority opinion. There is no appeal to any other court, because the parties agree to accept the decision of the court before bringing the case to the court.

The ICJ is presented here because it is the precursor of all of the international criminal courts or tribunals.

International Military Tribunal (IMT)

The International Military Tribunal (IMT) is a product of World War II. Long before the war ended, the leaders of the United States, Great Britain, and the Soviet Union, infuriated by the ruthless genocidal murder of European Jews and the torture and murder of Allied prisoners of war, announced in unequivocal terms that they were going to prosecute those who engineered the World War II for crimes against humanity and war of aggression. They came to a conclusion to hold an IMT.

The leaders of the Allied Forces: President Franklin D. Roosevelt (United States), Prime Minister Winston Churchill (Great Britain), and Josef Stalin (Soviet Union), signed an agreement in 1943, called the Moscow Declaration, during an armistice that those found to be responsible for war crimes would be sent back to the country where they committed the offense and tried according to the laws of that country. In addition, major war criminals whose crimes could not be pinned to any particular country would be tried and punished, on the basis of a joint decision of the Allied governments (USHMM, 2012).

The Post-World War II Military Trials: Nuremberg

There were two major IMTs at the end of the World War II. The first was the IMT at Nuremberg, Germany, which began on November 20, 1945, about six-and-a-half months after Nazi Germany surrendered to the Allied forces.

The IMT at Nuremburg was set up by the four Allied Nations: the United States, Great Britain, the Soviet Union, and France. Each of the four countries supplied a judge and an alternate, and a prosecution team. The presiding judge was Colonel Lord Justice Geoffrey Lawrence of Great Britain. Four languages (English, French, German, and Russian) were used simultaneously in the trial proceedings (USHMM, 2012). Most of the attorneys for the defendants were German lawyers (Davidson, 1997).

The Criminals of the Nuremberg Trial

The offenders charged at the Nuremburg trial were those considered to be the masterminds of the World War II. There were 24 of them. Only 21 appeared before the tribunal because Adolf Hitler, Himmler, and Joseph Goebbels had committed suicide before the end of the War.

On the whole, about 200 Nazi war-crime defendants were tried in Bavaria, Nuremburg, and 1,600 others who received lesser charges than the Nuremburg offenders, were tried in other locations. Leipzig, Munich, and Luxembourg were among the other locations (Overy, 2001).

Crimes Charged at the Nuremburg Trial

The Nazi defendants were charged with genocide, war crimes, crimes against peace, and crimes against humanity. The Nuremburg Tribunal defined crimes against humanity as "murder, extermination, enslavement, deportation, or persecutions on political, racial, or religious grounds" (MacLeod, 2010; Biddiss, 1995; Utley, 1948). Some of the Nuremburg war crime defendants were convicted. Some received the death penalty; some life imprisonment; and others were discharged and acquitted.

International Military Tribunal for the Far East (IMTFE): TOKYO

The second IMT after the World War II was the Tokyo Crimes Tribunal, which is also known as the IMTFE. This tribunal was set up on April 29, 1946, to try the leaders of Japan for war crimes. The Japanese World War II leaders, who were suspected of war crimes, were divided into three categories—Class A, Class B, and Class C. Class A crimes are charged to those who were privy to a joint conspiracy to wage the war and were in the highest decision-making echelon. Class B crimes were for those who committed heinous crimes, such as crimes against humanity. And Class C crimes were for those who engaged in organizing and executing the war plan or failed to prevent the war.

In the Class A crimes were 28 Japanese military men and political leaders, while more than 5,700 Japanese were charged in Class B and C crimes. Most of Class B and C offenders were involved in the ruthless abuse of war prisoners (Minear, 1971; Horowitz 1950; Roling & Ruter, 1977).

Judges of the Tokyo Tribunal

There were 11 judges, one each from United Kingdom, Australia, Canada, British India, New Zealand, Republic of China, the provisional government of the French Republic, the Kingdom of the Netherlands, Philippines, and the USSR, and two from the United States. Also, there were 11 prosecutors from the countries who served as judges. The chief prosecutor was Joseph Keenan of the United States, who was appointed by President Harry S. Truman (Maya, 2001; Piccigallo, 1979; Sherman, 2001).

Crimes Charged at Tokyo War Crimes Tribunal

The defendants were charged with conventional war crimes, crimes against peace, and crimes against humanity. The trial lasted over two-and-a-half years, because there were hundreds of witnesses and thousands of exhibits of evidence introduced in court. The Japanese suspects were further charged with depraved-hearted murdering; the maiming and ill-treatment of prisoners of war; and subjecting internees to work under inhuman conditions, plundering public and private property, recklessly destroying towns and villages, inflicting mass murder, rape, pillage, brigandage, torture, and the barbaric destruction of populations (Minear, 1971; Brackman, 1987). The Japanese defendants could not escape charges of waging unprovoked war against China, and waging aggressive wars against the United States, the British Commonwealth, the Netherlands, France (Indo China), and the USSR.

The Japanese Defense

The Japanese defendants were represented by 75 Japanese lawyers and 25 American attorneys. While it took the prosecution 192 days to present their charges, it took the defense 225 days to complete their presentation (Minear, 1971; Brackman, 1987; Horowitz, 1950; Piccigallo, 1979).

Judgment and Sentencing

It took the IMTFE six months to reach a decision and draft a 1,781 page opinion. There was no consensus among the judges on how to deal with the Japanese defendants. Five of the 11 judges issued separate opinions. There were some who wanted clemency; and there were others who saw the tribunals as a nonneutral court; and some did not countenance the exclusion of Emperor Hirohito and his family from the criminal indictments.

Sentencing

At the end, the majority of the judges' opinion prevailed. Eight of the Japanese defendants were given a death penalty for war crimes, crimes against humanity, and crimes against peace. There were two political leaders and six military commanders. Eighteen of the defendants were sentenced to years of imprisonment to life. A plea of clemency was granted in some cases.

The International Military Tribunals are presented here, because they paved the way for the emergence of International Criminal Tribunals (ICT), the International Criminal Court (ICC), and the "Special Court" for Sierra Leone of the United Nations.

International Criminal Tribunals (ICT)

Preamble to the Emergence of ICT

You have seen from above why and how the ICJ emerged and what led to the ad hoc IMTs at Nuremberg and Tokyo. The IMTs at Nuremberg and Tokyo emerged because of war crimes, crimes against humanity, crimes of aggression, and genocide during World War II, which were committed by states. And after the offenders in that World War II were indicted, convicted, and punished, what happened to the offenders in wars that occurred from 1946 through 1989? There have been many wars, all over the world, since the end of World War II in 1945, such as the Indo-China war between France and Vietnam (1946–1954), the Vietnam War between the United States and Vietnam (1959–1975), the Franco-Algerian War (1946–1962), the Angolan War of Independence (the Portuguese government vs. nationalist Angolans, 1961–1975), the Eritrean War of Independence (1961–1991), the Eritrea-Ethiopia War (1968–2000), the Iran-Iraq War (1980–1988), the Salvadoran Civil War (1980–1992), the Soviet war in Afghanistan (1979–1988), the Nigeria-Biafra War (1967–1970), to name but a few. Why didn't the UN set up an IMT or an International Criminal Tribunal (ICT) to investigate atrocities committed by some people in those wars that were war crimes, crimes against humanity, crimes of aggression, and acts of genocide? For example, why didn't the UN set up an IMT or an ICT after anyone of the so many wars since the end of the World War II? The reason can be found in the Nigeria-Biafra War in which the writer was a commanding Army Officer on the Biafran side.

Biafra seceded from Nigeria because of pogrom and acts of genocide that occurred throughout the north, west, and the southeast of Nigeria against an ethnic group, the Igbos, whom the British hated for spearheading and agitating in favor of Nigerian independence. As a result of the pogrom and the massacre of Igbo men, women, and children in all corners of Nigeria, the lgbos and the minority ethnic groups of Eastern Nigeria seceded from Nigeria and formed the Republic of Biafra on May 30, 1967. On July 6, 1967, Nigeria attacked Biafra.

In the war, Great Britain, the United States, and the Soviet Union supplied Nigeria with jet fighters and bomber aircraft, all kinds of tanks, and other weapons and ammunition. With the war planes, Nigeria bombed open-air civilian market squares, churches, refugee camps, and civilian village homes (Ebbe, 2010). Were all of these not crimes against humanity? Were they not war crimes, or crimes against peace? The answer is, whenever the so-called big powers in the Security Council of the UN have special interests in a war, there is no need to investigate for atrocities committed in the war (Ebbe, 2013).

Why did the UN and the North Atlantic Treaty Organization (NATO) pay attention to the wars in the former Yugoslavian areas in 1990–1992? The answer is simple. The demise of the Soviet Union, which had held Yugoslavia as a communist ally; the Federation of Yugoslavia is a reminder to the Allies of a communist economy and ideology and had to be dismantled as the ethnic groups thereon desired; the NATO members and their big powers in the Security Council saw better trade partners in a dismantled Yugoslavian federation; and the mass media sealed the Allies' intentions. Indeed, a German, Klaus Kinkel, Foreign Minister of Germany, originally came up with the idea of creating an ICT (Hazan, 2004). For the powers in the UN Security Council, that was the time to establish the ICT, and it had to start with the wars in the former Yugoslavia. ICT is a UN weapon to control states criminal excesses.

Remote Causes of Yugoslavia Conflict

Adolf Hitler sowed the seed of future disintegration in Yugoslavia. In 1941, Hitler captured the Kingdom of Yugoslavia and divided the country among the Axis states (Lukic & Lynch, 1996). Like the scramble for Africa in the 18th and 19th centuries, some ethnic groups in Yugoslavia were split into two and amalgamated with others. At the end of World War II, communist totalitarianism held them together. But, with the collapse of the Soviet Union, the newly independent states (NIS) of the Soviet empire began to emerge. For the Yugoslavian ethnic groups: Slovenia, Serbia, Croatia, Bosnia and Herzegovina, the desire for self-determination and nationalism led to ethnic cleansing and acts of genocide. The Bosnian Serb Army pursued Bosnian Muslims and Bosnian Croats. Against them were crimes of murder, rape, sexual assault, unlawful confinement, torture, robbery, beating and hunting down political leaders, crushing intellectuals and professionals, illegal trafficking in women and children, illegal deportation of civilians, illegal taking away of real personal property, destruction of homes and businesses, destruction of buildings of worship, and depraved-hearted genocide (Thackrah, 2008).

The atrocities being committed in the areas of Yugoslavia drew international attention and coupled with similar events that had happened over the years, the UN finally decided to establish an ad hoc ICT for the prosecution of individuals responsible for serious violations of International Humanitarian Law. Such a tribunal had to start with the former Yugoslavia. The second such a tribunal would be in Rwanda.

International Criminal Tribunal for the Former Yugoslavia

Given the events described above that took place in the former territories of Yugoslavia from 1991–1995, the UN Security Council passed Resolution 827 on May 25, 1993, to establish the International Criminal Tribunal for the Former Yugoslavia (ICTY) and gave it jurisdiction over the four classes of crimes committed in Yugoslavia since 1991, which are grave breaches of the Geneva Conventions, crimes against humanity, genocide, and violations of the law or customs of war (Hazan, 2004).

ICTY Organizational Structure

The headquarters of ICTY is at the Hague, the Netherlands. It has a courtroom and detention facilities. While it started with 200 staff, its employees now number over 900 (ICTY, 2012). ICTY is a part of the UN, and it is the first international court for criminal justice.

The tribunal has a president and a vice-president. At the ICTY headquarters are chambers, the court registry, and the office of the prosecutor.

Chambers

Judges and their aides are based at the chambers. There are three trial chambers and one appeals chamber. Unlike the ICJ, the decisions of the International Criminal Tribunals can be appealed.

Judges of the ICTY

The UN General Assembly elects the judges of the ICTY. First of all, the UN member states each submit two nominees to the UN Secretary General. The UN Secretary General compiles a list and submits it to the UN Security Council. The Security Council selects 28–42 nominees and submits those selected to the UN General Assembly, which elects 14 judges from the list (ICTY, 2009b).

An ICTY judge can serve for 4 years and may stand for reelection. The UN Secretary General can appoint a replacement in case of emergency. Sixteen permanent judges and nine *ad litem* judges serve on the ICTY.

Prosecutor

The prosecutor is the head of the office of the prosecution division. The UN Secretary General nominates the prosecutor and submits the name of the candidate to the UN Security Council. The UN Security Council makes the appointment (UN Security Council, 1993). He or she is responsible for investigating crimes, gathering evidence, and prosecuting the cases.

Registry

This is the administrative division of the tribunal. It maintains court records. It is responsible for transporting and accommodating witnesses, translating court documents, taking care of public information section, payroll administration, personnel and procurement administration. In addition, it takes care of the legal aid program and the detention unit for those indicted by the ICTY. The registry is headed by a registrar.

Detention center for the ICTY

The UN Detention Unit is on the Penitentiary Institution Haaglanden, Scheveningen, The Hague, the Netherlands, about 4 miles (6.4 km) from the ICTY chambers. Those indicted are kept in private cells, which have a toilet, shower, radio, satellite TV, personal computer, and so forth, (no Internet access). They have some social amenities and can telephone friends and relatives and can have family member visits. They can cook for themselves. Library, sports, and religious facilities are available. The inmates—enemies and friends—mix freely (Evans, 2009).

Indictments

The first indictment of the ICTY was issued in 1994 against the Bosnian-Serb concentration camp commander Dragan Nikolic. The next were two indictments on February 13, 1995, against 21 Bosnian-Serbs charged with committing atrocities against Muslim and Croat civilian prisoners.

Dusko Tadic, a Bosnian-Serb, was the tribunal's first trial. He was arrested by the German police in 1994 in Munich for his alleged crimes in Omarska, Irnopolje, and Keraterm detention camps. So far, the tribunal has indicted more than 166 persons and has completed proceedings on 126 of them. Among them, 13 have had their cases acquitted, 64 were sentenced, 13 have had their cases transferred to local courts, and 36 cases were terminated for lack of evidence (ICTY, 2013; BBC, 2008). The ICTY had, among its indicted suspects, ordinary common soldiers, police commanders, generals, and prime ministers. Among the top political and military figures indicted were General Ante Gotovina of the Croatian Army; Ramush Haradinaj, former prime minister of Kosovo; Radovan Karadzic, former president of the Republika Srpska; Ratko Mladic, former commander of the Bosnian-Serb Army; Milan Babic, former president of the Republika Srpska Krajina; and Prime Minister Slobodan Milosevic. Unmistakably, Slobodan Milosevic became the first sitting head of state to be indicted for war crimes in modern history. Of course, he was not the first head of state to commit war crimes.

Some of the cases tried have been appealed. Some of the indicted suspects are still at large. As of September 2012, some of the fugitives wanted by the Tribunal had been arrested (Al Jazeera, 2011).

Crimes Charged at the ICTY

The defendants were charged with one or more of the following crimes: genocide; persecutions on political, racial, or religious grounds (a crime against humanity); extermination (a crime against humanity); murder (a crime against humanity); a violation of the law or customs of war; unlawful deportation (a crime against humanity); inhumane acts of forcible transfer (a crime against humanity); acts of violence with the primary purpose of spreading terror among the civilian population (a violation of the laws or customs of war); unlawful attacks on civilians (a violation of laws or customs of war); and taking hostages (a violation of the laws or customs of war) (ICTY, 2009a).

Judgment and sentencing

The ICTY has the power to impose life imprisonment but not a death penalty. Some of those already indicted, tried, and found guilty received sentences ranging from 7 years to life.

The UN Security Council wants the ICTY to complete its trials and sentencing by December 31, 2014, and transfer its duties to the newly established International Residual Mechanism for Criminal Tribunals (IRMCT), which started working for the ICTY branch from July 1, 2013. The ICTY will finish all outstanding cases and appeals against their judgments or sentences, if filed before July 1, 2013. The ICTY and the defendants have been made aware that appeals filed after that date will be handled by the IRMCT (ICTY 2010). The ICTY plans to have all appeals heard and resolved by 2015, except those fugitives recently arrested (UN Security Council, 2011). Lastly, 17 member states of the UN have signed an agreement to provide prison facilities for persons convicted by the ICTY.

The relevance of ICTY

The ICTY has demonstrated that, henceforth, no head of state is beyond incrimination. The grounds for its indictments have sharpened the facts, reality, and the edges of international criminal law. The ICTY allowed the victims of domestic and international wars to have a voice in their grievances. The ICTY has awakened the importance of international criminal law, which had been lost since the Nuremberg and Tokyo trials. Finally, ICTY proceedings and evidence have strengthened the relevance of the rule of law in all societies.

International Criminal Tribunal for Rwanda (ICTR)

The second and last ICT is that for Rwanda. The bloody conflict that erupted in Rwanda in 1994 was started by the Belgian colonial administration of Rwanda, who gave political and economic power to the minority ethnic group of the Tutsi (only 14% of Rwandan population compared to Hutus, who form 85%). After the Rwandan independence, which was fought for by the Tutsi, Belgium sided with the Hutu in democratic political maneuvers to punish the Tutsi, reminiscent of the British colonial administration of Nigeria.

The Immediate Cause of Rwanda Genocide

As of April 1994, the Tutsi ethnic groups still held economic power in Rwanda, but a Hutu, Habyarimana, was the president of Rwanda. On April 6, 1994, an aircraft carrying President Habyarirmana was shot down in broad daylight and he was killed. Among the Hutu leadership, it was strongly believed that the Tutsi shot down the plane that killed President Habyarimana. In effect, the Hutu designed acts of genocide under the camouflage of a civil war. According to the United Human Rights Council, Belgium, France, the United States, the UN, and other European powers knew from the beginning that genocide was going on in Rwanda, but kept silent (United Human Rights Council, 2013). The genocide in Rwanda reached epidemic proportions when the Hutu began killing some other Hutu who were sympathizers of the genocidal killings of the Tutsi. In many cases, the Hutu and Tutsi had profoundly intermarried with each other over the centuries. Unmistakably, in many situations, it was relatives slaughtering a whole family of relatives. It was genocide of the majority against the minority, and at one point, the majority was also destroying itself because of the interethnic marriages.

The international media, the Human Rights Watch groups, and other nongovernmental organizations charged the UN and European powers connected with events in Rwanda with discrimination and a nonchalant attitude toward what was happening in Rwanda, given that the UN had created an ICT for the Former Yugoslavia in 1993. They wanted the same kind of tribunal to be created for Rwanda.

The Emergence of International Criminal Tribunal for Rwanda

Responding to the cries of public opinion and the international media, the UN Security Council recognized the seriousness of humanitarian law being violated with impunity in Rwanda. In effect, it acted on the basis of Chapter VII of the UN Charter and created the ICT for Rwanda in line with that of former Yugoslavia (ICTY) by Resolution 955 of November 8, 1994.

Purpose of ICTR

The primary aim of creating the ICT for Rwanda was to start a process of national reconciliation in Rwanda, and to maintain peace in the region. To achieve the set-out aim, the ICTR had to prosecute persons responsible for the Rwandan genocide and other serious violations of international humanitarian law committed in Rwanda from January 1, 1994 to December 31, 1994, including prosecuting Rwandan citizens who were responsible for the genocide and violations of international criminal law in the territory of neighboring states at the same period (ICTR, 2013a).

The structure of ICTR

There are three organs of the ICTR. These are as follows:

1. The chambers and the appeal chamber;
2. The office of the prosecutor; and
3. The registry.

There are three chambers of original jurisdiction (trial chamber I, trial chamber II, and trial chamber III).

There are 16 independent judges for the four chambers including the Appeal Chamber, and nine *ad litem* judges. Member states nominate their best judges to the Secretary General (S-G) of the UN. The S-G sends the compiled list to the UN Security Council, which sends a list to the UN General Assembly. The judges are then elected by the General Assembly. The judges serve for 4 years and may be reelected. As in the case of ICTY, no two judges from the same country will serve in the tribunal at the same time. Three judges sit in each of the trial chambers, and five judges sit in the appeals chamber. In all chambers, there is a presiding judge. The appeals chamber is shared with ICTY appeals. A maximum of four *ad litem* judges are attached to each trial chamber. By Resolution 1855 of December 19, 2008, the UN Security Council authorized the Secretary General to appoint additional ad litem judges upon the request of the president of the ICTR "in order to complete existing trials or conduct additional trials" (ICTR, 2013b).

Office of the prosecutor

The prosecutor is responsible for investigating the cases and prosecuting them. There are two sections in the office of the prosecutor. The investigation section investigates the cases and collects evidence against persons who committed war crimes in Rwanda in 1994. The prosecution section is responsible for indicting all Rwandan war crime criminals and prosecuting them before the tribunal.

The registry

The registry is headed by a registrar. The main duties of the registry are to provide all judicial and administrative support to all of the chambers, and to the prosecutor.

Headquarters of the ICTR

On February 22, 1995, the UN Security Council decided that the seat of the ICT for Rwanda will be located in Arusha, United Republic of Tanzania.

Jurisdiction of ICTR

The ICT for Rwanda has jurisdiction to try genocide, crimes against humanity, violations of Article 3 common to the Geneva Convention and of Additional Protocol II which shall be punishable, crimes committed by Rwandans in Rwanda, and crimes "in the territory of neighboring states as well as non-Rwandan citizens for crimes committed in Rwanda" (ICTR, 2013).

Defendants at ICTR

Most of the time, persons who commit genocide and crimes against humanity are individuals in power and positions of authority. The ICTR presents, for the first time, persons in positions of power who committed atrocities, including violations of human rights in Africa, who were prosecuted for their crimes.

The defendants in ICTR ran away and scattered across more than 15 countries before most of them were arrested. As of December 2011, the Tribunal has indicted 161 individuals. Proceedings have been completed for 97 of them, 67 were convicted and sentenced to terms of imprisonment, 17 were acquitted. Out of the 161 indicted persons, 36 were terminated because of death of the suspect, or the case was withdrawn. Out of the 67 indicted persons, 48 were convicted and sentenced, 34 have completed their prison sentences, and 3 died while serving their sentences. Also, there are seven ongoing trials; five cases were at the appeals stage, and 23 suspects were the subject of contempt proceedings (Al Jazeera, 2011).

Two persons in charge of Rwandan Radio Television Libre des Mille Collines, Ferdinand Nahimana and Jean Bosco Barayagwiza, and the director and editor of the Kangur newspaper, Hassan Ngeze, who were charged with genocide, incitement of genocide, and crimes against humanity because they used their media to incite genocide and other war crimes, were convicted in 2003. While Jean Bosco Barayagwiza was sentenced to 35 years of imprisonment, Ferdinand Nahimana and Hassan Ngeze received life imprisonment. The three convicts appealed their cases. The appeals chamber did not see any evidence of misdirection of justice in the decision of the trial chamber, and only reduced their sentences to 30 years of imprisonment for Ferdinand Nahimana, 32 years for Jean Bosco Barayagwiza, and 35 years imprisonment for Hassan Ngeze.

ICTR detention and prison system

African countries very strongly cooperated with the ICTR in helping to arrest the fugitives and incarcerating the convicted war criminals. In fact, on February 12, 1999, the Republic of Mali became the first African country to sign an agreement with the ICTR to provide prison facilities for the ICTR or the imprisonment of individuals convicted by the Tribunal. The Republic of Benin in West Africa followed, on August 28, 1999. Now, there are 15 African countries as well as countries outside of Africa, such as Italy, France, and Sweden, that have signed agreements with the ICTR to provide detention and incarceration facilities for the tribunal.

The relevance of ICTR

Since the eclipse of colonial hegemony around the world in the 1960s and the early 1970s, no continent has seen inter-ethnic wars and bloody political upheavals more than Africa and

Asia. In effect, no continent has seen its heads of state violate fundamental human rights and commit crimes against humanity, including genocide, more than the African continent.

Like the ICTY and the Eastern European countries, the ICTR is a warning to the present and future African countries' heads of state that no national leader is beyond incrimination. Also, the ICTR has brought back normal life in Rwanda and the Hutu-Tutsi reconciliation is almost complete. Both the ICTY and the ICTR made possible the creation of the IRMCT for each of them to take care of cases whose appeals may not be dealt with by their deadlines (2014 for ICTR and 2015 for ICTY). Finally, both the ICTY and the ICTR made the emergence of a permanent International Criminal Court (ICC) possible, which has started handling war crimes committed in Africa and elsewhere after the creation of the ICTR.

Next is the analysis of the first permanent international court of criminal justice, which the former Secretary General of the UN, Kofi Annan, described as "the best and the greatest achievement of the United Nations so far."

The Emergence of the International Criminal Court (ICC)

Introduction

Origin and development of the International Criminal Court

The idea for the establishment of a permanent International Criminal Court (ICC) goes back to the 1948 UN Convention on the Prevention and Punishment of the crime of Genocide (Genocide Convention). It was after the adoption of the 1948 UN Genocide Convention that the General Assembly engaged the International Law Commission (ILC) "to study the desirability and possibility of establishing an international judicial organ for the trial of persons charged with genocide" (Bantekas & Nash, 2003; Magnarella, 2004). This court, as envisaged, will not be an ad hoc tribunal. It will be a permanent criminal court.

The ILC met in 1949 and 1950 and reported to the General Assembly that the establishment of such a court was desirable and a possibility. However, there were tense disagreements about the ICC subject-matter jurisdiction over certain crimes. Even when four crimes were identified, the lack of a consensus over the definition of "crime of aggression" put the idea of establishing an international criminal court in limbo until more than three decades later.

In December 1989, Trinidad and Tobago was overwhelmed by high waves of illicit trafficking in drugs. In effect, they petitioned the Secretary General of the UN for establishing an international court with jurisdiction over illicit trafficking in drugs across international borders. In response, the UN General Assembly, once again, called upon the ILC to continue work on the establishment of an ICC. Also, the war in the former Yugoslavia, with the concomitant establishment of the ICTY, spurred the General Assembly on to making the emergence of the ICC a priority. Consequently, a draft statute of the ICC was produced in 1994 (Crawford, 1995), and the General Assembly created an Ad Hoc Committee on the Establishment of an International Criminal Court. This committee met more than once in 1995 (Morris & Bourloyannis-Vrailas, 1996; Bantekas & Nash, 2003; Magnarella, 2004). The General Assembly established the Preparatory Committee on the Establishment of an International Criminal Court.[15] After the preparatory committee completed its work, the General Assembly convened a diplomatic conference in Rome in July 1998 to give finishing touches to some of the articles of the statute. After some intensive debates, negotiations, and resolutions on various issues, the ICC Statute was signed on July 17, 1998 (Bantekas & Nash, 2003; Magnarella, 2004).

Signatories to ICC

The ICC Treaty was signed by 120 states who voted in favor of the treaty. Seven countries (United States, China, Libya, Iraq, Israel, Qatar, and Yemen) voted against the treaty, while 21 countries abstained. When the United States and Israel were criticized by some of the US and European allies for voting against the ICC treaty along with five dictatorships (China, Libya, Iraq, Qatar, and Yemen), they changed their stand. On December 31, 2000, the United States and Israel signed the ICC Statute (Thakur, 2004; Magnarella, 2004). On May 6, 2002, however, President George W. Bush unilaterally withdrew the United States' signature from the ICC treaty.

The purpose, statute, and ratification of ICC

The ICC was created as a permanent international criminal court, under the auspices of the UN General Assembly, to bring to justice individuals or groups who committed heinous crimes of profound concern to the international community, such as genocide, crimes against humanity, war crimes, and crimes of aggression.

For the ICC to operate as a legitimate court with a definite jurisdiction, its statute, which is officially captioned as the "Rome Statute of International Criminal Court,"[16] required ratification by 60 states. On April 11, 2002, the ICC received the required number of ratifications "when ten states presented their instruments of ratification at the UN Headquarters, bringing the total number of ratifying countries to 66" (Magnarella, 2004). The ICC Statute assumed an international, legal viable force on July 1, 2002.

Jurisdiction of the ICC

The jurisdiction of the ICC includes party and nonparty states. Party states are countries who signed the ICC treaty. The individuals, groups, or states, accused of any crimes under the jurisdiction of the ICC, may be residing in party states or nonparty states. The Rome Statute of the ICC provides that, if the state where the crime is alleged to have been committed (the "territorial state") is a party to the ICC Statute or consents to the jurisdiction of the court, "then the ICC would have authority to prosecute even if the defendant's state of nationality was not a party to the Statute and did not consent to the ICC jurisdiction"[17] (Thakur, 2004; Morris,

2004). The above provision gives the ICC "jurisdiction over non-party nationals." Giving the ICC power to prosecute the accused without the consent of their state of nationality speaks of the gravity of the seriousness of the subject matter jurisdiction of the crimes to the international community.

It is expected that the ICC and the national courts of states complement each other. The ICC may exercise jurisdiction in the subject matter crimes if states are incapable or reluctant to prosecute. The Rome Statute of the ICC Article 17 provides that "A case shall not be admissible before the ICC if the case is being investigated or prosecuted by a state which has jurisdiction over it, unless the state is unable or unwilling genuinely ·to carry out the investigation or prosecution."[18]

Under the system of complementarity of the ICC and the states, the ICC is the ultimate judge as to whether the national state has sincerely exercised jurisdiction over a case involving its citizen(s) (Morris 2004). Unmistakably, if the ICC observes that there is no bona fide exercise of jurisdiction by the state authority in the matter, the ICC can exercise jurisdiction even in spite of the objection of the state authority.

The subject matter jurisdiction of the ICC is over genocide, crimes against humanity, war crimes, and crimes of aggression. The crimes of aggression have been isolated in the ICC operations and scholarly writings. The reason will be explained later. In compiling the subject matter jurisdiction of the ICC, the inclusion of other crimes such as drug trafficking, terrorism, and offenses against the UN and associated personnel, was speculated before and during the Rome conference, but they were excluded because of the problem of investigation and the sensitive nature of drug trafficking and terrorism, and given the absence of an international definition of terrorism (Bantekas & Nash, 2003). Of the four crimes under the ICC jurisdiction, only three received a consensual definition.

Genocide. Article 6 of the Rome Statute of the ICC was taken verbatim from Article II of the 1948 Genocide Convention, and received a unanimous consensus (see Chapter 5).

Crime against humanity. The general definition of crimes against humanity is set out in Article 7(1) of the Statute, comprising any act contained in an exhaustive list of offenses when perpetrated "as part of a widespread or systematic attack" against any civilian population. Because not every inhuman act is a crime against humanity, the ICC Statute modified "attack" to mean "a course of conduct involving the multiple commission of acts pursuant to or in furtherance of a state or organizational policy to commit such attacks" (Bantekas & Nash, 2003; Thakur, 2004; Schabas, 2000; UN General Assembly Report, 1995).[19]

To prove a charge of crime against humanity, the prosecutor had to show that an attack against a civilian population involved multiple acts and a policy element, and had to show that the attack was either widespread or systemic (Robinson, 1999). The *mens rea* for crime against humanity requires that the defendant acts with knowledge that his/her offense was part of an overall widespread or systematic attack against a civilian population (Bantekas & Nash, 2003;

Maxted, 2004). In addition, the elements of the charged particular offense must be proved before the court. Crimes against humanity can be committed by states or their agents, as well as nonstate bodies.

Among the crimes against humanity are the offenses of apartheid and enforced disappearance. Apartheid is defined in Article 7(2)(h) as, "inhumane acts [intentionally causing great suffering, or serious injury to body or to mental health] committed in the context of an institutionalized regime of systematic oppression and domination by one racial group over any other racial group or groups and committed with the intention of maintaining that regime."

Before the Rome Statute of 1998, earlier conventions had criminalized apartheid as a crime against humanity—Article l(b) of the 1968 Convention on the Non-Applicability of Statutory Limitations to War Crimes and Crimes Against Humanity and Article I of the 1973 Convention on the Prevention and Suppression of Apartheid. The inclusion of apartheid in the ICC's subject matter jurisdiction shows the detest of the offense by the international community. In the same vein, "enforced disappearance" was a clandestine criminal policy of dictators such as former president Augusto Pinochet of Chile, Somoza of Nicaragua, the late president Abacha of Nigeria, the Saddam Hussein of Iraq, the late Idi Amin of Uganda, the late Milosevic of the former Yugoslavia, the late Mubutu Sese Seko of Zaire, the late Ferdinand Marcos of the Philippines, the late Stroessner of Paraguay, and so forth, using their thugs to kidnap their political opponents and bury them in cold blood and declare them as missing, or incarcerate them as political prisoners, or get them poisoned while in prison as President Abacha did so that they die in prison. The world has seen a lot of such political murderers as heads of state to the point that ICC was created to pursue them. The crime of enforced disappearance is defined in Article 7(2)(i) of the Rome Statute as, "the arrest, detention, or abduction of persons by, or with the authorization, support or acquiescence of, a State or a political organization, followed by a refusal to acknowledge that deprivation of freedom or to give information on the fate or whereabouts of those persons, with the intention of removing them from the protection of the law for a prolonged period of time."

Enforced disappearance is a crime of persecution. In the ICC statute (Art. 7), persecution is defined as "the intentional and severe deprivation of fundamental rights contrary to international law by reason of the identity of the group or collectivity." The crime of persecution that may sound like criminalizing discrimination is a type of "extreme forms of discrimination with a deeply criminal character" (Bantekas & Nash, 2003).

Other offenses included as crimes against humanity are "sexual slavery, enforced prostitution, enforced sterilization, and any other forms of sexual violence of comparable gravity."[20]

War crimes. Articles of the Rome Statute of the ICC deal with war crimes. Acts classified under war crimes include offenses against UN personnel and UN military personnel on peacekeeping missions for as long as they are not engaged in hostilities/use of poison or poisoned weapons, asphyxiating, poisonous or other gases, liquid or materials,[21] and use of bullets which expand or flatten after entering the body of human beings.[22] Also included as war crimes are the conscription or enlistment of children under 15 years of age into "national armed forces or other groups engaged in non-international armed conflicts" (Bantekas & Nash, 2003; Maxted, 2004; Thakur, 2004), destruction of buildings dedicated to education, religious worship, arts, science, and other historic monuments,[23] for as long as such buildings and monuments are not used for military purposes.

Attempts to include the use of nuclear weapons and land mines as war crimes were blocked by the nuclear state parties of the ICC Rome Convention. In the same vein, the prohibition of the development of new weapons received opposition from some powerful nations. However, some compromise was reached. The Rome Statute stated the compromise in three categories (see Bantekas & Nash, 2003, p. 338): First, new weapons are prohibited and their use criminalized, if they are of a nature to cause superfluous injury or unnecessary suffering or which are inherently indiscriminate; secondly, such weapons must be the subject of a comprehensive prohibition; and thirdly, they must be specifically included in an annex to the statute by a future amendment, in accordance with the constitutional arrangements of the statute under Acts 121 and 123.[24]

It must be noted that the 1949 Geneva Convention and the 1954 Convention for the Protection of Cultural Property in the Event of Armed Conflict included bombing or destruction of hospitals, schools, colleges, and civilian populations as war crimes for as long as such institutions are not being used for the production or storage of war materials. The Rome Statute of the ICC was a complement and an attempt to provide a watchdog for previous war crime conventions.

Crimes of aggression (crimes against peace)

The concept of crimes against peace or crimes of aggression is as old as the Nuremberg Charter. The 1998 Rome Statute made an attempt to include crimes of aggression as one of the ICC's subject matter jurisdiction. But, the permanent members of the Security Council objected to the inclusion of crimes of aggression as a war crime, because they argued as to "who would explain when a crime of aggression has been committed?" And "what is its definition?" Such an opposition, coming from powerful nations, led the Rome Statute to drop "crimes of aggression" from the list of crimes falling under the subject matter jurisdiction of the ICC.

Limitations and autonomy of the ICC

The authority of the ICC is highly limited by the interests of the powerful and industrialized nations of the Security Council. This group resisted the inclusion of many serious crimes in the subject matter jurisdiction of the ICC. The most serious area is the area of war crimes. As a result of the objection by some members of the Security Council, Article 124 of the ICC Statute allows ratifying state members to declare that it will not accept the jurisdiction of the ICC for a period of 7 years after the statute comes into effect with respect to war crimes perpetrated by its citizens or within its territorial integrity. Thereafter, ratifying states must accept the jurisdiction of the ICC in its totality (Magnarella, 2004; Bantekas & Nash, 2003; Forsythe, 2004).

The ICC exercises some degree of authority in dealing with genocide, crimes against humanity, and war crimes. The ICC can prosecute some nationals of member states and non-member states in the three crime areas without the approval of their governments. The court also exercises a high degree of authority in its decisions and prescription of penalty.

How cases reach the ICC

Cases reach the ICC in three ways: (1) on the basis of Chapter VII of the UN Charter, the Security Council can ask the ICC to investigate a matter in a particular state that the council feels threatens international peace and tranquility. All states under the UN flag are obliged to cooperate with the ICC investigations and surrender their accused citizens when requested to do so, because the ICC operates under the authority of the Security Council and assembly parties. Also, the orders of the court can "be enforced by the Security Council in the form of imposing embargos, the freezing of assets of leaders and their supporters, and the use of force" (Magnarella, 2004; Forsythe, 2004); (2) individual countries can bring a case to the court based on cooperation and complementarity of state parties to the ICC; and (3) the ICC prosecutor can bring an action against individuals or groups accused of crimes of genocide, crimes against humanity, or war crimes. As noted earlier, the court could bring an action against individuals or groups when a state's authorities are unwilling or unable to prosecute the offenders.

Judges of the ICC: Composition, qualifications, and selection

Article 36 of the Rome Statute spells out the rules for judicial nominations and selections. Any state party to the ICC can nominate one candidate to be elected judge of the court.

In the selection of the judges, the assembly state parties are required to take into account a fair representation of males and females, geographical diversity, and the principal world legal systems (Magnarella, 2004; Bantekas & Nash, 2003; Flinterman, 2004; Forsythe, 2004).

The Rome Statute provides that the judges of the ICC must be longstanding, experienced legal practitioners admitted to the bar association of their respective countries. They must be persons of sound, moral character, highly qualified, and impartial judges. Candidates for nomination to the position of judge of the ICC must have demonstrated competence in criminal law and international law, and possess extensive experience in the legal profession (Art. 36).

A list of candidates is submitted to state parties to the statute. From the list of candidates, state parties elect 18 full-time judges. It is required that a minimum of five judges must be experts in relevant areas of international law, such as international humanitarian law and human rights (Forsythe, 2004; Magnarella, 2004; Bantekas & Nash, 2003; Flinterman, 2004).

Article 35 provides that the term of service of the judges be 9 years, and the judges are not eligible for reelection. In addition, no two judges shall be citizens of the same state party to the statute. Article 40 provides that the judges of the ICC be independent in the execution of their duties. And, Article 41 stipulates that a judge of the ICC shall not participate in any case in which his/her impartiality might be taken with a grain of salt.

Prosecutor of the ICC

The prosecutor is an independent agent of the ICC. He/she may designate deputy prosecutors whose candidacy must be approved by the assembly state parties. The deputy prosecutors serve the court full-time. Like the judges, the prosecutor must be independent (Art. 42) and must not be involved in any activity that will interfere with his/her duties.

Both the prosecutor and deputy prosecutors are elected by the assembly of state parties for a 9-year term. Candidates for the position of prosecutor and deputy prosecutor must be highly qualified legal practitioners with high moral character and legal competence.

Defendant(s)

Individuals or groups or a country being investigated or prosecuted can, at any stage of the prosecution, demand that a prosecutor be disqualified to handle the case on reasonable grounds such as partiality. However, the ICC Statute provides safeguards against fabricated, politically motivated prosecutions.

Standard of proof

In all cases before the ICC, the standard of proof for criminal conviction is guilty beyond a reasonable doubt.

Registrar of the ICC

Article 43(4) of the Statute stipulates that the judges of the ICC are authorized to elect the registrar of the court for a five-year term. The registrar can be reelected only once.

United Nations Special Court for Sierra Leone

This court is also known as the "Special Court" (SCSL). This court was established on the basis of an agreement signed between the United Nations and the Government of Sierra Leone on January 16, 2002. The agreement was ratified by Parliament on December 15, 2011 and signed into law on February 1, 2012. The court has office in Freetown, The Hague, and New York City. The court was designed to try all those accused of war crimes and other atrocities during the Sierra Leone Civil War.

Jurisdiction

The court (SCSL) has jurisdiction to try persons who committed crimes against humanity, against civilians, such crimes as murder; extermination; enslavement; deportation; torture; imprisonment; rape; sexual slavery; forced prostitution; or any other form of sexual violence; prosecution on the basis of politics, race, ethnicity, or religion; and other "inhuman acts." In addition, the court has jurisdiction to prosecute anybody who violated the Geneva Convention of 1949, as well as Sierra Leone's Prevention of Cruelty to Children Act, 1926, for the abuse of girls and the Malicious Damage Act 1861.

The SCSL has no jurisdiction on persons younger than 15 years of age. And the court is superior to any court in Sierra Leone.

The structure of the SCSL

There are three institutions surrounding the court. They are the Registry, the Prosecutor, and the Chambers (for trials and appeals). Like in ICC, the Registrar of SCSL is responsible for the overall management of the court (SCSL, 2002).

Chambers. The statute of the court provides for 8 to 12 judges. Three of the judges serve in the trial chamber, and one of them is appointed by the government of Sierra Leone, and two by the United Nations Secretary General. Five of the judges serve in the appeals chamber, of which two are appointed by the government of Sierra Leone, and three by the United Nations Secretary General.[25]

Punishment. The sentences for all those convicted by the court will be carried out within Sierra Leone, except if there is no capacity to deal with the accused. In such a case, any state pursuant to the International Criminal Tribunal for Rwanda or the International Criminal Tribunal for the former Yugoslavia who have acceded a willingness to host the accused for the tenure of their sentence can hold the prisoner. The enforcement in such a situation will be carried out by the court.

The court can sentence those found guilty of a crime or crimes to terms of imprisonment or confiscation of property. Like in all other criminal tribunals of the UN, the SCSL has no power to impose the death penalty.

A total of 22 people have been indicted in the SCSL. Proceedings against 21 people have been completed: 9 are serving their sentences, 7 have finished their sentences, 2 have been acquitted, and 3 have died before the conclusion of the proceedings against them. Proceedings against one person, Johnny Paul Koroma, are ongoing; he is a fugitive, although he is believed to be deceased.

Charles Taylor, the former Liberian President, was among those found guilty of war crimes. On April 26, 2012, he became the first African head of state to be convicted of a crime.

The Victimology and Future of State Crime

Whenever a crime is committed, there must be a victim, directly or indirectly. Individuals may commit a crime that claims only one victim. But the victims of a state crime are many. Think about a state crime of omission to enforce pollution law, or deliberately dumping a nuclear material at a poor neighborhood. The victims are enumerable, because it could affect generations unborn. Even in a crime of political assassinations, the individual assassinated is not the only victim. His family members and other relatives are also victims. In war crimes, genocide, crimes against humanity, state terrorism, and so forth, so many people are victimized. Unmistakably, a state crime is the mother and father of all crimes, because it provides some people rationalization to engage in crimes against individuals and against the state.

The emerging interest among scholars in the study of state crime, and the surging interest in the use of cell phone cameras to secretly snap activities of state agents warn state authorities that future deviances and crimes will not be swept under the rug. Police brutality is no more hidden. Modern technology has put the state on notice that some of its actions, deviant and nondeviant, are under the public radar. State crimes had never been under the monitor of intellectuals and social media more than in the 21st century, and this is good for society.

Discussion and Conclusion

The establishment of a permanent international criminal court by the international community, to deal with three heinous global crimes, is a commendable progress to humanity. The mere existence of such a permanent world court has a deterrent effect throughout developed and developing countries. Unmistakably, no dictator (an individual, a group, or a state) will engage in acts of genocide, war crimes, or offenses against humanity, without realizing that there are watchdogs that would bring him to justice in a court beyond his control.

The ICC, by far, is better and more effective in deterrence than the IMT and the ICT in that both IMT and ICT are ad hoc courts. They exist for as long as the case assigned to it lasts. As soon as the case is decided, it ends the life of the tribunal. For instance, the IMT for the Nuremberg trial ended with the Nuremberg trial, and the ICT for the former Yugoslavia (ICTY), and the ICTR for Rwanda end their existence after the trial of the offenders and sentencing them is achieved. But the ICC exists forever and so is its effect on humanity.

Although the ICC has some degree of autonomy, its authority is controlled by the Security Council. The permanent members of the Security Council are broken rear axles on the wheel of the UN. If the General Assembly's decision, on any issue, does not favor any of them, they veto the bill individually or collectively. The 1998 Rome Conference that created the ICC Statute ran into road blocks set by the nuclear nations and land mine nations who are permanent members of the Security Council. In the same vein, the definition of war crimes was modified to accommodate the interests of France and some other permanent members of the Security Council who opposed the original definition of the crime. "Crime of aggression"was not submitted to the ICC because some of the permanent members of the Security Council could not come to terms with any consensual definition of the offense, even though "crimes against peace" was accepted as war crimes at the 1945 Nuremberg IMT Charter (Bantekas & Nash, 2003). "Crimes against peace" is the same as crimes of aggression.

Unmistakably, with the unpredictability of the permanent members of the Security Council, it is not good news that the Security Council has control over the ICC. Undeniably, the provision that an assembly state party can opt to refuse to accept the jurisdiction of the ICC for 7 years after the statute went into effect was to appease the minds of some permanent members of the Security Council. That provision is a slap on the face to the Rome Statute.

The assembly of state parties controls the administrative and substantive matters of the court. Although the assembly of state parties governs by majority rule, the permanent members of the Security Council (except the United States)are still part of the assembly of state parties. They can veto whatever ruling they want to veto.

The United States, which is the world peace maker, surprisingly declined to ratify the ICC statute. It is mindboggling that the United States refused to sign a treaty to establish a permanent international criminal court to hold dictators responsible for their crimes against humanity.

According to Forsythe (2004), the United States refused to sign the Rome Statute because the American policy makers could not countenance the American military personnel standing as defendants before the ICC. Worst of all, the fear that ICC could summon senior members of the U.S. military and Pentagon to the ICC to answer questions on U.S. military activities in Afghanistan, Iraq, and so forth, is hard to swallow in Washington, D.C. Some U.S. policy-makers argue that the ICC is not democratic, and that the court is not answerable to any political body. In other words, there is no political check over the ICC (Forsythe, 2004). The U.S. objection to the ICC stems from Jesse Helm's argument long ago as Chairman of the Senate Foreign Relations Committee that, "Nothing trumps our Constitution, no international court, unless we voluntarily, under our constitutional process, agree to submit to that court" (Forsythe, 2004). In the light of Helm's argument, and given that the U.S. Congress understood that the Rome Statute gives the ICC the power to prosecute persons or groups, including those whose countries are not signatories to the statute, who committed crimes that fall within its subject matter jurisdiction, a bill was passed in Congress and signed by President Bush into law in August 2002 to wedge the ICC. The law authorizes the American president to use force to free any U.S. citizen being held in custody by the ICC (Forsythe, 2004).

The U.S. argument that because it did not ratify the treaty, and therefore, American citizens should not be subject to the ICC, is not in order, for two reasons: First, other treaties, like the treaty on terrorism, contain similar provisions that some states did not ratify; yet, citizens of those non-ratifying states are legally bound under international law. Second, "the Nuremberg tribunal went forward without the consent of any German Government" (Forsythe, 2004).

In conclusion, adherence to international law and treaties is for world peace, and U.S. allies, such as France and the United Kingdom, realized that view and ratified the ICC statute. Nobody loses with the emergence of the ICC except dictatorial regimes. The ICC was not created to control the United States or impinge upon the American Constitution or the Constitution of any developed nation. The Rome Statute was intended to protect the "little people" all over the world who may be in danger of being slaughtered by greedy, authoritarian regimes.

Now it is unequivocal that the United Nations not only has a court for dealing with states' deviances in civil matters but it also has a permanent criminal court (ICC) to prosecute state authorities who took the law into their own hands. Undeniably, as Kofi Annan put it, the creation of the ICC is the greatest achievement of the United Nation, by realizing that states do, in fact, commit crimes.

Review Questions

1. (a) What led to the emergence of the United Nations? (b) What are the central terms of the Charter of the United Nations?
2. What is the rationale of the International Humanitarian Law?
3. What is meant by "Geneva Conventions"?
4. The Fourth Geneva Convention of 1949 provided four treaties. What are they?
5. The 1949 Geneva Convention was followed by two Protocols (Protocol I and Protocol II). Why did the two Protocols emerge after over 20 years of the 1949 Geneva Conventions?
6. Name at least five United Nations Conventions to control state crimes and deviance. What are the significance of those Conventions?
7. How did the United Nations recognize the contributions of the "Mirabal Sisters" to political science and freedom of speech?
8. Write a short essay on each of the following:
   The League of Nations (LN)

   International Military Tribunal (IMT)

   International Criminal Tribunal (ICT)

   International Criminal Court (ICC)
9. What are the four crimes under the ICC jurisdiction? Define them.
10. What are the limitations of the ICC?
11. How did the United Nations Special Court for Sierra Leone (SCSL) emerge?
12. Who are the victims of state crime? Explain in detail.

Notes

1. "Geneva Conventions 1864–1977" (http://www.britannica.com/EBchecked/topic/229047/GenevaConventions). Accessed April 14, 2015.
2. "Protocol I," (see http://www.icrc.org/ihl/INTRO/470). Accessed April 14, 2015.
3. **Protocol III** is a 2005 amendment protocol to the Geneva Convention relating to the Adoption of an Additional Distinctive Emblem. Under the protocol, the protective sign of the Red Crystal may be displayed by medical and religious personnel at times of war, instead of the traditional Red Cross, Star of David or Red Crescent symbols. People displaying any of these protective emblems are performing a humanitarian service and must be protected by all parties to the conflict.

4. See the United Nations Treaty Collection: "Convention on the Prevention and Punishment of the Crime of Genocide," (http://treaties.un.org/ages/ViewDetails.aspx?src=TREATY&mtdsg_no=IV-1&chapter=4&lang=en). Accessed April 15, 2015.

5. United Nations General Assembly *Session 47 Resolution 133.* "Declaration on the Protection of all Persons from Enforced Disappearance" A/RES/47/133 (http://www.un.org/ga/search/view_doc.asp?symbol=A/RES/47/133). 18 December 1992. Accessed April 15, 2015.

6. See "Convention against Torture," Article 27 (http://www2.ohchr.org/english/law/cat.htm). Accessed April 15, 2015.

7. See "United Nations Treaty Collection: Convention against Torture and Other Cruel, Inhuman or Degrading Treatment or Punishment." (http://treaties.un.org/ages/ViewDetails.aspx?src=TREATY&mtdsg_no=IV-9&chapter=4&lang=en). Accessed April 15, 2015.

8. General Assembly Resolution 317(IV). Also see "Convention for the Suppression of the Traffic in Persons and of the Exploitation of the Prostitution of Others," (http://www.ohchr.org/Documents/ProfessionInterst/trafficpersons.pdf). Accessed April 15, 2015.

9. "Signatories to the UNCAC" (http://www.unodc.org/unodc/en/treaties/CAC/signatories.html). Accessed April 16, 2015.

10. Nonmember states that have signed are the Cook Islands, the State of Palestine, and the European Union. The UN member states that have not ratified the convention are Barbados, Bhutan, Japan, New Zealand and Syria (see http://www.unodc.org/unodc/en/corruption/indes.html). Accessed April 16, 2015.

11. See "Convention on the Elimination of All Forms of Discrimination against Women" (http://www.un.org/womenwatch/daw/cedaw/cedaw.htm). Accessed April 16, 2015.

12. Ibid.

13. See "UN Convention against Transnational Organized Crime: Treaty Status," (http://treaties.un.org/ages/ViewDetails.aspx?src=TREATY&mtdsg_no=XVIII-12&chapter=18&lang=en). Accessed April 16, 2015.

14. UN General Assembly Resolution 44/39, December 4, 1989.

15. UN General Assembly Resolution 50/46, December 11, 1995.

16. UN Doc. A/CONF. 183/9, July 17, 1998.

17. Rome Statutes of the International Criminal Court, Art. 5, July 17, 1998; also see Art. 12.

18. Rome Statutes of the International Criminal Court, Art. 5, July 17, 1998; also see Art. 12.

19. ICC Statute, Art. 7(1)(h); Art. 7(1)(g).

20. ICC Statute, Art. 8(2)(b)(xvii).

21. ICC Statute, Art. 8(2)(b)(xvii).

22. ICC Statute, Art. 8(2)(b)(xvii).

23. ICC Statute, Art. 8(2)(b)(ix) and (e)(iv).

24. ICC Statute, Art. 8(2)(b)(xix).

25. "Statute of the Special Court for Sierra Leone," (http://www.sc.sl.org/LinkClick.aspx?
fileticket=cCInd1MJeEw%3d&tabid=70). Accessed April 17, 2015.

References

Abbott, E. (1988b). *Haiti: An insider's history of the rise and fall of the Duvaliers*. New York, NY: Simon & Schuster.

Abbott, E. (1988a. *Sugar: A bittersweet history*. New York, NY: Penguin.

Abrahamson, B. & Katz, J. (2009). The Persian conquest of Jerusalem in 614 compared with Islamic conquest of 638: Its messianic nature and the role of the Jewish Exilarch. Available from www.pdffactory.com. Accessed December 19, 2014.

Abu, B. D. (1988a, July 4). Death where's thy drum? *Newswatch* (Nigerian weekly magazine).

Abu, B. D. (1988b, July 11). Koko: To move or not to move. *Newswatch* (Nigerian weekly magazine).

Aburish, S. (1997). *A brutal friendship: The West and the Arab elite*. London, England: Indigo.

Acemoglu, D., Robinson, J. A., & Verdier T. (2004). Kleptocracy and divide-and-rule: A model of personal rule. *Journal of the European Association, 2*(2–3), 162–192.

Achebe, C. (1959). *Things fall apart*. New York, NY: McDowell, Obolensky.

Adewole, O. (1991). Africa: The waste basket of the West. *Business and Society Review, 67*, 48–50.

Adler, F., Mueller, G. O.W., & Laufer, W. S. (1991). *Criminology*. New York, NY: McGraw-Hill.

Adu, A. (1987). *African perspectives on colonialism*. Baltimore, MD: John Hopkins University Press.

Agren, D. (2012). Normalists fight changes in Mexico education system. *Florida Today* (Melbourne, Florida), p. 4A.

Al Jazeera. (2011). Serbia's last war crimes fugitive arrested. *Al Jazeera Media Network*. Retrieved from http://www.aljazeera.comlnews/europe/2011/07/201172074249705610.html

Akcam, T. (2012). *The young Turks' crime against humanity: The Armenian genocide and ethnic cleansing in the Ottoman Empire*. Princeton, NJ: Princeton University Press.

Akukure, O. (2012). How Babangida, Abacha, Obasanjo shared Nigeria's oil wells. *Masterweb Reports* (Citizen News). Retrieved from http://nigeriamasterweb.com/blog/index.p. Accessed April 4, 2015.

Alba, F. (1982). *The population of Mexico: Trends, issues, and policies*. New Brunswick, NJ: Transaction Books.

Alessandri, F. B. (2014, February 12). The fight to stop young Italians dying in police custody. *Vice News* (Television broadcast). Available from http://www.vice.com/en_us. Accessed February 25, 2015.

Alike, E. (2010). Nigeria: U.S. keeps $917 million bribe settlement. Available from All Africa. com. Also see http://www.respondanet.com/Africa/nigeria-us-keeps-917-million-bribe-settlement.html. Accessed April 3, 2015.

Allsen, T. T. (1987). *Mongol imperialism: The policies of the Grand Qan Mongke in China, Russia, and Islamic Lands* (pp. 1251–1259). Berkeley: University of California Press.

Allison, H. (1986). *The tragic saga of the Indians*. Paducah, KY: Turner Publishing Company.

Almond, G. (1946). The German resistance movement. *Current History, 10*, 409–527.

Ames, G. J. (2004). The globe encompassed: The age of European discovery, 1500–1700. New York: Prentice-Hall.

Anaclet, R. (1988, July 20). Africa: New dumping ground for toxic wastes. *Inter Press Service*.

Anderson, W. (1991). *Cherokee removal: Before and after*. Athens: University of Georgia Press.

Anderson, D. L. (Ed.). (1998). *Facing my Lai: Moving beyond the massacre*. Lawrence: University Press of Kansas.

Anderson, D. (2005a). *Histories of the hanged: The dirty war in Kenya and the end of empire*. New York, NY: W.W. Norton & Company.

Anderson, G. C. (2005b). *The conquest of Texas: Ethnic cleansing in the promised land, 1820–1975*. Oklahoma City: Oklahoma University Press.

Annan, K. (1998). The Establishment of the Court . . . (Speech), In *The International Criminal Court: History and Role*, – Parliament of Canada, Library of Parliament Research Publications. Retrieved from http://www.parl.gc.ca/content/LOP/Resear. Accessed January 10, 2015.

Ansari, Z. (2013). Rigging in Pakistan elections 2013: All evidence compiled. Retrieved from https://www.facebook.com/Rigging201. Accessed March 4, 2015.

Anueyiagu, A. (1997, January 4). Nsukka gripped by Otokoto saga: A six-year-old boy escapes kidnap. *This Day*, pp. 1–2.

Archer, C. I. (2007). *The birth of modern Mexico, 1780–1824*. Lanham, MD: Rowman & Littlefield Publishing Group.

Ariffin, L. (2014). Jais raid Bible Society, Malay bibles seized. Retrieved from http://www.free-malaysiatoday.com/category/nation/2014/01/02/jais-raids-bible-society-bibles-seized/. *Free Malaysia Today*. Accessed March 14, 2015.

Arnold, B. T. & Michalowski, P. (2006). Achaemenid period historical texts concerning Mesopotamia. In M. W. Chavelas (Ed.), *The ancient near east: Historical sources in translation*. London, England: Blackwell Publishing.

Atzili, B. (2012). *Good fences, bad neighbors: Border fixity and international conflict*. Chicago, IL: University of Chicago Press.

Austin, J., & Coventry, G. (2001, February). Emerging issues on privatized prisons: Bureau of Justice Assistance.

Avirgan, T. & Honey, M. (1982). *War in Uganda: The legacy of Idi Amin*. Wesport, CT: Lawrence Hill & Co. Publishers.

Ayandele, E. A. (1970). Holy Johnson, pioneer of African nationalism, 1836-1917. New York: Routledge.

Ayandele, E. A. (1979). Nigerian historical studies. London: Frank Cass.

Backman, C. R. (2014). *The worlds of Medieval Europe*. Oxford, England: Oxford University Press.

Baker, G. P. (1929). *Hannibal*. New York, NY: Dodd Mead.

Balebo, A., Nwafor, O., & Pants, E. V. M. (1994, January 10). Dele Giwa Affairs, *Newswatch*, p. 6.

Bantekas, I. & Nash, S. (2003). *International criminal law* (2nd ed.). London, England: Cavendish Publishing Limited.

Barak, G. (Ed.). (1991). *Crimes of the capitalist state: An introduction to state criminality*. Albany, NY: State University of New York Press.

Barrett, A. A. (1989). *Caligula: The corruption of power*. London, England: Batsford.

Bassiouni, M. C. (2010). Perspectives on international criminal justice. *Virginia Journal of International Law, 50,* 269–298.

Bassiouni, M. C. (2011). Introduction: Crime of state and other forms of collective group violence by nonstate Actors. In D. L. Rothe & C. W. Mullins (Eds.), *State crime: Current perspectives*. New Brunswick, NJ: Rutgers University Press.

Bassiouni, M. C. & Derby, D. (1981). Final report on the establishment of an international criminal court for the implementation of the apartheid convention and other relevant international instruments. *Hofstra Law Review, 9*, 523.

Bates, E. (1998, January 5). Private prison. *The Nation*, p. 13.

BBC News. (2008). Hague court acquits Kosovo ex-PM. Retrieved from http://news.bbc. co.uk/2/hi/7328148.stm. Accessed February 15, 2013.

BBC News (2010, October 11). Officer given life for boy's murder in Greek riot case. Also see http://www.bbc.co.uk/news/world-europe-11513309. Accessed February 26, 2015.

BBC News (2014, February 11). Retrieved from http://www.bbc.com/news/uk-northern-in. BBC News_Samuel Devenney. Accessed February 23, 2015.

Bealer, A. W. (1972, 1996). *Only the names remain: The Cherokees and the Trail of Tears*. Boston, MA: Little, Brown and Company.

Beane, M. E. (1995). Money laundering: A preferred law enforcement target for the 1990s. In J. Albanese (Ed.), *Contemporary issues in organized crime*. Monsey, NY: Criminal Justice Press.

Beechert, E. D. (1985). *Working in Hawaii: A labor history*. Honolulu: University of Hawaii Press.

Benedict, P. (2004). *Rouen during the wars of religion*. Cambridge, England: Cambridge University Press.

Benson, N. L. (1992). *The provincial deputation in Mexico: Harbinger of provincial autonomy, independence, and federalism*. Austin: University of Texas Press.

Bergen, D. (2003). *War and genocide: A concise history of the Holocaust*. Lanham, MD: Rowman & Littlefield.

Berkeley, B. (2002). *The graves are not yet full*. New York, NY: Basic Books.

Bethel, L. (1987). *The independence of Latin America*. Cambridge, England: University of Cambridge Press.

Bhorat, H. & Cassim, A. (2014, January 27). South Africa's welfare success story II: Poverty-reducing social grants. *Brookings Africa in Focus*. Retrieved from http://www.brookings. edu/blogs/africa-in

Biddiss, M. (1995). Victor's justice: The Nuremberg tribunal. *History Today, 45*, 40.

de Blij, H. J. & Muller P. O. (2003). *Geography realms, regions and concepts*. New York, NY: Wiley.

Block, M. (1941). *Current biography who's news and why*. New York, NY: The H W Wilson Company.

Blumrosen, A. W. & Blumrosen, R. G. (2005). Slave nation: How slavery united the colonies and sparked the American revolution. Naperville, ILL: Sourcebooks.

Boone, R. (2012). Idaho inmates claim gangs run prison. Retrieved from http://abcnews.go.com/ US/wireStory/apnewsbreak-idaho-inmates-claim-gangs-run-prison-17704975#. UKWvxoalCSo. Associated Press. Accessed March 20, 2015.

Boone, R. (2013). Judge CCA in contempt for prison understaffing. Retrieved from http://big-story.ap.org/article/judge-cca-contempt-prison-understaffing. Associated Press. Accessed March 20, 2015.

Bothe, M. & Partsch, K.J. (1982). *New rules for victims of armed conflicts, commentary on the two 1977 protocols additional to the Geneva Conventions of 1949.* London, England: Martinus Nijhoff Publishers.

Boulden, J. (2001). *Peace enforcement: The United Nations' experience in Congo, Somalia, and Bosnia.* Westport, CT: Praeger.

Bourne, H. R. F. (1903). *Civilization in Congoland: A story of international wrong doing.* London, England: P.S. King & Son.

Bower, Y. (2000). *Rethinking the Holocaust.* New Haven, CT: Yale University Press.

Brackman, A. C. (1987). *The other Nuremberg: The untold story of the Tokyo war crimes trial.* New York, NY: William Morrow and Company.

Braitwaite, T. (2011). *The jurisprudence of the living oracles.* Bloomington, IN: Trafford Publishing.

Braudel, F. (1995). *The Mediterranean and the Mediterranean world in the age of Philip II.* Berkeley: University of California Press.

Brehier, L. (1980). *Crusades. Catholic encyclopedia.* New York, NY: Robert Appleton Company.

Brooke, J. (1988, July 17). Waste dumpers turning to West Africa. *The New York Times.* Retrieved from http://www.nytimes.com/1988/07/17/world/waste-dumpers-turning-to-west-africa.html. Accessed March 21, 2015.

Bruce, R. V. (1989). *1877: Year of violence.* Chicago, IL: Ivan R. Dee Publisher.

Brundage, B. C. (1963). *Empire of the Inca.* Norman: Oklahoma University Press.

Brunet, J.-P. (2008). Police violence in Paris, October 1961: Historical sources, methods, and conclusions. *The Historical Journal, 51*(1), 195–204.

Brynjar, L. (2006). *The Society of the Muslim brothers in Egypt: The rise of an Islamic mass movement 1928–1942.* New York, NY: Ithaca Press.

Buchanan, B. J. (Ed.). (2006). *Gunpowder, explosives and the state: A technological history.* Aldershot, England: Ashgate Publishing.

Bullock, A. L. C. (1939). *Germany's colonial demands.* Oxford, England: Oxford University Press.

Bullock, A. (1999). *Hitler: A study in tyranny.* New York, NY: Konecky & Konecky.

Burns, A. (1967). History of Nigeria. London: Allen & Unwin Limited.

Burt, A. & Diederich, B. (1969). *Papa Doc: Haiti and its dictator.* Princeton, NJ: Markus Wiener Publishers.

Bushkovitch, P. (2001). *Peter the great: The struggle for power, 1671–1725*. Cambridge, England: Cambridge University Press.

Cahill, D. (2008). Genocide from below: The Great Inca Rebellion of 1780–1782 in the Southern Andes. In A. Dirk Moses (Ed.), *Empire, colony, genocide: Conquest, occupation, and subaltern resistance in world history*. New York, NY: Berghahn Books.

Campbell, D. (2002). *The Bush dynasty and the Cuban criminals*. London, England: Guardian. Retrieved from http://www.guardian.co.uk/world/2002/dec/02/usa.books

Campos, J. E. (2007). *The many faces of corruption: Tracking vulnerabilities at the sector level*. Washington, DC: World Bank.

Carassava, A. (2008, December 17). Greek protests unfurl banners at Acropolis. *The New York Times*. Also see http://www.nytimes.com/2008/12/18/world/europe/18greece.html?en. Accessed February 26, 2015.

Carland, J. M. (1985). The colonial office and Nigeria, 1898-1914. Oakland, CA: Hoover Press.

Carr, E. H. (1966). *The Bolshevik revolution*. New York, NY: Penguin.

Carter, P. (1976). *Mao*. London, England: Oxford University Press.

Cawthorn, N. (1999). *The world's worst atrocities*. London, England: Octopus Publishing Group.

CBC News. (2007, November 14). Taser video shows RCMP shocked immigrant within 25 seconds of their arrival, *CBC News*. Accessed February 25, 2015. Also see http://www.cbc.ca/canada/british-columbia/sotry/2007/11/14/bc-taservideo.html

CBC News. (2010, January 22). Vancouver police apologize after man beaten. Retrieved from http://www.cbc.ca/canada/british-columia/story/2010/01/21/bc-vpd-alleged-assault-yao-wai-wu.html. *CBC News*. Accessed February 25, 2015.

Chaliand, G. (2007). *The history of terrorism: From antiquity to Al Qaeda* (p. 185). Berkeley: University of California Press.

Chaliand, G. & Blin, A. (2007). *The history of terrorism: From antiquity to Al Qaeda*. Berkeley: University of California Press.

Chamberlain, M. E. (1974). *The scramble for Africa*. Hong Kong, China: Longman Group Limited.

Chambliss, W. J. (1974). The state, the law, and the definition of behavior as criminal or Delinquent. Chapter 1 in Handbook of Criminology by Daniel Glaser, (ed.). Chicago: RandMcNally.

Chambliss, W. J. (1975). Toward a political economy of crime. *Theory and Society*, vol.2, no. 2: 149–170.

Chambliss, W. J. (1976). *Whose law? What order?: A conflict approach to criminology*. New York, NY: John Wiley & Sons.

Chambliss, W. J. (1978). On the take: From petty crooks to president, First edition. Bloomington, IN: Uiversity of Indiana Press.

Chambliss, W. J. (1988). On the take: From petty crooks to president, Second edition. Bloomington, In: University of Indiana Press.

Chambliss, W. J. (2010). Forward. In State crime: Current perspectives, by Dawn L. Rothe & Christopher W. Mullins, (eds.). New Brunswick, NJ: Rutgers University Press.

Chan, M. (2012). Universal health coverage. *The Lancet, 380*(9845), 845–948.

Chang, I. (1998). *The rape of Nanking: The forgotten Holocaust of World War II*. New York, NY: Penguin.

Chase, K. W. (2003). *Firearms: A global history to 1700*. New York, NY: Cambridge University Press.

Chicago Daily Tribune. (1872, October 12). Police brutality: A prisoner shamefully maltreated by officers, kicked and pounded in cell . . . probably fatally injured.

Chizea, B. (1991, November 4). Bank fraud: Who is to blame. *Newswatch*, p. 61.

Chomsky, N. & Vltchek, A. (2013). *On western terrorism: From Hiroshima to Drone warfare*. London, England: Pluto Press.

Churchill, W. (1997). *A little matter of genocide: Holocaust and denial in the Americas, 1492 to the present*. San Francisco, CA: City Light Publisher.

Clarke, A. (2015). Switzerland to return $380 million to Nigeria in Abacha case. *AML/Financial Crime Tutor.* see http://www.int.comp.org/BlogEngine/post/2015/3/23/switzerland-abacha-case-aspx. Accessed April 3, 2015

Clarke, T. (1981). *By blood and fire*. New York, NY: G-P Puttnam's Sons.

Clinard, M. B. & Yeager, P. C. (1979). *Illegal corporate behavior*. Washington, DC: U.S. Government Printing.

Clinard, M. B. & Yeager, P. C. (2002). Corporate crime: Clarifying the concept and extending the data. In M. D. Ermann & R. J. Lundman (Eds.), *Corporate and governmental deviance: Problems of organizational behavior in contemporary society*.

Cocroft, W. (2000). *Dangerous energy: The archeology of gunpowder and military explosives manufacture*. Swindon, England: English Heritage.

Cohen, S. (1996). Review of controlling state crime. *British Journal of Sociology, 47,* 733–734.

Cohen, A. K. (1990). Criminal actors: Natural persons and collectives. In New dfirections in the study of justice, law, and social control. New York: Plenum.

Cohen, J. M. (1969). The four voyages of Christopher Columbus. Being his own log book, letter, and dispatches with connecting narrative drawn from the life of the admiral by his Hernando Colon and others. London (UK): Pengui.

Conquest, R. (1986). *The harvest of sorrow: Soviet collectivization and the terror-famine.* Oxford, England: Oxford University Press.

Constantakopoulous, C. (2012, January). Identity and resistance: The Islanders' league, the Aegean Islands and the Hellenistic Kings, *Mediterranean Historical Review, 27, 49–70.*

Coogan, T. P. (2002a). *Michael Collins: The man who made Ireland.* New York, NY: Palgrave.

Coogan, T. P. (2002b). *The troubles: Ireland's ordeal 1966–1996 and the search for peace.* New York, NY: Palgrave Macmillan.

Cook, N. D. (1998). *Born to die: Disease and new world conquest, 1492–1650.* Cambridge, England: Cambridge University Press.

Cook, N. D. (2002). Sickness, starvation, and death in early Hispaniola, *Journal of Interdisciplinary History, 32*(3), 349–386.

Corder, M. (2009). International court begins case of Congo Warlord. Retrieved from http://www.google.com/hostednews/ap/article/ALegM5jIIQpLKy3NrhJa50Xg3Wte4yxJwD95UPQG80. The Associated Press. Accessed January 9, 2015.

Corera. (2013, April 2). MI6 and the death of Patrice Lumumba. Security Correspondent, *BBC News Africa.*

Cosgrove, R. A. (1980). *The rule of law: Albert Venn Dicey, Victorian jurist.* London, England: Macmillan.

Costen, M. D. (1997). *The Cathers and the Albigensian crusade.* Manchester, England: Manchester University Press.

Cottrell, L. (1992). *Hannibal: Enemy of Rome.* New York, NY: Da Capo Press.

Crassweller, R. D. (1966). *Trujillo: The life and times of a Caribbean dictator.* New York, NY: Macmillan.

Crawford, J. (1995). The ILC adopts a statute for the International Criminal Court. *AJIL, 89,* 404.

Cribb, R. (2008). Political loyalties and the genocide of a settler community: The Eurasians in Indonesia, 1945–1946. In A. Dirk Moses (Ed.), *Empire, colony genocide: Conquest, occupation and subaltern resistance in world history.* New York, NY: Berghahn Books.

Crosby, A. W. (2002). *Throwing fire: Projective technology through history.* New York, NY: Cambridge University Press.

Crow, J. A. (1992). *The epic of Latin America* (4th ed.). Berkeley: University of California Press.

Crowley, R. (2006). *Constantinople: The last great siege, 1453.* London, England: Faber Publications.

Cruz, J. M. (2009). Police abuse in Latin America. America barometer insights Latin American Public Opinion Project (LAPOP), No. 11.

Cryer, R. & Friman, H. (2010). *An introduction to international criminal law and procedure* (2nd ed.). Cambridge, England: Cambridge University Press.

Curthoys, A. (2008). Genocide in Tasmania: The history of an idea. In A. Dirk Moses (Ed.), *Empire, colony genocide: Conquest, occupation and subaltern resistance in world history.* New York, NY: Berghahn Books.

Curtis, A. (1992). Interview with John Stockwell on "Black Power". *BBC Two* series, *Pandora's Box.*

Curzio, L. (2000). Organized crime and political campaign finance in Mexico. In J. Bailey & R. Godson (Eds.), *Organized crime and democratic governability: Mexico and the U.S.—Mexican Borderlands* (pp. 83–102). Pittsburgh, PA: University of Pittsburgh Press.

Darwin, J. (2008). *After Tamerlane: The rise and fall of global empires, 1400–2000.* New York, NY: Bloomsbury Press.

Datary, F. (2007). *The Ismailis: Their history and doctrines.* New York, NY: Cambridge University Press.

Davidson, E. (1997). *The trial of the Germans: An account of the twenty-two defendants before the international military tribunal at Nuremberg.* Columbia, MO: University of Missouri Press.

Davidson, R. & Wang, Z. (2000). The court system in the People's Republic of China. In O. N. I. Ebbe (Ed.), *Comparative and international criminal justice systems: Policing, judiciary, and corrections* (2nd ed.) Boston, MA: Butterworth Heinemann.

Davis, N. (1997). *Europe—A history.* London, England: Pimlico Publishers.

Davis, R. (2014, August 8). Marikana, two years on: Cape Town's protest artists remember the dead. *Daily Maverick.* Retrieved from http://www.dailymavreick.co.za/article/2014-08-15-marikana-two-years-on-cape-towns-protest-artists-rem . . . . Accessed March 2, 2015.

Dawar, A. (2008). Violence continues in Greece as rioters firebomb buildings. *The Guardian* (UK). Also see http://www.guardian.co.uk/world/2008/dec/21/greece-protests-athens-violence

Dawidowicz, L. S. (1975). *The war against the Jews, 1933–1945.* New York, NY: Holt, Rinehart, and Winston.

De Arrizabalaga Y. Padro, L. (2010). *The Emperor Elagabalus: Facts and fiction.* Cambridge, England: Cambridge University Press.

De Beer, G. (1969). *Hannibal: Challenging Rome's supremacy.* New York, NY: Viking Press.

Demarest, A. (2004). *Ancient Maya: The rise and fall of a rainforest civilization.* Cambridge, England: Cambridge University Press.

Diamond, J. (2005). *Collapse. How societies choose to fail or succeed.* New York, NY: Penguin.

Diederich, B. (1978). *Trujillo. The death of the goat.* New York, NY: Little, Brown and Co.

Diederich, B. (1999). *Trujillo. The death of the dictator.* Princeton, NJ: Markus Wiener Publishers.

DiLorenzo, T. J. (2012). *Organized crime: The unvarnished truth about government.* New York, NY: Create Space Independent Publishing Platform.

Dubstan, W. E. (2010). *Ancient Rome.* New York, NY: Rowman & Littlefield.

Dugard, J. (1973). Convention on the suppression and punishment of the crime of apartheid, *United Nations Audiovisual Library of International Law.* Retrieved from http://legal. un.org/avl/ha/cspca/htm. Accessed April 15, 2015.

Dunstan, W. E. (2010). Ancient Rome: Lanham, MD: Rowman & Littlefield.

Durkheim, E. (1964). *The division of labor in society.* New York, NY: Free Press.

Dyer, T. H. (1861). *The History of modern Europe: From the fall of Constantinople in 1453 to the war in the Crimea in 1857.* London, England: John Murray Publisher.

Eagle, W. (2012). Developing countries strive to provide universal health care, *Voice of America.* Retrieved from http://www.voanews.com/content/develo. . . . Accessed March 13, 2015. Also see *The Lancet, 380*(9845), 859–948.

Ebbe, O. N. I. (1977). *A study of foreign and United States' students perceptions of seriousness of selected criminal offenses: A cross-cultural iniquity.* Kalamazoo, MI: An Unpublished Master Thesis.

Ebbe, O. N. I. (1982). Crime in Nigeria: An analysis of characteristics of offenders incarcerated in Nigerian prisons. Ann Arbor, MI: University Microfilm International.

Ebbe, O. N. I. (1985). The correlates of female criminality in Nigeria. *International Journal Of Comparative an d Applied Criminal Justice,* 9(1): 84–95.

Ebbe, O. N. I. (1990). Heads of state: The vice kings and narcotic barons. *International Journal of Comparative and Applied Criminal Justice,*16(2): 112–124.

Ebbe, O. N. I. (1998). Police corruption in Nigeria. Paper presented at the annual meeting of the Academy of Criminal Justice Sciences held in Albuqurque. NM, March 10–14.

Ebbe, O. N. I. (1999). Political-criminal nexus slicing Nigeria's national cake: The Nigerian case. *Trends in Organized Crime,* 4(3), 29–59.

Ebbe, O. N. I. (2003). Slicing Nigerian's national cake. In R. Godson, (Ed.), *Menace to society: Political-criminal collaborations around the world.* New Brunswick, NJ: Transaction Publisher.

Ebbe, O. N. I. (2010). *Broken back axle: Unspeakable events in Biafra.* Bloomington, IL: Xlibris Corporation.

Ebbe, O. N. I. (2013). World Courts of Justice of the United Nations, In O. N. I. Ebbe (Ed.), *Comparative and international criminal justice systems: Policing, judiciary, and corrections* (pp. 185–200). Boca Raton, FL: CRC Press of Taylor & Francis Group.

Edgerton, R. (2002). *The troubled heart of Africa: A history of the Congo*. New York, NY: Macmillan.

Edwards, P. (2001). *One dean Indian*. Toronto, Canada: Stoddart Publishing Co. Ltd.

Edwards, T. L. (2008). *Argentina: A global studies handbook*. Santa Barbara, CA: ABC-CLIO.

Eke, E. (1997, January 12). Ripples of Otokoto Rock Aba. *The Guardian*, p. 2.

Ekeocha, O. (1993, May 17). A cry for justice or drum beats of treason, *The African Guardian*.

Elias, T. O. (1956). *The nature of African customary laws*. Manchester, England: Manchester University Press.

Elson, R. E. (2001). *Suharto: A political biography*. Cambridge, England: Cambridge University Press.

Ennis, P. H. (1967). National Opinion Research Center: President's Commission on lawenforcement and administration of justice. Washington, DC: Government Printing Office.

Etcheson, C. (1984). *The rise and demise of democratic Kampuchea*. New York, NY: Westview Press.

European Court of Human Rights. (2007). ECHR Jorgic v. Germany Judgment 47, 112. Retrieved from http://www.echr.coe.int/echr/—Jorgic v. Germany Judgment. Accessed January 7, 2015.

Evans, R. (2008). Crime without a name: The case of Indigenocide. In A. Dirk Moses (Ed.), *Empire, colony, genocide: Conquest, occupation, and subaltern resistance in world history*. New York, NY: Berghahn Books.

Evans, R. J. (2003). *The coming of the Third Reich*. New York, NY: Penguin Group.

Evans, R. J. (2005). *The Third Reich in power*. New York, NY: Penguin Group.

Evans, J. (2009). Radovan Karadzic cell life. *The Times* (London). Retrieved from http://www.timesonline.co.uk/tollnews/worldleurope/article6891319.ece. Accessed May 14, 2012.

Evans, R. (2010). Trafigura fined Elm for exporting toxic waste to Africa. Retrieved from http://www.guardian.co.uk/world/2010/jul/23/trafigura-dutch-fine-waste-export. London, England: The Guardian. Accessed March 23, 2015.

ExecutedToday.com. (2009). 1209: Massacre of Beziers, kill them all, let God sort them out. Accessed December 20, 2014.

Ezrow, N. & Frantz, E. (2013). *Failed states and institutional decay. Understanding poverty in the developing world* (Kindle Edition). London, England: Bloomsbury.

Farmer, P. (2005). *Pathologies of power: Health, human rights, and the new war on the poor*. Berkeley: University of California Press.

Farrington, P. (2013). Mirabal sisters of the Dominican Republic. Retrieved from http://www.therealdr.com/dominican-republic-history/mirabal-sisters-of-the-dominican-republic.html#.UmlzplrD_cs. *The Real Dominican Republic*. Accessed April 3, 2015.

Farwell, B. (1989). *The great war in Africa, 1914–1918*. New York, NY: W.W. Norton & Company.

Faust, K. L. & Kauzlarich, D. (2008). Hurricane Katrina victimization as a state crime of omission. *Critical Criminology, 16*(1), 85–103.

Fein, H. (1993a). Discriminating genocide from war crimes: Vietnam and Afghanistanreexamined. *Denver Journal of International Law, 22*(1), 29–62.

Fein, H. (1993b). *Genocide: Sociological perspective*. London, England: Sage.

Fest, J. (1973/1974). *Hitler*. London, England: Weidenfeld & Nicolson.

Finzsch, N. (2008). The Aborigines . . . were never annihilated, and still they are becoming extinct settlers. Imperialism and genocide in 19th century America and Australia. In A. Dirk Moses (Ed.), *Empire, colony genocide: Conquest, occupation and subaltern resistance in world history*. New York, NY: Berghahn Books.

Fischer, K. P. (1995). *Nazi Germany: A new history*. London, England: Constable and Company.

Flexner, S. B. (2010). *New Oxford American Dictionary*. New York, NY: Oxford University Press.

Flinterman, C. (2004). The international criminal court: Obstacles or contribution to an effective system of human rights protection? In R. Thakur & P. Malcontent (Eds.), *From sovereign impunity to international accountability: The search for justice in the world of states* (pp. 264–271). New York, NY: United Nations University Press.

Fogel, J. A. (2000). *The Nanjing massacre in history and historiography*. Berkeley: University of California Press.

Forbath, P. (1977). The Congo River: The discovery, exploration and exploitation of the world's most dramatic rivers. New York, NY: Harper & Row.

Ford, T. H. (1985). Albert Venn Dicey: The man and his times. Chichester: Rose.

Forde, D. (1965). Justice and judgement among the Southern Libo under colonial rule. In H. Kuper & L. Kuper (Eds.), *African Lavo: Adaptation and development*. Los Angeles: University of California Press

Foreman, G. (1932/1989). *Indian removal: The emigration of the five civilized tribes of Indians* (2nd ed.). Norman: University of Oklahoma Press.

Forsythe, D. P. (2004). International criminal justice and the United States: Law, culture, power. In R. Thakur & P. Malcontent (Eds.), *From sovereign impunity to international accountability: The search for justice in the world of states* (pp. 61–79). New York, NY: United Nations University Press.

Fort, T. H. (1985). *Albert Venn Dicey: The man and his times*. Chichester, England: Rose.

Franklin, B. A. (1981, April 28). Court says Agnew took bribes; orders repayment. *New York Times*.

Freisenbruch, A. (2010). *Caesars' wives: Sex, power, and politics in the Roman Empire*. London, England: Free Press.

French, H. (1997, April 18). The Great gold rush in Zaire. *New York Times*. Retrieved fromhttp://nytimes.com/1997/04/18/world/the-great-gold-rush-in-zaire-html. Accessed April 8, 2015.

Fromm, E. S. (1964). *The heart of man: Its genius for good and evil.* New York, NY: Harper & Row.

Fromm, E. (1973/1977). *The anatomy of human destructiveness.* London, England: Penguin Books.

Frontline. (1999, August 13). The Tirunelveli Massacre. Retrieved from http://www.frontline/in/static/html/fl1616/16160180.htm. *Frontline* (Tamil Nadu, India). Accessed February 28, 2015.

Furber, D. & Lower, W. (2010). Colonialism and genocide in Nazi-occupied Poland and Ukraine. In A. Dirk Moses (Ed.), *Empire, colony, genocide: Conquest, occupation, and subaltern resistance in world history* (pp. 372–400).

Fuson, R. H. (1992). The log of Christopher Columbus. Classics International Marine Publishing.

Gahia, C. (1990, May 7). Why they struck: Coup plotters flaunt their reasons to unseat Ibrahim Babangida. *The African Guardian*, pp. 21–22.

GaijinAss. (2011). 7 Brutal realities regarding arrest in Japan. *GaijinAss.com.* Also see http://gaijinass.com/2011/01/02/7-brutal-r

de Galindez, J. (1973). *The era of Trujillo, Domican dictator.* Tuscon: University of Arizona Press.

Gambrell, J. (2010, May 17). Nigeria police brutality: Cops kill and torture victim's genitals, group claims. *Associated Press.*

Gao, M. (2008). *The battle for China's past: Mao and the cultural revolution.* London, England: Pluto Press.

Garcia-Navarro, L. (2014). In Brazil, race is a matter of life and violent death. *NPR News.* Retrieved from http://www.npr.org/blogs/parallels/2014/11/09/362356878/in-brazil-race-is-a-matter-of-life . . . Accessed February 27, 2015.

Gary, G. B. & Litt, D. (1927). The foundation and extension of the Persian Empire. In *The Cambridge ancient history*, (Vol. IV, 2nd ed., p. 15). Cambridge, England: Cambridge University Press.

Gasiorowski, M. J. & Byrne, M. (Eds.) (2004). *Mohammad Mosaddeq and the 1953 coup in Iran.* Syracuse, NY: Syracuse University Press.

Gaunt, R. A. (2010). *Sir Robert Peel: The life and legacy.* London, England: I.B. Tauris Publishers.

Gellately, R. & Kieman, K. (2003). *The specter of genocide: Mass murder in historical perspective.* New York, NY: Cambridge University press.

Gerlach, C. (2010). *Extremely violent societies: Mass violence in the twentieth-century world.* Cambridge, England: Cambridge University Press.

Ghanta, P. (2009). Countries with universal health care by date. Retrieved from http://truec-ostblog.com/2009/08/09/countries-with-universal-healthcare-by-date. Accessed March 13, 2015.

Gibbon, E. (2003). *The history of the decline and fall of the Roman Empire.* New York, NY: Everyman's Library.

Giblin, R. W. (1928). *The early history of Tasmania: The geographical Era 1642–1804.* London, England: Vintage.

Gilbert, M. (1986). *The Holocaust: A history of the Jews of Europe during the Second World War.* New York, NY: Holt, Rinehart, and Winston.

Gilinskiy, Y. (2000). *Crime and deviance: Stare from Russia.* St. Petersburg, Russia: Center of Deviantology, Baltic University of Ecology, Politics and Law.

Gilinskiy, Y. (2003). Organized crime: A perspective from Russia: In J. Albanese, D. Das, & A. Verma (Eds.), *Organized crime: World perspectives* (pp. 146–164). Englewood Cliffs, NJ: Prentice-Hall.

Gilinskiy, Y. (2013). The criminal justice system and police in Russia: General overview. In O. N. I. Ebbe (Ed.), *Comparative and international criminal justice systems: Policing, judiciary, and corrections* (3rd ed., pp. 135–147). Boca Raton, FL: CRC Press of Taylor and Francis Group.

Glendinning, L. (2008, December 7). Greek youths riot after police shot boy. *The Guardian* (UK). See http://www.guardian.co.uk/world/2008/dec/07/greece. Accessed February 26, 2015.

Glendon, M. A. (2002). *A world made new: Eleanor Roosevelt and the universal declaration of human rights.* New York, NY: Random House.

Glenny, M. (1996). *The fall of Yugoslavia: The third Balkan war* (3rd ed.). New York, NY: Penguin.

Godson, R. (Ed.). (2003). *Menace to society: Political-criminal collaborations around the world.* New Brunswick, NJ: Transaction Publishers.

Goodman, M. (2008). *Rome and Jerusalem: The clash of ancient civilizations.* New York, NY: Vintage Books.

Gordon, D. A. (2000). World reactions to the 1961 Paris pogrom. *University of Sussex Journal of Contemporary History, 1.*

Gough, J.W. (1936). *The social contract.* Oxford, England: Clarendon Press.

Gould, D. (1980). *Bureaucratic corruption and underdevelopment in the third world: The case of Zaire.* Oxford, England: Pergamon Press.

Green, P. & Ward, T. (2000). State crime, human rights, and the limits of criminology. *Social Justice, 27*(1), 101.

Griffin, M. T. (1984). *Nero: The end of a dynasty.* New Haven, CT: Yale University Press.

Griffis, W.E. (1909). *The story of New Netherland: The Dutch in America.* Boston, MA: Houghton.

Grillo, I. (2012). *El Narco: Inside Mexico's criminal insurgency.* New York, NY: Bloomsbury Publishing Company.

Griske, M. (2005). *The diaries of John Hunton.* New York, NY: Heritage Books.

Grove, R. (1995). *Green imperialism: Colonial expansion, Tropical Island Edens and the origins of environmentalism, 1600–1860.* Cambridge, England: Cambridge University Press.

GSDRC (2013). Intwernational legal frameworks for humanitarian action: Topic guide. Birmingham (UK): GSDRC, University of Birmingham.

Guerard, A. (1959). *France: A modern history.* Ann Arbor: University of Michigan Press.

Gwyn, D. (1977). *Idi Amin: Death light of Africa.* Boston, MA: Little, Brown and Company.

Hall, B. S. (1954). *Weapons and warfare in Renaissance Europe: Gunpowder, technology, and tactics.* Baltimore, MD: John Hopkins University Press.

Hall, F. (1868). *Invasion of Mexico by the French, and the reign of Maximilian I., with a sketch of the Empress Carlota.* New York, NY: James Miller.

Handelman, S. (1994). The Russian Mafiya. *Foreign Affairs, the Council of Foreign Relations,* March/April issue. Retrieved from http://www.foreign/fairs.com/articles/496. Accessed April 4, 2015.

Handelman, S. (1995). *Comrade criminal: Russia's new Mafiya.* New Haven, CT: Yale University Press

Hanes, S. (2014, October 4). Jean-Claude Duvalier, ex-Haitian leader known as Baby Doc dies at 63, *Washington Post.*

Harding, L. (2011). Routine police brutality in Egypt. Retrieved from http://www.theguardian.com/world/2011/jan/28/egypt-police-brutality-torture . . ./. Accessed March 2, 2015.

Harris, B. (2011, November 12). More or less: Herdes and killers of the 20th century. Retrieved from http://www.webcitation.org/6380xTWzj. Archived from the original from http://www.moreorless.au.com/killers/trujillo.html. Accessed April 3, 2015.

Hart, P. (2007). *Mick: The real Michael Collins.* New York, NY: Penguin.

Hartman, C. & Squires, G. D. (Eds.). (2006). *There is no such thing as a natural disaster: Race, class, and Hurricane Katrina.* New York, NY: Routledge.

Haskin, J. M. (2005). *The tragic state of the Congo: From decolonization to dictatorship.* New York, NY: Algora Publishing.

Haslip, J. (1972). *The crown of Mexico: Maximilian and his Empress Carlota*. New York, NY: Holt, Rinehart and Winston.

Hatton, R. M. (1972). *Louis XIV and his world*. New York, NY: Putnam.

Hazan, P. (2004). *Justice in time of war: The true story behind the international criminal tribunal for the former Yugoslavia*. College Station, TX: Texas A & M University Press.

Hedican, E. J. (2008). The Ipperwash inquiry and the tragic death of Dudley George. *Canadian Journal of Native Studies, 28*(1), 159–173.

Heizer, R. F. (1993). *The destruction of California Indians*. Lincoln: University of Nebraska Press.

Hill, G. (2005). *What happens after Mugabe: Can Zimbabwe rise from the ashes?* Cape Town, South Africa: Zebra Press.

Hemming, J. (2003). *The conquest of the Incas*. New York, NY: Harvest Press.

Hirschfeld, K. (2015). *Gangster states: Organized crime, kleptocracy, and political collapse*. New York, NY: Palgrave Macmillan.

Hobbes, T. (1651/2008). *Leviathan*. Charleston, SC: Forgotten Books.

Hochschild, A. (1999). *King Leopold's ghost: A story of greed, terror, heroism in Colonial Africa*. New York, NY: Marina Books.

Hoffman, B. (2006). *Inside terrorism*. New York, NY: Columbia University Press.

Hoffmann, P. (1977). *The history of German Resistance, 1933–1945* (3rd ed.). Kingston, ON: McGill Queens University Press.

Holland, R. (2000). *Nero: The man behind the myth*. Stroud, England: Sutton Publishing.

Hollingworth, C. (1985). *Mao and the men against him*. London, England: Jonathan Cape.

Holt, M. P. (2002). The Duke of Anjou and the politique struggle during the wars of religion. New York: Cambridge University Press.

Horowitz, S. (1950). The Tokyo Trial. *International Conciliation, 465*(November), 473–584.

Horsley, R. (1979). The Sicarii: Ancient Jewish terrorists. *The Journal of Religion, 59*(4), 435–458.

Hughes, L. (1998). *Russia in the age of Peter the Great*. New Haven, CT: Yale University Press.

Hughes, L. (2001). *Peter the great and the west: New perspectives*. London, England: Palgrave Macmillan.

Hugo, V. (2008). *The memoirs of Victor Hugo*. Charleston, SC: BiblioLife, LLC.

Hull, I. V. (2006). *Absolute destruction: Military culture and the practices of war in Imperial Germany*. Ithaca, NY: Cornell University Press.

Human Rights Watch. (1999, August 7). People killings in Tamil Nadu, India. Retrieved from http://www.hrw.org/news/1999/08/05/police-killings-tamil-nadu-india. *Human Rights Watch*. Accessed February 28, 2015.

Hurley, D. W. (1993). *An historical and historiographical commentary on Suetonius' life of C. Caligula*. Atlanta, GA: Scholars Press.

Huttenbach, H. R. & Esparza, M. (Eds.). (2011). *State violence and genocide in Latin America: The cold war years (Critical Terrorism Studies)*. New York, NY: Routledge.

Hyde, H. M. (1946). *Mexican Empire: The history of Maximilian and Carlota of Mexico*. London, England: Macmillan & Co.

ICIJ. (2013). ICIJ, the global muckraker. Retrieved from http://www.icij.org/blog. Accessed March 6, 2015.

Icks, M. (2011). The crimes of Elagabalus. Library Review. Retrieved from http://focreviews,blogspot.com/2011/09/crimes-of-elagabalus-by-martjin-icks.html.   Accessed March 23, 2015.

ICRC. (1977, June 8). Protocol additional to the Geneva Conventions of 12 August 1949, and relating to the Protection of Victims of International Armed Conflicts. ICRC: *International Committee of the Red Cross*.

ICTY. (2001, August 2). The International Criminal Tribunal for the Former Yugoslavia found in Prosecutor v. Radislav Krstic - Trial Chamber I - Judgment - IT-98-33 (2001) ICTY 8 that genocide has been committed. Retrieved from http://www.worldlii.org/int/cases/ICTY/2001/8.html. Accessed January 7, 2015. Also see Bosnia Genocide http://wikipedia.org.wiki/Bosnia_Genocide. Accessed on January 7, 2015.

Innes, H. (2002). *The conquistadors*. London, England: Penguin.

International Criminal Tribunal for Rwanda (ICTR). (2013a). General information. Retrieved from http://www.unictr.org/AboutCTR/Generallnformation/tabid/101/Default.aspx. Accessed February 15, 2013.

International Criminal Tribunal for Rwanda (ICTR). (2013b). The chambers. Retrieved from http://www.unictr.org/tabid/I 03/Default.aspx. Accessed February 15, 2013.

International Criminal Tribunal for Rwanda (ICTR). (2013c). Press briefings. Retrieved from http://www.unictr.org/AboutCTR/Generallnformation/tabid/65/Default.aspx. Accessed February 15, 2013.

International Criminal Tribunal for the FormerYugoslavia (ICTY). (1995). Karadzic indictment. Retrieved from http://wwwJcty.org/x/cases/mladidind/en/kar-ii950724e.pdf. Accessed May 15, 2012.

International Criminal Tribunal for the Former Yugoslavia (ICTY). (2010). Resolution 1966. Retrieved from http://www.icty.org/x/file/About/Reports%20and%20Publications/Residual Mechanism/101222_sc_res1966_residualmechanism_en.pdf. Accessed February 15, 2013.

International Criminal Tribunal for the former Yugoslavia (ICTY). (2012). Employment and internships. Retrieved from http://www.icty.org/sid/106. Accessed May 14, 2012.

International Criminal Tribunal for the Former Yugoslavia (ICTY). (2013). Key figures. Retrieved from http://www.icty.org/sections/TheCases/KeyFigures. Accessed February 15, 2013.

International Criminal Tribunal for the Former Yugoslavia (ICTY). Retrieved from http://www.icty.org/x/file/Legal%20Library/Statute/statute_sept09_en.pdf. Accessed May 14, 2012.

Irwin, R. (2012). Genocide conviction for Serb General Tolimir. Retrieved from http://iwpr.net/report-news/genocide/conviction-serb-general-Tolimir. *Institute for war and peace reporting.* Accessed January 6, 2015.

Israel, J. I. (1989). *Dutch primacy in the world trade, 1585–1740.* New York, NY: Oxford University Press.

Jackson, K. D. (1992). *Cambodia, 1975–1978: Rendezvous with death.* Princeton, NJ: Princeton University Press.

Jacobs, F. (1992). *The Tainos: The people who welcomed Columbus.* New York, NY: G.P. Putnam's Sons.

Janowitz, M. (1946). German reaction to Nazi atrocities. *The American Journal of Sociology, 52*(2), 141–146.

Jenrola, K. (1990, April 23). The seamy side of banking: Fraud and bad loans cause problems for financial industry. *The African Guardian,* pp. 11–14.

Joes, A. J. (2006). *Resisting rebellion: The history and politics of counterinsurgency.* Lexington: University of Kentucky Press.

Johassohn, K. & Björnson, K. S. (1999). Genocide in the Middle Ages. In I. W. Charny (Ed.), *Encyclopedia of Genocide,* (Vol. 1, pp. 275–277).

Johnson, E. H. (2000). Guided change in Japan: The Correctional Association Prison Industrial Cooperative (CAPIC) and Prison Industry. In O. N. I. Ebbe (Ed.), *Comparative and international criminal justice systems: Policing, judiciary, and corrections* (2nd ed.) Boston, MA: Butterworth/Heinemann.

Johnson, M. S. (2004). *Street justice: A history of police violence in New York city.* New York, NY: Beacon Press.

Johnson, K. (2008, October 15). FBI: Justifiable homicides at the highest in more than . . . decade. *USA Today.*

Jonassohn, K. & Bjeornson, K. S. (1998). *Genocide and gross human rights violations.* Neward, NJ: Transaction Publishers.

Jones, A. (2006). *Genocide: A comprehensive introduction.* New York, NY: Routledge/Taylor & Francis Publishers.

Jones, B. W. (1984). *The Emperor Titus.* London, England: Palgrave Macmillan.

Jones, N. (2014). From Stalin to Hitler, the most murderous regimes in the world. Retrieved from http://www.dailymail.co.uk/home/moslive. Accessed January 24, 2015.

Joseph, A. (Ed.) (1971). *The horizon: History of Africa*. New York, NY: American Heritage Publishing Co.

Josephus, F. (2009). *The war of the Jews: The history of the destruction of Jerusalem*. W. Whiston (trans.).

Kan, P. (2012). *Cartels at war: Mexico's fuel-drug violence and the threat to U.S. national security*. Dulles, VA: Potomac Books.

Kant, I. (1795). Perpetual peace: a philosophical sketch. Retrieved from http://www.constitution.org/kant/perpeace.htm. Accessed April 12, 2012.

Kauzlarich, D., Mullins, C., & Matthews, R. (2003). A complicity continuum of state crime. *Contemporary Justice Review, 6*, 241–254.

Kelly, S. (1993). *American's tyrant: The CIA and Mobutu of Zaire*. Washington, DC: American University Press.

Khan, I. (2013, October 4). Justice is scarce in Arab countries where the rule of law is absent. *Global Post Blog*. Available from www.globalpost.com. Accessed January 24, 2015.

Khanbaghi, A. (2006). *The fire, the star and the cross: Minority religions in medieval and early modern Iran*. New York, NY: I.B. Tauris.

Kiernan, B. (2007). *Blood and soul: A world history of genocide and extermination from Sparta to Darfur*. New Haven, CT: Yale University Press.

Kirkham, C. (2012). With states facing shortfalls, private corporation offers cash for prisons. Retrieved from http://www.huffingtonpost.com/2012/02/14/private-prisons-buying-state-prisons-n-1272143.html. *Huffington Post*. Accessed March 20, 2015.

Kirkpatrick, F.A. (1934). *The Spanish conquistadores*. London, England: A & C Black.

Kirkpatrick, D. D. (2011, January 28). Egypt calls in army as protesters rage. *New York Times*. Accessed January 17, 2015.

Kirkpatrick, D. D. (2013, August 19). Islamists debate their next move in tense Cairo. *New York Times*. Retrieved from http://www.nytimes.com/2013/08/16/world/middleeast/egypt.html. Accessed March 2, 2015.

Kirkpatrick, D. D., Shadid, A., & Cowell, A. (2011, February 11). Mubarak steps down, ceding power to military. *New York Times*. Accessed January 17, 2015.

Knecht, R. J. (2001). *The rise and fall of Renaissance France, 1483–1610*. London, England: Blackwell Publishing

Komisar, R. (2001). *The monk and the riddle: The art of creating a life while making a living*. Boston, MA: Harvard Business Review Press.

Kotkin, S. (2014). *Stalin: Paradoxes of power, 1878–1928*. London, England: Allen Lane.

Kranacher, M.-J., Riley, R., & Wells, J. T. (2010). *Forensic accounting and fraud examination.* Hoboken, NJ: John Wiley & Sons.

Kuhrt, A. (1995). *The ancient near east: C. 300–330 BC.* New York, NY: Routledge Publishers.

Kuhrt, A. (2007). *The Persian Empire: A corpus of sources from the Achaemenid period.* New York, NY. Routledge Publishers.

Kuper, L. (1982). *Genocide: Its political use in the twentieth century.* New Haven, CT: Yale University Press.

Kwitny, J. (1986). *Endless enemies.* New York, NY: Penguin Books.

Kyemba, H. (1977). *A state of blood: The inside story of Idi Amin.* New York, NY: Ace Books.

Lachman, S. (1982). Arab rebellion and terrorism in Palestine 1929–39: The case of Sheikh Izz al_Din al-Qassam and his movement. In K. Elie & G. H. Sylvia (Eds.), *Zionism and Arabism in Palestine and Israel.* London, England: Frank Cass.

Laing, A. (2012). Striking South African miners were shot in the back. *The Telegraph.* Retrieved from http://www.telegraph.co.uk/news/worldnews/africaandindianocean/south southafrica/9501910/Striking-South-Af.... Accessed March 2, 2015.

Landers, B. (2011). Empires apart: A history of American and Russian imperialism. Available from Open Road Media website: http://www.openroadmedia.com.

Laquerue, W. (1999). *The new terrorism: Fanaticism and the arms of mass destruction.* New York, NY: Oxford University Press.

Lary, D. (2012). *Chinese migrations: The movement of people, goods, and ideas over four millennia.* New York, NY: Rowman & Littlefield.

Leadbetter, B. (1999). Genocide in antiquity. In I. W. Charny (Ed.), *Encyclopedia of genocide* (Vol. 1, pp. 272–275).

Lebedel, C. (2011). *Understanding the tragedy of the Cathers.* Rennes, France: Editions Quest-France.

Lee, M. (1990). *Great Britain's Solomon: James VI and I on his three kingdoms.* Urbana: University of Illinois Press.

Lemarchand, R. (1994). *Burundi: Ethnic conflict and genocide.* New York, NY: Cambridge University Press.

Lendering, J. (2012). Messiah - Roots of the Concept: From Josiah to Cyrus. Available from http://www.livius.org/men-mh/messiah/messia_04.htm, livius.org. Accessed January 9, 2015.

Lewis, B. (2002). *The assassins.* New York, NY: Basic Books.

Lewis, D. K. (2003). *The history of Argentina.* New York, NY: Palgrave MacMillan.

Lewis, P. (2011, August 7). Tottenham Riots: Weren't to be violent like they were, the suddenly all hell broke loose. *The Guardian.* Accessed February 21, 2015.

Lichtblau, E. (2013, March 1). The holocaust just got more shocking. *New York Times.*

Llifee, J. (1967). The organization of the Maji Maji rebellion. *The Journal of African History,* 8(3), 495–512.

Lincoln, B. (1989). Discourse and the construction of society: Comparative studies of myths in ritual and classification. New York: Oxford University Press.

Locke, J. (1689/2015). *The second treatise of government.* San Bernardino, CA: Maestro Publishing Group.

Locke, J. (1824). *Two treaties of government.* London, England: C. Baldwin

Longmire, S. (2013). *Cartel: The coming invasion of Mexico's drug wars.* New York, NY: Palgrave MacMillan Trade.

Lopez-Calvo, I. (2005). *God and Trujillo: Literary and cultural representations of the Dominican dictator.* Gainesville, FL: University Press of Florida

Lukic, R. & Lynch, A. (1996). *Europe from the Balkans to the Urals: The disintegration of Yugoslavia and the Soviet Union.* Oxford, UK: Oxford University Press and the Stockholm International Peace Research Institute.

Lunev, S. (1998). *Through the eyes of the enemy: The autobiography of Stanislav Lunev.* Houston, TX: Regency Publishing, Inc.

MacGaffey, J. (2014). *Entrepreneurs and parasites: The struggle for indigenous capitalism in Zaire.* London, England: Cambridge University Press.

MacGaffey, J. & Mukohya, V. (1991). *The real economy of Zaire: The contribution of smuggling and other unofficial actives to national wealth.* Philadelphia: The University of Pennsylvania Press.

MacLeod, C. (2010). Toward a philosophical account of crimes against humanity. *European Journal of International Law, 21*(2), 281–302.

Madden, T. F. (2005). *The new concise history of the crusade.* New York, NY: Rowman & Littlefield.

Magnarella, P. J. (2004). The consequences of the war crimes tribunals and an international criminal court for human rights in transition societies. In S. Harowitz & A. Schnabel (Eds.), *Human rights and societies in transition: Causes consequences, responses* (pp. 119–140). New York, NY: United Nations University Press.

Maja-Pearce, A. (2014). Changing Nigeria's Cruel Police Culture. *The New York Times.* http://www.nytimes.com/2014/10/08/opinion/adewale-maja-pearce-changing-nigerians-cruel-police. Accessed March 2, 2015.

Makambe, E. P. (1987). Marginalizing the human rights campaign: The dissident factor and the politics of violence in Zimbabwe, 1980 - 1987. Institute of Southern Africa Studies, National University of Lesotto.

Mallett, M. E. & Shaw, C. (2012). *The Italian wars 1494-111559: War, state and society in early modern Europe (modern wars in perspective)*. London, England: Longmans.

Manaut, R. B. (2000). Containing armed groups, drug trafficking, and organized crime in Mexico: The role of the military. In J. Bailey & R. Godson (Eds.), *Organized crime and democratic governability: Mexico and the U.S. –Mexican borderlands* (pp.126–158). Pittsburgh, PA: University of Pittsburgh Press.

Mancel, P. (1997). *Constantinople: City of world desire 1453-1924*. London, England: Penguin.

Mann, M. (2005). *The dark side of democracy: Explaining ethnic cleansing*. New York, NY: Cambridge University Press.

Manz, B. F. (1989). *The rise and rule of Tamerlane*. New York, NY: Cambridge University Press.

Markus, A. (2000). *Governing savages: Commonwealth and aborigines 1911 - 1939*. Sydney, Australia: Allen & Urwin.

Marozzi, J. (2004). *Tamerlain: Sword of Islam, conqueror of the world*. New York, NY: Harper Collins.

Marshall, A. (2005a). The social and ethical aspects of nuclear waste. *Electronic Green Journal, 21*, 1.

Marshall, C. (2005b). Gang wars plague Mexican drugs hub. http://news.bbc.co.uk/2/hi/americas/414486.stm, BBC news. Accessed April 9, 2015.

Marshall, A. (2008). Leaving messages about our radioactive wastes for future generations. In A. P. Latiffer (Ed.), *Nuclear waste research*. Hauppauge, NY: Nova Publishers.

Martin, J. J. (1984). *The many who invented genocide: The public career and consequences of Raphael Lemkin*. Colorado Springs, CO: Ralph Myles Publisher.

Maser, W. (1973). Hitler: Legend, myth, reality. London, England: Allen Lane.

Mason, C. (2013). International growth trends in prison privatization. http://www.sentencingproject.org/, The Sentencing Project: Research and Advocacy for Reform.

Masson, S. (2004). Remembering the Vendee . . . .Godspy.

Mattera, P., Khan, M., & Nathan, S. (2003). *Correction corporations of America: A critical look at its first twenty years*. Charlotte, NS: Grassroots Leadership. Available from http://grassrootsleadership.org/sites/default/files/uploads/CCAAnniversaryReport.pdf.   Accessed March 20, 2015.

Matthews, R. J. (2001). The 1980 convention of certain conventional weapons: A useful framework despite earlier disappointments. *International Review* of the Red Cross, 844.

Maxted, J. (2004). The international criminal court and the prohibition of the use of children in armed conflict. In R. Thakur & P. Malcontent (Eds.), *From sovereign impunity to international accountability: The search for justice in the world of states* (pp. 253–263). New York, NY: United Nations University Press.

Maya, T. P. (2001). *Judgment at Tokyo: The Japanese war crimes trials.* Lexington, KY: University of Kentucky Press.

Mba, N. E. (1982). *Nigerian women mobilized: Women's political activity in southern Nigeria, 1900–1965.* Berkeley, CA: Institute of International Studies.

Mbaku, J. M. (1994). Bureaucratic corruption and policy reform in Africa. *The Journal of Social, Political & Economic Studies, 19*(summer), 149–175.

Mbiti, J. S. (1990). *African religions and philosophy* (2nd ed.). New York, NY: Free Press.

McClenaghan, M. (2012). South African Massacre was the tip of an iceberg. *The Bureau of Investigation Journalism.* Available from http://www.thebureauinvestigates.com/2012/10/18/south-african-massacre-was-the-tip-of-an-iceberg/. Accessed March 2, 2015.

McEwan, G. F. (2010). *After collapse: The regeneration of complex societies.* Tucson: University of Arizona Press.

McKechnie, W. S. (1905). *Magna Carta: A commentary on the great charter of King John.* Glasgow, England: Robert MacLehose and Co. Ltd.

McKeon, R. (Ed.) (2001). *The basic works of Aristotle.* New York, NY: Random House.

McKittrick, D., Kelters, S., Feeney, B., & Thornton, C. (2001). *Lost lives: The stories of the men, women, and children who died as a result of the northern Ireland troubles.* Edinburg, TX: Mainstream Publishing.

McQuaid, J., Marshall, B., and Schleifstein, M. (2005). Human error blamed for making new Orleans' flooding worse. *Newhouse News.* Available from http://www.levees.org/research/sources/Newhouse%2011.htm. Accessed March 4, 2015.

Meierhenrich, J. (2014). Genocide: A reader. New York: Oxford University Press.

Melady, T. P. & Melady, M. B. (1977). *Idi Amin Dada: Hitler in Africa.* Kansas City, MO: Sheed Andrews and McMeel.

MeLaugh, M. (2010). Text of Sir John Steven's inquiry into collusion between the UK and loyalist terrorists. Available from http://www.cain.ulst.ac.uk/issues/collusion/stevens35ummary.htm. Cain.ulst.ac.uk. Accessed December 12, 2014.

Melendez, S. (2012). Remember: There was genocide in United States too. *Indian Country Today.* Accessed on December 30, 2014.

Mendez, J. E. (2012). Reports on torture and other cruel, inhuman, or degrading treatment or punishment. Office of the High Commissioner for Human Rights (OHCHR).

Meredith, M. (2006). *The state of Africa: A history of fifty years of independence.* London, England: The Free Press.

Meri, J. W. (2005). *Medieval Islamic civilization.* New York, NY: Routledge.

Merton, R. K. (1968). *Social theory and social structure.* New York, NY: The Free Press.

Michalowski, R. (1985). *Order, law and crime.* New York, NY: Random House.

Michalowski, R. & Kramer, R. (2006). *State-corporate crime: Wrongdoing at an intersection of business and government.* New Brunswick, NJ: Rutgers University Press.

Miller, C. (1974). *Battle for the Bundu: The first world war in East Africa.* New York, NY: Mac-Millan Pub. Company.

Miller, R. L. (2000). Controlling state crime in Israel: The dichotomy between national security and coercive powers. In J. I. Ross (Ed.), *Varieties of state crime and its control.* Monsey, NY: Criminal Justice Press.

Minear, R. H. (1971). *Victor's justice: The Tokyo war crimes trial.* Princeton, NJ: Princeton University Press.

Mitchel, P. (2007). The significance of the world court ruling on genocide in Bosnia. Available from http://www.wsws.org/en/articles/2007/03/icj-mi6.htm. World Socialist Web. Accessed January 7, 2015.

Mitchell, R. (1993). *The society of the Muslim brothers.* New York, NY: Oxford University Press.

Mizruchi, E. (1964). *Success and opportunity.* New York, NY: Free Press.

Modupe, I. (1997, January 12) God is on ourside: Otokoto family members say as they relocate to Lagos. *Sunday Vanguard.*

Mohsen, M. (2013, August 19). Health ministry raises death toll of Wednesday's clashes to 638. *Daily News Egypt.* Available from http://www.dailynewsegypt.com/2013/08/16/health-ministry-rasises-death-toll-of-wednesdays-clashes-to-6 . . . . Access March 2, 2015.

Mojzes, P. (2011). *Balkan genocides: Holocaust and ethnic cleansing in the twentieth century.* London, England: Rowman & Littlefield.

Molly, T. (2001). Russian Mafia: Organized crime. Available from http://www.youtube.com/watch?v=QAJwINIqvyI (TV). United States: The History Channel. Accessed April 6, 2015.

Monbiot, G. (2009, March 3). The revolting trade in human lives is an incentive to lock people up. Available from http://www.guardian.co.uk/commentisfree/2009/mar/03/prison-population-titan-jails. *The Guardian.* Accessed march 20, 2015.

Montefiore, S. S. (2005). *Stalin: The court of the red Tsar.* New York, NY: Vintage Books.

Morris, M. H. (2004). Democracy, global governance and the international criminal court. In R. Thakur & P. Malcontent (Eds.), *From sovereign impunity to international accountability: The search for justice in the world of states* (pp. 182–183) New York, NY: United Nations University Press.

Morris, V. & Bourloyannie-Vrailas, C. M. (1996). The work of the sixth committee at the fiftieth session of the UN general assembly. *AJIL, 90,* 491.

Morsink, J. (1999). *The universal declaration of human rights: Origins, drafting, and intent.* Philadelphia: University of Pennsylvania Press.

Moses, A. D. (2004). Genocide and settler society in Australian history. In A. Dirk Moses (Ed.), *Genocide and settler society: Frontier violence and stolen indigenous children in Australian history* (pp. 3–48). New York, NY: Berghahn Books.

Moses, A. D. (2008). Moving the genocide debate beyond the 'History Wars'. *Australian Journal of Politics and History, 54*(2), 263.

Munro, D. (2013). Universal coveris is not 'Single Payer' healthcare. Available from http://www.forbes.com/sites/danmunro/2013/12/08/universal-coverage-is-not-single-payer . . . . Accessed March 13, 2015.

Munro, D. (2014a). U.S. healthcare ranked dead last compared to 10 other countries. Available from http://www.forbes.com/sites/danmunro/2014/06/16/u-s-healthcare-ranked-dead-last-comp . . . . Accessed March 13, 2015.

Munro, D. (2014b). The first global symposium on health system research. Summary. Available from http://www.pacifichealthsummit.org/downloads/UHC/the%20political%20economy%of%20uhc.pdf. Accessed March 13, 2015.

Murphy, S. D. (1993). The basel convention on hazardous wastes. *Environment, 35*, 42–44.

Naing, U. M. (2000). *National ethnic groups of Myanmar* (trans. by H. Thant). Yangon, Myanmar: Thein Myint Win Press.

Neemuchwala, N. (2014, September 1). Police brutality in India. *Liberty Voice*. Available from http://guardianlv.com/2014/09/police-brutality-in-India. Accessed February 28, 2015.

Nicolle, D. (2003). *The first crusade, 1096 - 99: Conquest of the holy land*. Oxford, England: Osprey Publishing.

Nicolle, D. (2007). *The fall of Constantinople: The Ottoman conquest of Byzantium*. New York, NY: Osprey Publishing.

Niven, C. R. (1937). A short history of Nigeria. London: Longmans, Green & Co Ltd.

Norman, An. (2003). *Robert Mugabe and the betrayal of Zimbabwe*. Jefferson, NC: McFarland Company.

Norrell, B. (2004). Remembering Indian genocide in Texas. *Alternet.org*. Accessed on December 30, 2014.

Nwebo, O. E. & Ubah, C. B. A. (2015). Globalization of crime: Problems and challenges for world peace and security. *International Journal of Liberal Arts and Social Science, 3*(2), 91–100.

O'Connor, R. (1971). *The Cactus Throne: The tragedy of Maximilian and Carlota*. New York, NY: G. P. Putnam's Sons.

Okpa, E. (1995, September 12). I am not one of the corrupt Nigerian military officers. *Nigerian Times*, p. 9.

Oldenbourg, Z. (1961). *Massacre at Montsegur: A history of the Albigensian crusade*. Phoenix: University of Arizona Press.

Oneale, L. (2014). Police brutality continues to soar in South Africa. Available from http://guardianlv.com/2014/03/police-brutality-continues-to-soar-in-south-africa/. Accessed March 2, 2015.

Onwudiwe, I. D. (2001). *The globalization of terrorism*. Burlington, VT: Ashgate Publishing Limited.

Onwumere, O. (2007, February 14). Toxic waste dumping: Africa at the mercy of god *Nigerians in America (NIA)*. Also see http://www.nigeriansinameric.com/toxic-waste-dumping-africa-at-the-mercy-of-god/. Accessed March 22, 2015.

Orch, A. (1990, May 7). One coup, many issues. *The African Guardian*, pp. 22–24.

Orwin, C. (1994). *The humanity of Thucydides*. Princeton, NJ: Princeton University Press.

Osaghae, E. E. (1998). Crippled giant: Nigeria since independence. London: Hurst & Co.

Osifo-Whiskey & Ikoria, K. (1988, June 13). Deaths that defy defection. Mysterious killings send shock waves into a Hitherto peaceful community. *Newswatch*, pp. 8–15

Overy, R. (2001). *Interrogations: The Nazi elite in allied hands*. London, England: Allen Lane/The Penguin Press.

Pacepa, I. M. (2006, August 24). Russian footprints. *National Review Online*.

Paine, T. (1797). *Agrarian justice*. New York, NY: Penguin Edition.

Pakenham, T. (1992). *The scramble for Africa: White man's conquest of the dark continent from 1876 - 1912*. New York, NY: Avon Books.

Palmer, A. (1978). *The Kaiser: Warlord of the second Reich*. New York, NY: Charles Scribner's Sons.

Parry, R. L. (2010). Security increased at Christian churches as Allah row divides Malaysia. Available from http://www.timesonline.co.uk/tol/news/world/asia/article6990454.ece. *The Times*. Accessed March 14, 2015.

Partington, J. R. (1960). *A history of Greek fire and gunpowder*. Baltimore, MD: John Hopkins University Press.

Parvish, M. (1996). *The lesser terror: Soviet state security, 1939 - 1953*. Westport, CT: Praeger Press.

Pearl, J. I. (1998). *The crime of crimes: Demonology and politics in France 1560–1620*. Waterloo, ON: Wilfrid Laurier U. Press.

Perazzo, J. (2002, November 29). Iraqi horrors. *Front Page Magazine*.

Pereault, S. (2012). Homicide in Canada, 2011 *Juristat. Statistics Canada Catalogue* no. 85-002-x. Accessed February 21, 2015.

Pereault, S. (2013). Police-reported crime statistics in Canada, 2012. *Juristat. StatisticsCanada Catalouge* no. 85-002-x. Accessed February 22, 2015.

Phillips, T. (2013, June 24). Carlo Guiliani's relatives sue former police officer and deputy police commissioner. *Activist Defense*. Available from http://activistdefense.wordpress.com/2013/06/24/carlo-guiliamis-relatives-sue-former-police-police-officer-and-de . . . Accessed June 17, 2015.

Phillips, W. D. & Phillips, C. R. (1992). The world of Christopher Columbus. Cambridge: Cambridge University Press.

Piccigallo, P. R. (1979). *The Japanese on trial: The allied war crimes operations in the east, 1945-1951*. Austin: University of Texas Press.

Pilkington, E. (2009). Jailed for a MySpace parody, the student who exposed America's cash for kids scandal. Available from http://www.guardian.co.uk/world/2009/mar/07/juvenile-judges-cash-detention-centre. *The Guardian* (London). Accessed March 20, 2015.

Pimentel, S. A. (2000). The nexus of organized crime and politics in Mexico. In J. Bailey and R. Godson (Eds.), *Organized crime and democratic governability: Mexico and the U.S. - Mexican Borderlands* (pp. 33–57). Pittsburgh, PA: University of Pittsburgh Press.

Poplak, R. (2012). The murder fields Marikana. The cold murder fields of Marikana. *Daily Maverick*. Available from http://dailymaveerick.co.za/article/2012-08-30-the-murder-fields-of-marikana-the-cole-murder-fields-of-m . . . Accessed March 2, 2015.

Porterfield, S. & Weir, D. (1989). The export of U.S. toxic waste. *Nation, 245*, 344.

Prados, J. (2006). *Safe for democracy: The secret wars of the CIA*. Chicago, IL: Ivan R. Dee.

Pressly, L. (2006). Life as a secret Christian convert. Available from http://news.bbc.co.uk/2/hi/programmes/crossing_continents/6150340.stm. *BBC News*. Accessed March 14, 2015.

Proal, L. (1898). *Political crimes*. New York, NY: D. Appleton and Company.

Pulle, M. (2009). Texas watchdog. Available from http://www.texasprisonbidness.org/lobbying-and-influence/texas-watchdog-looks-big-bad-private-prisons-lobby. Accessed March 20, 2015.

Quinney, R. (1977). Class, state, and crime: On the theory and practice of criminal justice. New York: David McKay & Company.

Quinney, R. (2000). Bearing witness to crime and social justice. Albany, NY: SUNY Press.

Quinney, R. (2001). Eric Fromm and critical criminology. Urbana: University of Illinois Press.

Ramsey, G. (2011). Poverty a recruitment tool for Mexico's criminal gangs. *InsightCrime.org* Available from http://www.insightcrime.org/news-analysis. Accessed April 9, 2015.

Rawlins, C. G. (2014, February 24). Anti-government demonstrators run from tear gas during clashes with Riot police at Altamira Square in Caracas. *Reuters*.

Rawls, J. (1971). *A theory of justice*. Cambridge, MA: Harvard University Press

Rayfield, D. (2004). *Stalin and his hangmen: The tyrant and those who killed for him*. New York, NY: Random House.

Reinecke, J. E. (1997). *The Filipino piecemeal sugar strike of 1924 - 1925*. Honolulu: University of Hawaii Press.

Remini, R. V. (2001). *Andrew Jackson and his Indian wars*. New York, NY: Viking Press.

Reno, W. (1999). *Warlord politics and African states*. New York, NY: Lynne Rienner.

Retting, J. (2011). Death toll of 'Arab Spring'. Available from www.usnews.com/news/slide-shows. Accessed January 24, 2015.

Ridley, J. (2001). *Maximilian and Juarez*. London, England: Phoenis Press.

Riley-Smith, J. (1991). The first crusade and the idea of crusading. Philadelphia: University of Pennsylvania Press.

Riley-Smith, J. (1995). *The Oxford illustrated history of the crusades*. Oxford, England: Oxford University Press.

Robinson, D. (1999). Defining crime against humanity at the Rome conference. *AJIL, 93*, 51.

Rohl, J. (1994). *The Kaiser and his court: Wilhelm II and the government of Germany*. Cambridge, MA: Cambridge University Press.

Rohter, L. (1997, February 15) The three sisters, avenged: A Dominican drama. Available from http://www.nytimes.com/1997/02/15/world/the-three-sisters-avanged-a-dominican-drama.html. *New York Times*. Accessed April 3, 2015.

Rolfsen, C. (2007, November 18). Hundreds mourn Robert Dziekanski. *Vancouver Sun*. Available from http://www2.canada.com/cancouversun/news/story . . . html?id=297676bf-61e3-49d0-be35-806a823d2605. Accessed February 25, 2015.

Roling, B. V. A. & Ruter, C. F. (1977). *The Tokyo judgement: The international military tribunal for the far east (IMTFE) 29 April1946 - 12 November 1948*. Amsterdam, The Netherlands: APA - University Press.

Rome Statute. (2007). Crime of Apartheid, *Article 7*. Available from http://www.un.org/law/icc/statute/99_corr/2.htm of the Rome Statute of the International Criminal Court specifically lists the "Crime of apartheid" as one of eleven recognized crimes against humanity.

Roos, J. (2012, February 21). Spanish police brutalize student protesters in Valencia. *ROAR Magazine*. Also see http://roarmag.org/2012/spain-valencia. Accessed February 26, 2015.

Ross, J. I. (Ed.) (2000). *Varieties of state crime and its control*. Monsey, NY: Criminal Justice Press.

Rostwororwski, M. (1998). *History of the Inca Realm*. Cambridge, MA: Cambridge University Press.

Rothe, D. L. (2009). *State criminality: The crime of all crimes*. New York, NY: Lexington Books.

Rothe, D. L. & Mullins, C. E. W. (Eds.) (2011). *State crime: Current perspectives*. New Brunswick, NJ: Rutgers University Press.

Rouse, I. (1992). *The Tainos: Rise and decline of the people who welcomed Columbus*. New Haven, CT: Yale University Press.

Rousseau, J.-J. (1762/1968). *The social contract* (trans. M. Cranston). New York, NY: Penguin Group.

Ruffins, P. (1988, November). Toxic terrorism invaders third world nations. *Black Enterprise*, p. 19.

Runciman, S. (1965). *The conquest of Constantinople, 1453*. Cambridge, MA: Cambridge University Press.

Rusche, G & Kirchheimer, O. (1939). Punishment and social structure. New York: Columbia University Press.

Russell-Wood, A. J. R. (1993). A world on the move: The Portuguese in Africa, Asia, and America, 1415-1808. New York: Macmillan.

Sachar, H. (2007). *A history of Israel: From the rise of Zionism to our time*. New York, NY: Knopf.

Salvatore, N. (1980). Railroad workers and the great strike of 1877. *Labor History, 21*(4), 522–545.

Sanchez, A. N. (2011). Private prisons spend millions on lobbying to put more people in jail. Available from http://thinkprogress.org/justice/2011/06/23/251363/cca-geogroup-prison-industry/. Accessed March 20, 2015.

Sandison, A. T. (1958). The madness of the emperor Caligula. *Medical History, 2*, 202–209.

Satter, D. (2003). *Darkness at dawn: The rise of the Russian criminal state*. New Haven, CT: Yale University Press.

Schabas, W. (1998). Canada and the adoption of universal declaration of human rights. *McGill Law Journal, 43*, 403.

Schabas, W. A. (2000). Genocide in international law: The crime of crimes. New York, NY: Cambridge University Press.

Schabas, W. A. (2009). *Genocide in international law: The crime of crimes* (2nd ed.). New York, NY: Cambridge University Press.

Schatberg, M. G. (1991). *Mobutu or Chaos? The United States and Zaire, 1960 - 1990*. Lanhan, MD: University of America Press.

Schissel, H. (1988). The deadly trade: Toxic waste dumping in Africa. *Africa Report, 33*(Sept./Oct.), 47–49.

Schwartz, T. T. (2008). Travesty in Haiti: A true account of Christian missions, orphanages, fraud, food aid and drug trafficking. Charleston, SC: Booksurge Publishing.

Schwendinger, H. & Schwendinger, J. (1970). Defenders of order of guardians of human rights. *Issues in Criminology, 5*(2), 123–157.

Scott, J. (1972) *Comparative political corruption.* Englewood Cliffs, NJ: Prentice-Hall

SCSL. (2002). Statute of the special court for Sierra Leone. Available from http://www.sc-sl. org/LinkClick.aspx?fileticket=uClnolIMJeEw%3d4tabid=70. Accessed April 17, 2015.

Seeton, K. M. (Ed.) (1985). *A history of the crusades: The impact of the crusades on the near east.* Madison: University of Wisconsin Press.

Segev, T. (1999). *One Palestine, complete.* New York, NY: Metropolitan Books.

Sellin, T. (1938). Culture conflict and crime. New York: Social Science Research.

Selva, M. (2006, September 1) Toxic shock: How western rubbish is destroying Africa. *The Independent.*

Shakespeare, W. (1596/1988a). *Hamlet: Act 1, Scene 3.* Oxford, England: Clarendon Press.

Shakespeare, W. (1596/1988b). *The tragedy of Julius Caesar.* Oxford, England: Clarendon Press.

Sharer, R. (1994). *The ancient Maya* (5th ed.) Stanford, CA: Stanford University Press.

Sharer, R. J. & Traxler, L. P. (2006). *The ancient Maya* (6th ed.). Stanford, CA: Stanford University Press.

Sharkansky, I. (1995). A state action may be nasty but is not likely to be a crime. In J. I. Ross (Ed.), *Controlling state crime: An introduction* (pp. 35–52). New York, NY: Garland.

Shelley, L. I. (1995). *Privatization and crime: The post-Soviet experience.* Washington, DC: National Council for Soviet and East European Research.

Shelly, L. I. (1996). Post-Soviet organized crime: A new form of authoritarianism. In P. Williams (Ed.), *Russians organized crime. The new threat.* (special double issue), *Transnational Organized Crime 2,* 2/3 (summer/autumn), 122–138.

Shen, A. (2012). Private prisons spend $45 million on lobbying, rake in $51 billion for immigration detention along. Available from http://thinkprogress.org/justice/2012/08/03/627471/private-prisons-spend-45-million-on-lo . . . . Accessed March 20, 2015.

Shariat, S., Mallonee, S., & Stephens-Stidham, S. (1998). Oklahoma city bombing injuries. *Injuries Prevention Service, Oklahoma State Department of Health.*

Sherman, C. (2001). *War crimes: International military tribunal.* Paducah, KY: Turner Publishing Company.

Siddique, H. (2009). Gun attack injures Greek policeman. *The Guardian* (UK). Also see http:www.guardian.co.uk/world/2009/jan/05/greece-police-shooting. Accessed February 26, 2015.

Sifris, R. (2013). *Reproductive freedom, torture and international human rights: Challenging the masuclinisation of torture.* New York, NY: Routledge.

Simons, M. (2013). Genocide charge re-instated against wartime leader of Bosnian serbs. Available from http://www.nytimes.com/2013/07/12/world/europe/genocide-charge-reinstate-agaisnt-wartime-leader-of -the-bosnian-serbs.htm. *The New York Times*. Accessed on January 7, 2015.

Skinner, B. F. (1948). *Walden Two*. Indianapolis, IN: Hackett Publishing Company.

Smith, M. (1971). Zealots and Sicarii: Their origins and relation.. *The Harvard Theological Review, 64*(1), 1–19

Somervill, B. (2005). *Francisco Pizzaro: Conqueror of the Incas*. New York, NY: Compass Point Books.

Soto, E. (2013). Police beating a 17 year old student in Chile. Available from http://guardianlv.com/wp-content/uploads/2013/06/represion-2 . . . . Accessed February 26, 2015.

Spiedel, M. P. (1993). Commodus the god-emperor and the army. *Journal of Roman Studies, 83*, 109–114.

Spieman, D. G. (2007). *Katrinaville Chronicles: Images and Observations from New Orleans Photographer*. Baton Rouge: University of Louisiana Press.

Stannard, D. (1992a). *American holocaust: Columbus and the conquest of the new world*. New York, NY: Oxford University Press.

Stannard, D. E. (1992b). *Genocide in Americas. Nation, 19*, 430.

Staten, C. L. (2005). *The history of Cuba*. New York, NY: Palgrave MacMillan Trade.

Steinmetz, G. (2007). *The devil's handwriting: Precoloniality and the German colonial state in Qingdao, Samoa, and Southwest Africa*. Chicago, IL: University of Chicago Press.

Stevenson, M. (2011). *Mexican police guilty of widespread abuse: Human rights commission*. Associated Press, 10/12.

Stewart, J. (2003). Towards a single definition of armed conflict in international humanitarian law. *International Review of the Red Cross* 850: 313–350.

Stone, A. (2011). World justice project rule of law index ranks 66 countries on government rights. Available from http://www.huffingtonpost.com/2011/06/11. Accessed January 24, 2015.

Straauss, B. (2009). *The Spartacus war*. New York, NY: Simon and Schuster.

Struelens, M. (1978). *The United Nations in the Congo, and international politics*. Brussels, Belgium: Max Arnold.

Subrahmanyam, S. (1997). The career and legend of Vasco da Gama. Cambridge: Cambridge University Press.

Sutherland, E. (1947) *The principle of criminology*. Chicago, IL: J.B Lippincott Co.

Sutton, M. (1994). *Bear in mind these dead: An index of deaths from the conflict in Ireland 1969–1993*. Belfast, Northern Ireland: Beyond the Pale

Suvorov, V. (1984). *Inside Soviet military intelligence*. New York, NY: W.W. Norton.

Swedenburg, T. (2002). Islamic hip-hop versus islamophobia. In T. Mitchell (Ed.), *Global noise: Rap and hip hop outside the USA*. Middletown, CT: Wesleyan University Press.

Sykes, G. & Matza, D. (1957). Techniques of neutralization: A theory of delinquency. *American Sociological Review, 22*, 664–670.

Talbot, P. A. (1929). *The peoples of southern Nigeria*, (vol. 1). London: Frank Cass & Co.

Talbot, P. A., (1967). *The peoples of southern Nigeria*, (vol. 3). London: Oxford University Press.

Tallet, F. (1991). *Religion, society and politics in France since 1789*. New York, NY: Continnum International Publishing.

Taylor, I. A. (1913). *The tragedy of an army: La Vendee in 1793*. London, England: Hutchinson & Co.

Terrill, R. (1980). *Mao: A biography*. New York, NY: Simon & Schuster.

Thackrah, J. R. (2008). *The Routledge companion to military conflict since 1945: Routledge companion series*. New York, NY: Taylor & Francis.

Thakur, R. (2004). Dealing with guilt beyond crime: The strained quality of universal justice. In R. Thakur & P. Malcontent (Eds.), *From sovereign impunity to international accountability: The search for justice in the world of states* (pp. 272–292). New York, NY: United Nations University Press.

The Commonwealth Fund. (2014). Survey on overall health care. Available from http://www.commonwealthfund.org/publicaitons/fund-reports/2014/jun/mirror-mirror. Accessed March 13, 2015.

The Guardian (UK). (2012, July 21). £13tn: Hoard hidden from Taxman by Global Elite. *The Guardian* (UK).

The Hindu. (2003). Two killed as tribals, police clash. Available from http://www.hindu.com/thehindu/2003/02/20/stories/2003022004730700.htm. *The Hindu*. Accessed February 28, 2015.

Thompson, A. C. (2008, December 7). Katrina's hidden race war. *The Nation*. Available from http://www.thenation.com/article/Katrinas-hidden-race-war#. Accessed March 4, 2015.

Thompson, J. M. (1970). *English witnesses of the French revolution*. New York, NY: Associated Faculty PP. Inc.

Thornton, R. (1987). *American Indian Holocaust and survival: A population history since 1492*. Oklahoma City: University of Oklahoma Press.

Thucydides, T. (2013). *The history of the Peloponnesian war*. Oxford, England: Oxford University Press.

Thucydides, T. & Finley, M. I. (1954). *History of the Peloponnesian war*. New York, NY: Penguin Books.

Toal, G. (2011). *Bosnia remade: Ethnic cleansing and its reversal*. Oxford, England: Oxford University Press.

Tone, J. L. (2008). *War and genocide in Cuba 1895-1898 (envisioning Cuba)*. Chapel Hill: University of North Carolina Press.

Torstein, M. (1996). Child slavering, Nigerian human rights group reporting. Nigerian *Press Digest*.

Trinchero, H. H. (2006). The genocide of indigenous peoples in the formation of the Argentine Nation - state. *Journal of Genocide Research, 8*(2), 121–135.

Trump, D. J. & Kiyosaki, R. T. (2006) *Why we want you to be rich. Two men, one message*. New York, NY. Rich Press

Turits, R. L. (2004). *Foundations of despotism: Peasants, the Trujillo regime, and modernity in Dominican history*. Stanford, CA: Stanford University Press.

Ubah, C. B. A., Nwebo, O. E., & Ezeanyika, E. S. (2015). Transnational crime and international organization: The challenge of internal and international security. *Unpublished Research*.

Ubani, M. (1989, February 13). The Aba ring. *The African Guardian*, pp. 25–26.

Ubani, M. (1990a, April 16). War against drugs. *The African Guardian*, p. 15.

Ubani, M. (1990b, May 7). In the bangs of crisis: Awka-Etiti communal feud deepens following another murder. *The African Guardian*, pp. 8–11.

Uniform Crime Reports (2013). Crime in the United States. Washington, DC: Government Printing Press.

UN General Assembly Report. (1995).

UN Security Council. (1993). Annex, Article 16. Report of the secretary-general pursuant to paragraph 2 of Security Council Resolution 808. Retrieved from http://www.icty.org/x/file/Legal %20Library/Statute/statute_re808_1993_en.pdf. Accessed February 15, 2013.

UN Security Council. (2011). Assessment and report on Judge Patrick Robinson, President of the International Tribunal for the Former Yugoslavia, provided to the Security Council pursuant to paragraph 6 of Security Council resolution 1534. Retrieved from http://www.icty.org/x/file/About/Reports%20and%20PublicationsCompletionStrategy/completion_strategy_18may2011_en.pdf. Accessed February 15, 2013.

Ung, S. K. & McElroy, T. (2011). *I survived the killing fields: A true life story of a Cambodia refugee activities*. Seattle, WA: S & T Publishing.

United States Holocaust Memorial Museum (USHMM). (2012). International military tribunal Nuremberg. Retrieved from http://www.ushmm.org/wlc/en/articlephp?Moduleld=l0007069. Accessed May 10, 2012.

United Human Rights Council. (2013). Genocide in Rwanda. Retrieved from http://www.unitedhumanrights .org genocide/genocide_in_rwanda.btm. Accessed February 15, 2013.

Urin, P. (1999). Ethnicity and power in Burundi and Rwanda: Different paths to mass Violence. *Comparative Politics, 31*(3), 262.

Utley, F. (1948). *The Nuremberg judgment.* Chicago, IL: Henry Regency Company.

Uwechue, R. (1971). Reflections on the Nigerian civil war. New York: Africana Publishing Corporation.

Vanhanen, T. (1997). *Prospects of democracy: A study of 172 countries.* New York, NY: Routledge.

Vickery, M. (1984). *Cambodia: 1975 - 1982.* Boston, MA: South End Press.

Viorst, M. (1991, June 24). Report from Baghdad. *The New Yorker.*

Vir, A. K. (1989). Toxic trade with Africa. *Environment, Science & Technology Journal, 23*(1), 24–25.

Vulliamy, E. (2010). *America: War along the borderline.* New York, NY: Farra, Straus and Girouk.

Vyas, K. (2015). Protesters and state security agents. Available from www.wsj.com/articles/Venezuelas_tc. Accessed January 24, 2015.

Wakabayshi, B. T. (Ed.). (2008). *The Nanking Atrocity, 1937 - 38: Complicating the picture.* New York, NY: Berghahn Books.

Waldman, C. & Braun, M. (2009). *Atlas of the North American Indian.* New York, NY: Infobase Publishing.

Walker, P. & Lewis, P. (2012, July 19). Ian Tomlinson death: Simon Harwood cleared of manslaughter. *Guardian.* Also see http://www.guardian.co.uk/2012/jul/19/simon-harwood-not-guilty-ian-tomlinson. *The Guardian.* Accessed February 25, 2015.

Walsh, M. (1992). The global trade in hazardous waste: Domestic and international attempts to cope with a growing crisis in waste management. *Catholic University Law Review, 42,* 103–140.

Walvin, J. (2001). Black Ivory: Slavery in the British empire. New York: John Wiley & Son.

Wang, Z. (2000). The police system in The People's Republic of China. In O. N. I. Ebbe (Ed.), *Comparative and international criminal justice systems: policing, judiciary, and corrections* (2nd ed.). Boston, MA: Butterworth Heinemann.

Wang, J. Z. & Anderson, D. (2000). The Chinese criminal justice system. In O. N. I. Ebbe (Ed.), *Comparative and international criminal justice systems: Policing, judiciary, and corrections.* Boston, MA: Butterworth/Heinemann.

Ward, S. R. (2009). *Immortal: A military history of Iran and its armed forces.* Washington, DC: Georgetown University Press.

Warner, R. (1985). *Thucydides, history of the Peloponnesian war.* Suffolk, VA: Penguin.

Weber, M. (1947). *The theory of social and economic organization.* (trans by A. M. Henderson and T. Parsons) (Eds.). New York, NY: Oxford University Press.

Weir, A. (2003). *Mary, Queen of Scots and the murder of lord Darnley.* London, England: Random House.

Weier, C. (1999). *Athens, a portrait of the city in its golden age.* London, England: John Murray.

Weisbord, R. G. (2003). The King, the cardinal, and the Pope: Leopold II's genocide in the Congo and the Vatican. *Journal of Genocide Research, 5,* 35–45.

Wells, M. (2013). Why do Brazilian police kill? Available from http://insightcrime.org/news-analysis/why-do-brazilian-police-kill. Accessed February 27, 2015.

White, M. (2011). *Atrocities: Humanity's 100 deadliest achievements.* Edinburg, TX: Canongate Books.

Whitehead, N. L. (1999). The crisis and transformations of invaded societies: The Caribbean 1492 - 1580. In F. Solomon and S. B. Schwartz (Eds.), *The Cambridge history of the native peoples of the Americas* (Vol.3, south America, Part 1). Cambridge, MA: Cambridge University Press.

Whiteman, K. (1984). 475 Detainees-Idiagbon. *West Africa, 19*(March), 638.

WHO. (2014). Snapshots of health systems: The state of affairs in 16 countries in summer 2014 WHO. Available from http://web.archive.org/web/20100125175655/ http://www.euro.who.int/document/e85400.pdg. Accessed March 13, 2015.

Wilkinson, A. (2004). Mary Queen of Scots and the French connection. *History Today, 54*(7), 37–43.

Williams, N. (1964). *Thomas Howard: Fourth Duke of Norfolk.* London, England: Random House.

Williams, P. (1981). United Nations General Assembly: The international bill of human rights. New York, NY: Entwhistle Books.

Woolf, A. (2008). *A short history of the world: The story of mankind from prehistory to the present day.* London, England: Arcturus Publishing Ltd.

Wrage, A. A. (2007). *Bribery and extortion: Understanding business, governments, and security.* Westport, CT: Praeger Security International.

Wrong, M. (2009). *In the footsteps of Mr. Kurtz: Living on the brink of disaster in Mobutu's Congo.* New York, NY: Harper Collins.

Yakovlev, A. N. (2002). *A century of violence in Soviet Russia.* New Haven, CT: Yale University Press.

Yamamoto, M. (2000). *Nanking: Anatomy of an atrocity.* Westport, CT: Praeger Publishers.

Yearly, C. K. Jr. (1956). The Baltimore and Ohio railroad strike of 1877. *Maryland Historical Magazine, 51*(3), 118–211.

Young, P. (2007). *History of Mexico: Her civil wars and colonial and revolutionary annuals.* Sussex, England: Gardner Books.

Young, C. & Turner, T. E. (1985). *The rise and decline of the Zairian state.* Madison: University of Wisconsin Press.

Zeitlin, S. (1965). Masada and the Sicarii. *The Jewish Quarterly Review, 55*(4): 299–317.

Zito, M. (2003). Prison privatization: Past and present. Available from http://www.ifpo.org/articlebank/prison_privatization.html. The International Foundation for Protection Officers. Accessed March 20, 2015.

Appendix A

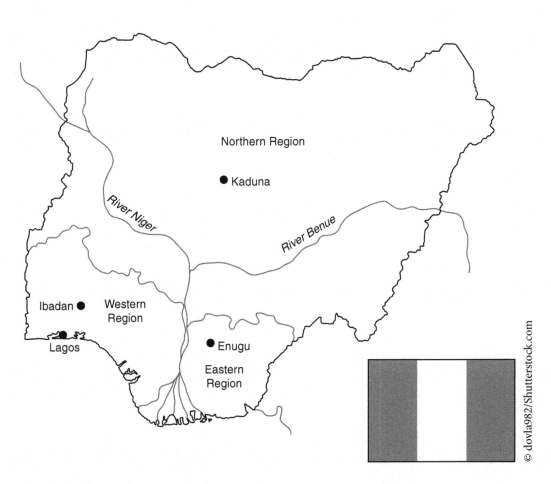

Northern Region

● Kaduna

River Niger

River Benue

Ibadan ●   Western
            Region

● Enugu

Lagos

Eastern
Region

© dovla982/Shutterstock.com

Index

CPSIA information can be obtained
at www.ICGtesting.com
Printed in the USA
LVOW04s0910190817
545286LV00022B/13/P